PATTON

PATTON

BATTLING WITH HISTORY

J. Furman Daniel III

UNIVERSITY OF MISSOURI PRESS

Columbia

Library of Congress Cataloging-in-Publication Data

Names: Daniel, J. Furman, III, author.
Title: Patton : battling with history / by J. Furman Daniel, III.
Other titles: Battling with history
Description: Columbia : University of Missouri Press, [2020] | Series:
  American military experience | Includes bibliographical references and
  index.
Identifiers: LCCN 2019041406 (print) | LCCN 2019041407 (ebook) | ISBN
  9780826222091 (hardcover) | ISBN 9780826223302 (paperback) | ISBN
  9780826274458 (ebook)
Subjects: LCSH: Patton, George S. (George Smith), 1885-1945. |
  Generals--United States--Biography. | United States. Army--Biography.
Classification: LCC E745.P3 D353 2020 (print) | LCC E745.P3 (ebook) | DDC
  355.0092 [B]--dc23
LC record available at https://lccn.loc.gov/2019041406
LC ebook record available at https://lccn.loc.gov/2019041407

Typefaces: Carlito and Minion

THE AMERICAN MILITARY EXPERIENCE SERIES
JOHN C. MCMANUS, SERIES EDITOR

The books in this series portray and analyze the experience of Americans in military service during war and peacetime from the onset of the twentieth century to the present. The series emphasizes the profound impact wars have had on nearly every aspect of recent American history and considers the significant effects of modern conflict on combatants and noncombatants alike. Titles in the series include accounts of battles, campaigns, and wars; unit histories; biographical and autobiographical narratives; investigations of technology and warfare; studies of the social and economic consequences of war; and in general, the best recent scholarship on Americans in the modern armed forces. The books in the series are written and designed for a diverse audience that encompasses nonspecialists as well as expert readers.

Selected titles from this series:

Lessons Unlearned:
The U.S. Army's Role in Creating the Forever Wars in Afghanistan and Iraq
Pat Proctor

Loss and Redemption at St. Vith:
The 7th Armored Division in the Battle of the Bulge
Gregory Fontenot

Military Realism: The Logic and Limits of Force and Innovation in the US Army
Peter Campbell

Omar Nelson Bradley: America's GI General, 1893–1981
Steven L. Ossad

The First Infantry Division and the US Army Transformed:
Road to Victory in Desert Storm, 1970–1991
Gregory Fontenot

Bataan Survivor: A POW's Account of Japanese Captivity in World War II
Frank A. Blazich

Dick Cole's War: Doolittle Raider, Hump Pilot, Air Commando
Dennis R. Okerstrom

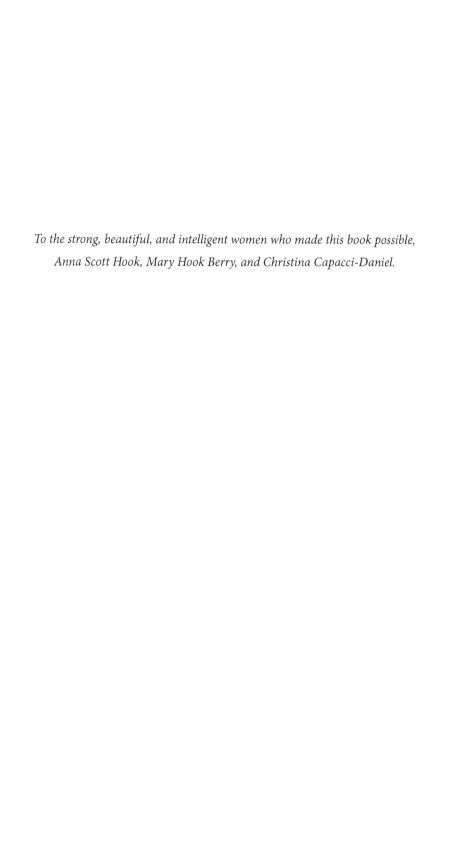

To the strong, beautiful, and intelligent women who made this book possible,
Anna Scott Hook, Mary Hook Berry, and Christina Capacci-Daniel.

CONTENTS

LIST OF FIGURES

LIST OF MAPS

ACKNOWLEDGMENTS

OVER THE PAST decade, many of my friends and colleagues have given me the heartfelt advice that writing is a lonely endeavor. I have not found this to be the case. On the contrary, this work would have been impossible without many generous people who were dedicated to my success and supported my efforts.

The entire team at the University of Missouri Press, especially Mary S. Conley, Andrew J. Davidson, Gary Kass, Drew Griffith, and series editor John C. McManus, have made extraordinary efforts to improve my writing, encourage me, and shepherd this book to production. Without their patience and dedication, this book would not have been possible.

Special thanks are in order for Amanda Morgan and the staff at the General George Patton Museum of Leadership at Fort Knox, Kentucky. Despite my procrastination, they went above and beyond to help me obtain many of the photos that brought this book to life.

I have been extremely blessed by my colleagues at George Washington University and Embry-Riddle Aeronautical University: Doug Evans, Thomas Field, Tom Foley, Tyrone Groh, Geoff Jensen, Phil Jones, Reg Parker, Brooke Shannon, Joanna Spear, and Lisa Stephenson. Each of them has made coming to work an intellectual challenge and true pleasure.

In addition to these colleagues, two other members of the Embry-Riddle community deserve special attention. Leanne Harworth filled dozens of interlibrary loan requests with an uncommon speed and joy, and Dale Perez provided edits and corrections with a much-needed sense of humor.

I am also blessed by my friends and mentors who helped me with the project and at times distracted me from it: Joe Collins, Elliott Fullmer, Gator

Greenwill, Paul Musgrave, Jay Parker, Richard Rodriguez, and countless others have made my life richer and more enjoyable.

Special thanks are due to Brian A. Smith. In addition to being one of my best friends, he is my best critic. Thanks for being the older brother I never had.

Most important, I want to thank the three women to whom this book is dedicated. My grandmother Anna Scott Hook was a brilliant lady and a true trailblazer. She earned two master's degrees in an era where educated females were not appreciated. She had the strength to serve as a minister's wife for parts of six decades and chose to teach in underprivileged and segregated schools because it was the right thing to do. She had a gift for history, and in 1991 she unknowingly put me on the path to where I am today by talking to me about Jackie Fisher.

My mother, Mary Hook Berry, is a similarly brilliant lady. She possesses a creativity and passion for education that I can only hope to emulate. She taught me kindness, faith, and pride in a job well done. While she often wondered about why her boy wanted to study conflict, she loved me for who I was. Even as a grown man, I look to her for inspiration.

Finally, my wife, Christina Capacci-Daniel, is my best friend and intellectual foil. We met on my first day of grad school while she was earning her doctorate in organic chemistry. She has loved, supported, and encouraged me from day one. She has helped me through difficult times of intellectual, financial, and personal hardship and has made every day a true blessing. She truly is my raison d'être.

PATTON

THE MYTH OF PATTON AS A NATURAL WARRIOR

There is always something to do. For example, read about war.

—George S. Patton Jr., "Obligations of Being an Officer,"
October 1, 1919

The Historian's Challenge

ACCORDING TO LEGEND, a young Captain Patton had one of his many inter-actions with the supernatural while riding to a secret meeting in early 1918. Despite his youth, he was one of the top officers in the newly formed tank corps, and his presence was required to help incorporate these untested units into the Allied strategy for the new year. The meeting was set to take place at night, some eighty miles from Patton's headquarters, in a part of France where he had never been. While he may have been nervous about serving as an advocate for the tank corps and interacting with many top Allied leaders, his mind was supposedly transported to visions of the past.

As his car crested a hill, Patton asked the driver "if the camp wasn't out of sight just over the hill and to the right." The driver was taken back by this question and replied, "No sir, our camp where we are going is further ahead, but there is an old Roman camp over there to the right. I have seen it myself." After his meeting with the senior Allied generals concluded, Patton was again purportedly struck by a sense of the supernatural. As he exited the meeting, he asked a French officer, "Your theater is over here straight ahead, isn't it?" Much like the driver, the officer was struck by the unusual question and replied, "We have no theater here, but I do know that there is an old Roman theater only about three hundred yards away."[1]

While these stories capture the popular imagination, they are at best difficult to verify. The story of the Roman camp and theater originated from Patton's longtime friend and confidant Harry Semmes, a successful lawyer in his civilian life who served with him in both world wars. In 1955, ten years after his friend's death, he wrote an extremely flattering biography titled *Portrait of Patton*. This book, which was written with the support and encouragement of the Patton family, venerates his old friend and makes repeated assertions that the famous general was guided by an uncommon connection to the past.[2] While this is not the only one of the early biographies that verges on hagiography, it has little in the way of outside sources and relies heavily on a series of anecdotes from their four-decade friendship. To accept Semmes's claims, we must rely on his memory of events that occurred decades prior to the publication of the book and must consider the fact that he was writing as a friend of the deceased hero, not as a professional historian. As such, it appears likely that Semmes passed on family lore and personal anecdotes without critically examining their veracity and directly contributed to the intriguing but unsubstantiated mythology.

The tales of the Roman camp and theater are perfect examples of this uncritical approach. By his own admission, Semmes was not present for the incidents and claims that he heard about it only because Patton recounted the incident to him in August 1918, approximately six months after this brush with the supernatural supposedly occurred. While it is certainly conceivable that the episode did transpire, it is also possible that the story was an exaggeration or outright fabrication.

Interestingly, this story is similar to the story told by Patton to his nephew, godson, and biographer Frederick Ayer. In his 1964 biography, *Before the Colors Fade*, Ayer claims that in early 1918 Patton had been offered a tour of Langres, France, by a young French liaison officer. The future general politely refused this generous offer and decided to survey the town's historic sites on his own. Not only did he find the Roman amphitheater and two temples, but he claimed that he precisely identified the exact location where Julius Caesar had pitched his tent some two millennia previously because he had actually been there during a past life! Here again, a close friend repeated Patton's unsubstantiated claim decades after the fact without outside sourcing. While the *New York Review of Books* criticized Ayer's work as "a rambling series of anecdotal sketches, about his uncle," it and Semmes's work remain critical parts of the Patton mythology and are still cited by modern historians who repeat these unsubstantiated legends as established facts.[3]

This interpretation of Patton as a romantic and atavistic warrior was propelled into the mainstream in the 1970 film *Patton*, starring George C. Scott. Much like the fictional Don Quixote, Scott portrayed the general as a tragic figure trapped between the past and the present and driven by a mythic sense of destiny. In one of the most iconic scenes of the movie, Patton is riding in a jeep to visit the Kasserine Pass battlefield when he demands that his driver "turn right, damn it," on the pretext that he could "smell a battlefield." The driver then turns off the main road and takes the general to the deserted ruins of a Carthaginian city where Scott, in a trancelike state, recounts a battle between Rome and the city's Punic defenders. With dramatic music setting the mood, he discusses his belief in reincarnation to an awestruck and incredulous General Omar Bradley and his staff, noting that "two thousand years ago, I was here." The fictitious Patton then recites a stanza from his actual 1922 poem "Through a Glass Darkly," where he asserts that he had "fought and strove and perished countless times upon a star," only to be reborn as a warrior.[4]

Despite the large number of biographies, memoirs, and primary source documents, there is no evidence that the incident where Patton diverted General Bradley and their staffs down a side road toward unseen Carthaginian ruins only to make claims of reincarnation and recite poetry ever occurred. It is not included in any of the major biographies of the general, General Bradley never mentioned it in either of his two memoirs, and despite hundreds of references to ancient sites in his diaries and letters Patton does not record this incident. Even more troubling, there is no documentation of his visiting ancient ruins during the narrow window of dates suggested by the movie's time frame. While Patton did write "Through a Glass Darkly," which the producers included in the scene, the rest is an example of Hollywood creative license.[5]

The film *Patton* has had a profound impact on popular legend. While the movie was more detailed and historically accurate than many of the films of its era, director Frank Schaffner and producer Frank McCarthy (himself a brigadier general in the US Army) made a series of creative decisions where actual events are altered or embellished (such as the slapping incidents during the Sicilian campaign), and some scenes were completely fictitious (such as the diversion to the ruined Carthaginian city). To help with the historical details, retired general Omar Bradley was hired as an assistant for the film. While Bradley had grown increasingly bitter toward Patton in the two and a half decades since the end of World War II, his involvement in the film did not keep the famous general from being portrayed as a pure and natural warrior.[6]

If anything, the juxtaposition of Bradley, the calm professional soldier who eschews glory, with the bold and bombastic Patton only serves to reinforce the myth that the protagonist was indeed a "pure warrior." For the uninformed viewer, the very fact that the film had high production values and did generally follow the course of events during World War II may make it more difficult to separate fact from fiction, as the film gives the outward appearance of presenting an unbiased "real" version of events.[7] For the biographer, the success of this film, like the books by Semmes and Ayer, further complicates the task of determining where legend and fact diverge.[8]

Another popular legend that distorts the truth centers on the bronze statue of Patton at the United States Military Academy at West Point. This larger-than-life statue, sculpted by American artist James Earle Fraser, was dedicated in 1950 by the general's widow, Beatrice. The eight-foot-tall bronze depicts a defiant Patton wearing the four stars of a full general, riding boots, and his famous ivory-handled pistols.[9] The general holds a pair of binoculars and grimaces at an unseen enemy, frozen in time at the pinnacle of his career. This statue has been reproduced for the "Hatch Shell" in Boston, where the general addressed a massive crowd for a war-bond drive in 1945, and at the George Patton Memorial Museum in Ettelbruck, Luxembourg, a town liberated by Patton's Third Army. This statue evokes a truly powerful image designed to inspire cadets, civilians, and foreign nationals alike with a vision of a larger-than-life hero.

The location of the statue at West Point is prominent, yet its physical presence contributes to one of the most enduring and incorrect of the Patton myths—that of a natural warrior. According to popular folklore, the statue faces the library because Patton never visited the building as a cadet. While it makes for a memorable anecdote and is consistent with the thesis that the general had an instinctive understanding of warfare, this story has no basis in fact.[10]

Far from being a natural warrior who did not need to study or who purposely neglected his grades, Patton was very well served by his military education at West Point and dedicated extraordinary time and effort to his academic pursuits. While it is true that he struggled initially and had to repeat his plebe year because of poor grades in mathematics, he managed to earn excellent marks overall. In fact, he consistently improved his standing at the academy, graduating in 1909 a respectable 46th in a class of 103, among them an impressive collection of future generals, including William Simpson, Jacob Devers, Robert Eichelberger, and Patton's personal rival John Lee.[11] Simply stated, the notion that he never visited the library as a cadet is unfounded and absurd.

Examining the Myth of a Natural Warrior

The challenge for any biographer of General George S. Patton Jr. is to separate legend from fact. Throughout his life, Patton cultivated an image of a natural warrior born to achieve military greatness. This mythic image was fueled by seemingly impossible examples of his physical exploits and military leadership, a public hungry for heroes, a press that embellished his exploits and exposed them to a mass audience, a best-selling posthumous memoir, an award-winning Hollywood biopic, and a series of biographies that retold his stories to eight decades of readers. In many ways, this popular image is both a blessing and a curse. The mythology ensures that his heroic deeds and colorful persona will long endure, yet it distorts his true character, perpetuates half-truths, and unintentionally obscures the more subtle elements of his success.[12]

Patton remains one of the finest examples of military leadership, yet the mythology that surrounds him comes with a price—it obscures the real man. While he was extremely gifted, the fact that he dedicated his life to the study of warfare and history is frequently lost. To neglect this insight is to perpetuate an incomplete view of a complex man and to implicitly endorse the view that he *was* the natural warrior of legend.

Patton in Proper Context: Dedication, Manipulation, Coup d'Oeil, and Determination

This book documents how Patton's life was shaped by his experiences as a student, writer, and maker of history and will use this insight to develop three overarching points.

First, he was a lifelong lover of history and was dedicated to learning all he could about the past, confident in the belief that this study would pay practical dividends. To make this claim that history profoundly shaped his life and career is a comparatively simple task. Indeed, there is ample evidence from friends, family, official documents, and the general's own writings to support such an interpretation.

Despite the fact that this is a comparatively easy claim to substantiate, the popular myth is that Patton was a natural warrior, not a serious scholar.

To fully appreciate his life and work, it is essential to understand that he worked diligently to achieve mastery of his chosen profession. Ultimately, this insight, not the popular myth, should lead to a greater appreciation of his true genius. Success was not preordained but based on a lifetime of dedication and hard work.

Second, the book will argue that despite his love of history, Patton frequently used his knowledge of the past for his own self-serving purposes. On the most benign level, he used his knowledge of history to influence and inspire others. He frequently employed his impressive knowledge of historical cases to reason by analogy and to win others over to his ideas on obscure points of doctrine or strategy. This tactic was particularly successful among his peers in the US Army, as it allowed him to establish himself as an authority on military affairs by speaking the lingua franca of military history.

Similarly, he used historical analogies to inspire others and exude confidence when faced with adversity. In times of crisis, Patton presented himself as a voice of calm, focused not on the troubles of the moment but instead buoyed by his long view of history. It stood to reason that Patton could make things right because he understood how great leaders throughout history had triumphed over their own seemingly inescapable circumstances. When others needed reassurance, the general could claim a mastery of the past and argue that he had a vision for shaping the uncertain future.

More cynically, Patton was very sensitive to his place in history and would on occasion purposely manipulate and distort the historiographic record. While it is unclear if this dishonesty bothered Patton, there are many prominent examples of his making unsubstantiated claims of reincarnation, falsifying official records, lying to the press, and editing his own written and oral statements in order to present a more flattering version of events. Because Patton understood the need to present an idealized version of himself for posterity, he embellished and falsified his own deeds with an eye toward shaping popular imagery and future historiography.

For a biographer, this use (and abuse) of history is quite interesting, as it exposes both a key element of Patton's professional success and his deep insecurities and character flaws. In Patton's mind, the past was not set in stone but rather a tool to win battlefield, bureaucratic, and personal victories. By interpreting it to serve his own ends, Patton hoped to make history on his own terms and establish himself as one of history's great leaders.

Despite his many successes, he was ultimately unsure about his place in history. He craved greater glory and did not like sharing accolades with other commanders who he believed were less talented. By the end of World War II he also had several significant failures that he wanted to hide. To protect his legacy, he manipulated the historical record to highlight his own success, blame others for his failures, and cover up his shortcomings. In contrast to the popular methodology, the general was not a warrior torn from ages past, but rather a man who understood the power of popular imagery and used his mastery of history to further his own career and legacy.

Finally, this book argues that Patton's lifelong obsession with history and the military profession allowed him to achieve both coup d'oeil as well as a determination to act decisively on his instincts.[13] The term *coup d'oeil* literally means "the strike of an eye," but has come to define military genius. While many military professionals can achieve proficiency in the arts of war, coup d'oeil describes an innate, instinctual, seemingly effortless vision for warfare. Rather than simply reacting to events, leaders who possess coup d'oeil have the flexibility of mind to anticipate an unfolding battle or campaign and shape events on their own terms.[14] Like his heroes Frederick the Great and Napoleon, Patton's mastery of history and the military profession provided him with coup d'oeil that gave him a decisive advantage over his opponents and made it seem as if he were acting effortlessly.[15]

While Patton often struggled to define or describe his so-called sixth sense for warfare, he clearly had a gift for rapidly understanding complex military problems and identifying a strategy to win.[16] This unique ability was not an accident but rather the result of his fanatical dedication to learning and practicing the military arts. The result was that by the time he was given command during World War II, he was so well versed in military thought that he could rapidly understand the complexities of a battle or campaign and rapidly draw on his vast historical and practical experiences to determine a course of action. In an undated letter to General Eisenhower, probably written in early February 1943, Patton described this ability: "For years I have been accused of indulging in snap judgements. Honestly, this is not the case because, like yourself, I am a profound military student and the thoughts I express, perhaps too flippantly, are the result of years of thought and study."[17]

This instinctive knowledge would have been useless had Patton not had the confidence and convictions to act boldly and decisively on his instincts. Here, his mastery of history again helped him by giving him confidence in his own views of warfare. While the senior Allied generals were all extremely well-educated military professionals, they frequently were risk adverse and missed opportunities to win decisive victories. Patton, on the other hand, felt empowered to take risks, confident that his aggressive style of fighting was supported by military principles going back many centuries. While Patton was frequently seen as an unstable liability by his superiors, no one doubted his desire to act decisively.

This unique combination of coup d'oeil and decisiveness was the key to Patton's success. In describing the military genius of Napoleon, Prussian theorist Clausewitz described this combination of traits as the key to his success:

> If the mind is to escape unscathed from this relentless struggle with the unforeseen, two qualities are indispensable: *first, an intellect that, even in the darkest hour, retains some glimmering of the inner light which leads to truth; and second, the courage to follow this faint light wherever it may lead.* The first of these qualities is described by the French term, *coup d'oeil*; the second is determination. . . . *Coup d'oeil* therefore refers not alone to the physical but, more commonly, to the inward eye. . . . Stripped of metaphor and of the restrictions imposed on it by the phrase, the concept merely refers to the quick recognition of a truth that the mind would ordinarily miss or would perceive only after long study and reflection. . . . Determination in a single instance is the expression of courage; if it becomes characteristic, a mental habit . . . the role of determination is to limit the agonies of doubt and the perils of hesitation when the motives for action are inadequate. . . . Determination, which dispels doubt, is a quality that can be aroused only by the intellect, and by a specific cast of mind at that.[18]

Like Napoleon, Patton had this unique combination of coup d'oeil and determination, and he worked his entire life to improve upon his understanding of history and warfare.

Patton directly contributed to his own mythology through his dress, frequent references to history, claims of psychic visions and reincarnation, and purposeful manipulation of the written record. Despite his claims of mysticism, reincarnation, and being the perfect warrior, the general was none of these things. Rather, he was so immersed with the past and so willing to provide his own thoughts on military subjects that he *appeared* to be a natural warrior. Patton understood that this appearance was beneficial for his career and his place in history, and he purposely played up this persona to his friends, fellow officers, and the press as well as in his private writings.

While much of the legend of a natural warrior was manufactured by Patton and his supporters, the mythos would not have survived if it was not supported by truly extraordinary accomplishments and a flamboyant personality. Indeed, the general's battlefield successes, combined with his inability to moderate his behavior during times of peace, lend veracity to the legends. The less glamorous truth is that the general's successes and failures were built on decades of historical study and an almost fanatical dedication to self-improvement. These intellectual exercises gave him the extraordinary knowledge to achieve coup d'oeil and the determination and confidence to boldly practice his unique vision of warfare.

Patton as a Student of History
Despite the fact that he struggled with reading, grammar, and spelling, Patton was a prolific consumer of books and articles on a broad array of subjects. Even on his honeymoon in England, the future general found that he could not help reading and thinking about military subjects. To this end, he made a series of purchases at London booksellers specifically designed to augment his growing library of books on history and the military arts.[19] The most notable of his book purchases was an abridged English translation of *On War* by Prussian military theorist Carl von Clausewitz.[20]

A few weeks after returning from his honeymoon, Patton and his cavalry troop were detached for extended field maneuvers. His unit traveled from Fort Sheridan outside of Chicago to a remote wilderness area in Wisconsin. Patton was tasked with moving the men, horses, mules, and other supplies to the training area in addition to planning and participating in a series of mock battles and practice maneuvers. In addition to his cavalry gear, the young lieutenant packed one additional item, his abridged copy of Clausewitz's *On War*, which he had purchased a few weeks before. In his downtime, he struggled with the Prussian master's dense text and wrote his wife, Beatrice, about his reading, noting, "Clausewitz is about as hard reading as any thing [*sic*] can well be and is as full of notes and equal abstruseness as a dog is of fleas."[21] The fact that he would read this difficult work when he was doubtless tired and busy trying to master the duties of a junior cavalry officer speaks to his drive to achieve a broader professional competency in the military arts and suggests that he was thinking far beyond the tasks of the moment.

He would return to the reading of Clausewitz in 1926 while stationed in Hawaii and frustrated with the slow pace of army life on the island during the interwar period. By this time, Patton had obtained a complete version of the work, divided into a three-volume set. He made extensive notes in the first two volumes, often disagreeing with the Prussian theorist. For example, he refused to accept Clausewitz's theory of economy of force, which asserted that the total destruction of an enemy was unnecessary and counterproductive.[22] Instead, Patton scribbled in the margin of page, "Bunk—always go to the limits," a clear assertion of his own views of warfare.[23]

The most prominent manifestation of the future general's continued study of military history was his personal library. He was particularly interested in collecting classic primary sources on military theory so that he could learn directly from the great military strategists. Indeed, he collected multiple translations of Clausewitz's *On War* (a book written in an archaic style of academic German that is notoriously difficult to translate) as well as other classics ranging from Thucydides to Napoleon. Because Patton wanted to learn directly from great commanders, he was particularly careful to avoid reading edited or digest forms of these works.[24]

Patton's library grew to impressive proportions, and as early as the 1930s his collection numbered several hundred volumes, many of which he had custom bound to his demanding specifications in order to protect their contents. He carefully annotated these books, highlighting key themes he thought worthy of further thought and reflection. Like many great thinkers, he was a self-directed lifelong learner who read broadly, a fact that does not match the popular image of a natural warrior.

Patton as a Writer of History
Patton was also a prolific writer. Starting as a cadet at West Point, he kept a private diary. Here he recorded his daily routines, scribbled short notes, composed some of his early poetry, and began to record his observations about the nature of war. Despite its informal style and frequent grammatical errors, his diary is an unparalleled source of insight into the mind of a young cadet who was attempting to master the complex tasks of being a military officer.

He continued to keep private diaries during his honeymoon and his campaign in Mexico, and these writings also provide key insights into his active mind and his views on a wide range of military and historical subjects. During the First World War, he continued to make extensive notes on military subjects and wrote hundreds of letters to friends and family detailing both his career progression and his evolving views on warfare.[25]

Patton resumed his formal diary entries on August 5, 1942, as he was beginning the planning for the Allied invasion of North Africa.[26] These diary entries were much more formal and complete than his previous efforts,

Figure 1. Patton class photo from
The Howitzer, 1909. United States
Military Academy. West Point
Digital Archive.

reflecting not only his increased maturity but also his belief that he was making history. If Patton won the fame he so desperately craved, he anticipated that his "private" thoughts and comments would be of interest to historians and that he could shape the historiographic record.

For this reason, the post-1942 diary entries must be read critically. While the thousands of unflattering examples of racial bias, expressions of self-doubt, and insubordinate comments about the Allied High Command give the appearance of an unbiased account, the tone and framing of issues are frequently self-serving and defensive. Similarly, while the diaries provide a chronicle of his outstanding career and document his theories on a wide range of military subjects, they typically present Patton as having a unique vision of warfare grounded in a deep appreciation for history and the arts of war. Other Allied commanders often serve as a dynamic foil to the brilliant Patton, ultimately lacking his understanding of the unfolding strategic situation and keeping him from achieving even greater military triumphs. The result is a biased account where Allied failures are the fault of others, while successes are often credited to Patton and his subordinates.

Despite the fact that he was writing these entries with an eye toward future publication, he was quite protective of their contents during his lifetime. In fact, the Hurst Corporation offered him $250,000 for exclusive rights to publish the diaries in the fall of 1944, an offer he promptly refused.[27] While Patton's significant family wealth allowed him to spurn this generous offer (the rough equivalent of $3.5 million in today's money), it is likely that he was primarily motivated by a desire to retain editorial control over the contents of his writings and feared that the release of these unedited diaries would threaten both his career and his historical legacy.[28]

In addition to his diaries and private notes, Patton also composed poetry. These poems focused on military and historical themes and were written in a style similar to the ballads of Patton's favorite poet, Rudyard Kipling.[29] Even as a boy he could cite long passages of the British poet's *Barrack-Room Ballads* from memory, and it is clear that he styled his own works on these military-themed stanzas.[30] While he was dedicated to the poetic art form, composing approximately eighty known poems, only a handful were published during the general's lifetime. In fact, it is fair to assume that they would have certainly been forgotten had their author not achieved lasting fame on the battlefield.[31] Although these literary efforts frequently touched on themes of death, reincarnation, and battles past, they were primarily for his own amusement and personal succor in times of crisis and uncertainty. Patton frequently composed or recited verse as a means of distraction and amusement but made no effort to expose his poetry to anybody other than close family and friends until his fame and reputation were firmly established. As such, Patton's poetry is best seen as an interesting element of his character, but not as a serious attempt to better understand history, advance his theories of warfare, or win future glory.

Starting as a young second lieutenant, Patton also began to write a series of articles designed to promote his views to a broader professional audience. While Patton frequently wrote on seemingly obscure technical and doctrinal points, he used his excellent knowledge of historical cases to support his arguments.[32] Then as now, military history was a common language for military officers and a major element of the professional military education system.[33] By using the common language of military history, Patton could not only prove his professional credentials to senior officers, but also use historical analogies to speak directly to their potential objections. The future general would master this technique early in his career, and he would continue to employ it to convince others and win arguments for the remainder of his life.

His first article, "The Form and Use of the Saber," which appeared in the March 1913 issue of *Cavalry Journal*, is an excellent example of this approach.[34] This piece applied lessons from military history to argue that the current cavalry sword was a poor copy of an outdated eleventh-century form and that Patton's own design for a straighter bladed sword optimized for stabbing should be adopted by the Army Ordnance Department. Although the young lieutenant was challenging the orthodox views on the proper design and use of the sword, his argument was well received and quickly influenced army doctrine, training, and procurement, thanks in no small part to the fact that he was able to appeal to the historically minded, and notoriously conservative, members of the Army Ordnance Department.

Building on this early success, Patton wrote numerous articles and delivered countless lectures during the period prior to the outbreak of World War I and again during the long peace that followed. While Patton struggled mightily during the two decades of peace following World War I, he continued to refine his thinking and promote his ideas to a broader audience. In a series of articles, lectures, and private notes, he formalized his theories about the evolving nature of war and produced first-rate analyses on a myriad of topics, including armored doctrine, training, force structure, small-unit leadership, and the vulnerability of Hawaii to a Japanese surprise attack.

The most impressive of Patton's published efforts during the interwar period was his 1932 Army War College thesis, titled "The Probable Characteristics of the Next War and the Organization, Tactics, and Equipment Necessary to Meet Them." This remarkable piece of scholarship accurately predicted the advances in mechanized warfare that would come to define the next war and argued that the United States was uniquely well suited to adapt to future contingencies because of its superior industrial base and the American fascination with automobiles and aircraft.[35] These views so impressed the War College faculty that they circulated the thesis within the War Department. Although the Depression-era army did not have the financial resources to implement Patton's suggestions, he accurately predicted the nature of the fighting nine years prior to America's involvement in World War II. Even when his career seemed to be stalled by lean budgets, slow promotion, and a lack of action, Patton used his writings to garner attention and respect among senior officers and defense planners.[36]

The US entry into the war on December 7, 1941, gave Patton the opportunity to serve in a more active capacity but did not end his literary contributions. Even while he was busily preparing US troops for deployment to North Africa, he found time to publish a short piece in *Cavalry Journal* titled "The Desert Training Corps." Here, he expounded on the need for tough, realistic training to prepare citizen soldiers for battle and the need to sustain these men with the best food and equipment available. While Patton would not publish any official works for the remainder of the war, he continued to faithfully write in his diary, correspond with his family and friends, and publish a series of unofficial "Notes on Combat," which were pithy lessons learned designed to convey practical advice about combat operations to his officers and men and to win his critics over to his views on warfare.[37]

After the end of World War II, Patton returned to writing in both an official and an unofficial capacity, efforts that were inadvertently aided by scandals of his own making. After halfheartedly implementing Allied denazification policies and making a series of ill-advised statements to the press, the disgraced general was transferred to the US Fifteenth Army. Here, he was tasked with writing official lessons learned from fighting in the European theater. During the post–World War II period, Patton also worked diligently to edit portions of his diary into a publishable memoir. For both the memoir and the official history, he solicited historical, editorial, and promotional assistance from a wide range of friends, family, military contacts, and professional historians. He saw these works as critical to formalizing the hard-earned lessons of modern warfare while also cementing his legacy as one of history's greatest commanders.

Although Patton made substantial progress on these projects, his work was cut short by a debilitating and ultimately fatal car wreck on December 9, 1945. After his death, the work of the Fifteenth Army proceeded along the guidelines that he had set out two and a half months before and helped indoctrinate a wide range of Patton's theories of war into the official US Army history. While largely forgotten today, they are impressive in both their scope and their candor. Building on Patton's belief that the lessons of war should be thoroughly analyzed, these reports objectively highlighted the successes and failures of the American efforts in Europe.

While Patton had completed an initial draft of his memoirs just a few days before the tragic accident, this project also remained unfinished at the time of his death. The book was completed posthumously by his wife, Beatrice, and his longtime friend and military aide Colonel (later General) Paul Harkins. While some of the general's salty language and personal grievances were edited out of the final version, this memoir provides a clear picture of how Patton wanted to be remembered and boldly presents his views regarding success in modern warfare.

The resulting book, *War as I Knew It*, was published in 1947 while Patton's fame was still fresh in the minds of the American people, and it quickly became a commercial and critical success. With a keen eye to shaping the historical record, this memoir presents Patton as the most innovative and daring commander of World War II. It also presents a very selective view of history by purposely omitting controversial comments to the press, making a virtue out of his slapping of shell-shocked troops in Sicily, and providing misleading accounts of failures, such as the raid on a prison camp in Hammelburg, Germany. The book has remained in print and continues to contribute to the Patton mythos, while perpetuating a biased version of history. As such, it is extremely important for a historian to critically analyze this text and understand that it was Patton's attempt to solidify his reputation and theories of war for future generations.

Patton as a Maker of History

For Patton, history was more than a collection of facts—history contained lessons with a direct application to the battlefield. During his campaigns, he was able to draw from his corpus of historical knowledge to inspire his troops, reason by analogy, and apply the lessons of history to an unfolding battle. This ability to apply history in real time was so effective that it convinced many that he was a natural warrior, but the truth was that Patton worked hard to develop his professional knowledge and eventually became such a master of the military arts. The product of these years of study was that he could almost instantaneously apply his knowledge of the past to an unfolding battle or campaign and act faster and more decisively than his opponents.

In 1917 Patton received his first taste of combat in Mexico.[38] Building on the lessons he learned as a small boy listening to the legendary Confederate partisan leader Colonel John Singleton Mosby, he was able to lead his men deep into enemy terrain, cut enemy communications, and avoid ambushes. During the campaign, he remembered that during the Civil War horses were a tool to provide mobility but that cavalry was often more effective when fighting dismounted. He used this knowledge of the past and combined it with the technology of the present, experimenting with the use of automobiles as a new means for riding into battle.[39]

This led to what Patton described as the first mechanized assault in American history. His forces used their cars to surround and surprise a suspected Mexican leader's house and approached on foot, a modern adaptation of Civil War tactics. In the midst of the ensuing firefight with Mexican banditos, he was again able to apply his study of the past, remembering to shoot at the horse of a mounted rider, not the man himself, a tactical insight gleaned from his friendship with many local cowboys who had passed on their knowledge of local bandits and their tactics. This practical lesson from history allowed him to kill a Mexican rider who was attempting to flee the ambush and was able to win recognition for his coolness under fire. In an otherwise inconclusive campaign, the young lieutenant's actions were some of the only good news for the Americans, and Patton was quickly dubbed "Pershing's bandit killer" and became something of a minor celebrity.[40]

As a tank commander in World War I, the future general drew from his knowledge regarding the value of active leadership, technical expertise, and the importance of initiative in following up an initial breakthrough. He compared his historical studies with French and British tank experts and was able to improve upon their hard-earned expertise and develop a training regime and doctrine that were truly revolutionary. While the war ended before Patton could fully test these theories, he was able to get his first taste of modern war and win several significant victories for the American tank force. During World War I, he frequently used historical analogies to elucidate his own views for the armored force and became increasingly comfortable with his claims of reincarnation that would come to define his legacy.[41]

During the Second World War, Patton's mastery of history was on full display. As he sailed to Morocco to participate in the Operation Torch landings, the general took the time to reflect on his knowledge of Middle Eastern history and began to read the Koran.[42] During his time in North Africa, he leveraged this knowledge to help him manage the potentially hostile Muslim population and avoid a potentially disastrous insurgency in his rear areas. Additionally, he used the language skills that he had perfected on various trips to France and his expert knowledge of French history to adroitly manage the egos of his defeated Vichy opponents and to lessen the administrative burden on the Allies by incorporating the defeated French forces into his own plan for pacification and administration of the region.[43]

When he was given the task of relieving Lloyd Fredendall as commander of American II Corps after the disaster at Kasserine Pass, Patton again relied on his study of history. While the tactical deployment of the American forces was poor, he also sensed that the Americans lacked discipline and inspired leadership.[44] By combining his belief that discipline, pride, and personal leadership were essential to success with historical analogies to the Civil War and Napoleon, he was able to inspire his men, reorient their efforts, and rapidly reverse the Allies' fortunes.[45] This understanding allowed him to reason by analogy and win a series of battles against the Axis forces. These early successes established him as one of the top American field commanders during his brief actions in North Africa and further contributed to his growing mythology.

Building on these successes, Patton was pulled away from the North African campaign and assigned to assist planning the invasion of Sicily. With a keen eye toward history, the general was eager to fight in the same places as Alcibiades and Scipio, but quickly became frustrated with the politics of the Allied High Command. He was particularly upset by the British dominance of the planning process and felt personally slighted that the American forces were being tasked to serve in a supporting role during the upcoming campaign.[46]

These frustrations led Patton to believe that the only way to improve the standing of the US Army was to seek decisive action and win victories on his own. This desire to make history would create problems in the Sicilian campaign, as it caused him to push extremely hard and take unnecessary risks as well as exacerbating tensions within the Allied High Command. While he would ultimately capture Palermo and win his "horse race" with the British to Messina, these actions were extremely costly professionally. Not only did his obsession with outdoing the British strain his relationship with General Omar Bradley, but he also jeopardized his career by slapping two shell-shocked enlisted soldiers who had been evacuated to rear-area hospitals. While these incidents did not cost Patton his career, they tarnished his reputation, obscured his many successes during the Sicilian campaign, and may have cost him the opportunity to lead the American invasion of France in June 1944.[47]

The Allied invasion of France provided Patton with a much-needed opportunity for personal and professional redemption. On a trip to the region in 1913, he had predicted that he would fight a decisive battle in Normandy, but when the newly activated US Third Army entered combat two months after the Normandy landings, the prospects for success appeared dim.[48] The drive inland had stalled due in part to a lack of intelligence on the local road network, and the Allies faced the possibility of a bloody stalemate. Once again, Patton relied on his mastery of history to win victory. Remembering that he had conducted a personal survey of the region's roads while visiting the region three decades before, he requested a copy of his original study. A copy was located in the army archives and became the basis of the planned Normandy breakout. Relying on this study and his understanding of history, the general was able to anticipate the outcome of the campaign with uncanny accuracy up to their advance to the German border.[49]

In what was perhaps his greatest military achievement, Patton used his knowledge of the 1918 and 1940 German offensives in France to anticipate and react to the Ardennes offensive in December 1944. Utilizing an almost uncanny ability to grasp the unfolding operational situation, Patton was able to begin planning his counterattack against the German forces prior to being briefed regarding the specifics of the German assault. He anticipated that the key to the American defensive position was the town of Bastogne, Belgium.[50] This critical road junction was being defended by the 101st Airborne Division and scattered elements from other units, but they were quickly outnumbered and surrounded. Despite their bravery, it was uncertain how long these forces could hold out against a determined Nazi assault, and the Allies faced the possibility of a major military defeat.[51]

While the mood at Allied headquarters was tense, Patton remained calm and promised that he could shift his forces and begin an attack to relieve Bastogne in forty-eight hours.[52] This struck most of the Allied generals as impossible, but lacking any better options Eisenhower allowed Patton to proceed with his daring plan.[53] Once given the orders, the Third Army was able to extract itself from an ongoing battle, pivot ninety degrees, maneuver to the decisive point some one hundred miles distant, attack into the German flank, and relieve the 101st Airborne.[54] This achievement was a testament to not only the courage and commitment of the men of the Third Army, but also their commanding officer's unique mastery of modern warfare.[55]

In the war's final weeks, Patton's knowledge of history and desire to act proactively again shaped his decision making, as he anticipated that the Soviet Union would emerge as a geopolitical rival. In an attempt to limit Soviet gains in Central and Western Europe, he drove his men into Bavaria, Austria, and Czechoslovakia as rapidly as possible in an attempt to deny these critical regions to the Red Army.[56] During this period, the Third Army rescued the world famous Lipizzaner stallions and prevented looted art treasures from falling into communist hands, a testament to their commanding officer's cultural acumen as well as his fear of future Soviet aggression.[57]

While Patton's distrust of the Soviet allies was grounded in an appreciation of history, it would ultimately be self-destructive. He seemed trapped in the past and unable to reconcile his powerful convictions with the new realities of the Cold War. This pattern continued when Patton was named the military proconsul of Bavaria and tasked with the denazification and de-industrialization of Germany. The general fundamentally disagreed with the mission of punishing his defeated foe and instead focused on reviving the local economy and providing food and heating for ordinary German citizens. Here, the general's knowledge of the past informed his actions but ultimately led to his disgrace and relief from command of Third Army.

Plan for the Book

This book will attempt to contradict many of the myths surrounding General Patton by showing how his command of history enabled him to succeed. The first chapter will provide a short overview of Patton's early life and show how his dedication to history and professional studies paid dividends during his campaigns in Mexico and World War I. The second, third, and fourth chapters examine the general's most famous campaigns in World War II and show how history both informed his decisions on the battlefield and motivated him to make history on his own terms. Chapter 5 will examine how the past informed the general's views of the early Cold War and explains many of his struggles to adapt to the uncomfortable realities of the new peace. The sixth chapter discusses Patton's transfer to the Fifteenth Army and documents how he used this opportunity to write and study history as a means of rebuilding his reputation and passing on his vision of warfare to future generations. Chapter 7 explores how he attempted to revive his reputation through writing history and will assess the historical accuracy and objectivity of the official history and his memoirs. The conclusion re-examines the myth of a natural warrior and makes recommendations for modern scholars and practitioners.

· ·

NOTES

1. Harry H. Semmes, *Portrait of Patton*, 38.

2. Semmes, *Portrait of Patton*, vii–x.

3. Fred Ayer Jr., *Before Colors Fade: A Portrait of a Soldier, George S. Patton Jr.*, 94–95; Clancy Sigal, "Blood and Guts," *New York Review of Books, August 20, 1964.*

4. Franklin J. Schaffner, dir., *Patton* (Los Angeles: 20th Century Fox, 1970).

5. Nicholas Evan Sarantakes, *Making "Patton": A Classic Film's Epic Journey to the Silver Screen*, 58.

6. Sarantakes, *Making "Patton,"* 15.

7. Despite the fact that this scene is fictitious, it contains an element of truth regarding Patton as a student of history. As such, it has been used as part of the Marine

Corps Combat Development Command course taught at Quantico, Virginia, to impart the lesson that "a properly schooled officer never arrives on the battlefield for the first time, even if he has never actually trod the ground, if that officer has read wisely to acquire the wisdom of those who have experienced war in times past." See Paul K. Van Riper, "The Relevance of History to the Military Profession: An American Marine's View," in *The Past as Prologue: The Importance of History to the Military Profession*, ed. Williamson Murray and Richard Hart Sinnreich, 52–53.

8. On the challenge of separating fictitious accounts of history and politics from actual events, see J. Furman Daniel III and Paul Musgrave, "Synthetic Experiences: How Popular Culture Matters for Images of International Relations"; Daniel T. Gilbert, Romin W. Tafarodi, and Patrick S. Malone, "You Can't Not Believe Everything You Read"; and Norman N. Holland, "Spider-Man? Sure! The Neuroscience of Suspending Disbelief."

9. www.usma.edu/pv/pointer%20view%20archive/09may21.pdf.

10. Steve E. Dietrich, "The Professional Reading of General George S. Patton, Jr."; James Kelly Morningstar, *Patton's Way: A Radical Theory of War*, 123.

11. Edward M. Coffman, *The Regulars: The American Army, 1898–1941*, 114–45. Another prominent general from World War II, General Courtney Hodges, would have graduated in the class of 1909 but was found deficient in mathematics. Despite this failure, Hodges would go on to a very distinguished army career and would be a close personal friend of Patton.

12. On the mixed blessing of the 1970 George C. Scott film, see Winston Groom, *The Generals: Patton, MacArthur, Marshall, and the Winning of World War II*, 16; Agostino Von Hassell and Ed Breslin, *Patton: The Pursuit of Destiny*, ix–xx. For a well-written, in-depth account of the making of the film, see Sarantakes, *Making Patton*.

13. Roger H. Nye, *The Challenge of Command: Reading for Military Excellence*, 72.

14. On the concept of military genius and coup d'oeil, see Jon Tetsuro Sumida, *Decoding Clausewitz: A New Approach to On War*, 117, 130–31, 170.

15. On Napoleon's mastery of coup d'oeil, see David G. Chandler, *The Campaigns of Napoleon*; and William Duggan, *Napoleon's Glance: The Secret of Strategy*. For a description of Patton as a commander who was an exception to the otherwise plodding Allied High Command because he "inferred enemy intentions intuitively," see Eitan Shamir, *Transforming Mission Command: The Pursuit of Mission Command in the U.S., British, and Israeli Armies*, 63, 138, 156, 200.

16. Patton would famously confide to his son, "Leadership is the thing that wins battles. I have it—but I'll be damned if I can define it. Probably it consists in knowing what you want to do and then doing it and getting mad if any one stepps [sic] in the way. Self confidence and leadership are twin brothers." Martin Blumenson, *The Patton Papers*, vol. 2, *1940–1945*, 625; John Nelson Rickard, *Advance and Destroy: Patton as Commander in the Bulge*, 303.

17. Blumenson, *The Patton Papers*, 2:169.

18. Carl von Clausewitz, *On War*, 102–3 (emphasis in the original).

19. Martin Blumenson, *Patton: The Man behind the Legend, 1885–1945*, 68; John Gooch, "History and the Nature of Strategy," in *Past as Prologue*, ed. Murray and Sinnreich, 137, 149.

20. On Patton's disdain for abridgements of classic texts, see Beatrice Patton, "A Soldier's Reading." On the inadequacy and rarity of early English translations of Clausewitz's *On War*, see Christopher Brassford, *Clausewitz in English: The Reception of Clausewitz in Britain and America, 1815–1945*; and Roger H. Nye, *The Patton Mind: The Professional Development of an Extraordinary Leader*, 27–28.

21. Nye, *Patton Mind*, 27–28; Carlo D'Este, *Patton: A Genius for War*, 120.

22. Based on this note, it would appear that Patton fundamentally disagreed with (or perhaps misunderstood) the central theme of Clausewitz that war tends toward extremes but should be limited. For a discussion of Clausewitz as an advocate for limited warfare, see J. Furman Daniel III and Brian A. Smith, "Burke and Clausewitz on the Limitation of War," 313–30.

23. Nye, *Patton Mind*, 71.

24. B. Patton, "A Soldier's Reading."

25. Diaries, 1910–45, George S. Patton Papers, Manuscript Division, Library of Congress, Washington, DC.

26. Diaries, 1910–45, Patton Papers.

27. Rick Atkinson, *The Guns at Last Light: The War in Western Europe, 1944–1945*, 342.

28. US Department of Labor, Bureau of Labor and Statistics inflation calculator, www.bls.gov/data/inflation_calculator.htm.

29. B. Patton, "A Soldier's Reading."

30. See Rudyard Kipling, *Kipling: Poems*; and Carmine Prioli, ed., *Lines of Fire: The Poems of General George S. Patton Jr.* See also Blumenson, *The Patton Papers*, 2:524, 846; and D'Este, *Patton*, 40, 261, 780.

31. During the final months of World War II, Patton instructed his wife, Beatrice, to attempt to get his poems published as a means of promoting his fame. Ultimately, her efforts paid off as *Cosmopolitan* published the poem "Fear" and paid the general $250 for his work. Chronological File, 1901–77, Patton Papers; Blumenson, *The Patton Papers*, 2:654.

32. For an example of Patton's writing on the obscure point of the US Army polo team, see George S. Patton Jr., "Report of Operations of the Army Polo Team of 1922," 230–33.

33. On this point, see generally Murray and Sinnreich, *Past as Prologue*.

34. George S. Patton Jr., "The Form and Use of the Saber."

35. Patton's fascination with automobiles began in 1911 when he purchased his first car while stationed at Fort Sheridan, outside Chicago. He loved tinkering with the engine and driving fast and would continue his love of speed and fancy cars for the remainder of his life. Martin Blumenson and Kevin M. Hymel, *Patton: Legendary World War II Commander*, 25.

36. Indeed, as early as 1922, the military budget was drastically reduced, and severe austerity measures were introduced. For an overview of the effect these cuts had on army doctrine and procurement, see Michael R. Matheny, *Carrying the War to the Enemy: American Operational Art to 1945*, 45–49.

37. Military Papers, 1903–76, Patton Papers.

38. For an overview of the campaign, see generally Eileen Welsome, *The General and the Jaguar: Pershing's Hunt for Pancho Villa, a True Story of Revolution and*

Revenge. For a detailed account of Patton's experiences in Mexico, see Vernon L. Williams, *Lieutenant Patton: George S. Patton, Jr. and the American Army in the Mexican Punitive Expedition, 1915–1916.*

39. Brian McAllister Linn, *The Echo of Battle: The Army's Way of War*, 65.

40. John J. Pershing, "Punitive Expedition Report."

41. D'Este, *Patton*, 199–266; Morningstar, *Patton's Way*, 57.

42. George S. Patton Jr., *War as I Knew It*, 5.

43. J. Furman Daniel III, "Patton as a Counterinsurgent? Lessons from an Unlikely COIN-Danista," 1–14.

44. Martin Blumenson, *Kasserine Pass.*

45. See Rick Atkinson, *An Army at Dawn: The War in North Africa, 1942–1943*, 358–484; and Leo Barron, *Patton's First Victory: How General George Patton Turned the Tide in North Africa and Defeated the Afrika Korps at El Guettar.*

46. Rick Atkinson, *The Day of Battle: The War in Sicily and Italy, 1943–1944*, 124–27; H. Essame, *Patton as Military Commander*, 90–97.

47. D'Este, *Patton*, 549–51; Blumenson, *The Patton Papers*, 2, 345.

48. Ruth Ellen Patton Totten, *The Button Box: A Daughter's Loving Memoir of Mrs. George S. Patton*, 96.

49. Ladislas Farago, *Patton: Ordeal and Triumph*, 66.

50. Interestingly, the road network around Bastogne was a result of the governments of Belgium and Luxembourg investing heavily in roads and autotourism during the interwar period, not from any broader strategic purpose. See Rickard, *Advance and Destroy*, 20.

51. Hugh M. Cole, *United States Army in World War II, the European Theater of Operations, the Ardennes: Battle of the Bulge*, 305, 445–85; Patton, *War as I Knew It*, 190.

52. Patton, *War as I Knew It*, 190.

53. Dwight D. Eisenhower, *Crusade in Europe*, 350.

54. For an excellent overview of the drive to Bastogne, highlighting the courage and dedication of the 4th Armored Division, see Leo Barron, *Patton at the Battle of the Bulge: How the General's Tanks Turned the Tide at Bastogne.*

55. Some have claimed that the Bastogne operation was an example of Patton's experience in the cavalry and his "cavalry to the rescue" mentality. While it is important to note the general's formative experiences in the horse cavalry, it would be too simple of an interpretation and would neglect his broader study of initiative, mechanization, surprise, and leadership. For an example of this "cavalry army" thesis, see Jerry D. Morelock, *Generals of the Bulge: Leadership in the U.S. Army's Greatest Battle*, 104, 133. For a more nuanced view of how Patton's experiences in the cavalry shaped his approach to war, see Essame, *Patton as Military Commander*, 142; David E. Johnson, *Fast Tanks and Heavy Bombers: Innovation in the U.S. Army, 1917–1945*, 33, 124–25; and Linn, *Echo of Battle*, 6, 136–37.

56. Atkinson, *Guns at Last Light*, 617.

57. Elizabeth Letts, *The Perfect Horse: The Daring U.S. Mission to Rescue the Priceless Stallions Kidnapped by the Nazis.*

CHAPTER ONE

EARLY BATTLES WITH HISTORY

The Young History Lover

GEORGE S. PATTON JR. was born on November 11, 1885, in San Gabriel, California, and raised on his family's ranch outside of Pasadena. The Patton family moved to the area from Virginia shortly after the end of the American Civil War in an attempt to escape the devastated southern countryside and to restore their fortunes. Despite the inauspicious circumstances surrounding their departure from Virginia, the family was extremely proud of its history, particularly its military traditions. According to family lore, their relatives had distinguished themselves as military leaders for centuries fighting in conflicts such as the Jacobite Rebellion, the American Revolution, and the American Civil War.[1]

History was the favorite topic of discussion in the Patton household, and the oral history of his family's military exploits made quite an impression on the youth.[2] Even though he would listen attentively for hours to these stories, he soon grew interested in more complex subjects. While he was a poor reader initially, his family happily indulged him with countless hours of reading from classic works of literature on military themes, including the Bible, Shakespeare, Homer, Walter Scott, and Julius Caesar, as well as a wide range of secondary sources on topics ranging from the Middle Ages to the Napoleonic Wars.[3]

These lessons were supplemented by visits from many former soldiers, both friends and relatives alike, who frequently stayed as guests at the Patton family home for extended periods. Two of the most notable visitors were the Confederate partisan leader Colonel John Singleton Mosby, and Patton's step-grandfather, Colonel George Hugh Smith, both of whom had distinguished themselves during the American Civil War. Mosby had a gift for storytelling and imparted colorful anecdotes as well as practical advice about how to fight on horseback, exploit initiative, and use unconventional tactics to achieve battlefield success.[4] Colonel Mosby also had a playful side and would indulge the young Patton for hours riding across the family estate on horseback, reenacting battles and taking orders from "Robert E. Lee," played by George.

Colonel Smith taught Patton to revere both his military ancestors and Confederate heroes such as Robert E. Lee and Thomas J. "Stonewall" Jackson.[5] Perhaps more than any other person, Smith instilled in Patton a belief that he was destined to continue the family tradition of being a soldier. While the pro-Confederate bias may strike contemporary audiences as anachronistic, this worship of the past and the veneration of the "Lost Cause" had a profound impact on the young boy, encouraging him to learn history and to seek a military career.[6] This indoctrination into the mythology of the Lost Cause was so complete that he apparently prayed every night to a picture of Confederate generals Lee and Jackson that hung above his bed, believing that they were God and Jesus. While he would eventually be corrected as to the identity of these two men, he continued to venerate them and his Confederate ancestors, later reflecting that they "have ever inspired me [to be] true to the heroic traditions of their race."[7] As he matured, he continued to read and study the American Civil War and would frequently use examples from the conflict to understand unfolding campaigns and explain his views of warfare to his fellow officers.

Even in his childhood play, Patton was committed to living history and mastering the military arts. George and his younger sister, Nita, spent countless hours dressing up as Civil War soldiers and reenacting battles on the family ranch. While Nita was generally a willing participant in these games, she did refuse to serve as the defeated Trojan hero Hector, despite George's insistence that he would tie her to a horse and drag her body around the family farm in a modern reenactment of his favorite scene from *The Iliad*.[8]

One day, when Patton was still a young boy, his father bought him a .22-caliber rifle. The youth and his rifle quickly became inseparable. Patton hunted small game and practiced his marksmanship until he could shoot oranges off fence posts from a respectable distance, much to the amusement of the family and their houseguests. He would carry his love of firearms for the remainder of his life as an Olympic athlete and onto battlefields in Mexico, Africa, and Europe.

Young George particularly enjoyed staging mock sword fights with his father. He crafted many swords and primitive weapons out of wood and scraps of metal, including one on which he wrote "Lt. Gen. G. S. Patton." When a local surplus store ran a sale on model 1870 French bayonets, his father proudly presented one of these weapons to his young son, who used it to attack local cacti with ferocious abandon.

These early childhood experiments with swordplay would also serve Patton well in future days.[9] He displayed his world-class fencing skill as a pentathelete at the 1912 Olympics, was twice invited to study fencing at the French cavalry school, was named the "Master of the Sword" for the US Army Mounted Service School, redesigned the US Army saber, rewrote the saber manual, and taught swordsmanship at Fort Riley, Kansas.[10] Because Patton had to serve as a swordsmanship instructor to officers more senior in rank, he would often use the wooden swords from his youth as an icebreaker, claiming, "But gentlemen . . . I have been an expert on the sword, if nothing else, for at least fifteen years, and in that respect I am your senior."[11]

In his early days, Patton also became an accomplished horseman. He learned to ride on the bloodstained saddle of his Confederate grandfather, Colonel George S. Patton. The blood, which was believed to be from the mortal wound that killed his grandfather at the Third Battle of Winchester, connected him to his family history while reminding him of the sacrifice of a warrior who had gone before him. Initially, Patton struggled at horse riding. The many falls he experienced hardened both his body and his mind, but did not diminish his desire to engage in military-style exercises. He persevered and became not only an excellent rider but also a ferocious polo player and a lover of horses. In the final days of World War II, this appreciation of the equine arts led him to divert forces to prevent the famous Spanish Riding School's Lipizzaner stallions and their trainers from falling into Soviet hands.[12]

While Patton recognized the anachronistic nature of cavalry in modern warfare, he simultaneously reveled in the romantic past. Throughout his professional life, he used his knowledge of horses to further his career, connect with the cavalrymen of the past, achieve excellence in another field of military endeavor, and perpetuate his warrior image. The spirit of the cavalry became an essential part of his own theories of warfare. Much like his mounted predecessors, he was comfortable with a fluid operational environment, used mobility to arrive at decisive points on the battlefield, and maintained the initiative by vigorously pursuing retreating foes.

Patton's story time and playtime during his youth amounted to much more than idyllic diversions of an overindulged child. Rather, these early exposures to the military profession reveal much about his character and later success. Even as a boy, he studied history and the military arts, confident that these games and historical reenactments had a practical use.

Formal Military Education at the
Virginia Military Institute and West Point

Given this early indoctrination into military history and his family's veneration of warriors from previous generations, it was perhaps natural that the young Patton would choose a military career. Despite his passionate desire to attend the United States Military Academy at West Point, he was initially denied an appointment. Undeterred, he attended the Virginia Military Institute (VMI) for a year before reapplying and ultimately gaining admission to West Point.

Despite his excellent military deportment and passionate desire to succeed, Patton struggled at West Point. He failed mathematics and was required to repeat his plebe year. The young cadet was devastated by his academic failures and seriously questioned his abilities. Several prominent historians claim that these academic struggles were the result of undiagnosed dyslexia, and significant anecdotal evidence exists for this interpretation. He had been slow to learn how to read as a child, struggled with spelling his entire life, lost his temper easily, believed that he was stupid, and frequently expressed doubts about his own abilities. All of these traits are common with dyslexics but are inconclusive speculation without a formal diagnosis.[13]

On the contrary, it is also well documented that Patton lacked a comprehensive formal education prior to attending VMI and West Point. He was late to enter school, changed schools several times in his formative years, focused his energies almost exclusively on history and literature, and was indulged by friends and family who would read to him and tell stories rather than force him to study or read on his own. That he was never exposed to a rigorous education in science and mathematics prior to attending West Point may be an equally valid reason for these early struggles.[14]

Whatever the cause of these deficiencies, Patton was neither lazy nor dismissive in his studies at West Point, and he was keenly aware that his early shortcomings risked jeopardizing his military career. Contrary to the cocksure image of legend, he harbored deep feelings of self-doubt. He would admit to these insecurities only in his diary and private letters, but the sense that he was never good enough would follow him for the remainder of his life.[15]

Instead of discouraging him, however, these private struggles drove his studies and broader pursuit of excellence. In a letter to his father, the young cadet revealed his insecurities by describing a dream: "Every body [sic] was pointing their fingers at me and calling me stupid. I was so scared that I woke up." In this same letter, he went on to propose a solution, noting that he believed the soldier's duty was to be "so thoroughly conversant with all sorts of military possibilities. . . . To attain this end I think it is necessary for a man to begin to read military history in its earliest and hence crudest form and to follow it down in natural sequence permitting his mind to grow with his subject until he can grasp with out [sic] effort the most abstruse question of the science of war."[16]

To help formalize these early studies, Cadet Patton began to compose a series of notes and observations regarding military history and strategy. These notes were a mixture of names and dates, quotes from famous military figures, and his own set of pithy maxims and turns of phrase. While many of these entries reflect a deep sense of loneliness and self-doubt, they also reveal a firm belief that if he worked hard he could achieve his dreams of fame and high command.

In 1905 he wrote, "By perseverance and study and eternal desire any man can be great," and "I hope and pray that whatever it cost I shall gain my desire." This powerful motivation was supported by numerous quotes from Napoleon and Frederick the Great about the need to act decisively and dedicate oneself entirely to the mastery of the military profession. With an eye toward his own career, he reproduced this quote from Napoleon in his diary: "To command an army well a general must think of nothing else."[17]

Even at this early stage of his career, it was clear that Patton believed that he needed to study military history and extract enduring principles of war. In an entry that would presage the offensive tactics he would apply four decades later, he noted the importance of aggressiveness and initiative: "In making an attack make only one and carry it through to the last house holder. Make the men who have gained ground lay down and hold it. What folly to let them fall back and to take part in a fresh assault. . . . Remember Fredrick [sic] the Great [who said to his faltering troops] 'Come on men do you want to live for ever [sic]?'"[18] Such entries provide a revealing insight into the mind of the future general. He was already using the study of the past and the written word to improve himself because he was confident that it would pay future dividends.

While Patton had few close friends during these years, he was already being viewed as a young officer with a soldierly bearing, a fierce competitive streak, a desire to attain the highest ranks in the army, and a love of military history. The cadet yearbook, *The Howitzer*, joked that he could stop an earthquake with an order, noted his penchant for accidents on the athletic field and his fastidious appearance, and even mentioned his private studies, noting, "It is said that Georgie Patton has compiled for future generals, a rule for winning every battle under any combination of circumstances."[19]

For the remainder of his time at West Point, Patton worked hard to improve his class standing and master the military arts. He was never a top student in the classroom, but he steadily improved his grades and was promoted to the position of regimental adjutant in recognition of his outstanding military bearing. In 1909 these efforts paid off, as he graduated 46th out of 103 after six years of formal military education at VMI and West Point.

One month prior to graduation, Patton and his classmates traveled to Gettysburg, Pennsylvania, to conduct a two-day study of the Civil War battlefield. This experience made such a powerful impression on the young cadet that he even spent his free time during the trip exploring the battlefield in greater detail. He believed that seeing the ground and reliving the events of the three-day clash made "one understand what men do in battle.[20]" Patton would return to this historical site and countless others over the course of his life because he believed that being in the physical spot where history occurred was the best way to glean a true understanding of the past. These studies of battlefields allowed the future general to place himself into the mind of past warriors and helped develop his "sixth sense" of how battles would unfold as a result of the geography and the positioning of troops. While this class trip to Gettysburg is often neglected by biographers, it clearly had a powerful impact on Patton's approach to war.

After graduation, he married his childhood sweetheart, Beatrice Ayer, the daughter of a Boston millionaire, in a lavish ceremony that was the talk of the New England elite. After the wedding, the couple embarked on a honeymoon tour of England prior to Patton beginning his army career. The couple visited sites from Arthurian legend, and Patton made notes on this history of the region in his diary.[21] While in London, he made a special effort to visit bookshops and purchase titles to augment his growing private library on history and military theory. Here, he purchased the first of several copies of Carl Von Clausewitz's *On War*, a book that he would return to read and quote countless times over his life.

The next six years would be a whirlwind for the young couple. In the fall of 1909, Patton reported to his first assignment with 15th Cavalry at Fort

Sheridan, Illinois. Army life in those days was often bleak and the post was far from glamorous, yet despite her aristocratic upbringing Beatrice was extremely supportive of her husband. For the remainder of their marriage, she was his fiercest and most dedicated supporter, acting as a confidante and intellectual foil. Her family wealth also provided the family with a considerably higher standard of living than most military couples, and they enjoyed significant leisure time for reading, riding, and hosting dinner parties.[22]

After two years at Fort Sheridan, Patton was reassigned to Fort Myer, Virginia. The young lieutenant served as a quartermaster for the cavalry unit there and was responsible for hosting various parties and social events. Beatrice's wealth and social status opened doors for George as he befriended influential figures in Washington society, most notably Secretary of War Henry Stimson. While stationed at Fort Myer, Patton was chosen to represent the United States in the modern pentathlon at the 1912 Olympics in Stockholm, Sweden. Patton was renowned throughout the army as an excellent all-around athlete and was particularly skilled in horseback riding, running, shooting, and fencing four events, which in addition to swimming constituted the competition.

While he only had a few weeks to ready himself for the competition, he trained extremely hard, quit smoking, and subsisted on a diet of raw steak and salad.[23] At the Olympic Games, Patton impressed his fellow competitors with his fiery competitiveness, which at least partially compensated for his lack of training and coaching. He pushed himself so hard that he nearly died after the cross-country run and after the swim had to be dragged from the pool with a boat hook to save him from drowning. His aggressive fencing technique almost completely neglected defense but kept his opponents off balance and made him a crowd favorite. Despite an unexpectedly poor showing in the shooting event, he finished fifth overall, an impressive accomplishment for the young officer.

While these exploits won the young officer accolades, Patton was apparently disappointed by his poor showing with the pistol. Although he insisted on using his service revolver rather than a specialized target pistol, he believed that he was truly a world-class marksman and that he had something to prove to his friends and fellow officers. These insecurities most likely led him to lie about the results of the Olympic Games and falsify his official report to the army. For the remainder of his life, he claimed that he did not actually miss the target and was denied an Olympic medal because his

Figure 2. Patton fencing in the 1912 Stockholm Olympics. His aggressive fencing style almost completely neglected defense but made him a crowd favorite. Official Olympic Report, 1912.

shooting was so accurate that two bullets passed through the same hole and were scored misses.

On Patton's insistence, Olympic judges searched for his missing rounds but could not find them in the target area. This issue did not affect any of the other world-class shooters, and it seems unlikely that a systematic flaw in the Olympic scoring system would have impacted only the young lieutenant. More troubling, Patton's report to the army reveals multiple discrepancies, and in each case the official score is less favorable to him than his own written accounts. Although Patton should have been extremely proud of his accomplishments, he was surprisingly insecure about his performance and falsified the historical record to further his career and ego.[24] While the facts of the case were not widely known for many decades, it is revealing that even in his moment of triumph, Patton saw that the writing of history could be applied to self-serving ends.[25]

This Olympic success won Patton widespread praise and attention and provided him with an opportunity of a lifetime. With the blessing of the army, the young officer quickly began making plans to study under the world-famous Charles Cléry at the French Cavalry school in Saumur while on extended leave following the Stockholm Olympics. After a whirlwind sequence of stops in Berlin, Dresden, and Nuremberg with Patton's parents and sister, Beatrice and George left the family and departed to Saumur. Here, he took two weeks of intensive instruction from Cléry, focusing on épée and saber, greatly improving his techniques, and kindling his desire to further learn the anachronistic arts of swordsmanship.[26]

After returning to the United States, Patton was assigned to a staff job at Fort Myer, Virginia. Here, he began his first formal attempt at applying his study of the past to improving the army cavalry saber. Based on his research and practical experience, he concluded that the current army sword was poorly designed for fighting on horseback. While the heavy, curved blade of the existing model was easy to swing in a downward motion, it was ill-suited for inflicting a single killing strike. In his view, this saber encouraged slashing attacks and repeated the mistakes that had been passed on without serious reflection since the eleventh century, "when the Cossacks, Poles, and Turkish horsemen were the only examples of the un-armored horse which men had to copy." His view was that "retention of an illogical weapon seems without basis in history," yet the military weapon was retained by unreflective bureaucrats and traditionalists who "clung to [it] as fondly as . . . the inaccurate Civil War musket."[27]

Based on his reading of Napoleon, who famously implored his troops at Wagram, "Don't cut! The point! The point!" and his study of Prussian general Verdy du Vernois, Patton concluded that only a strike with the point of a sword could deliver a single lethal blow.[28] On his own initiative, he applied this knowledge to design a new sword with a lighter, straighter blade designed for striking with the point, not the edge, and wrote an article for *Cavalry Journal* titled "The Form and Use of the Saber" to support his views. Armed with the article, which combined both technical expertise and historical insights, he lobbied senior army leaders to adopt his redesigned weapon over the existing model. These efforts paid off, and in 1913 the army adopted the Model 1913 Cavalry Saber, which is known to this day as the "Patton Sword."

Fresh off the triumph of redesigning the cavalry saber, Patton requested to return to Saumur to resume his studies in swordsmanship. In June he received the good news that he was granted his request to continue his studies at Saumur "for the purpose of perfecting yourself in swordsmanship." Under these orders, Patton was permitted to travel at his own expense until

October 1, 1913, when he was to report to the Mounted Service School at Fort Riley, Kansas. While this opportunity might have been prohibitively expensive for many officers, Patton relied on his wife's family's wealth to ensure that the couple would not need to sacrifice comfort or convenience. The Pattons traveled in luxurious style, even shipping their personal automobile to France at the cost of $300, an expense that was nearly twice the $157 monthly pay he received as an army second lieutenant.[29] The couple relished this opportunity to take their third trip to Europe in four years and considered it an opportunity to have another honeymoon in Europe.

The Pattons landed in Cherbourg, France, in mid-July and journeyed through Normandy toward Saumur at a leisurely pace. Along the way, they visited castles and other sites of historic interest, and George had his first look at the *bocage* where he would fight with the Third Army more than thirty years later. The couple arrived at Saumur in late July, and Patton resumed his instruction in swordsmanship under his master, Cléry, with a vigorous passion.

In many ways, this summer in France was the happiest period of the Pattons' married life. Both enjoyed traveling in the romantic and pastoral French countryside without their children or family to distract them.[30] George was particularly happy not only to be studying swordsmanship, but also to be improving his knowledge of history. The couple quickly became immersed in the history and culture of the region surrounding Saumur, visiting "museums and out-of-the-way towns."[31] These historical studies were conducted entirely on Patton's initiative and were greatly enriched by Beatrice, who was an active participant throughout the trip.

Beatrice was particularly intrigued by the story of the Fulke family, which had ruled the surrounding area since the Middle Ages. This family was notorious for their Machiavellian reign and their personal eccentricities. The Pattons scoured local town-hall records for additional information about the Fulkes and amassed an impressive amount of primary source material and knowledge on the subject. According to Patton's daughter Ruth Ellen, George would eventually use these materials to draft "the most horrible novel for us children. With his tremendous knowledge of history and life in the Middle Ages, he put in plenty of detail. We learned history the interesting way—because he 'told it like it was.'"[32]

In addition to the personal and historical connections, Patton made an unusually strong bond with the French landscape.[33] For Patton, the land was intimately tied to the course of French history. While people had come and gone, the land had remained largely unchanged:

> The terrain around Saumur had been fought over for a thousand years. Caesar and his legions marched through it in 40 BC, Attila the Hun ravaged the land, and many other lesser men followed their bloody trails. Georgie and Ma followed their routes by foot, by horseback, and by car. Georgie was convinced that he had fought over this terrain before, and would fight there again. His intention was to study it "for the next time around." He said that wars had been lost and won in these fields and hills through knowledge of the country; that history had already picked the battlefields, that it was the greatest teacher. One of his mottos was "There are no practice games in life."[34]

Here, Patton was building on his study of geography and battlefields that he first experienced during his class trip to Gettysburg, which had impressed upon him the practical value in studying battlefields with an eye toward extracting useful military knowledge.

Although this region of France lacked obvious strategic value and had not seen a major battle since the protracted struggle between Fulke and Henry I in the twelfth century, Patton was convinced that he would some-day fight a decisive battle on this very ground. As part of his studies, he began to analyze the region's road network during his spare time. With assistance from Beatrice, Patton drove countless miles along the local road network to reconnoiter the region's key points. He used the same roads William the Conqueror had used to move his forces through the region, stopping in sleepy towns such as St. Lô, Falaise, and Caen. Although the gruesome battles of the Normandy campaign that would make these towns famous were more than three decades in the future, Patton made careful notes on the region and its terrain.[35]

After Patton reported for duty at Fort Riley in October 1913, he sum-marized his findings on the geography and roads of the region. While he believed that the countryside was well suited for defense because the hedgerows provided natural barriers, the extensive road network would help overcome these defenses and allow for rapid transport of men and matériel. This insight is particularly impressive given that mechanization of armed forces was in its infancy and that railroads, not automobiles, were the mode of military transportation preferred by most military planners.[36]

Although the Normandy region was typically wet and rainy, Patton had already anticipated this contingency, concluding that the "watershed roads would always be firm enough to carry military transports no matter how much it rained."[37] Patton was thinking several steps ahead, not only predicting a campaign that would not happen for another three decades but also accounting for the potential difficulties, or "friction," that elements such as weather could incur on his forces.[38] While Patton has been often criticized as neglecting logistics, he took the time to survey several key ports that would prove to be vital embarkation points and supply centers during both world wars, again anticipating future needs decades in advance.

After his second summer in France, Patton returned to a more traditional army posting in the Mounted Service School at Fort Riley, Kansas. There, he was given the title of "Master of the Sword" and tasked with teaching army officers how to use his new weapon. Despite his busy training schedule, he continued to refine his theories on swordsmanship and on his own initiative rewrote the drill manual for the saber. The new manual, titled *Saber Exercise*, was a guide for using the redesigned sword as a weapon on the modern battlefield. To make his words come to life, he happily posed for drawings in the manual to depict proper sword-fighting techniques, exactly as he had envisioned them.[39] In 1915 selections from his diary were published as *Diary of the Instructor in Swordsmanship*, an informal set of observations designed to show the best methods for mastery and instruction of swordsmanship.

Armed with these publications, Patton began formerly consulting with the Ordnance Department on the production of the new "Patton Sword" and traveled multiple times to the Springfield Armory to inspect the quality of the new blades being produced. While these early successes have been overshadowed by more colorful events, they are an excellent example of how a very junior officer could force meaningful change for the army through an understanding of history.

Patton's First Taste of Action

Despite his many accomplishments, Patton craved action. As tensions with Mexico were rising, the second lieutenant was transferred to Fort Bliss, Texas, in mid-September 1915 and assigned to the 8th Cavalry. This posting, on the outskirts of El Paso, was desolate, but provided the potential for action that the young officer so desperately wanted. Since the collapse of the Porfirio Díaz dictatorship in 1910, US-Mexico relations had been increasingly strained by a series of military coups, cross-border raids, and attacks on American businesses. President Woodrow Wilson had made relations with Mexico a key point of American foreign policy, but his actions were interpreted as heavy-handed and imperialistic and fomented animosity and resentment south of the border.[40]

Out of the turmoil of the Mexican Revolution came an almost mythic Robin Hood figure, Francisco "Pancho" Villa. Part revolutionary, part bandit, Villa opposed the ruling governments of General Victoriano Huerta and Ventustiano Carranza and formed his own political movement, the Conventionalist Party. Villa and his supporters employed a mixture of violence, theft, intimidation, and charity to undermine the legitimacy of the ruling government and to win support for the cause. Ironically, Villa had initially looked to the United States for support for his revolution but became increasingly angered by US interference in Mexican politics. When President Wilson officially recognized the Carranza government in October 1915, Villa swore revenge on the United States and began an increasingly bold series of raids across the US-Mexico border.[41]

Sensing the potential for conflict, Patton immediately began to befriend local cowboys and lawmen in an attempt to gain practical advice on desert warfare and gather intelligence on the Mexican incursions into the area. The young officer was particularly close to the town marshal of Sierra Blanca, Dave Allison.[42] Allison was a legendary lawman who had once killed a bandit named Orasco and several members of his gang. Despite his advancing age and long white hair, he cut an impressive figure and became an instant hero for the starstruck junior officer. The two would talk for hours about mounted combat, and the young officer wrote to Beatrice about him in glowing terms, noting, "He kills several Mexicans each month. He shot Orasco and his four men each in the head at sixty yards. He seemed much taken with me."[43] Patton hoped that he would be able to measure up to his hero when his time came, and he spent countless hours practicing his pistol and rifle shooting, scouting the area, and thinking about the likely characteristics of the brewing conflict.

The conflict that Patton craved became a certainty in the early morning of March 9, 1916, when Villa and his men raided Columbus, New Mexico. In a surprise attack, Villa and approximately five hundred men attacked the small border town, looting and terrorizing the civilian population before withdrawing across the Mexican border. Eighteen Americans were killed, including eight soldiers from the 13th Cavalry Regiment.[44] The size and boldness of the raid made it impossible to ignore, and the American people demanded a military response, a prospect that Patton relished. Sensing that action was imminent, he quickly canceled his plans to travel to Rock Island, Illinois, for a planned lecture to the Cavalry Board on the 1913 model "Patton Sword" and began preparing for action.[45]

After receiving the news of the Columbus raid, the commanding officer at Fort Bliss, General John J. Pershing, began to immediately prepare for action. Despite his passionate desire to participate in the coming campaign, Patton soon heard a camp rumor that the 8th Cavalry would not be sent to Mexico because its commanding officer was obese and physically unfit for active service. He noted in his diary that "there should be a law killing fat colonels on sight," but he did not let this setback thwart his opportunity for action.[46]

Unwilling to accept the fact that he would be left behind, Patton personally lobbied General Pershing's staff for inclusion on the Mexican Expedition. Pershing got word of these lobbying efforts and telephoned Patton to discuss the matter, yet made no firm promises to include him. The next day, Patton appeared, uninvited, at Pershing's headquarters to personally lobby for a position on the general's staff. Pershing questioned the young Patton: "Everyone wants to go. Why should I favor you?" to which the young lieutenant replied, "Because I want to go more than anyone else."[47]

The gamble paid off. Pershing called the next morning and asked how soon he could be ready to leave, to which Patton responded that he had already packed his belongings and could leave immediately. This show of initiative impressed the tough-minded Pershing, and he made the enterprising officer his aide-de-camp.[48] Thrilled to be chosen for the mission, Patton immediately threw himself into the task of preparing Pershing's headquarters for their move first to Columbus, New Mexico, and then into hostile territory. He proved so indispensable to Pershing that even after one of his official aides, Lieutenant James L. Collins, returned to headquarters following an authorized absence, he retained Patton in an unofficial capacity.[49]

Despite the fact that he was busy drafting orders, censoring mail, making logistical preparations, and running messages to various commands, Patton was already applying his knowledge of military history to assess the strategic situation. In a letter to his father dated March 19, 1916, he correctly predicted the difficulty of the task at hand: "I think that we will have much more of a party than many think as Villa's men at Columbus fought well. . . . There are no roads and no maps and no water for the first 100 miles. If we induce him to fight it will be all right but if he breaks up it will be bad. . . . They

Figure 3. A young Lieutenant Patton strikes a jaunty pose for the camera during the 1916 Punitive Expedition in Mexico. Even at this early date, Patton understood the importance of cultivating the press and the power of imagery. Courtesy the General George Patton Museum of Leadership, Fort Knox, Kentucky.

can't beat us but they will kill a lot of us. Not me though."[50] For such a junior officer, this level of understanding and foresight is truly impressive. Here, he correctly anticipated that he faced a battle-hardened foe, that transportation and logistics would be a challenge, and that it would be difficult to use regular troops to counter a dispersed band of guerrillas.

Complicating these military realities was the fact that General Pershing's mission was vague; his force was split into two columns, which created numerous command-and-control issues; and he was not authorized to move into Mexico until March 15, giving Villa's force a six-day head start.[51] Despite these limits, Pershing did his best to execute his orders and bring his forces to bear on the bandits.[52]

The general drove himself relentlessly, going days without sleep, personally exposing himself to dangers, and being seemingly everywhere at once. The young Patton was impressed by Pershing's leadership, noting that he embodied Caesar's maxim that "fortune favors the bold."[53] Despite their differences in age and rank, the two officers quickly developed a mutual admiration and respect, and for the remainder of his life, Patton viewed Pershing as his greatest mentor.[54]

As the expedition moved south, Patton noted the poverty of the Mexican peasants and understood how they could be seduced by a figure such as Villa. "I really think that Villa bad as he is . . . was the man for us to have backed; he was the French Revolution gone wrong." He then voiced his frustration with guerrilla warfare, noting that "old Villa is Damned hard to find."[55] Little did he know how prophetic his words would be. On March 28, Pershing received an intelligence report that Villa had been wounded in the leg during a gunfight with forces loyal to Carranza on or about the twenty-seventh.[56] Villa was near death and chose to hide from his enemies rather than continue fighting. While his wounds put the Mexican bandit out of action, the inability to kill or capture Villa frustrated the American forces. Rumors and misinformation made it appear that he was everywhere, but try as they might they could not locate their quarry.[57]

This lack of accurate and timely intelligence regarding Villa's whereabouts was exacerbated by the fact that local guides and scouts were often unreliable. The official reports indicate numerous incidents when local guides led US forces on circuitous routes or purposely sent them in the opposite direction of the Mexican forces.[58] This lack of local cooperation forced the US Cavalry to rely heavily on its own scouts to reconnoiter the area of operations in advance, a job that Patton eagerly accepted as one of his additional duties. He enjoyed these operations and was particularly impressed that General Pershing often accompanied his men on these dangerous missions.

With Villa out of action, American attention quickly shifted to killing or capturing one of his top subordinates, Julio Cárdenas. Cárdenas had served as Villa's personal bodyguard and was believed to have helped plan and execute numerous raids including the attack on Columbus, New Mexico. While Patton enjoyed working closely with General Pershing, he desperately wanted to be part of the team tasked with hunting down this notorious Villaist leader. He lobbied the commanding general for a temporary assignment to one of the units assigned to this mission and was sent to serve in Troop C, 13th Cavalry, commanded by First Lieutenant Innis Swift.

Acting on intelligence reports, Troop C believed that Cárdenas was likely hiding in an area near the San Miguelito Ranch.[59] While the ranch had been searched unsuccessfully by US forces, Patton believed that Cárdenas was still nearby. A second search of the ranch conducted by Troop C found Cárdenas's wife, baby, and uncle. Patton and his men attempted to extract a confession from Cárdenas's uncle, but as he noted in a letter to his father dated April 17, "The uncle was a very brave man and nearly died before he would tell me anything."[60] While the letter does not explicitly indicate if or how torture was used, it paints a grisly image of the future general's willingness to flaunt international law by using violence on noncombatants. Despite the fact that they did not have actionable intelligence as to Cárdenas's location, Patton deduced that the presence of his family indicated that the Mexican leader was still in the area or may have reason to return to the ranch. Based on this military judgment, US forces remained in the immediate area and maintained a close watch on the San Miguelito Ranch.

On May 14, 1916, General Pershing assigned Patton to a foraging detail tasked with buying corn from local farmers. Patton commanded a force of ten soldiers from the 6th Infantry Regiment as well as two civilian guides. The party traveled in three Dodge touring cars, intended to help them quickly accomplish their mission and carry the corn back to Pershing's headquarters. The party traveled to Rubio, where they spotted a group of approximately sixty Mexican men. One of Patton's guides recognized some of the men as known members of Villa's band and noted that they were a "bad lot."[61]

After purchasing the corn as ordered, Patton decided to use the mobility provided by their automobiles to take the initiative and conduct a surprise raid on the San Miguelito Ranch. His plan was to surround the ranch, prevent any of its occupants from escaping, and possibly capture Cárdenas. In a scene worthy of a western movie, the Americans approached the ranch house at high noon, Patton leading one car from the northwest while the remaining two cars approached from the southwest. When he was about fifteen yards from the house, he saw three armed men on horseback. The mounted men turned away and went around the corner of the house but quickly reversed their course when they saw the rest of the American force approaching from the opposite direction.

The three mounted men began to fire at Patton, their rounds kicking up dirt but doing no damage. He returned fire with his pistol, shooting five times, also without result. The Americans approaching from the southwest then opened fire, and Patton was forced to seek shelter from the cross fire behind the corner of the house. He quickly reloaded his pistol and reentered the fight with the three Mexican riders, who were now trapped in the ranch's courtyard between the two groups of Americans.

Just as he returned to action, one of the mounted men rode directly into Patton's path. The wildly turning rider presented a difficult target, but in the heat of battle the young lieutenant remembered a valuable bit of age-old advice. "I started to shoot at him but remembered that Dave Allison had always said to shoot at the horse of an escaping man and I did so." He fired at the horse, breaking its hip and sending the bandit tumbling to the ground. According to Patton's earliest testimony, he and his men quickly fired on the dismounted rider before he had a chance to recover: "We all hit him. He crumpled up."[62]

As Patton and his men killed the first rider, a second bolted from the courtyard and attempted to flee to safety. The Americans unleashed a fusillade of rifle fire on the bandit, dropping him dead approximately one hundred yards away from their position. This left at least one, and possibly many more, armed fighters to contend with, and the Americans quickly refocused their attention toward neutralizing the remaining gunman and securing the ranch house. To obtain a more advantageous observation and firing position, Patton climbed up onto the roof of the house. The dirt roof collapsed under his feet, burying him up to his armpits and temporarily rendering him defenseless, but he quickly pulled himself out of the broken roof and returned to action. While Patton was extracting himself, the third gunman who had been wounded in the battle attempted to flee on foot into the nearby fields, but was intercepted by one of the Americans' local guides, E. L. Holmdahl. The bandit feigned surrender but tried to shoot Holmdahl as he approached. The bandit missed and was quickly gunned down and killed by the guide.[63]

Patton wanted to search the house but was wary of a potential ambush. To shield him and his men, he quickly abducted four Mexicans who had been skinning a cow near the ranch and used them as human shields for the search of the residence. The search of the house revealed no additional fighters but did locate Cárdenas' mother, wife, and infant baby as well as a number of elderly women. No harm was done to these civilians, and attention soon shifted to examining the bodies of the three combatants for possible intelligence.

As they exited the house and began to inspect the carnage in the courtyard, the ornate saddle and saber still hanging on one of the dead fighter's horses quickly aroused suspicion that one of the fighters had been a high-status member of the Villa entourage. This was confirmed by the Mexican cow skinners, who identified the man killed by Holmdahl as none other than

Julio Cárdenas. Based on the empty slots in the bandit's gun belt, Patton's men determined that he had fired some thirty-five rounds at the Americans before he was silenced. Before being finished off by the Americans' guide, Cárdenas had also suffered four wounds, a tribute to his rugged constitution and determination to fight. The two other Mexicans were unnamed but identified as a Mexican captain and private.[64]

Patton and his men promptly collected Cárdenas's saddle and saber, tied the bandits' corpses to the hoods of their vehicles, and fled the scene before Mexican reinforcements could arrive. Just as they were leaving, the Americans spotted a group of about fifty men on horseback headed in their direction. A few shots were exchanged, but Patton and his band made good their escape. As they retreated, they cut several telephone lines to ensure that Villa's forces could not call ahead and plan an ambush, a tactic that had been perfected by cavalry units during the American Civil War.[65]

At approximately 1600 hours, Patton and his men returned to Pershing's headquarters, where they were greeted as conquering heroes. Pershing was presented the bodies of the dead Mexicans as trophies of war, and a sunset burial was hastily arranged. Patton was able to keep Cárdenas's sword and saddle, but, more important, he had proved himself in battle and won the respect and attention of his commanding general. Pershing soon nicknamed him the "Bandit Killer" and "Bandito" and mentioned him by name, with a brief description of his actions in his official report on the expedition, further advancing his reputation within military circles.[66] Their already close relationship deepened, and for the remainder of their lives Pershing would take a keen interest in Patton's career.

The American press was hungry for news and quickly seized on this relatively minor action. Almost overnight, Patton was a hero to millions, as papers across the nation told of his exploits. He personally befriended the *New York Times* reporter Frank Elser, who described him as "a thin, reedy-voiced lieutenant who strove to look like John J. Pershing" and credited him as having "initiated motorized warfare in the US Army."[67]

Patton loved the accolades and attention that this incident brought him and was pleased to learn that his family had saved many of the newspaper clippings documenting his adventures. This love of press clippings would continue throughout his long career, and he instructed his wife, Beatrice, to continue sending him newspaper stories regarding his exploits. Even at this early stage, Patton could clearly appreciate the power of the popular press in shaping public opinion and telling his story to a broader audience.

For the remainder of the Mexican campaign, Patton saw little action due to both the inactivity of Villa and his men as well as an injury he sustained from an exploding lantern that severely burned his face.[68] While recovering from this accident, he received a letter from Pershing wishing him a full and speedy recovery, but also counseling him on his career: "Do not be too insistent on your own personal views. . . . Our first duty is toward our own government, entirely regardless of our own views. . . . We are at liberty to express our personal views only when we are called upon to do so or else confidentially to our friends, but always confidentially and with the complete understanding that they are in no sense to govern our actions."[69] While it is unclear precisely what caused Pershing to provide this advice, it would prove to be extremely wise. For the remainder of his career, Patton would struggle to control his tongue, and it would ultimately prove his undoing.

Despite Pershing's advice to keep his thoughts and opinions more private, Patton wanted to be heard and express his insights on warfare to a broader audience. To this end, he composed a brief series of lessons learned that appeared in *Cavalry Journal* in 1917 under the title, "Cavalry Work of the Punitive Expedition." This short piece represented a significant break from his previous publications. Rather than simply using history to lobby for his theories regarding the design and use of the cavalry saber, this article attempted to pass on his experiences regarding scouting, stealth, fire discipline, and small-unit tactics for cavalry forces. For Patton, the lessons of the American Civil War were that cavalry forces typically rode to battle but then fought as dismounted light-infantry units:

> If our cavalry is to be limited to mounted work, then it has failed to profit by the lessons of the Civil War. For open warfare, under modern conditions, it is more necessary than ever to have troops that are able to move rapidly from one place to another over any kind of country and to arrive at the point of action fit for a fight. In addition to the important functions or reconnoitering and screening, and the dashing sphere of mounted combat, the cavalry must know how to fight on foot. Perfect control of the horse and expert use of the pistol or saber are demanded for successful mounted attack, while thorough training in rifle firing and mastery of the principles of fire tactics are equally essential in the dismounted fight. Our cavalry should be prepared to fulfill both these requirements in the future, or it may expect to receive scant consideration either in or out of the service.[70]

These observations were grounded in both his own experiences fighting in Mexico as well as the historical experiences of guerrilla fighters such as John S. Mosby and Dave Allison, who used horses to ride to battle but often chose to fight on foot.[71] Like his cavalry predecessors, Patton used the mobility of horses and automobiles to maintain initiative and achieve surprise, but chose to fight dismounted to present a smaller target and better conform to the surrounding terrain.[72]

Using history as a guide, Patton was able to adapt these tactics to fit the time. He understood that most cavalry battles were fought dismounted and insisted that the cavalry needed to relearn the lessons from the Civil War, yet he adopted the new technology of the automobile to extend their range and provide additional speed for his scouting missions and raids. For Patton, the cavalry would retain its relevance only if it could be adaptive to the needs of the moment. While he relished the opportunity to "meet the thunderous squadrons of a civilized foe . . . [and] charge them with as headlong an ardor as animated the troops of Seidlitz or Murat," he recognized that it was only a small and increasingly anachronistic part of the cavalry's mission. The less glamorous reality was that the cavalry would be used as it had during the Civil War and the recently concluded Punitive Expedition to "hold the foe at bay while our citizens arm . . . as did the men of [Nathan Bedford] Forrest" or to "pursue an enemy, as cruel and elusive as a coyote," as his troops had in Mexico.[73]

While a relatively small part of Patton's career, these actions in Mexico whetted his appetite for further adventures, brought him his first taste of fame, and marked him as a junior officer of exceptional ability. On a more private level, they seemed to confirm the value of both his childhood play on his family's California ranch as well as his engagement with history. These pursuits paid practical dividends, as he was able to ride, shoot, and think to achieve his first battlefield victory.

Patton would soon move on to larger and more complex military challenges in World War I, yet he would return to his glories in Mexico countless times during his life. He loved to tell the story and appears to have purposely embellished it to perpetuate his mythical image. The best evidence of this evolving narrative is Patton's own written retelling of the story from 1928. Here, he altered his account to provide a more flattering version of his killing of the man whose horse he had shot out from underneath him as he rode in front of Patton's pistols. In 1916 Patton clearly claimed that he and his men fired on the man immediately after he fell from his horse and that "we all hit him."[74] Twelve years later, he omitted the contributions of his men and injected an element of sport into the shooting, claiming that he was "impelled by misplaced notions of chivalry" and "did not fire until on the Mexican who was down until he had disentangled himself and rose to fire."[75]

Whether motivated by a desire to embellish the historical narrative or simply by the passage of time, this recasting of history is troubling. Not only does it perpetuate the myth that Patton was a pure warrior adhering to an anachronistic warrior ethos, but it also makes him the central figure in the drama at the expense of his brave comrades. While he would repeat this pattern of using history to help him win his battles, he would also continue to write and rewrite history for more self-serving ends. This troubling rewriting of history indicates that, even as a junior officer, Patton relished fame and glory and understood that crafting a compelling narrative of a perfect warrior had the power to make his dreams a reality.

Anticipating World War I

Even before his adventures in Mexico, Patton wanted to fight in World War I. This desire stemmed not only from his thirst for action and yearning to test himself, but also from two trips that he took to France in 1912 and 1913.[76] During both of these trips, Patton traveled with his wife, Beatrice, and the couple had ample downtime to explore the romantic French countryside, visit historical sites, and interact with locals. Perhaps the most interesting of these interactions was George's friendship with Lieutenant Jean Houdemon, a descendant of one of Napoleon's marshals and a fellow fencing enthusiast. These two young warriors were indeed kindred spirits: both would become heroes during the two world wars, both would reach the rank of general, both had a passion for history, and they would remain close friends for the remainder of Patton's life.[77]

Patton's feelings of friendship and desire for action would prove so strong that he would unsuccessfully request an assignment to fight in the French Army during the early days of World War I. The United States remained neutral for the first two years of the conflict, and for political reasons his request was denied by General Leonard Wood, who responded, "Don't think of attempting anything of the kind. . . . We don't want to waste youngsters of your sort in the service of foreign nations."[78]

Despite this rejection, the young lieutenant felt a deep connection and sympathy to the French people. According to his family, the deaths of much of the prewar French officer corps in the war's opening month had a powerful impact on Patton, and he compared them to his Confederate heroes: "The flower of the French Army, so soon to be mowed down by the trampling Bosch hordes. These were the men of legend. There will never be their like again. They reminded Georgie of the descriptions of the Southern cavaliers who had fought in the Civil War, and had been immortalized for him by his step-grandfather, Colonel Smith."[79] In the meantime, Patton would have to content himself with fighting a small and frustrating campaign in Mexico and studying wars in preparation for battles yet to come.

The war in Europe added urgency and focus to his academic and professional studies. Prior to the US entry into the conflict, Patton read broadly on subjects such as Saxon England, the Holy Roman Empire, and an account of the 1898 campaign in the Philippine Islands. He also made a concerted effort to read as many of the intelligence reports on the unfolding war in Europe as possible as well as many of the primary sources on German military techniques. On his own initiative, he purchased *A Critical Study of German Tactics and of the New German Regulations*, by Major de Pardieu; a two-volume work titled *Tactics*, by Colonel William Balck; and *How Germany Makes War*, by Friedrich von Bernhardi, and made extensive studies and notations on each of these works.[80]

During this period, he also read a book on mass psychology, *The Crowd: A Study of the Popular Mind*, by Gustave Le Bon.[81] This work argued that people behave differently when emboldened by the collective will of a group and could be manipulated by charismatic leadership. With an eye toward improving his leadership style, he noted in the margin notes, "The will to Victory thus affects soldiers. It must be inculcated. G." On page 148, he earmarked a passage that read: "Prestige is the mainspring of all authority. Neither gods, kings nor women have ever reigned without it." Then, adding his own note in the margin, Patton concluded, "Hence, it must be acquired."[82]

While Patton had always been a book lover, this self-imposed professional reading list is revealing. Frustrated by his inability to fight, he decided to use his time to learn, trusting that his moment for glory would come. Although largely unnoticed, this ability to study the realities of the new conflict, distill its lessons, and think about how he could do things better was a critical element of Patton's success. In studying intelligence reports and German sources, he was trying to know the enemy, and in studying the psychological underpinnings of leadership, he was trying to know himself and the minds of the men he would one day lead into battle.[83]

World War I

America's entry into World War I would rapidly accelerate Patton's development as an officer and allow him the opportunity to test himself in modern combat. By the end of the war, he had risen to the rank of colonel; commanded one of the first American tank battalions; demonstrated his courage and leadership; won several medals, including the Distinguished Service Medal, the French Croix de Guerre, the Purple Heart, and the Distinguished Service Cross; and had successfully tested many of his theories regarding tanks and mechanized warfare.

Patton was able to achieve these impressive feats in part because of his skills as a leader and his ability to rapidly absorb technical details, but also because of his more academic qualities. The new realities of modern trench warfare had frustrated many of the top generals and resulted in the deaths of millions, yet Patton would quickly see the tank as the means for breaking this bloody stalemate. By applying ancient principles such as concentration of force, initiative, and surprise to the new armored doctrine, he was able to achieve what many of the top Allied commanders had been unable to do for nearly four years—break the German lines, exploit this penetration, and allow the Allies to advance.

When America finally entered the First World War, Patton was overjoyed. News of the war served to distract him from the fact that his father had recently lost his race for US Senate in California and that his wife and father-in-law were both seriously ill.[84] On May 18, 1917, Patton received a telegram to report to General Pershing's headquarters in Washington, DC. Pershing had recently been selected to command the American Expeditionary Force and begin the task of moving American forces to Europe and preparing them for combat. Pershing's promotion was excellent news for the young officer, as it ensured that his idol and mentor was going to play the leading role in the coming conflict. To help assist his boss in the gargantuan task of preparing the US Army for war on the European continent, Patton was promoted to captain and given command of sixty-five enlisted personnel, including drivers, orderlies, signalmen, and medical corpsman, as part of the advance party of General Pershing's headquarters.

Patton sailed for England on May 28, 1917, and arrived in Liverpool ten days later. Seemingly everywhere they went, the Americans were treated as heroes. In both Liverpool and later in London, they were cheered, entertained by dignitaries, and given military honors. Much to his delight, Patton received a personalized tour of the Tower of London, signed the king's guest book at Buckingham Palace, and was treated to numerous dinners and toasts before sailing to Paris with Pershing and his advance staff five days later.

In Paris the Americans were again greeted as heroes. In a letter to Beatrice, Patton described their journey through Paris as "the most inspiring drive I ever took." The Americans' located their headquarters near Napoleon's tomb and began to prepare for the arrival of hundreds of thousands of additional troops to the European continent. Despite the fact that the battle lines were less than sixty miles distant, Patton lived in comfort, settling into a routine that provided him ample leisure time. This fact was not lost on him, as he made frequent references to the unusual disconnect between his plush surroundings and the horrors of war. To fill his time, he enjoyed his first flight in an airplane, dined at fancy restaurants, and made plans for bringing his wife to Paris. While Pershing would ultimately prohibit officers from bringing their wives into the theater, Patton attempted to persuade Beatrice to traveling to Paris by claiming, "We are just as safe here as you are at Avalon [Massachusetts]   It is hard to think that a war is going on so near."[85]

While Patton enjoyed the luxuries and comforts of Paris, he quickly tired of scheduling visits for VIPs, censoring mail, and accompanying Pershing to various meetings. On June 28, he complained to Beatrice, "With my present job I am bound to live long even if I am not happy. . . . Perhaps some time [sic] I shall get a real job."[86] Frustrated in his current capacity, the eager young officer began to seek out and lobby his chain of command for a role in a combat unit. Pershing moved the American Expeditionary Force's headquarters to Chaumont in September, yet Patton's role changed little and he remained desperate to escape the boredom of his administrative duties.

One possibility for an active posting was in the new tank corps, an opportunity he discussed in a September 1917 letter to Beatrice:

> There is a lot of talk about "Tanks" here now and I am interested as I can see no future in my present job. The casualties in the Tanks is [sic] high that is lots of them get smashed but the people in them are pretty safe as safe as we can be in this war. It will be a long time yet before we have any so don't get worried. . . . I love you too much to try to get killed but also too much to sit on my tail and do nothing.[87]

A few weeks later, while recovering from a case of jaundice, he shared a hospital room with Colonel Fox Conner, and the two discussed the future of the tank corps and the relative opportunities for action and advancement in each branch. While Conner is known as the "man who made Eisenhower," he apparently had a powerful impact on Patton as well by encouraging his interest in tanks.[88]

Although Patton does not record the exact date of the momentous decision, he noted in his diary, "Some time [*sic*] about the end of September Col. [LeRoy] Eltinge asked me if I wanted to be a Tank officer. I said yes and also talked the matter over with Col. McCoy who advised me to write a letter asking . . . that my name be considered[.] I did so."[89] Patton's letter on his own behalf dated October 3, 1917, was addressed to General Pershing and made an impressive case for why he should be reassigned to the tank corps:

> I have used Gas Engines . . . and have used and repaired Gas Automobiles since 1905. . . . I speak and read French better than 95% of American officers. . . . I have also been to school in France and have always gotten on well with Frenchmen. I believe I have quick judgement and that I am willing to take chances . . . have taught this for two years at the Mounted Service School where I had success in arousing aggressive spirit in students. . . . [and he was] the only American who has ever made an attack in a motor vehicle.[90]

While presumptuous, this letter made an excellent case that he was the ideal candidate for an assignment to the new tank corps.

What Patton left out was that he had also been thinking about armored vehicles in various forms for decades. As a boy, Patton converted farm wagons into armored vehicles inspired by the war wagons of John the Blind of Bohemia. On one memorable occasion, Patton pushed his armored cart down a hill into the family turkeys. The flock was devastated by the careening wagon, but Georgie avoided punishment by claiming that he was reenacting the fifteenth-century battle tactics. When questioned about how he knew about John the Blind and his deeds, the precocious youth simply replied, "I was there." This unlikely explanation apparently satisfied his parents and may have been the first example of the future general using a claim of reincarnation to further his own interests.[91]

While Patton may not have literally served with John the Blind, he clearly had thought about the potential for motorized vehicles to transform war. He was particularly fond of automobiles and enjoyed driving fast. He owned various automobiles prior to World War I and had even paid to have his car shipped to France during the summer of 1913, so that he and Beatrice could explore the back roads of Normandy. When combined with his youthful experiments, his creative mind, his experience using cars as scout vehicles and troop carriers in Mexico, and his desire for action, it is obvious in retrospect that he was a uniquely good choice for the armored corps.[92]

On November 10, 1917, the day before his thirty-second birthday, George S. Patton Jr. became the first member of the US Tank Corps. He was assigned an assistant, First Lieutenant Elgin Braine, a former artillery officer, and was instructed to report to Langres, France, and establish a tank school. Here, the only two members of the United States Tank Corps were given broad latitude to establish the training, support, and logistics system that would help make American armored forces an actual fighting force in the months to come.

Patton immediately threw himself into the task of learning all he could about tanks.[93] He visited the French tank school in Chamlieu and, for two weeks, immersed himself in tank training. He drove and fired the weapons of Renault tanks and noted that his experiences with automobiles helped ease this transition, claiming, "It is easy to do after an auto . . . though you can see nothing at all."[94] During this period, Patton used his knowledge of French to begin translating the curriculum into English. Despite his reliance on the French expertise, he did not blindly accept the existing doctrine as the final word on the subject and instead adopted a critical approach to the accepted wisdom. He continually bombarded his hosts with a series of practical and theoretical questions about tank design and doctrine, a clear indication that he was intellectually absorbed by the potential for tanks to play a key role in future battles.

Patton and Braine were even allowed to tour the Renault tank factory, where they talked directly to the designers and manufacturers about their design and its strengths and weaknesses. This visit proved invaluable for the fledgling American armored forces, as Patton was able to incorporate his insights into training and doctrine, while Braine was able to help expedite the American manufacture of French Renault tanks under license.[95] While a relative newcomer to tanks, Patton actually suggested a number of improvements to the Renault team, including an armored bulkhead and a self-starter, that were eventually adopted into subsequent variants.[96]

While Patton was learning from the French at Chamlieu, the British sent 324 tanks into battle at Cambrai. It was the largest use of tanks to date, and despite the numerous troubles with vehicle reliability, infantry support, planning, and doctrine, the battle proved that tanks had the potential to revolutionize war. Patton studied this campaign with interest and met with the British armored pioneer Colonel J. F. C. Fuller to discuss their views on armored warfare. The two men focused on the problem of coordinating tank movements with artillery fire. While both men believed that indirect-fire support was important, they agreed that it deprived the tanks of their striking power and limited the speed of their advance. Both agreed that, despite the current doctrine, tanks should be provided the freedom of action to push forward on their own initiative and force decisive action.[97] Fuller's expertise would prove invaluable for Patton, and the two would continue to exchange ideas for the remainder of the war.[98]

Patton incorporated both this technical knowledge and his study of the British campaign at Cambrai to produce a fifty-eight-page document titled "Light Tanks."[99] This document dated December 12, 1917, was a truly impressive synthesis of theory and practice. The document was broken into four sections in which he outlined technical specifications and requirements of tanks, proposed an organizational structure for American tank units, outlined the brief history of armored warfare and provided tactical lessons learned from these experiences, and outlined a plan for training and deploying an American tank corps.[100]

Of these sections, the third section was particularly impressive from the perspective of a historian. Patton briefly summarized the drive to overcome the defensive stalemate of the trenches and then transitioned to a critique of the success and failures of British and French tank pioneers. Despite the limited information and outside analysis available to him, he was able to quickly determine that lack of numbers, support, and mobility often doomed the Allied tank operations. To avoid these pitfalls, American tanks must use initiative and mobility to keep driving forward: "Mobility is a most essential feature in all arms and is the chief place where the light tank has an advantage. . . . [T]hey must have maximum mobility. . . . The best defense against any and all . . . methods of attack is constant movement and watchfulness." While rooted in basic military principles, this recognition that initiative and movement were keys to the success of the tank forces was a critical breakthrough. Although maintenance issues would often derail tank attacks during the Great War, many of the early pioneers could not appreciate the need to move rapidly and exploit their advantages. These theorists could not conceive of armored vehicles as anything more than an infantry support platform and thus did not prioritize speed as a key element in their approach.

For Patton, the tank's combination of protection, firepower, and speed meant that it could fundamentally change warfare. While he would not be able to fully implement these theories until World War II, this initial insight was extremely impressive, given that he had never seen an actual tank battle prior to reaching these conclusions and that tank doctrine was in its infancy. At an unknown later date, Patton would write across the top of his copy of the report, "This paper was and is the Basis of the U.S. Tank Corps. I think it is the best Technical Paper I ever wrote," a clear indication that he was proud of his analysis and wanted to be remembered for his pioneering work on armored warfare.[101]

The next months were filled with recruiting, training, and equipping the infant tank corps. While he pushed his men at a frantic pace, Patton brooded about the lack of action and attempted to find relaxation by visiting historical sites and composing poetry. During this period of inaction, he also reflected on his understanding of history and study of British and French tank tactics. These lessons not only helped him to create the tank corps from scratch, but also helped him refine his broader understanding of warfare throughout the ages. For Patton, history repeatedly proved that new weapons technologies were important but that technology itself was useless without active leadership and brave warriors willing to risk their lives to achieve victory.

Acting on these historical lessons, Patton began to display his obsessive zeal for discipline, cleanliness, and professional pride that would become a trademark for the remainder of his career. The Tank Corps commanding officer insisted that his men develop the same warrior spirit as their Greek and Roman predecessors. In making these declarations, he also praised the tenacity of their German enemy, noting, "The reason the Bosch has survived so long against a world at arms is because he is disciplined. Since 1805 he has bred this quality as we breed speed in horses." He continued to underscore that the American tank force must do everything possible to develop this same warrior spirit: "It is by discipline alone that all your efforts, all your patriotism, shall not be in vain. Without it heroism is futile. You will die for nothing. With DISCIPLINE you are IRRESISTABLE."[102]

While Patton would return to these themes for the remainder of his career, he enjoyed his first successes in inspiring his men in the months prior to their baptism of fire. The Tank Corps quickly developed into a close-knit community that reflected the spirit of its commanding officer. In fact, they even developed a nickname for a snappy salute—a "George Patton."[103] To augment the dressy appearance of his men, Patton also sponsored a contest

Figure 4. LTC Patton standing in front of a tank in France in 1918. Courtesy the General George Patton Museum of Leadership, Fort Knox, Kentucky.

to design a shoulder patch for the American tankers. A pair of lieutenants won with a design that combined blue, yellow, and red into a single triangle (the traditional colors of the infantry, cavalry, and artillery branches respectively). He approved the winning design and gave the two junior officers $100 of his own money to go into town and have patches made for the entire unit. This seemingly minor addition to the uniform had an immediate impact on unit morale and was so popular with the troops that it is still used as an insignia in the US Army to this very day.[104]

Patton's promotion to lieutenant colonel at the beginning of April 1918 further whetted his desire to test his new unit and tactics. He staged a series of mock battles beginning on April 16, 1918, that he described as "the first Tank Maneuver ever held in the US Army."[105] In these exercises, two tank battalions spearheaded an attack, while a third remained in reserve to provide follow-on support and fill in any gaps in the American lines. This built on the British experiences at Cambrai, where armored forces were placed behind the infantry reserve and often responded too slowly to requests for support from the front. Patton considered the British doctrine "no longer applicable" and was happy to see his theories pass their first field test when one of his reserve tanks filled in a gap left by a vehicle that had become stuck in a shell hole and the attack was able to continue.[106]

Patton's First Taste of Modern War
Patton was ultimately given the opportunity to apply his theories on tanks during the final months of World War I. In September 1918 he led his unit into two major battles, the Battle of St. Mihiel, and the Meuse-Argonne Offensive. Patton's men joined the American attack at St. Mihiel on September 12, 1918. Here was a critical test for Patton as a tank theorist and a field-grade officer, and he did not disappoint.

At St. Mihiel, the American tank force was tasked with capturing the German-held town of Essey, a key road juncture in the region. As they approached the town, Patton walked in front of his tanks and helped coordinate their movements. During the advance, he worked closely with members of the 84th Brigade of the 42nd Infantry Division commanded by Brigadier General Douglas MacArthur. The two young officers worked well together and were both impressed by the other's coolness under fire.[107] Spearheaded by Patton's tanks, the Americans liberated Essey and with MacArthur's blessing pushed onward to the town of Pannes. As the tanks approached the town, Patton rode on top of one of the American Renault tanks to both keep pace with the advance and to serve as a visible symbol to inspire his men. This bold action was successful, and the Americans were able to capture Pannes as well, far exceeding their original objectives.[108]

It was a very impressive baptism of fire for the tank corps and one that helped to cement in Patton's mind the soundness of his new doctrine as well as his belief that fighting spirit and hands-on leadership remained critical in modern warfare. Despite this success, his willingness to expose himself to fire angered his commanding officer, General Samuel Rockenbach, who maintained that a field-grade officer's duty was to not take foolish risks. Rockenbach was particularly piqued by his belief that Patton had violated the spirit of his orders to not ride in a tank under any circumstances by riding on top of the tank as it approached Pannes.

Despite these internal disagreements, the American tanks and their ambitious leader had exceeded all expectations during their initial baptism of fire. After just a day and a half of fighting at St. Mihiel, the offensive was over, and the Allied High Command was already looking for the next opportunity

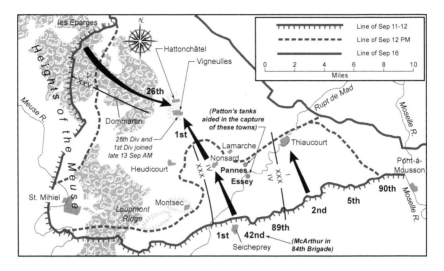

Map 1: St. Mihiel. Fighting alongside Douglas MacArthur's 42nd Infantry Division, Patton's tanks spearheaded the successful attack at St. Mihiel on September 12, 1918. The attack far exceeded the expectations of the Allied commanders and won Patton his first accolades as a field-grade officer. Map by Chris Robinson.

to employ the American tankers. Patton complained privately that he had wished for a longer and tougher first battle, but he would not have to wait long for this opportunity. In his short amount of downtime, he toured the battlefield in an attempt to distill whatever lessons he could from the recent fighting, again acting on his belief in the value of touring battlefields to learn from the past. He wrote his father that he enjoyed "a most interesting walk over the battlefield. . . . Like the books but much less dramatic."[109]

The American tankers were quickly reassigned to an even more ambitious operation, the Meuse-Argonne Offensive, planned for September 26, 1918. This battle would commit more than a million American soldiers to attacks on German defensive positions and would be the largest and most costly US operation during the entire war. Patton's unit was deployed in support of the 28th and 35th Infantry Divisions as they drove toward the French villages of Cheppy and Varennes. The American tankers had difficult terrain for their advance, and their mission was further complicated by the fact that the tanks lacked an adequate means for refueling in the field. Patton overcame these challenges by personally scouting the terrain for his unit's attack and ordering that two twenty-liter gas cans would be carried by each tank to supplement their own fuel supplies. He had already anticipated the issue with refueling during the St. Mihiel campaign and worked diligently in the intervening days to create this ad hoc means of extending the range and independence of his tanks.[110]

The Meuse-Argonne Offensive began at 0230 on September 26, 1918, with a massive artillery barrage intended to soften up the German defenders. Among the thousands of Americans who watched in awe was a National Guard captain from the 35th Infantry Division, Harry S. Truman, who commanded a four-gun team that provided artillery fire for the American advance. With Patton leading on foot, his tanks began their drive toward the town of Cheppy at 0530. The tanks, as well as their supporting infantry units, used the smoke and fog that covered the battlefield to help conceal their movements and attempted to follow as closely as possible behind a creeping artillery barrage designed to sweep away any Germans and obstacles in their path.[111]

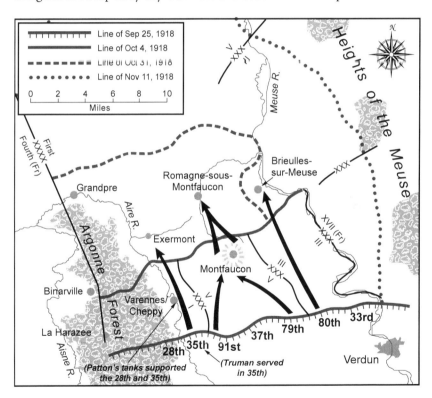

Map 2: Meuse-Argonne Offensive. On September 26, 1918 Patton again led his tanks into battle in the opening phases of the Meuse-Argonne Offensive. While Patton was wounded on the first day of fighting and would not return to action before the end of the war, his bold leadership helped keep the American assault moving despite fierce German resistance. Map by Chris Robinson.

Aided by dense fog cover, by about 1000 Patton had advanced to within a half kilometer of Cheppy. As the fog began to lift, however, he soon realized that the German fire was becoming much more deadly, and that the majority of his men were straggling far behind. Whether it was because of the literal fog of war, his own eagerness to advance toward the enemy, or the fact that the tanks had difficulty crossing German obstacles, he was approximately 125 yards ahead of his tanks and the main body of his men when the fog began to lift and expose his position. With their cover gone, "The tanks as well as the Infantry, were subject to intense fire from the front, flanks and sometimes from the rear."[112]

In the deadly German cross fire, chaos and confusion reigned. Tanks were stuck in the mud, infantry units were lost, the chain of command was broken, and the attack appeared to be disintegrating. Patton recognized that he needed to restore order and initiative to the American attack. As the German shells began to find the range, he initially struggled to find the courage to force himself to move forward. According to his daughter Ruth, he found personal inspiration from his ancestors whom he had so worshiped as a small boy:

> He was afraid. His hands were sweating and his mouth was dry. There was a low bank of clouds behind the rising ground, and he looked up and saw, among the clouds, his ancestors. The ones he had seen in pictures looked like the daguerreotypes and their paintings; there was General Hugh Mercer, mortally wounded at the Battle of Princeton; there was his grandfather, Colonel George Patton; mortally wounded at the Battle of Cedar Creek; there was his great-uncle, Colonel Waller Tazewell Patton, mortally wounded at Gettysburg. . . . They were all looking at him, impersonally, but as if they were waiting for him. He knew what he had to do, and continued the tank action.[113]

His courage screwed to the breaking point by the "visions" of his ancestors, Patton personally led a party to dig out the stranded tanks. He did so at great personal risk, exposing himself to fire the whole time, but was able to dig out the trapped tanks and restart the American advance.

With his tanks now free from the mud, Patton personally organized a mixed force from the infantry and armor units available and resumed the attack. Despite his own private fears, he led from the front of the ragtag formation and inspired the men forward by example. The men followed, but once again Patton rushed too far forward. As he paused to rally his men to catch up with him, he was suddenly struck in the upper-left thigh by a machine-gun bullet fired from about fifty meters away. The bullet produced a tremendous wound that was "about the size of a dollar where it came out."[114]

He attempted to move forward, but his legs quickly gave out and he was unable to continue. His batman, Private First Class Joe Angelo, dragged him to the relative safety of a shell crater and provided lifesaving first aid. Here, he lay in shock for between one and two hours as "the Bosch shot over the top as fast as he could."[115] A medic came by and changed Patton's bandages, but could not evacuate him because the same German machine gun that had inflicted his wound remained intact. Only after the Americans silenced the machine gun was he moved to the rear, barely clinging to life. He spent nearly a month in the hospital and was not returned to a combat role prior to the Armistice on November 11, 1918.

While his body was recovering, Patton's mind was working overtime to understand the lessons of the recent battles. During his hospitalization, he began to write a 249-page essay, "A Study of the Combat of Cavalry Up to and Including the World War," which he hoped would drive doctrine and thinking on armor during the interwar years. This impressive report highlighted both the technical advances of the American tankers and the softer skills such as training, doctrine, and fighting spirit.[116] While the American tank forces had suffered extremely high casualties (as high as 90 percent in the First Tank Brigade), they had been generally effective in silencing German machine guns, helping support infantry assaults, and exploiting breakthroughs. Furthermore, the tankers "established [their] reputation for not giving ground. They only went forward. And they are the only troops in the attack of whom that can be said."[117] This ability to combine the ancient principles of courage and the warrior ethos with the latest developments in technology would become a Patton trademark. For the remainder of his career, he would highlight the importance of both human factors and technology in his writings and analysis, a clear indication that he understood the complex and fluid nature of war.[118]

Preparing for the Next War

Although the war ended before he could fully test his theories on armored warfare, Patton believed that careful thought must be given to institutionalizing this hard-earned expertise and exploiting it for future conflicts. After World War I, he was assigned to Camp Meade, Maryland, and given the opportunity to create the army tank doctrine and study advances in mechanized technology. Here, he met a young Dwight Eisenhower, and the two quickly became friends. Both men skirted the new Prohibition laws, Eisenhower distilling bathtub gin and Patton brewing beer, and they spent many hours sampling the fruits of their labor and discussing the views on modern warfare. Ironically, despite their own casual observance of Prohibition, the two men would conduct their own vigilante missions and attempt to intercept local bootleggers, dressing up like bandits and driving Patton's Pierce-Arrow down local back roads in search of action. In spite of their enthusiasm, they never encountered any bootleggers in their short careers as amateur lawmen.[119]

In their official capacities, Eisenhower worked as Patton's deputy. The two men shared a common belief that tanks would play a key role in future warfare, and they worked diligently to build the American tank force. As part of their efforts to better understand the technical aspects of tanks, they completely disassembled and rebuilt a British Mark VIII. So exacting was this experiment that "no pieces were left over and the machine operated when we were finished," an excellent result, since this was the only tank at Camp Meade.[120]

Despite the two men's zeal for armored warfare, they suddenly found that the army was uninterested in indoctrinating the lessons learned or investing in further research and development of tanks. Patton and Eisenhower lobbied hard for their beloved Tank Corps and repeatedly made the case that it should be an independent branch of the army. Despite their convictions, they soon realized they faced budgetary and bureaucratic resistance from the army and politicians alike. In an attempt to use his writings to convince the army of the soundness of his ideas, Patton published two articles detailing his experiences during the Great War, but these efforts won him little professional recognition.[121]

In fact, Patton's advocacy for an independent Tank Corps may have had the unintended effect of stifling the development of armored doctrine, as it led to an unofficial censorship of future articles in the pages of *Infantry Journal* and *Cavalry Journal*. As the editors of these journals sought to restrict such disruptive thinking, articles advocating for wholesale changes soon disappeared from the pages of these publications, and the academic discourse suffered as a result.[122]

Like the rest of the US Army, the Tank Corps was gutted in terms of budget and manpower in the years following the Great War. While Patton was a true believer in the power of armored forces to transform warfare, he recognized that the anachronistic horse cavalry had better promotion and career potential and transferred to the 3rd Cavalry at Fort Meyer, Virginia, in September 1920. Although his transfer back to the horse cavalry helped perpetuate the notion that he was a romantic warrior from ages past, he never stopped thinking about the evolution of military technology and the potential characteristics of future wars. Despite his foresight and continued embrace of new technology, Patton was put in the uncomfortable position of actually having to advocate that the horse cavalry was the ideal means for missions such as patrolling the Mexican border and scouting. While this was a self-serving and careerist choice, it should not be interpreted as a rejection of mechanization or a sudden refusal to learn. Rather, it was Patton acting as a loyal member of the horse cavalry and conforming to the bureaucratic demands of his organization.[123]

In the years following the end of World War I, Patton was particularly interested in reading firsthand accounts of the recent war as a means of comparing his experiences with other key players. His old friend J. F. C. Fuller's 1920 book, *Tanks in the Great War*, was a personal favorite, and he made extensive underlining and notes in his copy.[124] In addition, he also read the studies from other British experts, including General Douglas Haig's *Cavalry Studies, Strategical and Tactical*, Lieutenant Colonel R. M. P. Preston's *The Desert Mounted Corps*, and W. T. Massey's *The Desert Campaigns*. In an effort to understand the thinking of his enemies, he dedicated significant time to reading German perspectives on the Great War, including General Erich Ludendorff's multivolume memoirs, Field Marshal Colmar von der Goltz's *The Conduct of War*, General Friedrich von Bernhardi's *The Future of War*, and General Hugo von Freytag-Loringhoven's *Deductions from the World War*.[125]

During the 1930 Christmas season, he celebrated in his own unique manner by reading works by General Hans von Seeckt and Ernst Jünger.[126] His study of von Seeckt, combined with intelligence reports of German armored tests, reinforced his belief that tanks would be an increasingly important part of any future war in Europe. In 1935 he would again take inspiration from German sources with his reading of Adolf von Schell's *Battle Leadership*. This book argued for a combination of active leadership and flexibility in modern war and developed the concept of *Auftragstaktik*. This approach was already well established in the German Army, but would become a key element in Patton's understanding of war and his future enemies.[127] These self-directed studies clearly indicate that the young officer valued deep theoretical engagement with foreign military writings and was actively learning about the impact of mechanization on war, despite the fact he remained in the horse cavalry.[128]

Whereas the war-weary Allies were satisfied to rest on the laurels of victory and their doctrine and military thought remained largely stagnant, the taste of modern warfare led Patton to craft some of the most original and clairvoyant military writings in American history. Between the wars, he anticipated nearly every major tactical and strategic change that would be encountered in World War II, writing and lecturing on subjects such as the development of armored doctrine, the role of mass armies in modern war, combined-arms warfare, logistics, road networks, training as a force multiplier, military psychology, leadership, and forward-air observation, and he even predicted a surprise Japanese attack on Pearl Harbor.[129]

While Patton's efforts to influence the thinking of the interwar army were largely ignored, he did achieve significant attention in 1932 for his Army War College thesis titled "The Probable Characteristics of the Next War and the Organization, Tactics, and Equipment Necessary to Meet Them." As part of his studies at the War College, the young officer was provided significant intellectual freedom to explore a "topic of interest to the War Department." While the War College was seen as a leisurely diversion from the rigors of military life and not a rigorous academic program, Patton used this opportunity to refine his understanding of mass armies and the effect of technology on warfare.[130]

In his thesis, Patton's mastery of history and exceptional strategic mind were on full display. Going back to 2500 BC, he noted the tension between small professional armies and mass formations and detailed the strengths and weaknesses of each force composition. While noting the successes of the Greek city-states and other mass armies at defending their homelands, he concluded that professional armies were generally more successful because of their superior discipline, ability to master complex tactics and weapons systems, and greater capacity to conduct protracted campaigns far away from their homes. Based on this analysis, he concluded that training and professionalism were essential elements to success in future war and argued that the United States should build a professional army and warrior culture of its own.[131]

On the issue of technology, he likewise traced the development of weapons to ancient times and claimed that changes in weaponry were an enduring element of war. While superior weaponry was critical, Patton repeatedly highlighted that new technologies must be supported with proper organization and training, as well as inspired leadership. Using examples that included the Thirty Years' War and the American Civil War, Patton concluded that without inspired and enlightened leadership, "similarity of organization, tactics, and equipment produced a long indecisive war." This trend was even more pronounced during recent conflicts such as the Franco-Prussian War and the Boer War: "Great mobility in a large theater of war, combined with new weapons and methods and opposed to stupid leadership and obsolete tactics, is bound to secure results out of all proportion to the means used."[132]

According to Patton's thesis, the general's job was to understand the tension between mass and professionalism and to properly implement new technologies to achieve victory. To make his point, he noted that during the Franco-Prussian War, Helmuth von Moltke was victorious because he mastered "novelty of organization, combined with usable numerical superiority and good leadership," and stated, "If the commanders had been swapped a year before the war started, the results would possibly have been reversed."[133]

After developing his theories about the role of professionalism and technology in war, Patton used the remainder of his thesis to predict the likely characteristics of a future war in Europe. While he noted the attempt of the Allies to limit German militarism after the end of World War I, he accurately predicted that Hans von Seeckt and other German generals were preparing the nation for war. The troubling development for Patton was that the Germans were able to subvert the spirit of the Versailles Treaty by creating a small professional cadre of soldiers that would form the basis for a larger and more dangerous German Army. He cited von Seeckt's "Armies of Today" and suggested that the Germans were doing more than simply "making the best of a bad bargain" but instead trying to revolutionize warfare. In contrast to the German efforts, Patton highlighted the writings of French military writers who noted the German advances but did not fully comprehend their extent and were constrained by budgetary and political realities.[134]

Patton was similarly critical of the austerity and malaise he witnessed in the interwar US Army. He argued that the modest cost savings of having a 130,000-man force with outdated equipment paled in comparison to the cost of fighting the First World War and made the case that it would pay a high price for its lack of professionalism in future conflicts. Having made this statement, he believed that the United States had an inherent advantage in modern warfare because of its superior industrial base and the American fascination with automobiles and aircraft. In contrast to the stalemate of

World War I, he argued that these small professional units could help restore mobility to the battlefields and win decisive victory. This mechanization, "if JUDICIOUSLY used, can materially lighten the amount of battle equipment carried by men and animals; if and only if we limit ourselves to small forces grouped in small units."[135]

Anticipating the budgetary limitations of the interwar army, Patton even proposed a system to purchase limited numbers of new weapons. He argued that the army should continually be purchasing and evaluating limited numbers of new weapons systems, but should not commit to any specific platform until the technology was mature and could be adopted into the army in sufficient numbers. In addition to saving money, the limited acquisitions would allow for experimentation without burdening the force with maintaining large numbers of legacy platforms (an issue that particularly hampered the development of French armored forces during the period).[136]

These views so impressed the War College faculty that the commandant classified it as a "work of exceptional merit" and circulated it within the War Department. Although the Depression-era army did not have the financial resources or the political support to implement Patton's suggestions, he anticipated the rise of the German Army and predicted the adoption of blitzkrieg tactics nine years before America entered World War II. This thesis, combined with Patton's excellence in the classroom, ensured that he graduated with honors from the War College in 1932 and established him as one of the top majors in the army.[137]

Despite the success of this impressive work, it sometimes uses history in a selective manner. In his effort to demonstrate the inferiority of mass armies versus professional ones, he highlights the battlefield successes of Carthaginian general Hannibal and his small professional army. To explain the eventual Roman triumph over Hannibal, he then attempts to recharacterize the Roman forces under Scipio as a professional force rather than a mass army. This slippery application of the term *professional* blurs the distinction between mass and professional armies, a flaw that Patton compounds further by conveniently blaming the Carthaginian defeat at Zama on the "bad behavior of the Carthaginian Cavalry, which, in this case, was not professional."[138]

This selective view of history helped maintain the internal logic of Patton's thesis, yet the fact that he would interpret history in such a manner is troubling. Despite his love of the past, he clearly was not above using it for his own ends. To win professional respect in the army, he had already falsified his report from the 1912 Olympics and in 1928 had altered his account of the gun battle with Julio Cárdenas. Now, he was mischaracterizing the causes for Roman victory in the Punic Wars to better fit his desire to build a professional army. While these manipulations of history will be discussed in greater detail, it is worth noting that Patton could be a biased source and was not above crafting history to promote his career.

Despite these personal flaws, Patton's early military study, writings, and applications are extremely impressive. They reveal a man who possessed a first-rate mind for history and strategic thought, passionately wanted to succeed in the interwar army, and believed that a mastery of the past was an essential element for success as a warrior.

- -

NOTES

1. Robert H. Patton, *The Pattons: A Personal History of an American Family*, 3–86.
2. R. Patton, 3–86.
3. B. Patton, "A Soldier's Reading."
4. Indeed. Mosby would also serve as a mentor to Patton's West Point classmate and future general William H. Simpson. Like Patton, Simpson's family also had deep Confederate roots, a fact that supposedly led Mosby to say of the young Simpson, "It'll seem kind of funny seeing you wearing a blue uniform. I still don't like it too doggone much, but it's all right." Coffman, *The Regulars*, 145.
5. Blumenson and Hymel, *Patton*, 6.
6. D'Este, *Patton*, 40–41; Groom, *The Generals*, 62; R. Patton, *The Pattons*, 87–122.
7. Blumenson and Hymel, *Patton*, 1, 6.
8. Blumenson and Hymel, 7.
9. D'Este, *Patton*, 42–43.
10. George S. Patton Jr., "War Department Document No. 463, 'Saber Exercise.'" The observation that stabbing was a more effective means for killing than slashing has deep roots in military history. "Not to Cut, but to Thrust with the Sword," in Flavius Vegetius, *On Roman Military Matters: A 5th Century Training Manual in Organization, Weapons and Tactics*, 15–16.
11. D'Este, *Patton*, 143–45.
12. Letts, *Perfect Horse*.
13. D'Este, *Patton*, 45–49, 74, 76, 80, 84–87, 90–93, 107–08, 201, 209, 830, 835.
14. For a brief discussion of the rigors of the West Point curriculum at the time and how it challenged even the brightest students, see Coffman, *The Regulars*, 147–48.
15. Diaries, 1910–45, George S. Patton Papers, Manuscript Division, Library of Congress, Washington, DC.
16. D'Este, *Patton*, 94.
17. D'Este, *Patton*, 91–93.

18. D'Este, *Patton*, 93.

19. United States Military Academy, *The Howitzer, 1909 Edition*, 76, 232.

20. Coffman, *The Regulars*, 149.

21. Diaries, 1910–45, Patton Papers.

22. Totten, *Button Box*, 35–120.

23. Totten, 94.

24. Erik Bergvall, ed., "The Fifth Olympiad: The Official Report of the Olympic Games of Stockholm, 1912," 647; D'Este, *Patton*, 132–33; George S. Patton Jr., "Report on the Olympic Games," September 19, 1912, Chronological File 1901–77, Patton Papers; Harold E. Wilson Jr., "A Legend in His Own Mind: The Olympic Experience of General George S. Patton Jr."

25. Although it is impossible to prove, Patton may have felt pressured to distort the historical record because of the excellent showing of the army's equestrian team in the 1912 Olympics. The team, led by Patton's former riding instructor at West Point Guy V. Henry, finished an impressive third, winning the bronze metal, while he went home empty-handed. Coffman, *The Regulars*, 158.

26. Richard Cohen, *By the Sword: A History of Gladiators, Musketeers, Samurai, Swashbucklers, and Olympic Champions*, 221.

27. Patton, "Form and Use of the Saber."

28. Patton, "Form and Use of the Saber."

29. D'Este, *Patton*, 140.

30. Totten, *Button Box*, 96.

31. Totten, 96.

32. The fate of this "novel" is uncertain. Neither archival sources nor secondary sources provide evidence of such a novel. Totten, *Button Box*, 96.

33. Ayer, *Before the Colors Fade*, 81; D'Este, *Patton*, 326.

34. Totten, *Button Box*, 96; Blumenson and Hymel, *Patton*, 27.

35. Farago, *Patton: Ordeal and Triumph*, 66.

36. For the importance of railroads on European armies during the period, see Dennis E. Showalter, *Railroads and Rifles: Soldiers, Technology, and the Unification of Germany*; A. J. P. Taylor, *War by Timetable: How the First World War Began*. During World War II, the majority of the German Army was moved by horse-drawn transport, not automobiles. See Richard L. DiNardo, *Mechanized Juggernaut or Military Anachronism? Horses and the German Army of World War II*; and Karl-Heinz Frieser, *The Blitzkrieg Legend: The 1940 Campaign in the West*.

37. B. Patton, "A Soldier's Reading"; Farago, *Patton: Ordeal and Triumph*, 66.

38. On the concept of friction in war, see Clausewitz, *On War*; and Barry D. Watts, *Clausewitzian Friction and Future War*. For a work that argues that Patton was keenly aware of Clausewitzian thinking, see Daniel, "Patton as a Counterinsurgent?," 1–14. On weather as a source of friction, see Harold A. Winters et al., *Battling the Elements: Weather and Terrain in the Conduct of War*; and C. E. Wood, *Mud: A Military History*.

39. Patton, "War Department Document No. 463."

40. Welsome, *The General and the Jaguar*, 27, 34.

41. Frank Ninkovich, *The Wilsonian Century: U.S. Foreign Policy since 1900*, 51–52.

42. Williams, *Lieutenant Patton*, 15.

43. D'Este, *Patton*, 158.

44. Welsome, *The General and the Jaguar*, 108–35.

45. Diaries, 1910–45, Patton Papers.

46. Pershing insisted on physical fitness and distrusted overweight officers. Patton shared this assessment and would insist on physical fitness for the remainder of his career. D'Este, *Patton*, 162–63.

47. Welsome, *The General and the Jaguar*, 167.

48. In these efforts, Patton was similar to a young Winston Churchill. As a junior officer, Churchill jumped at every opportunity he could to leave his unit, the 4th Hussars, and attach himself to units that expected active engagement. Churchill's antics won him few friends, but paid off by placing him in a position to win fame and glory. Winston S. Churchill, *My Early Life: 1874–1904*.

49. Williams, *Lieutenant Patton*, 50.

50. Chronological File, 1901–77, Patton Papers.

51. For a copy of Pershing's orders, see Pershing, "Punitive Expedition Report."

52. Welsome, *The General and the Jaguar*, 200.

53. See Patton's "Personal Glimpses of Pershing," Military Papers, 1903–76, Patton Papers.

54. Welsome, *The General and the Jaguar*, 199.

55. Military Papers, 1903–76, Patton Papers.

56. Pershing, "Punitive Expedition Report," 13–14.

57. Welsome, *The General and the Jaguar*, 189–90.

58. Pershing, "Punitive Expedition Report."

59. Welsome, *The General and the Jaguar*, 261.

60. D'Este, *Patton*, 173.

61. Undated Patton after-action report, "Report on the Death of Col. Cardenas," Military Papers, 1903–76, Patton Papers. According to Patton expert Carlo D'Este, the report was, "written immediately afterward," but the exact date is unknown. D'Este, *Patton*, 848n10.

62. "Report on the Death of Col. Cardenas," Military Papers, 1903–76, Patton Papers.

63. "Report on the Death of Col. Cardenas."

64. "Report on the Death of Col. Cardenas."

65. "Report on the Death of Col. Cardenas"; Harry Yeide, *Fighting Patton: George S. Patton Jr. through the Eyes of His Enemies*, 6–11.

66. Pershing, "Punitive Expedition Report."

67. Frank B. Elser, "Cardenas's Family Saw Him Die at Bay," *New York Times*, May 23, 1916; and D'Este, *Patton*, 176.

68. Welsome, *The General and the Jaguar*, 306.

69. D'Este, *Patton*, 181.

70. George S. Patton Jr., "Cavalry Work of the Punitive Expedition."

71. Mosby's memoirs make numerous references to fighting on foot. See John S. Mosby, *The Memoirs of Colonel John S. Mosby*, 94, 136, 153, 159, 329.

72. Despite the romantic notion of mounted cavalry actions, modern secondary sources confirm that Civil War–era cavalry typically fought dismounted. See Robert W. Black, *Cavalry Raids of the Civil War*, 10, 27, 30–31, 59, 67, 88, 144–48, 159–63, 182, 198, 202, 210, 217.

73. Patton, "Cavalry Work of the Punitive Expedition."

74. "Report on the Death of Col. Cardenas," Military Papers, 1903–76, Patton Papers.

75. D'Este, *Patton*, 174.

76. Martin Blumenson, *The Patton Papers*, vol. 1, *1885–1940*, 233; Cohen, *By the Sword*, 220–21; D'Este, *Patton*, 136; Totten, *Button Box*, 96.

77. Essame, *Patton as Military Commander*, 5–6.

78. Groom, *The Generals*, 84.

79. Totten, *Button Box*, 96.

80. B. Patton, "A Soldier's Reading"; Nye, *Patton Mind*, 35.

81. While Patton's study of military psychology was unusual, he was not the only US Army officer influenced by LeBon. In fact, Captain LeRoy Eltinge read this work as well and wrote a monograph titled *Psychology in War*, which attempted to incorporate these insights into US Army doctrine and training. During World War I, Eltinge, then a colonel, would meet Patton and encourage his interest in the Tank Corps. While Eltinge is largely forgotten today, his studies on military psychology and his mentorship clearly had a profound impact on the young Patton. J. P. Clark, *Preparing for War: The Emergence of the Modern U.S. Army, 1815–1917*, 233.

82. Clark, *Preparing for War*, 35–37; Roger H. Nye, "Whence Patton's Military Genius?"

83. Patton's friend and mentor General George Marshall was also a believer in the value of psychology and deep historical knowledge of the enemy. Marshall's and Patton's influence on their subordinates is difficult to quantify, but it did result in some significant converts such as General Gilbert Cook who would serve as a corps commander in Patton's Third Army. Cook followed the lead of Patton and Marshall and would pass around books on military history and psychology to his junior officers. Jörg Muth, *Command Culture: Officer Education in the U.S. Army and the German Armed Forces, 1901–1940, and the Consequences for World War II*, 141.

84. D'Este, *Patton*, 190–91.

85. Chronological File, 1901–77, Patton Papers.

86. Chronological File, 1901–77, Patton Papers.

87. Chronological File, 1901–77, Patton Papers.

88. See generally Edward Cox, *Grey Imminence: Fox Conner and the Art of Mentorship*, iii–xxi, 62–65, 81–83, 95–100. In an interesting twist of fate, it was Patton who first introduced Eisenhower to his future mentor. See Coffman, *The Regulars*, 231; and Matheny, *Carrying the War to the Enemy*, 77.

89. Diary entry, n.d., Diaries, 1910–45, Patton Papers.

90. Family Papers, 1857–1979, Patton Papers.

91. R. Patton, *The Pattons*, 94–95.

92. Johnson, *Fast Tanks and Heavy Bombers*, 33, 124–25.

93. Coffman, *The Regulars*, 211.

94. Blumenson, *The Patton Papers*, 1:444.

95. D'Este, *Patton*, 207.

96. Blumenson, *The Patton Papers*, 1:446.

97. Morningstar, *Patton's Way*, 57.

98. Blumenson, *The Patton Papers*, 1:735. In 1952 Patton's wife, Beatrice, would write a short article for *Armor* where she said Patton loved "anything by J. F. C. Fuller," a true testament to their mutual friendship and continued influence on each other's thinking. B. Patton, "A Soldier's Reading."

99. Johnson, *Fast Tanks and Heavy Bombers*, 34.

100. D'Este, *Patton*, 448–57.

101. D'Este, *Patton*, 448.

102. Military Papers, 1903–76, Patton Papers.

103. Semmes, *Portrait of Patton*, 42. While no prude, Patton was particularly concerned with the ill effects of venereal disease on his troops. As a result, he prohibited prostitution, limited his troop's access to local females, and punished homosexuality. See Richard S. Faulkner, *Pershing's Crusaders: The American Soldier in World War I*, 383–90, and 397–406.

104. Blumenson and Hymel, *Patton*, 33.

105. Blumenson, *The Patton Papers*, 1:523.

106. D'Este, *Patton*, 224–25.

107. William Manchester, *American Caesar: Douglas MacArthur, 1880–1964*, 101–2, 150.

108. Johnson, *Fast Tanks and Heavy Bombers*, 36–37.

109. D'Este, *Patton*, 241.

110. D'Este, *Patton*, 252–53. It would not be the last time that fuel supplies impeded Patton's movements. See Albin F. Irzyk, *Gasoline to Patton: A Different War*.

111. Robert H. Ferrell, *America's Deadliest Battle: Meuse-Argonne, 1918*, 44.

112. Military Papers, 1903–76, Patton Papers.

113. Totten, *Button Box*, 117–18. See also Michael Keane, *Patton: Blood, Guts, and Prayer*.

114. Family Papers, 1857–1979, Patton Papers.

115. Family Papers, 1857–1979, Patton Papers.

116. Morningstar, *Patton's Way*, 29.

117. Family Papers, 1857–1979, Patton Papers.

118. This seeming tension between Patton as a prophet of both technology and personal courage makes him hard to classify. Indeed, even after rejoining the horse cavalry, he would argue both elements matter. Ultimately, he concluded that "war is an art, and as such is not susceptible of explanation by fixed formula." Linn, *Echo of Battle*, 6.

119. Jean Edward Smith, *Eisenhower in War and Peace*, 56–57; Matthew F. Holland, *Eisenhower between the Wars*, 14, 16–17, 77–80.

120. Morningstar, *Patton's Way*, 62.

121. See George S. Patton Jr., "Tanks in Future Wars" and "Comments on Cavalry Tanks."

122. Johnson, *Fast Tanks and Heavy Bombers*, 74–75.

123. Johnson, *Fast Tanks and Heavy Bombers*, 75, 126–27; Alexander M. Bielakowski, "The Role of the Horse in Modern Warfare as Viewed in the Interwar U.S. Army's *Cavalry Journal*"; Linn, *Echo of Battle*, 6, 136–37.

124. Blumenson, *The Patton Papers*, 1:735. See also J. F. C. Fuller, *Tanks in the Great War, 1914–1918*.

125. Morningstar, *Patton's Way*, 64; Nye, *Patton Mind*, 49–60.

126. Nye, *Patton Mind*, 90–92.

127. Yeide, *Fighting Patton*, 2.

128. Morningstar, *Patton's Way*, 65, 92. See generally James S. Corum, *The Roots of Blitzkrieg: Hans von Seeckt and German Military Reform*.

129. See J. Furman Daniel III, ed., *21st Century Patton: Strategic Insights for the Modern Era*.

130. Coffman, *The Regulars*, 285; Martin Blumenson, "George S. Patton's Student Days at the Army War College." Despite the relatively leisurely pace of the War College in Patton's day, it had undergone significant reform by his time and was more rigorous than it had been in previous generations. See Clark, *Preparing for War*, 203–15.

131. This thesis was in many ways a refinement and an expansion of his 1931 article in *Cavalry Journal* titled "Success in War" that similarly used historical analysis to argue for the creation of an American warrior culture. See also Linn, *Echo of Battle*, 137.

132. George S. Patton Jr., "The Probable Characteristics of the Next War and the Organization, Tactics, and Equipment Necessary to Meet Them."

133. Patton, "Probable Characteristics of the Next War."

134. Yeide, *Fighting Patton*, 47; Corum, *Roots of Blitzkrieg*.

135. Patton, "Probable Characteristics of the Next War" (emphasis in the original).

136. Patton, "Probable Characteristics of the Next War."

137. Blumenson, "Patton's Student Days"; Coffman, *The Regulars*, 285.

138. Patton, "Probable Characteristics of the Next War."

CHAPTER TWO

BATTLES WITH HISTORY IN THE DESERTS

Training the Force for Action in North Africa

WHILE THE UNITED STATES was slowly beginning the process of rearmament in the months prior to the outbreak of World War II, Patton saw the gathering war clouds as an opportunity to finally win the fame he craved and prove his theories on modern warfare. As early as 1937, he began to study translations of writings on mechanized warfare by the future German generals Erwin Rommel, Heinz Guderian, and Walter Warlimont, and in 1938 he began to reconstruct German maneuvers in his own sand table.[1] After the war broke out, he took particular interest in the German blitzkrieg campaigns in Poland and France and read every Military Intelligence Bulletin he could find on the subject. The speed and decisiveness of the German advances inspired Patton and seemed to validate many of his theories regarding mechanized warfare. To keep his subordinates fresh on the unfolding developments, he made a special effort to brief his men on these events and incorporate these insights into his unit's training regime.[2]

Patton's ability to study the recent blitzkrieg campaigns and analyze them through a historical lens was clearly displayed in his September 1940 lecture to his troops at Fort Benning. He began his lecture with an overview of the failure of strategic thinking exhibited by the Poles in the recent campaign:

> You all remember that west Poland sticks into Germany in much the same way that Brazil protrudes into the Atlantic. To remove this pimple, the Germans used the oldest plan in the world. It was invented by the caveman when they surrounded the mammoth to destroy him . . . . [It is called] a Cannae, a double envelopment. There is an old latin [*sic*] saw to the effect that "To have a Cannae,

71

you must have a Varro." . . . [In other words] in order to win a great victory you must have a dumb enemy commander. From what we know at the moment, the Poles qualified with such a high command.

He then noted that his troops must not only trust his as their commanding officer, but also learn the arts of warfare to successfully carry out these strategies:

In a former geological era when I was a boy studying latin [*sic*], I had occasion to translate one of Caesar's remarks which as nearly as I can remember read something like this.

"In winter time, Caesar so trained his legions in all that became soldiers and so habituated them in the proper performance of their duties, that when in the spring he committed them to battle against the Gauls, it was not necessary to give them orders, for they knew what to do and how to do it."

This quotation expresses very exactly the goal we are seeking in this division. I know that we shall attain it and when we do, may God have mercy on our enemies; they will need it.[3]

While the Allies squandered many opportunities in the months prior to Pearl Harbor, Patton used this time wisely: reading, writing, and studying history, with an eye toward applying it during the next war. He was already hard at work formulating his own views on modern warfare, and he craved the opportunity to apply them in an active capacity.

In the months prior to the war, Patton distinguished himself in a series of military exercises in Tennessee, Louisiana, and the Carolinas. During these maneuvers, he acted as both a player and an observer and was able to test many of his theories regarding the role of tanks and mechanized forces in modern war.[4] By aggressively employing his tanks and maintaining the initiative, he was able to defeat more senior commanders, such as General Hugh Drum, an accomplishment that put him on the path toward higher command in the coming conflict.[5] His friend and mentor General George Marshall took particular interest in these war games, noting that they ensured "mistakes [were] made in Louisiana, not over in Europe."[6] In addition to marking Patton as a bold and decisive leader, these maneuvers convinced him that armor, not the horse cavalry, was the decisive instrument in modern warfare. Sensing that the horse cavalry was fast becoming an anachronism, he applied for and was granted a reassignment to the armored corps.[7]

Despite these incremental improvements, the outbreak of hostilities in December 1941 caught the American military woefully unprepared for a major war. The US military was still attempting to overcome the inertia and malaise of the Depression-era budgetary constraints and was an embryonic force of only 300,000 men, a far cry from the 8.7 million men American planners estimated would be needed to win a future world war.[8] To make this a reality, the United States would need to man, train, and equip a massive military of citizen soldiers, and it relied on General Patton to get its first units prepared for combat.

Patton's first assignment after the outbreak of war was to command the 1st Armored Corps. In addition to getting his unit ready for battle, he was also instructed to prepare a training center where other units could be sent for realistic exercises prior to overseas deployment. Given his well-known zeal for training and discipline, Patton was given wide latitude to create a Desert Training Center to his own specifications and to implement his views on mechanized warfare. Sensing an opportunity to exert a lasting influence on the future force, he eagerly threw himself into the task, personally scouting locations for the center in light aircraft and making detailed notes as to possible locations. The general selected a desolate stretch of California and Arizona desert he had remembered from his youth. This vast area would toughen the men by exposing them to extreme desert conditions and would also be remote enough to avoid unwanted attention.[9]

Patton also designed the curriculum for the training that included strenuous physical training in the desert heat; limited food, water, and sleep; and an insistence on wearing full uniforms in spite of the desert conditions. To observe and critique these training efforts, the general installed a radio and lookout post on the top of a prominent hill in the center of the training area. This hill, which became known as the "King's Throne," allowed him to critique his men throughout the training process and made them feel as if they were continually watched and judged by their commanding officer.[10]

Because of the rigors of training in such an unforgiving locale, Patton received many complaints from the officers and men, yet he insisted that this strict regime would pay dividends in battle, often repeating the phrase he adapted from eighteenth-century Russian general Alexander Suvorov: "A pint of sweat will save a gallon of blood."[11] While this remark could easily be dismissed as bluster, it was in fact a key part of his philosophy of war. Based on both his reading of history and his experiences in Mexico and France, the general believed that human factors often made the difference in battle. For the remainder of his career, he would insist on excellent physical conditioning of his troops and would often ask that this physical strength be translated into seemingly extraordinary feats on the battlefield.

Before being assigned to command part of the invasion force for Operation Torch, Patton personally oversaw the training of about sixty thousand men at the Desert Training Corps. Even after his departure, the regime of discipline

Figure 5. Patton preparing his troops for battle at the Desert Training Center in 1942. National Archives.

and physical toughness that he instilled endured a testament to the lasting impact of his theories of training and leadership. Before closing in May 1944, the Desert Training Corps would train more than one million American troops from more than four hundred units for battle and would help them transition more smoothly to the harsh conditions of combat.[12]

While often overshadowed by his later battlefield victories, Patton's tenure as the commanding officer of the Desert Training Corps should not be overlooked. In fact, building human capital and developing leaders was a key element in his military philosophy and was an underappreciated element of his success. He felt so strongly about the value of this training that he took the time to write a short article about the Desert Training Corps, which appeared in the October 1942 issue of *Cavalry Journal*.

Although this article appeared after he had already moved on to more active commands, it clearly expresses his conviction that that demanding training was a force multiplier. The article exuded confidence, claiming, "If the platoon commanders know their duty and carry it out, and if the higher commanders maintain discipline and supply and have a rugged determination to close with the enemy and kill him, the answer to successful combat against armored units has been found."[13] While the US Army was untested, its physical conditioning, fighting spirit, and mastery of desert warfare were as good as Patton and the Desert Training Corps could make them.

Opening Rounds in North Africa

Patton's first taste of action in World War II would come during the Operation Torch landings in Morocco. These landings were part of a hastily prepared effort, made on the insistence of President Roosevelt, who asserted that "it is of the highest importance that the U.S. ground forces be brought into action against the enemy in 1942."[14] While the political need to support the British and Soviet allies in the fight against the Nazis drove American decision making, many senior military leaders were wary of the impending operations. In fact, both the chief of staff, George Marshall, and the secretary of war, Henry Stimson, opposed Operation Torch, believing that it was overly ambitious and could lead to disaster.[15] Senior generals such as Dwight Eisenhower and Mark Clark were similarly concerned about the feasibility of the operations. Patton shared these concerns but was more willing to accept the risks, noting, "I feel we should fight. . . . We must do something now. I feel that I am the only true gambler in the whole outfit."[16]

Despite this bluster, the untested American Army faced myriad logistical and operational challenges. Serious questions remained unanswered about the ability of the Germans to resist the landings, the true intentions and fighting spirit of the Vichy French regime, and the peaceful cooperation of the local Arab populations. These challenges weighed heavily on the mind of American commander General Eisenhower, who despite the support and mentorship of General George Marshall was an untested combat leader.

Further complicating Eisenhower's decision making was the fact that he was surrounded by British generals who all had their own ideas about how to conduct the operations as well as the fact that British prime minister Winston Churchill also insisted on inserting himself into the planning process.[17] The British dominance of the planning process was tolerated by the Americans on the grounds that they were a critical ally and had combat experience against the Germans. Nevertheless, many, including Patton, believed that the British were patronizing and demeaning to their American comrades and would harbor hurt feelings and rivalry for the remainder of the war. In fact, the British would dominate Allied grand strategy until August 1944, when the Americans would finally insist on Operation Dragoon/Anvil, much to the dismay of Churchill, who then complained of US "bullying."[18]

The stress of planning took quite a toll on Eisenhower, who was happy to have Patton, his old friend and confidant, as part of the team. During this period, the two worked extremely well together, and Patton's swagger often buoyed Eisenhower's confidence. While Eisenhower was happy to have Patton serving as his subordinate, he was initially apprehensive about having a man who was his senior in age serving under him. Despite these misgivings, he repeatedly stated that he wanted lucky generals (a reference to Napoleon's preference for lucky subordinates) and believed Patton fitted that requirement perfectly.[19]

During the planning phases for Operation Torch, Eisenhower focused his efforts on the larger strategic and logistical problems of coalition warfare, while Patton busied himself with more operational-level planning tasks, such as creating a full working staff, military organization, landing and embarkation schedules, and the tactical problems of securing the beachheads and having enough firepower to neutralize any Axis opposition. Despite their different roles, the two often shared ideas and helped each other refine their thinking on critical elements of the Torch plan.

This working relationship was successful because their mutual trust and admiration allowed them to be surprisingly candid in their private interactions. Once, when Eisenhower asked Patton what he thought of the plan, he responded frankly that he believed that it was far too complex and needed major revisions.[20] Both men shared serious reservations about the US Navy's ability to transport the invasion fleet across the Atlantic Ocean, properly escort them in route, neutralize any Axis opposition in the landing areas, deliver them to the beaches on schedule, and then provide logistical support to the forces ashore.[21] While Patton would ultimately praise the navy for its efforts after the campaign, he fought a series of vicious interservice battles during the entire planning and training phase of the operation.

The main disagreement centered on the navy's perceived lack of attention to the landing phase of the operations and their desire to protect their ships from shore-based artillery fire. Here, Patton escalated a bureaucratic turf war unnecessarily and risked his career by attracting the attention of the chief of naval operations, Admiral Ernest King. Ultimately, General Marshall had to intervene to defuse the controversy by stating to the navy brass that Patton was "indispensable to Torch," the first of many times that Marshall would save Patton's career from his self-destructive tendencies.[22]

Patton's first headquarters was in the old Munitions Building on Independence Avenue in Washington, DC. He did his best to impose professionalism and calm in a hectic and cramped office and to move forward with the myriad technical and operational details of the upcoming operation. While in Washington, he selected Colonel Hobart "Hap" Gay to be his chief of staff. Gay was not widely liked outside of Patton's headquarters, but he quickly became indispensable to the general and would remain in the position until Patton's death in 1945. Gay was hardworking, loyal, and completely dedicated to serving his commanding officer, and the two quickly developed a mutual admiration and respect for each other. In addition to Gay, Patton also selected many other key staff officers during this period that would provide him exemplary service in the years to come. These included his deputy commander, General Geoffrey Keyes; Colonel Paul Harkins, who served as Gay's assistant chief of staff; and Captain Richard "Dick" Jenson, the son of a high school sweetheart, who would serve as his personal aide.[23]

Despite the fact that he was busy with a vast array of organizational and operational tasks related to the planning of Operation Torch, Patton was keenly aware that he was part of history. To this end, he began to keep a more organized and formal diary, starting with his first new entry on August 5, 1942.[24] While he had kept diaries of his cadet years, honeymoon, and battles in Mexico and France, and had kept copious notes on his reading and travels over the years, this diary was a much more ambitious and purposeful under-taking. Rather than simply a series of personal reflections or outlines of his thinking on military subjects, these entries were much more complete, as they attempted to document the entirety of his daily routines and his actions as a commanding general. As such, they provide a comprehensive record regarding his specific opinions on a given day or topic and are an invaluable insight into his perspective on World War II.

Patton's diaries give the appearance of complete candor and are often un-flattering to him, so it would be easy to conclude that they were not written with any other purpose in mind. Indeed, the fact that he frequently made comments that were insubordinate, racist, anti-Semitic, self-deprecating, or petty makes these entries seem as if they were nothing more than an outlet for his personal frustrations and amusement. However, despite their frequently raw tone, it would be a mistake to conclude that Patton did not intended them for a broader audience. While they became the basis for his posthumous memoirs, he clearly wrote them knowing that they would attract the broader interest of historians and military strategists.

While it is impossible to definitively know *how* Patton intended these dia-ries to be used by historians, a close inspection of their contents reveals that he was trying to justify his actions, document his decision-making process, and prove that his theories of war were correct. Over the course of the war, their tone alters between triumphant and defensive, and he frequently ex-pressed his belief that he alone could clearly see the correct course of action. When he was victorious, success was a product of his genius, but when he struggled, failure was often because he was blocked by others who did not share his bold vision of modern warfare. This tendency was exacerbated over time. As his professional frustrations mounted, Patton became more convinced that he was one of the greatest commanders in military history but was being held back by lesser talents or risk-averse superiors. However, during the planning phases of Operation Torch, he mostly documented his contributions to the plan and lamented the complexities of coordinating such a complex operation dominated by the British.

After a few days in the nation's capital, Patton and his staff embarked for a more permanent headquarters in London. The wartime austerity of London clearly made an impression on Patton, as he remarked in his new diary on the "hideous" appearance of the local women, but he quickly began to develop more professional reasons for his Anglophobia. Patton and Eisenhower both believed that they were being forced to rush their operational planning based on the political pressure from the British. They both feared that this would compromise their operational efficiency and put lives at risk unnecessarily, and they argued unsuccessfully for additional time and resources. Despite being overruled, Patton put on a brave face in his diary, noting, "We are told to do it and intend to succeed or die in the attempt. . . . [W]ith a little luck it can be done at a high price."[25] While Patton was publicly silent about these Anglo-American squabbles, he would remain suspicious of British motives for the remainder of his life.

Once the final decision on the Torch Operation was approved, Eisenhower confessed to his friend, "The past six weeks have been the most trying of my life," but he stated that he was satisfied with the final plan, noting, "You can well imagine that my feelings at the moment are those of great relief that a final decision [regarding the specifics of the Allied plan] now seems assured."[26]

The Allied plan was to send three task forces to strike simultaneously along the North African coast. The goal was to overwhelm the French defenders while seizing three major bases for launching future operations. The Western Task Force, commanded by Major General Patton, was composed of the 3rd Infantry Division and elements of the 2nd Armored and 9th Infantry Divisions. These forces were tasked with capturing the Moroccan port of Casablanca and securing this critical resupply center in the American area of operations.[27] The Center Task Force, commanded by Major General Lloyd Fredendall, was composed of the 1st Infantry Division and the 1st Armored Division and was given the mission of capturing the vital port of Oran, Algeria. Finally, the Eastern Task Force, under the command of British lieutenant general Kenneth Anderson, was composed of elements from the 9th and 34th American Infantry Divisions as well as the 78th British Infantry Division. This mixed British and American force was assigned the role of taking the key port of Algiers while also securing French government buildings and command centers within the city.[28]

While Patton's command was expected to encounter minimal resistance from the French defenders (an assumption that would prove wrong), his mission was critical to Allied success. Casablanca was slated to be the principal Allied port for sustaining their operations in North Africa, and to keep the Allied invasion on schedule it was essential for him to quickly capture this port and ensure that its docking and repair facilities remained undamaged. It was also critical to neutralize or capture the French naval squadron based

Map 3: Operation Torch landings. While Patton's troops landed far from the German defenders, his troops had the critical missions of seizing the port of Casablanca, neutralizing Vichy land, naval and air forces, and securing the Allied rear-areas. Map by Chris Robinson.

in Casablanca to ensure that it would not fall into Nazi hands or be used by the Vichy forces to threaten the Allied landings.

While it was assumed that the Vichy French would put up little or no resistance, the political situation was tense.[29] The French Navy was still reeling from the British Royal Navy attack on their base at Mers-el-Kébir in July 1940. This attack resulted in the deaths of more than twelve hundred sailors, but prevented the French fleet from falling into Nazi hands. Despite the fact that Churchill and the British admirals had sound strategic reasons for this strike, the death of so many French sailors perpetuated a deep sense of mistrust and betrayal between France and Great Britain.[30] The Germans skillfully exploited this friction for propaganda purposes that made frequent references to the British perfidy in attacking their former ally. In addition to feeling betrayed, the French legitimately feared that the Germans would enact reprisals if they failed to resist an attack on their sovereign territory by the Allies. In an effort to help convince the French not to resist the invasion, the Allies chose to de-emphasize the British role, on the belief that "America, on the other hand, had escaped this opprobrium."[31] While it was assumed that the French would offer only token resistance to mollify the Germans, the actual motivations of the French forces were unclear.[32]

Further complicating this political milieu were the relations with the local Arab leaders, whose loyalty and motivations were at best uncertain. While they had chafed under French colonial rule for decades, it was unclear if they would welcome the Americans and British or would use this opportunity to foment unrest and assert control over their traditional territories. German propaganda attempted to manipulate Arab opinion by insisting that the Americans and British would strip the Arabs of their rights and establish a Jewish state in North Africa.[33] While the thought that the Allies were invading French North Africa to promote Jewish interests is laughable in hindsight, it was clearly on the minds of the local Arab population. According to Patton's future aide Charles Codman, he was told that it was on "good authority" that "the chief objective of our landing was to foment uprisings of the Jews against the Arabs and in the ensuing confusion assume control of Morocco. . . . After all, your President Rosenfeldt [sic] is a Jew."[34] In such a toxic atmosphere, the potential for an Arab insurgency in this key Allied rear area was worth guarding against, as it would threaten the Allied logistical bases and pull many much-needed troops away from fighting the Germans.

Despite all of these potential pitfalls, Patton was optimistic as he embarked on the cruiser *Augusta* on October 24, 1942, bound for North Africa and his first taste of command as a general officer. He did his best to put on a brave face and maintain his warrior image but feared that he would "get fat" on the voyage due to the difficulty of exercising aboard ship.[35] His private writings reveal a mixture of boredom and tension, as he felt as if there was little more he could do to prepare for the operations at this point other than read and reflect on the lessons of history.

On his own initiative, Patton read the Koran and reflected in his diary that it was "a good book and interesting."[36] While he had been fascinated by religion for his entire life, the fact that he would devote significant time and effort to engage with this text is revealing.[37] While he read historical fiction titles, including *Three Harbors*, by F. Van Wyck Mason, and *The Sun Is My Undoing*, by Marguerite Steen, and the detective story *The Cairo Garter Murders*, also by Mason, to relax during the long voyage, his engagement with the Muslim holy book was clearly different. This episode demonstrates the general using his downtime to glean whatever insights he could on his future operating environment and its human terrain. This learning not only improved Patton's mind but also provided him with the comfort that he was doing something productive during the uneventful voyage. He noted that the mix of uncertainty and boredom caused "some of my people [to] worry. I could myself, but won't."[38]

Even as the Allies approached the shores of Africa, reports varied considerably as to the intentions of the French military, their readiness and fighting spirit, and the political situation on the ground. On the eve of battle, Patton was frustrated by this, noting, "In forty hours I shall be in battle, with little information, and on the spur of the moment will have to make the most momentous decisions," but he took comfort in his study and preparation: "It seems that my whole life has been pointed to this moment."[39] Taking additional solace from history, he reflected that even Napoleon entered battle with an incomplete view of the situation, writing, "Perhaps when Napoleon said, 'Je m'engage et puis je vois' [I start the fight and then I see], he was right."[40]

Patton's address to his troops on the eve of battle underscores the ambiguity of the situation at hand, as it simultaneously emphasized the fighting spirit of the American troops but also underscored the need for political sensitivity and compassion:

Soldiers: We are to be congratulated because we have been chosen as the units of the United States Army best trained to take part in this great American effort. . . .

It is not known whether the French African army . . . will contest our landing. It is regrettable to contemplate the necessity of fighting the gallant French who are at least sympathetic towards us, but all resistance by whomever offered must be destroyed. However, when any of the French soldiers seek to surrender, you will accept it and treat them with the respect due a brave opponent and future ally. . . .

When the great day of battle comes, remember your training, and remember above all that speed and vigor of attack are the sure roads to success and you must succeed—for to retreat is as cowardly as it is fatal. Indeed, once landed, retreat is impossible. Americans do not surrender.

During the first few days and nights after you go ashore, you must work unceasingly, regardless of sleep, regardless of food. A pint of sweat will save a gallon of blood.

The eyes of the world are watching us; the heart of every American beats for us; God is with us. On our victory depends the freedom or slavery of the human race. We shall surely win.[41]

Patton's task force's first action came at 0701 on November 8, 1942, when the US Navy engaged French aircraft off the coast of Casablanca. The

French planes were unable to damage the American flotilla, but lost one of their number to the American naval gunfire. Unwilling to surrender in the face of a superior force, the French naval squadron, composed of seven destroyers, one light cruiser, and the incomplete battleship *Jean Bart*, attacked the Allied invasion force at approximately 0704. The Americans wasted no time in returning fire, focusing their attention on the *Jean Bart*, and by 1150 the French squadron was neutralized with minimal American losses. The Vichy navy would resume their attack later that afternoon, but by 1530 was again neutralized by US Navy forces. The result was a victory described as "very one-sided." The French lost four destroyers and eight submarines sunk as well as two destroyers, a light cruiser, and the battleship *Jean Bart* disabled. American naval losses were three killed onboard the USS *Murphy* and about twenty-five wounded.[42]

Despite the Allied success, the French resistance was unexpected, and it delayed the American landings and signaled a tougher fight than planned.[43] In addition, the naval battle had the unintended effect of knocking out a small boat on board the *Augusta* that was scheduled to take Patton ashore at the head of the invasion force at 0800. While the general's famous ivory-handled pistols were saved by an orderly who retrieved them just before the boat was blown over the side, the loss of this small boat turned the commanding officer into an unwilling spectator and delayed his landing until 1320.[44]

Patton was not the only American who was behind schedule. In fact, many of the Allied forces arrived at their landing zones late, and the Second Armored division was soon bogged down on the beaches by unexpectedly heavy resistance from the French defenders. When the general did finally reach the shore, he threw himself immediately into the action. He approached the stunned Americans on the beach and exclaimed, "On your feet. . . . What the hell is the matter with you men anyway. . . . You heard me, You've got guns. Use them. If I see another American soldier lying down on this beach I'll court-martial him."[45] These bold actions helped restart the stalled American landings, and eventually superior American firepower and close-air support helped clear the landing zones. Despite the successes on the beaches, much work remained to be done to neutralize the French garrison in Casablanca. The French had enough troops to defend the city streets, and the Allies faced the very real possibility of having to choose between costly house-to-house fighting or a protracted siege of the city. Either of these options was incompatible with the American goals of moving rapidly to secure the city and its port facilities.

Patton's mission quickly shifted from securing the beaches to establishing relations with the French colonial leaders and persuading them to end their resistance. Understanding that further delay would risk the overall success of their operations, the general acted quickly. He used his forces to encircle the French garrison in Casablanca and immediately began to negotiate. Acting on his own initiative, he directly contacted the French defenders and proposed that they surrender or face a direct assault. At 1340 he "met with a French colonel, who suggested I send to Casa[blanca] to demand a surrender. He said that the French did not want to fight."[46] Based on his previous knowledge of the French officer corps, Patton realized that national and institutional prestige motivated the defenders, despite the fact that their military situation was untenable. Given these insights, he decided to play to French vanity and offered very generous terms that plainly outlined the futility of the defenders' situation and offered them full military honors even in defeat.

By negotiating his own terms for surrender of the French garrison, Patton was exceeding his authority from Washington and risking his position as commanding officer of the American invasion force. The gamble paid off, however, as the French accepted the generous terms approximately a half hour before the planned assault on Casablanca.[47] Patton treated his fallen enemies with dignity and respect by ordering his troops to extend full military courtesies to the captured French. He justified these actions with the observation that it was "no use kicking a man when he's down."[48] To ensure French compliance and goodwill, "I inspected the town and port and all the French soldiers except the marines saluted and grinned."[49] By preserving French honor and dignity, the general was able to avoid further bloodshed and delay and instead focus on securing Casablanca as a base of operations.

Although he was privately dismissive of French military capabilities, Patton took the additional step of incorporating the French forces into his security operations by employing them in his rear areas to guard against sabotage and help preserve the rule of law. Just hours after the fall of Casablanca, French forces began to protect the streets that they had recently been defending: "We put on a mixed Military Police, half American and Half French, with a Lieutenant of *chasseures a cheval*, a Moroccan, as assistant Provost Marshal."[50]

In the weeks that followed, French forces were given increased responsibilities in protecting the region, and they repeatedly proved their loyalty to the American forces. This benevolence allowed Patton to use his own force more effectively by freeing them to move against the Axis.[51] He explained his reasoning: "Let the French police the country, and let *us* get on with the war."[52] By his own estimation, the use of French forces to maintain order was necessary to achieve his mission, and "I have never had reason to regret that decision. Had I done otherwise, I am convinced that at least sixty thousand American troops would have had to occupy Morocco; thereby preventing our using it to the maximum and reducing our already inadequate forces."[53]

Patton was similarly adept in his relations with the local Arab population and their leaders. During his time in Morocco, he met frequently with the local Arab leaders, including the sultan of Morocco and his relatives, advisers, and viziers.[54] Patton's outreach to these local power brokers helped pacify the potentially unfriendly Arab population and ensure their cooperation with Allied efforts. Patton's December 8, 1942, meeting with the sultan's principal adviser, the grand vizier, set the tone for Patton's relations with the local authorities:

> I talked practically directly to the old man. He said that His Majesty was very anxious for me to know that the whole life of Morocco depended upon maintaining peace. I assured him that I was a profound student of history; that since my earliest infancy my whole idea had been to maintain peace in French Morocco, and that I intended to do so by consulting the wishes of His Majesty. . . . He said that when His Majesty heard these remarks from me he would be overcome with joyous emotion. He then talked about race antipathies. . . . I understood perfectly about race antipathies, and therefore I would do nothing about it because . . . the Sultan's ancestors have handled such questions for thirteen hundred years, they were better fitted than I was to continue their management. He said that this was completely to his way of thinking and that no racial or tribal troubles would ever stick their heads above the surface. . . . I then told him that, in spite of my most diligent efforts, there would unquestionably be some raping, and that I should like to have the details as early as possible so that the offenders could be properly hanged. He said that this was a splendid idea, and that the hanging of such miscreants would unquestionably bring great joy to all Moroccans. This conversation took about fifteen minutes, at the end of which time the Grand Vizier assured me that the complaisance had given him the happiest fifteen minutes of his life.[55]

Through meetings such as these, Patton was able to build trust with the local Arab leaders and accommodate their needs. While this was insufficient for achieving victory, it was necessary for avoiding a potentially debilitating insurgency in the Allies' occupation zones. Indeed, this quiet and understudied success clearly demonstrates the importance of working with local leaders even during a high-intensity campaign such as Operation Torch. He summarized this mastery by noting, "It took me a long time to realize how much a student of medieval history can gain from observing the Arabs."[56]

Figure 6. Patton with the sultan of Morocco and his son after the Operation Torch landings. Meetings such as this were critical in maintaining amicable relations in Patton's rear areas. National Archives.

These nonkinetic successes were noticed by General Eisenhower, who repeatedly praised Patton in his official after-action report on the Torch campaign. According to Eisenhower, "Lacking such an engagement on their part we would have been faced with the necessity of undertaking complete military occupation, for which we had neither the time nor the resources. In MOROCCO alone, according to General Patton's calculations, we would have required 60,000 men to keep the tribes quiet, and would have been faced with the danger that any tribal disturbance might tempt SPAIN to intervene against our very insecure lines of communication."[57] While it is impossible to prove that such a contingency would have occurred without Patton's leadership, Eisenhower certainly believed that he had the best commander for this difficult task.[58]

Throughout the Torch campaign, Patton's knowledge of the French language and culture, his extensive travels in France, his love of the French officer corps and their military traditions, his knowledge of Middle Eastern history, and his willingness to understand the Muslim religion and read religious texts such as the Koran all helped him to master this tricky political challenge.[59] Failure to do so could have prevented the later successes of the Americans and British in surrounding and destroying Rommel's Afrika Korps and may have significantly impeded the Allied war efforts.

In light of some of his later political failures, this attention to detail is particularly interesting. While he would struggle in his job of overseeing German reconstruction and denazification after World War II, during Operation Torch he clearly understood the need for care in dealing with the French and Arab authorities in the context of furthering the broader success of the Allied cause. Through a mastery of history and an understanding of the strategic context, Patton was able to carefully navigate the complex political situation and provide himself the opportunity to lead his forces in a more active role. While his efforts in Germany at the end of World War II would be much more controversial, this episode proves that he was able to work in a challenging political environment and leverage his understanding of history to achieve victory.

Battling the Germans in North Africa

Patton's administration of Morocco was adroit, but it was not the active combat command that he so passionately craved. Because the other Allied commands had landed farther east and were closer to the German bases in Tunisia, they were in the middle of the unfolding battles, while he had comparatively little to do. Frustrated by the lack of action, he noted that "for 26 days we have not had any fighting. This is regrettable."[60] He confronted his boredom by reading and visiting historical sites in the region. While time seemed to drag, he would not have to wait long for an opportunity to prove himself, as the Allies would soon need his skills as a combat leader.

The first indication of trouble was a relatively small series of battles from February 14 to 17, 1943, at Sidi Bou Zid. In a carefully executed surprise attack, elements of two German panzer divisions commanded by General Hans-Jürgen Von Arnim engaged and defeated the American II Corps commanded by American general Lloyd Fredendall. Using surprise and initiative, the battle-hardened Germans attacked at 0400 and never allowed the inexperienced American forces time to regroup and organize an effective defense. By late morning, the American forces were in retreat.[61]

The one exception to the Allied panic and disorder was a reinforced battalion under command of Lieutenant Colonel John Waters, George Patton's son-in-law. Waters was well respected by both Patton and his men for his calm and professional demeanor and his ability to inspire confidence. Task Force Waters would rely on this inspirational leadership, as it was positioned on the prominent Lessouda hill that dominated the plain over which the German forces were advancing. While Waters and his men could clearly see the importance of this position, General Fredendall was far from the front, and command could not grasp the importance of this terrain feature. Without an accurate picture of the unfolding battle, the Americans did not prioritize holding this key position and let a potential opportunity for victory slip away. Waters asked for support, but Fredendall dithered. Lacking support, Task Force Waters fought bravely but was quickly surrounded and subjected to a ferocious artillery barrage. Under the weight of the German attack, Waters's men held out as long as they could in the hope of reinforcement. Some of his men were able to break out of the German trap and escape, but the majority, including Waters, were eventually forced to surrender.[62]

Despite the fact that he had fought bravely, Waters doubted his own courage and leadership as he faced an uncertain future in German captivity. While he could not know it at the time, Waters had delayed the German attack long enough for much of the American force to escape greater destruction and regroup, actions that would earn him the Distinguished Service Cross.[63] The Americans' counterattack the next day was poorly coordinated and ineffective, and the Germans were able to stage a counterattack of their own that netted an additional 1,400 American prisoners. All told, the Battle of Sidi Bou Zid cost the Americans 2,546 captured, 103 tanks, 280 vehicles, 18 field guns, 3 antitank guns, and 1 antiaircraft battery.[64]

Axis forces soon followed up this small victory at Sidi Bou Zid with a much larger one. In a five-day battle lasting from February 19 to 24, 1943, the German and Italian forces under command of Field Marshal Erwin Rommel attacked a combined British and American force defending Kasserine Pass. The inexperienced Allies were taken by surprise, and panic quickly ensued. In their first major engagement with the Axis forces, the Americans were routed and retreated in disorder.[65] In some places, they were pushed back more than fifty miles and abandoned much of their heavy equipment in their attempt to escape. Only a combination of German overextension that limited their ability to pursue the fleeing Americans, the determined resistance of an outnumbered group of American defenders at the Thala Pass, and some exemplary leadership by field-grade officers prevented a total disaster.[66]

While many American soldiers had fought bravely, their sacrifices were undermined by inadequate senior leadership. The Allied command was divided between British lieutenant general Kenneth Anderson and American major general Lloyd Fredendall. In the confusion and chaos of battle, this bifurcated command structure led to miscommunication and a fundamental lack of coordination between the Allies, as both generals had difficulties managing the unfolding battle. Fredendall in particular struggled to obtain an accurate picture of the unfolding battle because he spent it in his command bunker some seventy miles behind the front. This physical distance exacerbated the lapses in communications and imperfect information that were all too common in combat and led to charges of cowardice and ineptitude.[67]

Patton followed the news of the Sidi Bou Zid and Kasserine Pass battles with a mixture of professional and personal interest. Based on intelligence reports and his discussions with Eisenhower and other top generals, he studied the lessons learned from the battles in anticipation that he would soon have the opportunity to command in a more active capacity. In the context of a broader defeat, he paid particular attention to the American success at the Thala Pass sector of the battlefield. Here, a mixed force of American units from the 26th Infantry Division, the 26th Armored Brigade, and artillery units from the 9th Infantry Division fought a fierce holding action against the 10th Panzer Division under the command of General Hans-Jürgen von Arnim. Taking advantage of their strong defensive position and their effective artillery fire, they slowly gave ground and eventually halted the Axis advance until nightfall. These efforts that potentially saved the American Army were encouraging to Patton because they proved that if properly led, these same men could fight on equal terms with the vaunted Afrika Korps. He analogized their sacrifice to the defense of Fort Stedman during the final weeks of the Petersburg campaign in the American Civil War, remarking to Eisenhower, "Well, Von Arnim should have read about Lee's attack at Fort Stedman."[68]

This analogy was particularly apt, as the Union defenders were initially surprised and disorganized and their commanding officer, General George Meade, was away from the front at a conference with General Ulysses Grant and other Union dignitaries at City Point, Virginia. Despite the initial surprise, the Union forces regrouped and prevented the Confederates from breaking the key portion of their line. They then used their artillery support to inflict massive casualties on the attacking Confederates and checked their last major assault of the Petersburg campaign.[69]

Based upon his study of this minor success, Patton quickly came to the conclusion that American troops had fought bravely but had been let down by their commanding officer, General Lloyd Fredendall.[70] In his diary, he recounted his frank discussion with Major General Ernest Harmon, who had observed the battle of Kasserine Pass: "According to Harmon, Fredendall is a physical and moral coward. Harmon did well. . . . And [Harmon] drove the Germans from the pass of Kasserine. He said it was due to what I had told him on a fishing trip about clearing a pass by capturing the heights. That is what he did with the infantry. Fredendall never went to the front at all and tried to make Harmon the goat."[71]

Patton's bitterness was exacerbated by the news that his beloved son-in-law John Waters had been captured. He first learned that "John's battalion was destroyed" on February 22, but on this date he had no news regarding his status.[72] The next day, in a letter to his wife, he broke the news, claiming that "John's battalion was practically wiped out" but adding that "he is thought to be safe."[73] In fact, the general had no knowledge of Waters's condition at this point and was purposely distorting the facts to his most trusted friend to make the news appear more hopeful.

Patton wrote two letters on March 2 to Beatrice and his brother-in-law, Frederick Ayer, that were more candid and truthful. To his wife he noted that he had sent a letter to his daughter "Little B. which is not a success as I am not too good a liar" but noted, "There is still a chance that John too may turn up. . . . If George [Patton's son] had been in John's place, I could not feel worse. . . . I feel terribly sorry for B." To Fred Ayer, the general was more realistic, noting, "There is still a chance that he may have escaped. . . . Personally knowing John, I do not think that he surrendered, but it is very important to make little Bea and also Bea senior believe that he did. . . . Eisenhower . . . considered his action one of the finest of this war and has given him the Distinguished Service Cross."[74] While he was doing his best to maintain a brave face, Patton was clearly upset by the loss of Waters and was doing his best to control his own emotions. Although he would soon have greater responsibilities as the new commander of II Corps, Patton would never forget Waters. In his diaries and letters, he frequently mentioned his son-in-law, blamed the ineptitude for the American generals for his capture, and was continually seeking additional information regarding his fate.

The twin defeats at Sidi Bou Zid and Kasserine were unacceptable for General Eisenhower. After conferring with Major General Ernest Harmon, who had observed the battles, as well as Major General Omar Bradley, Eisenhower decided to relieve Fredendall as commander of II Corps and replace him with Patton, effective March 6, 1943. While the two generals had been rivals and Patton blamed Fredendall for the loss of Waters, the two met for breakfast and attempted to be as professional as possible. Fredendall was "very nice and conducted himself well." Despite this conviviality, Patton was extremely critical in his assessment of the headquarters: "His staff in general [is] poor. Discipline and dress poor. . . . I think Fredendall is either a little nuts or badly scared."[75]

While meeting with Fredendall, he also inquired about his son-in-law Lieutenant Colonel John Waters. Waters's fate was clearly weighing heavily on his mind, as he relayed this conversation to his wife, Beatrice, in a letter dated the same day: "[Fredendall] says he is sure John [Waters] is alive, a prisoner, and Omar Bradley who is here feels the same so I am much more encouraged."[76]

To address the deficiencies of the American command, Patton immediately defaulted to his tried-and-true approach—discipline. On his first day of command, "I issued some orders on dress, saluting, etc. None had ever been issued. It is absurd to believe that soldiers who cannot be made to wear the proper uniform can be induced to move forward in battle."[77] While it would become a cliché, the general's insistence on dress and discipline was based on both his personal experiences leading men and his view of history. Just as Napoleon and Frederick the Great had insisted on pride and professionalism, Patton would insist that his men live up to his own demanding standards of deportment.

Consistent with this up-front leadership and his assessment that Fredendall had lost control over the battle, Patton also made a point to abandon his predecessor's command post and spend more time at the front with his troops. This leadership had an immediate impact on their morale and fighting readiness.[78] Unlike the distant Fredendall, who lived more than an hour's drive from the front lines, the new commander of II Corps was leading the unit through force of will and imparting his own unique leadership style to his men. Over the next few days, he would personally inspect many of his combat units. While he believed in the underlying quality and bravery of his troops, he found their attention to detail fundamentally lacking. "The discipline, dress, and condition of weapons at 34th [Division] very bad—terrible. On the other hand, elements of the division have fought well. Inspected their positions and found it weak, particularly in the emplacement of the 37 [mm] anti-tank guns, which are on the crest instead of on the reverse slope where they belong."[79]

In preparing his men for battle, Patton drove himself at a frantic pace. Despite this almost fanatical devotion to the men and the mission, he did take a moment to savor his promotion to lieutenant general on March 12. In his diary entry on the same date, he preserved his feelings for history:

> We have a done a lot but much remains to be done. Fredendall just existed—he did not command. . . . [General Manton S.] Eddy called at 2100 to tell me he had heard on the radio that I am a Lieutenant General. Dick Jenson [his aide] brought me a flag he had been carrying with him for a year. I am sleeping under the three stars. When I was a little boy at home, I used to wear a wooden sword and say to myself, "George Patton, Jr., Lieutenant General." At that time I did not know there were full generals. Now I want, and will get, four stars.[80]

He had come down off this high a bit the next day, when he wrote Beatrice, "Well at last I am a Lt. Gen. but there are so many of them that it has lost its zest. Still of course I am quite pleased. . . . Lots of love. George. Lt. Gen. (FIRST TIME)."[81]

El Guettar

Now that Patton had achieved his childhood dreams of becoming a three-star general, he had to make good on his promises to restore American fortunes and defeat the Germans. While he wanted to attack as soon as possible, the date for an American advance was delayed until March 17 to allow the American forces additional time to prepare. Patton wanted to attack as quickly as possible to obtain surprise and initiative. He believed that the Germans had overextended themselves and that the topography around Gafsa would allow him to sneak up and achieve tactical surprise. He then hoped to crush the Germans between his forces and the British and win a decisive victory.

Using history as his inspiration, Patton modeled his planned campaign on the Confederate victory at Second Manassas. Building upon his childhood fantasies, he cast himself as Confederate general Stonewall Jackson. In 1862

Jackson had achieved surprise by sneaking through the Manassas Gap and threatening the flanks of the Union forces. The Union forces responded by hastily attacking Jackson, who held on to an excellent defensive position known as Stoney Ridge. The remainder of the Confederate forces under the command of General James Longstreet attacked into the exposed Union flank and crushed the Northern forces between the two rebel armies, achieving one of the most complete victories of the war.[82]

Patton had read extensively on General Stonewall Jackson in the years prior to World War II, and, like the eccentric Confederate commander had done eight decades before, he planned to use a mix of geography, surprise, and hammer-and-anvil tactics to destroy the Germans.[83] Reflecting on this in his diary, Patton noted, "I fear Rommel will take the initiative, but I shall not assume defensive. Sent Bradley to 34th Division to preach bloody war. 34th is too defensive. 9th has 'Valor of Ignorance.' 1st is good. 1st Armored is timid. . . . Having a big problem with discipline. . . . I will have discipline— to do otherwise is to commit murder. . . . I am just the same since I am a Lieutenant General."[84]

On March 17, Patton's 1st Infantry Division moved forward and captured the town of Gafsa after encountering little resistance from the Italian defenders.[85] While the town was of minimal military significance, its capture was symbolic of a new spirit permeating through II Corps. The Americans were advancing and bringing the fight to the enemy. The press heralded Patton's exploits, and, with a whiff of irony, he was keen to note the successes of winning the "great and famous battle of Gafsa" in his diary entry.[86]

The next day, spearheaded by the 1st Ranger Battalion, American forces pushed forward to the desert oasis of El Guettar, capturing several hundred Italian prisoners but again meeting little resistance.[87] Even in the middle of the campaign, General Patton had a difficult time ignoring his sense of history. In a letter to his wife dated March 18, 1943, he stated:

The Roman ruins are wonderful and all over one get quite used to passing huge cities and not even knowing their names. . . . I have found out why all the pillars are broken: the Romans pinned them together with bronze pegs, and the Arabs pushed them over to get the metal. . . . It is hard to realize that the Romans were here 700 years. . . . The great city of Thelepte is near here but I have not had time to investigate it. It is supposed to have the finest temple to Minerva in the world. I can see the columns sticking up from the road. There are Roman mile posts in the yard of this building with dates and distances all over it. I could get some wonderful relics if I could move them, but they are all too big. There is a fine torso of a senator laying in the yard too. It is life size and probably weighs a ton.[88]

As Patton was reflecting about the Roman ruins in Tunisia, his forces consolidated their positions around El Guettar. While the American efforts were hindered by mud so severe that even tanks and tracked vehicles had difficulty moving, their commanding officer made great efforts to visit the front and personally inspect his troops positions, finding "countless Roman ruins along the way."[89]

At midnight on March 20, Patton received news from General Bradley that his son-in-law John Waters had been captured at Sidi Bou Zid but was alive. His trusted aide Dick Jenson relayed the news to Beatrice the very same day that "Johnnie Waters is safe" and noting, "It certainly lifts a dark feeling we all had. . . . Next job on the calendar is to get him back."[90] While the news clearly lifted his spirits, it would take another two years, countless lives, and a controversial raid to get Lieutenant Colonel John Waters back into American hands.

In the meantime, Patton had grown tired of the slow pace of advance and the anticlimactic capture of the dispirited Italians, whom he dubbed "additional Roman ruins."[91] He craved an opportunity to prove the fighting capabilities of the American Army in a pitched battle with Rommel's Afrika Korps. While Rommel had left the African theater and returned to Germany, II Corps would not have to wait long to fight their German foes. At that very moment, General von Arnim was planning a spoiling attack on the American forces that was designed to preempt the American advance. Arnim's attack was premised on the assumption that the Americans had gained little in the way of combat proficiency and senior leadership since their defeat at Kasserine Pass a month before.

At 0600 on March 23, the German 10th Panzer Division attacked Patton's forces defending El Guettar. Emerging through the El Guettar Valley, the Germans aimed their advance at the US 1st Infantry Division that was anchoring the American position on top of a hill. While the Germans did achieve some limited successes in the opening phases of the battle, they faced a vastly improved American force. Rather than panicking or fighting in uncoordinated small groups, the Americans held their ground and fought as a team.[92]

The critical moment of the battle came when German tanks advanced to within range of the 1st Infantry Division's headquarters. Sensing that the battle turned on his leadership, the 1st Division's commander, Major General Terry Allen, held firm. Allen refused to evacuate his headquarters, exclaiming, "I will like hell pull out," and threatened to "shoot the first bastard who does."[93] While crass, this example of bravery inspired his men to hold their positions and continue the fight. The tattered remains of the 1st Infantry Division held fast and beat back the Germans.[94]

After failing to overrun Allen's headquarters and then running into a minefield, the German attack lost the initiative. The Americans fought back and used their antitank guns and tank-destroyer units to inflict devastating losses on the German armor as they retreated to the cover of the El Guettar Valley. By 1000 the first German attack was effectively neutralized, and much of their armored striking power was destroyed.[95]

At approximately 1645, the Germans made a second attack on the American positions, this time leading with their infantry units.[96] Unlike at Kasserine a month before, the American artillery was well positioned and quick to respond. Accurate long-range fire took a devastating toll on the exposed German foot soldiers, who were too far away to effectively engage with their lighter weapons. Sensing that any further attacks would be fruitless, von Arnim ordered a retreat.

After a series of humiliating losses, II Corps had at last won a major victory. While the victorious general reflected that "the Lord helped a lot today," the II Corps' success was due in no small part to his influence.[97] Unlike at Kasserine, the Americans were properly positioned to exploit their excellent defensive positions, had active and inspiring leadership at every level of command, and did not panic under the stress of battle. While it was not a perfect replay of Second Manassas, each of these elements reflected Patton's commitment to the ageless fundamentals of warfare—the value of terrain, unity of command, and personal courage. Even Terry Allen's brave but tactless insistence that he would shoot the first person to desert his headquarters bore the hallmarks of General Patton's rough but inspiring language designed to motivate frightened men to endure the stress and fear of battle.

For the newly promoted three-star general, the Battle of El Guettar was critical because it validated his leadership philosophy and gave him a victory to build upon. The effect on morale was immediate. No longer were the Americans afraid to face the Germans in open battle, and the men began to have confidence in themselves. Their commanding officer was proud of what his men had accomplished, and he looked forward to building upon this first success.[98]

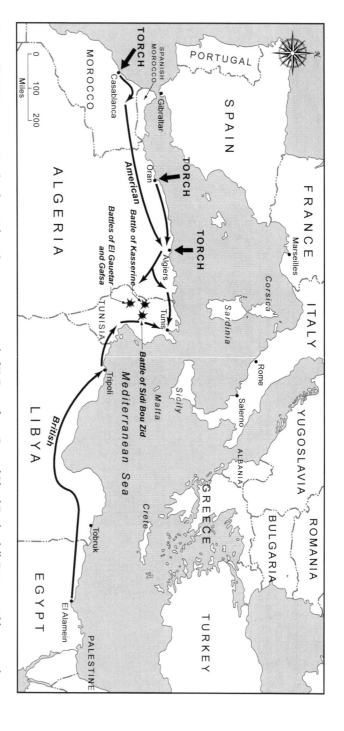

Map 4: Allied Drive across North Africa. After taking over command of II Corps from General Lloyd Fredendall, Patton quickly restored American fighting spirit and resumed the Allied drive across North Africa. Map by Chris Robinson.

Over the next week, II Corps consolidated its position and advanced along a narrow front, making slow but steady progress. Patton believed that he should act more aggressively but that British general Harold Alexander was favoring the British forces while also micromanaging the placement and operations of American forces in the area of operations.[99] By the end of March, II Corps was attacking the Germans along the Gabes Road line, despite terrain that was "almost impossible for armored vehicles." This failure to achieve a rapid breakthrough due to poor weather and the realities of coalition warfare frustrated Patton, who complained that he was "stuck everywhere," a reference to not only the mud but also the relationship with his British allies.[100]

This frustration paled in comparison with the raw emotion that Patton felt after the death of his aide Dick Jenson on April 1, 1943. While on an assignment to deliver instructions for an advance to General Bradley, Jenson was killed when a flight of German Junkers Ju-88 bombers attacked the general's command post.[101] While everybody jumped into a slit trench during the raid, a five-hundred-pound bomb dropped right on the edge of Jenson's trench, and the concussion from the blast killed him instantly.[102] In stark contrast to the popular "blood-and-guts" image of an insensitive warrior, Patton blamed himself for his aide's death and repeatedly mentioned him in his private letters and diary entries.[103] Jenson was like a son to the general, and he would carry the sadness of his death for the remainder of the war.[104]

· ·

NOTES

1. Yeide, *Fighting Patton*, 54.

2. Morningstar, *Patton's Way*, 37; "Address to officers and men of the Second Armored Division," Military Papers, 1903–76, George S. Patton Papers, Manuscript Division, Library of Congress, Washington, DC.

3. Blumenson, *The Patton Papers*, 2:12.

4. Peter R. Mansoor, *The GI Offensive in Europe: The Triumph of American Infantry Divisions, 1941–1945*, 68–69.

5. While it is important not to overstate Patton's accomplishments, they provided a testing ground for some of his theories and allowed Patton to distinguish him from more conservative and plodding leaders, such as Hugh Drum. Christopher R. Gabel, "The 1941 Maneuvers: What Did They Really Accomplish?"

6. D'Este, *Patton*, 392–407.

7. Johnson, *Fast Tanks and Heavy Bombers*, 141.

8. September 1941 estimate, "Victory Program," cited in Allan R. Millett, Peter Maslowski, and William B. Feis, *For the Common Defense: A Military History of the United States from 1607 to 2012*, 418; Johnson, *Fast Tanks and Heavy Bombers*, 115.

9. Sidney L. Meller, *The Desert Training Center and C-AMA, Study No. 15*, 1–2, 5.

10. Meller, *Desert Training Center*, 16.

11. Blumenson, *Patton*, 168; Essame, *Patton as Military Commander*, 38.

12. David C. Henley, *The Land That God Forgot: The Saga of Gen. George Patton's Desert Training Camps*, 26.

13. George S. Patton Jr., "The Desert Training Corps."

14. Roosevelt quoted in Millett, Maslowski, and Feis, *For the Common Defense*, 439.

15. Kent Roberts Greenfield, *American Strategy in World War II: A Reconsideration*, 14–15.

16. Blumenson, *The Patton Papers*, 2:83.

17. Millett, Maslowski, and Feis, *For the Common Defense*, 439–40. See also Arthur L. Funk, *The Politics of Torch: The Allied Landings and the Algiers Putsch, 1942*.

18. Winston S. Churchill, *The Second World War*, 57.

19. Yeide, *Fighting Patton*, 109.

20. D'Este, *Patton*, 419.

21. D'Este, *Patton*, 419.

22. D'Este, *Patton*, 421.

23. D'Este, *Patton*, 420–21.

24. Diaries, 1910–45, Patton Papers.

25. Diaries, 1910–45, Patton Papers.

26. Smith, *Eisenhower in War and Peace*, 215.

27. Mansoor, *GI Offensive in Europe*, 85.

28. Dwight D. Eisenhower, "Report of the Commander-in-Chief Allied Forces to the Combined Chiefs of Staff on Operations in North Africa," 3–9; Matheny, *Carrying the War to the Enemy*, 171.

29. Charles R. Codman, *Drive*, 9–10.

30. Yeide, *Fighting Patton*, 114.

31. D. Eisenhower, "Report of the Commander-in-Chief," 4.

32. On these points, see generally Robert O. Paxton, *Vichy France: Old Guard and New Order, 1940–1944*; and David Wragg, *Sink the French: The French Navy after the Fall of France, 1940*.

33. This anti-Semitism proved to be so strong that even after defeating the French, the Americans chose not to restore Jewish political rights in the region for fear of inciting an Arab revolt. Groom, *The Generals*, 278.

34. Codman, *Drive*, 38–39.

35. Patton, *War as I Knew It*, 5.

36. Patton, *War as I Knew It*, 5.

37. Keane, *Patton*.

38. Diaries, 1910–45, Patton Papers.

39. Patton, *War as I Knew It*, 8.

40. Blumenson, *The Patton Papers*, 2:98. In 1945, during some frustrating fighting around Trier, Patton would again boost his self-confidence by referring to this Napoleonic maxim.

41. Blumenson, *The Patton Papers*, 2:102.

42. Samuel Eliot Morison, *History of United States Naval Operations in World War II*, 2:93, 110.

43. Atkinson, *Army at Dawn*, 130–40.

44. Patton, *War as I Knew It*, 8–9.

45. Codman, *Drive*, 22.

46. Diaries, 1910–45, Patton Papers.

47. Matheny, *Carrying the War to the Enemy*, 173.

48. Patton, *War as I Knew It*, 10.

49. Diaries, 1910–45, Patton Papers.

50. Diaries, 1910–45, Patton Papers.

51. Blumenson, *Patton*, 173–75.

52. Codman, *Drive*, 51.

53. Alan Axelrod, *Patton on Leadership: Strategic Lessons for Corporate Warfare*, 250.

54. Blumenson and Hymel, *Patton*, 49.

55. Patton, *War as I Knew It*, 22–24.

56. Patton, *War as I Knew It*, 46.

57. D. Eisenhower, "Report of the Commander-in-Chief," 16–17.

58. See also Robert W. Komer, *Civil Affairs and Military Government in the Mediterranean Theater*.

59. An official report, "Memorandum for All Ground General and Special Staff, Headquarters Army Ground Forces, Subject: Lessons Derived from Operations at Casablanca and Oran," highlighted the need for more interpreters and greater fluency with the local culture. C. P. Bixel, "Memorandum for All Ground General and Special Staff, Headquarters Army Ground Forces, Subject: Lessons Derived from Operations at Casablanca and Oran."

60. Blumenson, *The Patton Papers*, 2:135.

61. Staff Group D, Section 4, *CSI Battle Book 4-D: The Battle of Sidi Bou Zid*.

62. Staff Group D, Section 4, *CSI Battle Book 4-D*.

63. Steven Thomas Barry, *Battalion Commanders at War: U.S. Army Tactical Leadership in the Mediterranean Theater, 1942–1943*, 114–21.

64. Charles R. Anderson, *Tunisia, 17 November 1942 to 13 May 1943*, 16.

65. Charles E. Heller and William A. Stofft, eds., *America's First Battles, 1776–1965*, 226–65.

66. Barry, *Battalion Commanders at War*, 116–41.

67. Blumenson, *Kasserine Pass*.

68. D. Eisenhower, *Crusade in Europe*, 159–60.

69. Noah Andre Trudeau, *The Last Citadel: Petersburg, Virginia, June 1864–April 1865*, 333–402; Earl J. Hess, *In the Trenches at Petersburg: Field Fortifications and Confederate Defeat*, 245–63.

70. Mansoor, *GI Offensive in Europe*, 90.

71. Diaries, 1910–45, Patton Papers.

72. Diaries, 1910–45, Patton Papers.

73. Blumenson, *The Patton Papers*, 2:175.

74. Blumenson, *The Patton Papers*, 2:177.

75. Diaries, 1910–45, Patton Papers.

76. Blumenson, *The Patton Papers*, 2:181.

77. Diaries, 1910–45, Patton Papers.

78. Gerald Astor, *Terrible Terry Allen, Combat General of World War II: The Life of an American Soldier*, 164.

79. Diaries, 1910–45, Patton Papers.

80. Diaries, 1910–45, Patton Papers.

81. Blumenson, *The Patton Papers*, 2:189.

82. D'Este, *Patton*, 472; Essame, *Patton as Military Commander*, 76. On the Battle of Second Manassas, see generally John J. Hennessy, *Return to Bull Run: The Campaign and Battle of Second Manassas*.

83. Indeed, one of Patton's favorite books was G. F. R. Henderson's *Stonewall Jackson and the American Civil War*, and he also bought the multivolume studies by Douglas Southall Freeman on General Robert E. Less and his subordinates as soon as they were released. B. Patton, "A Soldier's Reading."

84. Diaries, 1910–45, Patton Papers.

85. Barron, *Patton's First Victory*, 1–24.

86. Diaries, 1910–45, Patton Papers.

87. Barron, *Patton's First Victory*, 34.

88. Blumenson, *The Patton Papers*, 2:193.

89. Family Papers, 1857–1979, Patton Papers.

90. Blumenson, *The Patton Papers*, 2:196.

91. Blumenson, *The Patton Papers*, 2:197.

92. Barron, *Patton's First Victory*, 69–128.

93. Astor, *Terrible Terry Allen*, 168.

94. Atkinson, *Army at Dawn*, 440.

95. Atkinson, *Army at Dawn*, 441.

96. Atkinson, *Army at Dawn*, 442.

97. Diaries, 1910–45, Patton Papers.

98. Blumenson and Hymel, *Patton*, 52.

99. Blumenson, *The Patton Papers*, 2:200.

100. Diaries, 1910–45, Patton Papers.

101. For an excellent overview on Jenson's death, see Kevin M. Hymel, "'The Bravest and Best': Patton and the Death of CAPT. Richard Jenson in North Africa."

102. Codman, *Drive*, 88.

103. Blumenson, *The Patton Papers*, 2:203–5.

104. D'Este, *Patton*, 480.

CHAPTER THREE

BATTLES WITH HISTORY IN THE FOOTSTEPS OF HANNIBAL

Planning Operation Husky and Reflecting on the Recent Campaigns

WHILE SIGNIFICANT GERMAN forces remained in North Africa, command of II Corps was transferred to General Omar Bradley on April 14, 1943. Patton was reassigned to begin planning for the Allied invasion of Sicily, which was scheduled for that summer.[1] While he had been frustrated with the slow pace of the advance and perceived Anglo micromanagement, he had mixed emotions about the news, writing in his diary, "I hate to quit the fight but feel that I had best do so as I fear that on the north flank, where Alexander has put us, there is no future."[2] Sensing the need to praise his famous general, Eisenhower sent George a letter of congratulations dated April 14. Eisenhower highlighted his successful turnaround of the American efforts during "that phase of the Tunisian operations for which I placed you temporarily in command of the II Corps" and thanked him for his "outstanding example of leadership you have given us all."[3]

On April 15, Patton reflected on his growth as a leader and his hopes for the upcoming campaign in his diary: "It takes a simple, direct, and ruthless man to wage war. . . . I have developed a lot and my never small self-confidence has vastly grown. I am sure with God's help I will succeed at 'Husky' [the Allied code name for the invasion of Sicily] and so on to the end, which is far distant."[4] Despite his distrust of reporters, Patton even enjoyed excellent relations with the press during this period, noting that he was in fact "too popular with the press," as they heaped praise on the conquering general.[5] In a April 17 diary entry he summed up his role in the campaign: "I have been gone 43 days, fought several successful battles, commanded 95,800 men, lost about ten pounds, gained a third star and a hell of a lot of poise and confidence, and am otherwise the same."[6]

After defeating the Germans in North Africa, the Western Allies faced a series of tough strategic decisions. In January Roosevelt and Churchill met in Casablanca to coordinate strategy for 1943. Despite their differences, they agreed on three main objectives: neutralize the U-boat threat, provide maximum military aid to the Soviets, and expand the strategic bombing of German industry. While all of these objectives were considered essential for victory, they left the American and British ground forces without a clear mission. An attack on Sicily was the plan favored by the British, who argued that it was the best option to attrit Axis forces, relieve pressure on the Soviets, clear the Mediterranean of potential threats to Allied shipping, and potentially knock Italy out of the war. Echoing a phrase he used in the First World War, Churchill sold the plan as a "strike into the underbelly of the Axis."[7] Given the fact that the Allies lacked sufficient strength to invade France, the Americans begrudgingly accepted the indirect approach favored by the British.[8] Although senior American leaders, such as Secretary of War Stimson, criticized the Sicily invasion as "periphery pecking," planning for Operation Husky began in early 1943 while the Allies were still mopping up some of the last German units in Africa.[9]

Despite his private beliefs that the Americans were blindly following the British lead, Patton relished the opportunity to fight in Sicily. As the most successful American field commander in North Africa, he was the obvious choice to plan the American ground operations and command the newly formed Seventh Army in the upcoming campaign. While the overall commander for Operation Husky would be the British general Harold Alexander, Patton was pleased to be given this increased responsibility and hoped to have a prominent role in the upcoming campaign.

In addition to professional advancement, the general also wanted to fight in Sicily for more romantic reasons. As a student of history, he was eager to fight in a land so rich with military history and to follow in the footsteps of conquerors such as the Greeks, Carthaginians, Romans, Muslims, Vikings, Normans, Bourbons, and countless others. Of particular interest to Patton were the campaigns of the Greeks during the Peloponnesian War and the Romans during the Punic Wars. Since his childhood, he had been raised on these classic tales and frequently mentioned them in his writings and speeches. Now he would have the opportunity to fight where Alcibiades, Hannibal, and Scipio Africanus had and make his own mark on the military history of the island.[10]

As the Allies began preparing for the Sicilian campaign, Patton was hard at work both institutionalizing his notes from the Tunisian Campaign and planning Operation Husky. Like the two-faced Roman god Janus, the general was looking backward and forward simultaneously. To understand the meaning of the recent campaigns, he wrote down his observations, confident that they would be of practical value for the future. To anticipate the future campaign, he not only studied the present military situation but also looked to the past for inspiration and guidance.

On April 20, he finalized his observations from the Tunisian Campaign in one of his "Notes on Combat" that he forwarded to each of the units in his command. This document reemphasized the general's belief that speed, initiative, and fighting spirit were essential to achieving victory on the modern battlefield. Based on his experiences, officers should not spend their time "sitting in front of a map, plotting situations," but should instead "go to critical points to see that orders are being executed on time" and to "set the example in courage." In addition to instilling courage in their men, Patton reasserted his fervent belief in the need for standards and discipline in battle, claiming, "Officers who fail to perform their duty by correcting small violations and in enforcing proper conduct are incapable of leading." As part of this philosophy, officers must be easily identifiable to their men: "When men see a marked helmet they know it is an officer. These markings are not visible at a range beyond 200 yards, therefore the timid excuse that they produce sniping is of no value." In addition to arguing for inspirational leadership, he also made the case for rapid movement: "Death in battle is a function of time. The longer troops remain under fire, the more get killed. Therefore everything must be done to speed up movement." Once troops were moving forward, it was essential to keep them moving and avoid reverting to a defensive posture. "During an attack, infantry must not dig in until the final objective is reached. If they do, they cannot be restarted."[11] While he would continue to refine his theories on modern warfare, Patton had gained confidence in himself as a leader and was eager to build on his experiences.

During the spring of 1943, Patton was also very active at exploring archaeological ruins in North Africa, making many notes in his diary and letters of various sites he explored. After a detour to the Roman city of Timgad, he reflected in his diary about the Arch of Trajan and the wagon ruts that were "six inches deep" but concluded with the immodest boast, "Yet I have fought and won a bigger battle than Trajan ever heard of."[12] On April 17, he wrote Beatrice with a vivid description of his trip to Timgad, calling it "the finest ruin I have ever seen," making particular note of the baths, temples, theater, library, and "whore house."[13] These historical diversions would prove increasingly important to the general in the coming weeks as he grew disgruntled with a lack of action and the realities of managing the Anglo-American alliance.

While Patton was eager to fight the Axis, he was increasingly wary of what he saw as British domination of the planning process. Unlike the more pragmatic Eisenhower, he could not understand the political elements of coalition warfare and complained frequently that "this war is being fought for the benefit of the British Empire and for post-war considerations."[14] This inability to comprehend the need for inter-Allied cooperation and political tact would remain a near-constant theme for the remainder of Patton's career. In the coming Sicilian campaign, these frustrations would have a profound effect and ultimately cost him higher command and tarnish his reputation, but for the moment they were more a source of aggravation.

From an early stage in the planning process, Patton (and most of the American generals) had favored a two-pronged invasion of Sicily where one portion of the Allied force would land in the west, near Palermo, and the other in the east, near Catania. The British were afraid that a divided force would cause logistical nightmares, divide Allied striking power, and make coordinating air support more difficult. They insisted on a more conservative approach where British and American forces landed in closer proximity on the south of the island and advanced northward in parallel. Both sides made sound military arguments for their preferred plans, but seemed unable to convince their coalition partners. Lacking a clear plan, inter-Allied squabbling continued for three months. Sensing the futility of making his points in a planning process dominated by the British, Patton remained a spectator during many of the official meetings and chose to keep his opinions to himself in an uncommon display of passivity.

Ultimately, General Bernard Montgomery, the commander of British ground forces for the operation, broke the indecision. In a gambit that bordered on insubordination, Monty told his boss, General Alexander, that he was going to proceed with planning for landing on the southeast of the island no matter what the rest of the planners decided. He took this ploy one step further by cornering Eisenhower's chief of staff, Walter Bedell Smith, in a bathroom at the Allied headquarters. After Montgomery fogged a bathroom mirror with his own breath, he drew a simple map of his proposal and demanded that Smith approach Eisenhower with the plan for final approval.

Desperate to avoid continued squabbling, Eisenhower approved the plan, and the rest of the Allied High Command quickly followed suit.[15]

The compromise plan that was ultimately adopted did not please Patton. According to the plan, both the British and the American forces would land on the southeast of the island and move north in parallel. The British force would constitute the eastern wing and land near Syracuse and drive north to capture the key cities of Catania and Messina. The American force would land to the west in the Gulf of Gela and move in conjunction with the British to guard their flank against potential attacks. This plan gave the British the greatest opportunity to dictate the pace of the campaign, capture major cities, and win glory, while the Americans were restricted in their freedom of movement, forced to advance through the rugged mountain terrain inland, and reduced to a less glamorous supporting role. While the Allied commanders were happy to be moving forward with a plan, the Americans felt as if they had been insulted by the British and were understandably frustrated by the politics of coalition warfare.

Perhaps no one was frustrated by the Operation Husky plans more than George Patton. While he did his best to hide his feeling of animosity toward the British, he believed that they had hijacked the operational planning. The fact that his Seventh Army would be tied to the British in a supporting role limited its opportunities to achieve individual glory, and the need to remain in a position to guard the British flank directly contradicted Patton's recently published theories about the value of initiative, movement, and speed in achieving victory.

While he did his best to play the role of a loyal officer in public, his diary entry of May 22 tells a different story and was already providing excuses and assigning blame:

> Under the present arrangement for Husky, we have pro-British straw men at the top [Eisenhower], A British chief admiral and senior vice admiral. . . . Alexander commands all the ground troops. His chief of staff is British. . . . General Montgomery, a full general, commands [British Eighth Army]. I command—a poor last. I cannot see how the people at home don't see it. The U.S. is getting gypped. All Seventh Army supplies come either over beaches or else through Siracusa, a British port, and I am told to arrange with Monty. . . . On a study of form, especially in higher command, we are licked. Churchill runs this war and at the moment he is not interested in Husky. The thing I must do is to retain my SELF-CONFIDENCE. I have greater ability than these other people and it comes from, for lack of a better word, what we must call

greatness of soul based on a belief—an unshakable belief—in my destiny. The U.S. must win—not as an ally, but as a conqueror. If I can find my duty, I can do it. I must.[16]

While Patton did his best to control these emotions, his frustrations began to show themselves prior to the Husky landings. While observing the First Infantry Division conduct a practice landing, in the company of Generals Marshall, Eisenhower, and Bradley, Patton exploded in rage at the troops who had come ashore, yelling, "And just where the hell are your goddamned bayonets?" This display shocked the other senior generals, and an officer reportedly whispered to Bradley, "Well there goes Georgie's chance for a crack at higher command. That temper is going to finish him yet."[17]

Unsatisfied with his inability to shape the invasion plan, Patton yet again turned to his pen to win others over to his views on the impending combat operations. On June 5, just over a month prior to the invasion of Sicily, he issued a letter of instructions to his subordinate commanders outlining his strategy for the coming campaign. Despite the supporting role that the Seventh Army would play, he insisted on aggressive offensive movement and maintaining the initiative in pursuit of a defeated enemy.[18] Borrowing heavily from his recent "Notes on Combat," this document indicates that Patton wanted nothing more than to implement his theories of offensive warfare and was unwilling to accept a plodding support role by default.

Fighting in Sicily

Operation Husky began on the evening of July 9, 1943. Severe winds hampered both the airborne drop and the landings on the invasion beaches, yet the Americans met little organized resistance when they came ashore on the morning of July 10. The Italians made a few halfhearted attacks with their obsolete Renault tanks, targeting the 82nd Airborne and the 1st Infantry Division, but these advances were quickly halted by the men of the 82nd and direct naval gunfire from the cruisers USS *Savannah* and *Boise* and the destroyers USS *Jeffers* and *Shubrick*.[19] Under this crushing firepower, many of the Italians surrendered en masse much to the amusement of their American captors. The Germans were unable to mass their armored forces for an attack on the first day, and the Americans were able to consolidate their positions and prepare for movement inland.[20] In terms of troops put ashore on the first day of the invasion, the landings were the largest of World War II, and beach congestion, not Axis resistance, proved to be the biggest single challenge.[21] In total, Seventh Army landed three divisions, the 1st Infantry, 3rd Infantry, and 45th Infantry on the invasion beaches, and landed the 82nd Airborne Division behind the coast, while keeping the 2nd Armored Division in reserve to be landed and fed into the battle as needed.

When the Germans did counterattack, on July 11, they did so with the halfhearted support of their Italian allies. The attack was poorly coordinated, but the weight of Axis armor threatened to overwhelm the American 26th Infantry and 1st Infantry divisions and drive them off their narrow beachhead.[22] After a tense couple of hours, the Americans were able to halt the advance of the vaunted Herman Göring Division with the help of close air support and naval gunfire from the USS *Boise* and *Savannah*.[23] Patton arrived at the beleaguered beachhead after the most intense portion of the fighting was already over, smoking a cigar and imploring his men to advance inland. He ate a K ration with Brigadier General William J. Donovan, the director of the Office of Strategic Services (OSS), and stated bluntly, "You know Bill, there are two things in life I love to do—fucking and fighting." Donovan nodded and replied, "Yes, George, and in that order, too."[24]

The Axis defenders realized that they would be unable to push the Allies off the invasion beaches and shifted their strategy to a delaying effort aimed

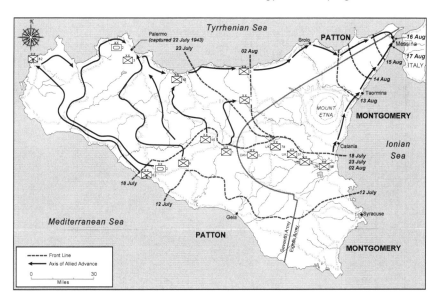

Map 5: Sicilian campaign. After successful landings on the southern coast of Sicily, Patton's Seventh Army was quickly reduced to a supporting role for the British. Hungry for fame and glory, Patton turned this setback into an opportunity and began to push further north and west than originally planned. This culminated with his famous "horse race" with General Montgomery to Messina. Map by Chris Robinson.

at trading space for time and inflicting as many casualties as possible while minimizing their own losses. They concentrated their forces in front of the eastern port city of Catania in an effort to block the British advance by denying them the vital coastal road that was needed to support their drive up the coast toward Messina. These efforts were successful, and the British advance quickly ground to a halt. Recognizing the need for another road to support his advance north, General Montgomery asked that General Alexander reassign Highway 124, which had been reserved for the Americans, to the British so that they could shift their forces farther to the west and resume the drive to the north. Alexander approved Montgomery's plan and gave access to Highway 124 to the British on July 13. While this decision helped restart Montgomery's drive, it infuriated Patton and the American command.[25] This highway was to be the key to the American drive north toward Messina, the Allies' main objective for Operation Husky.

Without this road, the Americans would be forced to advance farther west through the mountainous central part of the island. This portion of Sicily lacked any significant military value and was ideal ground for the German defenders to conduct a fighting retreat. In addition, this sector lacked a modern road network sufficient for military vehicles, a factor that would drastically limit American fighting power and mobility. By reassigning this critical road to the British, the Americans would have a much more difficult advance and would potentially lose any ability to act on their own initiative and shape the campaign.[26]

The fact that General Alexander appeared to make this decision, which clearly favored the British commanders, without consulting the Americans and then presented it as a matter of fact further deepened the sense of betrayal. In his diary entry from July 13, Patton described the meeting where Alexander broke the news to the Americans: "Went to lunch at 1250. General Alexander . . . and members of his staff arrived at 1310, so I had to quit eating and see them. They gave us the plan of operations, which cuts us off from any possibility of taking Messina. It is noteworthy that Alexander, the Allied commander of a British and American Army, had no Americans with him. What fools we are."[27]

While Patton was clearly upset by this development, he dutifully accepted this order and quickly looked for an opportunity in the midst of disappointment. Noting that the planned route of advance for the Seventh Army had been altered, "I asked General Alexander permission to advance and take Agrigento which is beyond the line specified for the front of the Seventh

Army. He stated that if this could be done through the use of limited forces, in the nature of a reconnaissance in force, he had no objection."[28]

By authorizing the Seventh Army to advance beyond the planned lines in a reconnaissance in force, Alexander had unwittingly given Patton the official, if unintended, sanction to rewrite the American campaign plan for Operation Husky. Freed from the role of protecting the British flank, Patton wasted no time in acting. The very same day that he received his order from Alexander, he reassigned Highway 124 to the British, ordered an advance toward Agrigento, and directed General Bradley to move the 45th Infantry Division toward the mountainous interior of the island.[29]

General Bradley was extremely upset by the actions of his superiors. He believed that his forces were entitled to use Highway 124 and that Patton should have more rigorously opposed the change in plans. In his later writings, Bradley would assert that Patton was hungry for personal glory and had purposely used the British need for a road as a means of creating a more ambitious mission for the Seventh Army.[30] This moment signaled a change in the relationship between these old friends, and Patton's actions for the remainder of the campaign seemed to confirm Bradley's suspicions that his commanding officer was hungry for glory and was willing to bend the rules and take unnecessary risks to make himself famous.[31]

Perhaps sensing the need to proactively defend his historical legacy, the Seventh Army's commander justified the drive toward Agrigento in his diary on military grounds, arguing, "It is very essential to capture this port as, by so doing, we can obviate the necessity of using Siracusa as a base, thus saving a turn around of 140 miles over bad roads, and also obviating the necessity of using a port in conjunction with the [British] Eighth Army. . . . This will permit abandonment of the beaches which are difficult and distant."[32] Despite the sound military logic of capturing Agrigento, there is good evidence that Patton was already thinking several moves ahead. As early as July 14, he was talking about capturing Palermo and had openly made a bet of "a bottle of whisky against a bottle of gin" with British vice air marshal Philip Wigglesworth that "we would take Palermo by midnight on the 23rd."[33]

Freed of its mission to stay in close contact with the British, the Seventh Army moved at a rapid pace, gobbling up territory and moving so fast that it was able to capture thousands of Italian and German prisoners. Agrigento fell on July 16 with little resistance, and George had time to write his wife his first letter since the start of the campaign. He complained that "Monty is trying to steal the show and with assistance of Devine Destiny [Eisenhower] may do so but to date we have captured three times as many men as our cousins. . . . My CP [command post] is on the site of a pagan temple. There is one pillar left and that fluted. I would class it as Egyptian as its capital is like a lotus pod. No one here knows any thing [sic] about it except that Pliny wrote of it."[34]

Despite these successes, and his ancient surroundings, Patton's mood was uneasy. He still believed that the American Army was playing a subordinate role in comparison to the British. These fears were exacerbated, as Alexander attempted to rein in Seventh Army's advance and ensure that the British flank and rear were properly protected. Patton flew to Alexander's headquarters and argued that "it would be inexpedient politically for the Seventh Army not to have equal glory."[35] When presented with a detailed plan of the Seventh Army's proposed advance, the British general relented and "gave me permission to carry out my plan if I would assure him that the road net near Caltanissetta would be held."[36] Patton believed that the British were still being too cautious, but agreed to this concession and continued his drive toward Palermo with renewed energy.

For both military and nonmilitary reasons, Patton wanted to capture Palermo quickly. From a purely strategic sense, he wanted to make contact with and destroy as many Axis units as possible to prevent them from buying the time they needed to evacuate men and matériel from the island.[37] On a more political level, he wanted to prove what his forces could do by demonstrating how fast they could move once they were untethered from British control. This would help build American prestige while showing the British that the US Army was fully capable of independently planning and executing complex military operations. Personally, Patton craved fame and attention, and he believed that the capture of Palermo would ensure his place in history as one of the greatest American commanders of the war.

For each of these reasons, Patton pushed his men and himself at a ferocious pace, instituting his policy of "continuous attack." Despite the "truly terrible country" over which Seventh Army advanced, they were able to achieve impressive results because they were able to move faster than their opponents. Under this constant pressure, the Axis forces were unable to effectively implement a well-ordered fighting retreat and were forced to abandon much of their heavy equipment. While the Italian forces were fighting well up to this point, he believed that "they must crack soon" under the ceaseless pressure of Seventh Army.[38]

As the US Seventh Army continued its rapid drive toward Palermo, Patton became increasingly confident that his views about the conduct of modern war were being vindicated and that he was making a place for him and his men in the history books. In contrast to the slow, plodding pace of the British Army, he crowed in his diary, "We can go twice as fast as the British and hit harder. . . . They attacked Catania with a whole division . . . and only made 400 yards. . . . Our method of attacking all the time is better than the British system of stop, build up, and start, but we must judge by the enemy reaction. I can do it here—Alex[ander] can't in Tunis." Recalling his bet with the British general a few days prior, Patton noted that "we may get to Palermo by the 23rd, and I will win my bet with Wigglesworth."[39]

In addition to maintaining near-constant pressure on his retreating foe, Patton also applied his own personal leadership throughout the Sicilian campaign. By leading from the front and seeming to be everywhere at once, he inspired his men to keep pushing forward. In a controversial incident, he cleared a bridge that had been blocked by a farmer's mule cart by shooting the beast and having the cart dumped over the side to clear the road and resume the stalled advance. While Patton never fully conquered his fear of being shot, he continually exposed himself to fire and shared the dangers of his men, noting that "one dies but once and I am on a high spot . . . but I do hate to be shot at as much as I ever did."[40]

Patton's pressure and presence paid off when on July 22, 1943, the US Seventh Army captured Palermo. This action not only won the general his bottle of whiskey from Vice Air Marshal Wigglesworth, but also won lasting fame and adulation for the Seventh Army. Local citizens and dignitaries mobbed the triumphant Americans, relieved to be liberated from fascist rule. Even General Alexander radioed to congratulate, "You and your splendid soldiers."[41] With great satisfaction, he noted in a letter to Beatrice, "We have out blitzed the Bosch."[42]

While the capture of Palermo had dubious military value, it had a tremendous propaganda value and appealed to Patton's sense of history.[43] Not only was the city rich in history and culture, but by moving rapidly across the island of Sicily to capture Palermo, Patton's Seventh Army had proved the capabilities of the American Army to fight decisively and win victories independent of British support. In his moment of triumph, the conquering general reflected in his diary, "The Command and General Staff School will study the campaign as a classic example of the use of tanks."[44] Likewise in his report on the capture of Palermo, he claimed, "I believe . . . that historical research will reveal that General Keyes' Corps moved faster against heavier resistance over worse roads than did the Germans during their famous blitz."[45] The fame and attention only whetted the general's desire for further

Figure 7. Lieutenant General George S. Patton discussing strategy with Lieutenant Colonel Lyle Bernard shortly after an amphibious landing behind enemy lines on Sicily's north coast. National Archives.

glory. Moreover, the rapid drive over unforgiving terrain seemed to confirm the general's theories regarding modern war and emboldened him to take greater risks in the next phases of the campaign.

Building on the momentum, Patton planned to drive east from Palermo toward the port city of Messina. This city was the key to the enemy position because it was the last major port in Axis control and was the planned embarkation point for evacuating their forces to the Italian mainland. If the Allies could capture Messina rapidly, they could cut off the escape route of the enemy forces and keep these battle-tested units from fighting again. In addition to these strategic reasons, Patton wanted to rapidly move toward Messina to build upon his growing fame and to reinforce the point that the

American forces were superior to their British allies and that they should be given greater opportunities to act independently. To this end, the general repeatedly emphasized his distaste of coalition warfare in his private letters and diary entries.

While future generations of historians would eventually portray the Seventh Army's drive to Messina as a race with the British, the contest was very much a figment of Patton's imagination. He became increasingly focused on proving that he and his men were superior to the British and began to put pressure on himself and his commanders to drive forward at a rapid pace. In a July 28 letter to General Troy Middleton, he described the operations as a "horse race, in which the prestige of the U.S. Army is at stake," insisting that the Americans "must take Messina before the British."[46] The general was also keenly aware that the press was focused on his drive and was kept up to date on the reports by both his staff and his wife, who kept press clippings and frequently reported on the media coverage.[47]

To win the "horse race" to Messina, Patton pushed himself and his men extremely hard. He slept little, frequently visited the front, and kept the pressure on the retreating Germans. Despite this constant action, he took time to ponder the lessons of the unfolding campaign with the idea of building upon these observations in future campaigns. In letters to his friends, he highlighted the utility of American amphibious vehicles (DUKWs) in surrounding German positions, the ability of the two-and-a-half-ton trucks to keep his frontline units supplied, and the combination of mobility and firepower provided by the 4.2-inch mortar. In a letter to General Leslie McNair, the commander of Army Ground Forces, he briefly summarized his views about the need for more realistic training, better shoes, reforming the replacement system, and larger-caliber tank guns, as well as noting the "devastating" firepower of the M-1 rifle.[48]

Even in the midst of battle, Patton could not escape the rich history of Sicily. He set up his headquarters in a lavish palace that apparently made his home at Green Meadows, Massachusetts, appear, "pretty measley [sic]" in comparison. In multiple letters to his wife, he described the history of his headquarters, noting that the central portion was built prior to AD 1000, the chapel was added by a Norman duke in about 1040, the frescos depicted the labors of Hercules, and the carved head of Christ was "the finest I have ever seen."[49] Despite these luxurious surroundings, he worried that he might not beat the British to Messina and that he may lose his position as the top combat commander in the American High Command.[50] Sensing this insecurity,

General Eisenhower sent a cable to Patton via General Alexander's headquarters with an eye toward reassuring his historically inclined subordinate: "The Seventh Army has already made a name for itself that will live in American history. Within the next few days it will add immeasurably to the luster of its fame. I personally assure you that if we speedily finish off the German in Sicily, you need have no fear of being there in the backwater of the war." Despite these reassurances, Patton was uneasy, and he began to show signs of strain, repeatedly mentioning the race to Messina in letters to his friends and family. He continually worried about his historical legacy and wondered if Hannibal had trod over the same terrain. In a letter to Beatrice, he noted that he visited "an ancient olive grove where Hannibal may have wondered if he ever came this way" and said that the land was the "God damdest [*sic*] . . . I have ever seen."[51] Even on the eve of one of his greatest triumphs, Patton's private writings reveal a deep insecurity regarding his place in history.

In retrospect, Patton's actions over the final weeks of the campaign threatened to destroy his reputation and negate a lifetime of dedication to the study and practice of the military arts. Over the objection of General Bradley and others, he ordered a series of amphibious landings behind the German lines in an effort to use American naval power to outflank the enemy. If not properly supported, the landings could have been easily overwhelmed by the German defenders, a fact that greatly concerned General Bradley, who repeatedly argued against such risky tactics versus a foe that was already in retreat. Bradley believed that Patton was taking unnecessary risks in order to beat Montgomery and, despite being overruled, did his best to ensure that these landings were provided with air support and rapidly relieved by troops advancing overland. In his private writings, Patton justified these risks to his potential detractors as necessary to maintain pressure on the Germans and achieve surprise. While it is impossible to know if these landings were in fact necessary, they were masterpieces of planning and execution. In a letter to Beatrice, Patton took particular delight in recounting one of these nighttime landings that captured more than four hundred Germans who were sleeping in an orchard.[52]

Despite these successes, there was a very real chance that Montgomery would win the race to Messina. The British had captured Catania, and the Germans in their sector began a full-scale retreat. The British were now significantly closer to Messina and had the advantage of better roads and shorter supply lines. Sensing that he may lose the "race," Patton redoubled his attacks. Believing that Bradley was wasting time on maneuvers, Patton ordered him "to get to Messina just as fast as you can. I don't want you to waste time on these maneuvers, even if you've got to spend men to do it. I want to beat Monty into Messina." Bradley claimed that Patton was "nearly irrational in his determination to beat Monty to Messina," and Patton's actions left Bradley "shocked" and "sickened." Bradley refused to execute what he believed was an immoral order, "to waste lives merely for the sake of winning a meaningless race."[53]

On August 16, Patton again came into conflict with General Bradley, who begged him to postpone a final amphibious operation designed to capture Messina. Patton overruled Bradley and the commander of the 3rd Infantry Division, General Lucian Truscott, who argued that the plan was too risky. In an attempt to embolden his subordinate, Patton used a combination of historical analogy and flattery: "Remember Fredrick [sic] the Great: L'audace, toujours l'audace! . . . I then told Truscott I had complete confidence in him, and, to show it, was going home and to bed, and left." Despite this bold display, Patton understood that this amphibious operation was potentially risky and used historical analogies to calm his own nerves. "On the way back alone [from visiting Truscott] I worried a little, but feel I was right. I thought of Grant and Nelson and felt O.K. That is the value of history." Then, as if to explain his actions to future historians, Patton concludes, "I may have been bull-headed, but I truly feel that I did my exact and full duty and under rather heavy pressure and demonstrated that I am a great leader."[54]

While the incident would later be sensationalized in the 1970 film *Patton*, the actual landing was anticlimactic, as the Germans had already begun their retreat from the landing area and had left the path to Messina thinly defended.[55] In his diary, Patton minimized the concerns of his subordinates and justified the operation by claiming, "I have a sixth sense in war and am willing to take chances." He then further justified his decision on tactical grounds, noting that the operation allowed him to "get an extra regiment to the front without effect."[56]

Thanks to these extraordinary efforts, Seventh Army won the race to Messina. American forces entered the city at 2200 on the evening of August 16, and Patton immediately sent an uncoded radio message announcing the capture of the city to Generals Alexander and Eisenhower. The conquering general entered the city at 1000 the next morning. There he encountered a small detachment of British tanks that he believed "Montgomery sent . . . for the purpose of stealing the show. . . . I think the general was quite sore that we had gotten there first, but since we had been in for 18 hours when he arrived, the race was clearly to us." Patton and Truscott toured the captured city, met with the mayor and local dignitaries, and inspected the devastation. In contrast to his "blood and guts" reputation, the general was particularly sensitive to collateral damage, noting in his diary, "I do not believe that this indiscriminate bombing of towns is worth the ammunition, and it is unnecessarily cruel to civilians."[57]

In the immediate aftermath of his victory, Patton was again focused on protecting his place in history. In his diary, he stated, "If I had to fight the campaign over, I would make no change in anything I did. Few generals in history have ever been able to say as much."[58] He returned to bragging about his place in history in a letter to Beatrice the next day: "The Sicilian campaign has joined the countless others which this island has known and become history. . . . The obstacles in the way of terrain and demolitions were appalling and the valor and tenacity of the enemy was great but we were greater. . . . Few people, especially generals, have no regrets, but in this case I have none. . . . I fought a perfect campaign."[59]

Patton's triumphalism was on full display in his Seventh Army General Order #18, which he published on August 22:

> Soldiers of the Seventh Army: Born at sea, baptized in blood, and crowned in victory, in the course of 38 days of incessant battle and unceasing labor, you have added a glorious chapter to the history of war.
>
> Pitted against the best the Germans and Italians could offer, you have been unfailingly successful. . . .
>
> As a result of this combined effort, you have killed or captured 113,350 enemy troops. You have destroyed 265 of his tanks, 2,324 vehicles, and 1,162 large guns, and in addition, have collected a mass of military booty running into hundreds of tons.
>
> But your victory has a significance above and beyond its physical aspect— you have destroyed the prestige of the enemy. . . .
>
> Your fame shall never die.[60]

Despite the exultant tone of this message and his private writings, Patton had good reason to worry about his place in history. The "perfect campaign" was anything but, as approximately 110,000 Axis troops had been able to escape to the Italian mainland.[61] In addition, his much-publicized race to Messina had exposed serious flaws in the ability of the Americans and British to fight as equal partners, a fact that would hamper the Allied coalition and frustrate Patton for the remainder of the war.[62] Even after he had left the Italian theater, these problems would haunt the Americans, as their new commander, General Mark Clark, would engage in a similar race to capture Rome and would likewise sow discord among his British allies, suggesting that they were slow and plodding in their approach to war.[63]

On a more personal level, the campaign had also exposed many of Patton's less savory flaws. He permanently strained his relationship with Generals Bradley and Eisenhower, had dismissed reports of his troops killing German prisoners of war, and had slapped two enlisted personnel who had been evacuated to army field hospitals. While Bradley would privately seethe about the news of the murder of German POWs, these potentially explosive incidents would not become public knowledge for decades.[64]

Given these brewing controversies, Patton's bold and seemingly unreflective claims of perfection take on a new light. Rather than actually believing that he had achieved perfection, it would appear that he was attempting to highlight his military accomplishments as a means of protecting himself against future troubles. This proved to be a wise strategy, as his fame and reputation as a bold fighter would ultimately save his career in spite of his difficult personality and rash actions.

The Slapping Incidents

In two separate incidents, on August 3 and 10, Patton visited field hospitals as part of his tour of the front. In both cases, he came across two enlisted soldiers who were suffering from shell shock. The general became enraged when the soldiers admitted that they had not suffered any physical injuries, and he slapped the two men and demanded that they be returned to the front lines. While he would later defend these actions as an act of compassion in his memoirs, the simple fact is that the general temporarily lost control of his temper. The general had always been privately afraid of facing enemy fire, but prided himself on his ability to overcome these fears. When he saw what he believed to be cowardice in others, he snapped.[65]

This behavior was unacceptable for a general officer and would jeopardize his future in the army, yet Patton initially seemed unconcerned by his actions. He justified these events in his diary as a matter of fact, apparently not recognizing, or unwilling to admit, that he had erred. His August 3 entry described the encounter: "In the hospital I also met the only arrant coward I have ever seen in this Army. This man was sitting, trying to look as if he had been wounded. I asked him what was the matter, and he said he just couldn't take it. I gave him the devil, slapped his face with my gloves, and kicked him out of the hospital. Companies should deal with such men, and if they shirk their duty, they should be tried for cowardice and shot. I will issue an order on this subject tomorrow." His description of the August 10 incident was even more terse: "Saw another alleged nervous patient—really a coward. I told the doctor to return him to his company and he began to cry so I cussed him well and he shut up. I may have saved his soul if he had one."[66]

Word of these two incidents quickly reached General Eisenhower. He recognized the severity of Patton's actions and did his best to suppress news of the incidents. Eisenhower met privately with the members of the press corps in Sicily and explained that it was in the best interest of the war effort to censor this story and avoid controversy. He argued that if news of this incident reached the American public, he might be forced to remove his best field commander and insisted that he would handle the matter privately. The local press was convinced by Eisenhower's pleas and agreed to quash the story.

Eisenhower made good on his promise to discipline Patton privately. On August 17, he sent his general a strongly worded letter where he admonished him for the "shocking . . . allegations against your personal conduct" and said that it had caused him to "seriously question your good judgement and your self discipline." He assured Patton that "it is *not* my present intention to institute any formal investigation," yet he was clear that future indiscretions would not be tolerated. Eisenhower implicitly acknowledged that he was protecting Patton because his leadership during the Sicilian campaign was of "incalculable value" and "fully vindicated to the War Department your pre-eminent qualifications for the difficult task to which you were assigned." He then ordered Patton to apologize to his men and the hospital staff and closed his letter: "No letter that I have been called upon to write in my military career has caused me the mental anguish of this one, not only because of my long and deep personal friendship for you but because of my admiration for your military qualities, but I assure you that conduct such as described in the accompanying report will *not* be tolerated in this theater no matter who the offender may be."[67] While Eisenhower had done his best to protect Patton, this was nevertheless a stinging professional reprimand.

Patton quickly followed through with the apologies, addressing both the small groups of personnel and individual soldiers who had witnessed the incidents as well as each division of the Seventh Army. In his small-group interactions, he attempted to explain his actions by telling the story of a friend during World War I who was allowed to shirk his duty. The friend "was let get by with it, and eventually killed himself . . . [and] I had to correct such a future tragedy."[68]

These apologies struck some as insincere and defensive, but they are entirely consistent with Patton's desire to use historical analogies to explain and justify his actions. One of the soldiers who has been struck, Private Charles Kuhl, shook hands with the general, publicly accepted his apology, and later defended the general's actions, claiming that "he didn't know that I was as sick as I was. . . . [Patton was] a great general. . . . I think he was suffering from a little bit of battle fatigue himself."[69]

After these apologies, it appeared as if the slapping incidents had blown over, and Patton eagerly returned to studying the lessons learned from the recent campaign and preparing for the invasion of France. He was rudely awakened in late November 1943 when journalist Drew Pearson learned of the story and sensationalized it to the American public on his weekly radio program. A firestorm of public outrage ensued, and multiple senators and representatives demanded that Patton be punished. Eisenhower was also criticized for his role in censoring the press and protecting his friend, and a Senate investigation was launched into the affair. Secretary of War Stimson intervened, sending a personal letter to the US Senate in which he defended Eisenhower's decision on the basis of military necessity. He saved Patton's career by highlighting his "aggressive, winning leadership in the bitter battles which are to come for final victory." This pragmatic approach was echoed by President Roosevelt at a press conference a few days later. Misquoting Abraham Lincoln's defense of Ulysses S. Grant's drinking, FDR recalled, "It must be a good brand of liquor," a clear sign that he understood Patton's flaws but wished to retain his fighting abilities.[70]

With the backing of Roosevelt and Stimson, Generals Marshall and Eisenhower decided to endure the public controversy and save Patton's career. Had they not needed his fighting abilities to win the war, it is likely that they would have caved to the public outcry and sacked their longtime friend. While Stimson, Marshall, and Eisenhower presented a unified public face on the incident, privately they were extremely critical of Patton's actions and let him know that further indiscretions would not be tolerated. Much to his credit, he responded with humility and did his best to focus on the upcoming invasion of Europe.[71] In his crude and self-deprecating manner, he even took ownership of his status as a "son-of-a-bitch." For the remainder of his life, he would joke about his reputation as an uncompromising fighter proceeding him.[72]

An Uneasy Probation and Operation Fortitude
While he had survived the political uproar surrounding the slapping incidents, Patton was disappointed that he was not included in the planning process for the upcoming invasion of France. Despite the fact that he warned Allied planners about the Norman hedgerows and lack of access to deepwater ports for resupply, his advice was largely ignored. Rather than attacking into Normandy, he advocated for a direct assault on Calais, France. This plan would have had the advantages of crossing the English Channel at its narrowest point and avoiding some of the difficult terrain in Normandy, yet it would have been directed into a more heavily defended portion of the German defenses. This attack would have been riskier in many ways, and even at the time it played into the misperception that Patton was insensitive to casualties. He made a sound military case for his preferred plan, yet these repeated attempts to influence the invasion planning annoyed many of the top Allied generals. Bradley and others resented the second-guessing of their operational planning from somebody outside of their chain of command and did their best to simply ignore Patton's advice.

Instead of being included in the initial invasion effort, he was given a dual mission of standing up the newly created Third Army and acting as a decoy to convince the Germans that he was planning to land his forces at Calais. Patton believed that he was being ignored, but attempted to focus his efforts on preparing the Third Army for battle. He threw himself into this task with vigor, spending countless hours overseeing training, supply, and organizational details.

It was during this period that he gave his famous speech that was immortalized (and sanitized) in the 1970 film *Patton* starring George C. Scott. The speech reflected the general's firm belief in the value of building morale through directly addressing his men. However, at this point, preparing his men for future battles was all he could do to impact the course of the war. Despite its later fame, there is not a universally agreed-upon version of this speech. In fact, Patton gave the speech from memory on at least four and possibly six occasions, and several different accounts of the work exist.[73] While the speech has dominated popular imagination ever since the 1970 film as an example of a triumphant and confident Patton, it actually reflected his frustration with his inability to directly influence events.

In addition to preparing Third Army for battle, Patton also played a key role in the Allied deception effort, Operation Fortitude. While the Allies had decided to invade France in the lightly held Normandy sector, they attempted to convince the Germans that Patton was preparing to lead an Allied landing at Calais. The hope was to pin down a large portion of the Wehrmacht in Calais and keep these forces away from the Normandy front during the critical first days of the invasion. German strategists believed that Calais was the most logical invasion point and, in an amazing case of mirror imaging, failed to recognize that the Allies would act more cautiously and that they were purposely being deceived.[74]

The Allies went to great lengths to create the illusion of a massive American Army poised to strike at Calais, creating dummy aircraft, tanks, and invasion craft and also simulating radio traffic and troop movements that they hoped would be discovered by the Germans. King George VI even played his part in the deception efforts by visiting Patton and his paper army, a fact that was reported widely by the press.[75] The Allies also fed the Germans false intelligence from their own spy network that had been compromised in the years prior to the Normandy invasion. Unaware that most of their spies in England were now working as double agents for the Allies, the Germans did not question their reports.[76] When these reports were combined with the fake invasion force and radio traffic, their false belief about the Allied intentions was confirmed.

Patton played his role in the deception efforts by purposely being conspicuous.[77] Prior to his arrival in England, he took a much-publicized tour of the Mediterranean theater, where the general visited Algiers, Tunis, Corsica, Cairo, Jerusalem, and Malta, with the intent of deceiving the Germans that he was planning on leading an invasion into southern Europe by way of Trieste.[78] While Patton took copious notes of the various historical sites he visited, it is clear from his writings that he was worried about his future in the army and was less interested in distilling the potential lessons of the past for future campaigns. He noted that the pyramids were "thrilling" but then vented his frustrations on the Egyptian peasants, whom he crudely described as "definitely lower than the Sicilian WHOM I have thought was the bottom." In a similarly sardonic vein, he also noted that the knights of Malta had taken vows of poverty, chastity, and obedience, and "They only kept the last vow."[79]

In England the general was also on display as he traveled broadly and gave a series of public appearances. During one of his visits to Knutsford, England, he was perhaps too conspicuous, as he created a controversy by claiming that "it is the evident destiny of the British and Americans, and, of course the Russians to rule the world."[80] While the general was speaking in an unofficial capacity, these comments were quickly seized upon by the press, who suggested that he had insulted the Soviet allies.[81] In reality, Patton had done nothing wrong, but the controversy, coming on the heels of the slapping incidents, again threatened his future in the army. Eisenhower seriously considered relieving his general, but again chose to retain him because of his value as a combat leader. In a cable sent directly to Patton, Eisenhower explained, "I M ONCE MORE TAKING THE RESPONSIBILITY OF RETAINING YOU IN COMMAND IN SPITE OF DAMAGING REPERCUSSIONS RESULTING FROM A PERSONAL INDISCRETION. I DO THIS SOLELY BECAUSE OF MY FAITH IN YOU AS A BATTLE LEADER AND FOR NO OTHER MOTIVES."[82]

Recognizing that any further incident would result in his termination, Patton purposely keep out of the headlines and focused his efforts in preparing for the campaigns in France. He compared his own status to that of his hero Wellington, who had similarly struggled during periods of inactivity, and encouraged his aide Charles Codman to use the period of calm to read about the Iron Duke. Patton and his aide shared their observations on Wellington's life, and later Codman would compare his boss to the Napoleonic-era hero: "[T]hose waiting periods are harder on army commanders than any number of strenuous campaigns. . . . [T]he Iron Duke had more than his share of frustrations—of being kept in ignorance, pushed around, passed over, and generally stymied. Being a great man, he managed through it all to retain that most invaluable of all assets—his self-confidence—and in the end came through magnificently. But it does seem queer that in war times a fighting leader should not be used to the fullest extent."[83] While Patton and his aide could take some comfort from the past, they nevertheless believed that the Allies were wasting the talents of a truly great general.[84]

In an attempt to connect with the history of the region, Patton read the massive multivolume *History of the Norman Conquest*, by Edward Augustus Freeman, and consulted with the historian James van Wyck Osborne, author of *The Great Norman Conquest*.[85] He paid particularly close attention to the roads and lines of advance used by William the Conqueror nine centuries before, reasoning, "The roads used in those days had to be on good ground which was always practicable. Therefore, using these roads, even in modern times, permits easy by-passing when the enemy resorts, as he always does, to demolition."[86]

Based on this study of history and geography, Patton privately marked a map with a series of key terrain features where he anticipated to fight. His forecasts would be amazingly prescient, as the eventual path of the Third Army's advance nearly matched his predictions.[87] In his memoirs, Patton himself would gloat about the accuracy of his predictions, claiming, "In fact, I told Mr. J. J. McCloy, the Assistant Secretary of War . . . that the first big battle of the Third Army would be at Rennes. Actually it was the second big battle."[88]

Patton coordinated these planning efforts with his capable head of intelligence, Colonel (later Brigadier General) Oscar Koch. Koch was frustrated by the lack of good maps and the ambiguity of Allied operational planning and asked for a clear mission. Patton ordered Koch to direct Third Army's advance toward Metz, France. This ancient fortified city had played a key role in the Franco-Prussian War and was strategically located for an advance into the industrial heart of Germany, but was located more than three hundred miles from Normandy.[89] Thinking several steps into the future, the general hoped to drive directly toward Germany and avoid crossing the Loire River, a task that he feared would cause him to lose the initiative. According to Koch, this foresight was "based on a lifetime of professional training and on thinking," a clear indication that Patton had convinced his head of intelligence of his own innate grasp of warfare.[90] Despite the farsightedness of their commanding officer and his staff, the Third Army would have to wait to implement these ambitious plans.

· ·

NOTES

1. Atkinson, *Army at Dawn*, 484.

2. Diaries, 1910–45, George S. Patton Papers, Manuscript Division, Library of Congress, Washington, DC.

3. Blumenson, *The Patton Papers*, 2:220.

4. Diaries, 1910–45, Patton Papers.

5. Blumenson, *The Patton Papers*, 2:224.

6. Diaries, 1910–45, Patton Papers.

7. Greenfield, *American Strategy in World War II*, 5, 31.

8. On the importance of the Mediterranean to British and American planners, see generally Douglas Porch, *The Path to Victory: The Mediterranean Theater in World War II*.

9. Greenfield, *American Strategy in World War II*, 31, 35.

10. On the military history of Sicily during the Peloponnesian and Punic Wars, see generally Donald Kagan, *The Peace of Nicias and the Sicilian Expedition*; and Robert

L. O'Connell, *The Ghosts of Cannae: Hannibal and the Darkest Hour of the Roman Republic*.

11. Military Papers, 1903–76, Patton Papers.

12. Diaries, 1910–45, Patton Papers.

13. Blumenson, *The Patton Papers*, 2:223–34.

14. Diaries, 1910–45, Patton Papers.

15. D'Este, *Patton*, 493.

16. Diaries, 1910–45, Patton Papers.

17. D'Este, *Patton*, 496.

18. Blumenson, *The Patton Papers*, 2:262.

19. Morison, *United States Naval Operations*, 9:102–5; Yeide, *Fighting Patton*, 202.

20. Atkinson, *Day of Battle*, 81–87.

21. Andrew J. Birtle, *Sicily 1943, the U.S. Army WWII Campaigns, 24;* Morison, *United States Naval Operations*, 9:105.

22. Essame, *Patton as Military Commander*, 90–93.

23. Atkinson, *Day of Battle*, 96–105; Mansoor, *GI Offensive in Europe*, 103.

24. Atkinson, *Day of Battle*, 104.

25. Atkinson, *Day of Battle*, 124; Essame, *Patton as Military Commander*, 96–97.

26. Atkinson, *Day of Battle*, 124–27.

27. Diaries, 1910–45, Patton Papers.

28. Diaries, 1910–45, Patton Papers.

29. Mansoor, *GI Offensive in Europe*, 103.

30. Omar N. Bradley and Clay Blair, *A General's Life*, 191–92.

31. This feeling would only grow as Bradley aged and would be exacerbated in 1974 with the release of Patton's diaries and personal letters, which were frequently critical of Bradley and Eisenhower. Jonathan W. Jordan, *Brothers, Rivals, Victory: Eisenhower, Patton, Bradley, and the Partnership That Drove the Allied Conquest in Europe*, 551.

32. Diaries, 1910–45, Patton Papers.

33. Blumenson, *The Patton Papers*, 2:287–88.

34. Blumenson, *The Patton Papers*, 2:289.

35. Patton also noted in a July 18 letter to Beatrice that his plane flew over the ruins of Carthage.

36. Diaries, 1910–45, Patton Papers.

37. *The Seventh Army in Sicily*, after-action report, Staff of the Seventh Army, 1943, B-20.

38. Diaries, 1910–45, Patton Papers.

39. Diaries, 1910–45, Patton Papers.

40. Diaries, 1910–45, Patton Papers.

41. Diaries, 1910–45, Patton Papers.

42. Blumenson, *The Patton Papers*, 2:296.

43. Mansoor, *GI Offensive in Europe*, 104.

44. Diaries, 1910–45, Patton Papers.

45. Blumenson, *The Patton Papers*, 2:299.

46. Blumenson, *The Patton Papers*, 2:306.

47. See, for example, the July 30, 1943, letter from Beatrice to Patton. Blumenson, *The Patton Papers*, 2:307–8.

48. Blumenson, *The Patton Papers*, 2:309–10, 317.

49. Family Papers, 1857–1979, Patton Papers.

50. Atkinson, *Day of Battle*, 142.

51. Family Papers, 1857–1979, Patton Papers.

52. Family Papers, 1857–1979, Patton Papers.

53. Bradley and Blair, *A General's Life*, 199.

54. Diaries, 1910–45, Patton Papers.

55. Yeide, *Fighting Patton*, 213.

56. Diaries, 1910–45, Patton Papers.

57. Diaries, 1910–45, Patton Papers. For a similar comment from Patton's aide Charles Codman, see Codman, *Drive*, 271.

58. Diaries, 1910–45, Patton Papers.

59. Family Papers, 1857–1979, Patton Papers.

60. Blumenson, *The Patton Papers*, 2:334–35.

61. Interestingly, the Germans believed that Patton's drive was impressive in its speed but was militarily irrelevant, as it mostly captured unimportant terrain and allowed them to evacuate the island. Yeide, *Fighting Patton*, 212–14.

62. Mansoor, *GI Offensive in Europe*, 107.

63. Andrew Roberts, *The Storm of War: A New History of the Second World War*, 385.

64. Stanley Hirshon, *General Patton: A Soldier's Life*, 1–3.

65. Essame, *Patton as Military Commander*, 103–8.

66. Diaries, 1910–45, Patton Papers.

67. Blumenson, *The Patton Papers*, 2:329, 330.

68. Diaries, 1910–45, Patton Papers.

69. Blumenson, *The Patton Papers*, 2:336–37.

70. D'Este, *Patton*, 543, 546. When told that General Grant was a prodigious consumer of whiskey, President Lincoln famously said, "I then began to ask them if they knew what he drank, what brand of whiskey he used, telling them most seriously that I wished they would find out . . . for if it made fighting generals like Grant, I should like to get some of it for distribution." Ron Chernow, *Grant*, 293.

71. Despite the fact that they jeopardized Patton's career, the slapping incidents seem to have had minimal impact on his popularity with the American public. According to a survey of the general's personal fan mail, the response was approximately 89 percent pro and 11 percent con. Charles Codman reflected, "Taken as a whole, it [the survey] forms quite an illuminating human document . . . about the importance of backing a leader, specially one who has the rare quality of making people *want* to fight." Codman, *Drive*, 134, 272.

72. D'Este, *Patton*, 546.

73. See Terry Brighton, *Patton, Montgomery, Rommel: Masters of War*, 260–68. The 1970 film presented a highly sanitized version of Patton's words cobbled together from several different speeches. Despite the iconic imagery, George C. Scott was apparently unhappy with the scene. Sarantakes, *Making "Patton,"* 2–4, 56–57.

74. Robert M. Citino, *The Wehrmacht's Last Stand: The German Campaigns of 1944–1945*, 128–29; Matheny, *Carrying the War to the Enemy*, 197.

75. Roberts, *Storm of War*, 463.

76. Michael Howard, *Strategic Deception in the Second World War*, 120–21.

77. While the German intelligence forces noted Patton's movements, his role in the deception efforts probably had a minimal impact on German decision making. According to one recent study of German perceptions of Patton prior to the invasion, "Patton was simply one blip in a noisy pattern of very dangerous commanders, many of whom, such as Montgomery and Soviet marshall [*sic*] Georgi Zhukov, probably loomed much larger in their thinking." Yeide, *Fighting Patton*, 215–17.

78. Anthony Cave Brown, *Bodyguard of Lies: The Extraordinary True Story behind D-Day*, 448; Blumenson and Hymel, *Patton*, 60; Codman, *Drive*, 125.

79. Diaries, 1910–45, Patton Papers.

80. Blumenson, *The Patton Papers*, 2:441.

81. Brown, *Bodyguard of Lies*, 477.

82. Blumenson, *The Patton Papers*, 2:452.

83. Codman, *Drive*, 135.

84. During this period, Patton was also busy studying the Napoleonic era. In April 1944, he read Arthur Bryant's *The Years of Endurance*, which he wrote Beatrice was a "swell book." Blumenson, *The Patton Papers*, 2:437.

85. Morningstar, *Patton's Way*, 160; Essame, *Patton as Military Commander*, 125, 142; Diaries, 1910–45, Patton Papers.

86. Patton, *War as I Knew It*, 92; Atkinson, *Guns at Last Light*, 150; D'Este, *Patton*, 612. This is not the first time that Patton used a history book to trace roads and supply lines. In fact, during the interwar period, Patton used Liddell Hart's accounts of General William T. Sherman's campaigns in Georgia and the Carolinas as a guide to trace the Union lines of march and supply while on a vacation. See Essame, *Patton as Military Commander*, 125–26.

87. In a 1962 memo written by his son, Lieutenant Colonel George Patton wrote, "To any biographer—This is a historic document since GSP, Jr. marked it well before the campaign plans had developed. He was very close to his prediction." Speeches and Writings File, 1900–1947, Patton Papers.

88. Patton, *War as I Knew It*, 91.

89. This was also the same route that General Pershing planned to advance during the final days of World War I. It is also possible that Patton was hoping to complete his mentor's planned advance. See Essame, *Patton as Military Commander*, 190.

90. Oscar W. Koch and Robert G. Hayes, *G-2: Intelligence for Patton*, 53, 71.

CHAPTER FOUR

BATTLES WITH HISTORY ON THE EUROPEAN CONTINENT

Winning in Normandy with the Help of History and Honeymoons
ALTHOUGH THE INITIAL Allied landings on the coast of France on June 6, 1944, were an unparalleled success of military planning, naval and air domi-nance, and personal courage, the larger Normandy campaign was very much in doubt in the weeks that followed. Indeed, the main emphasis of the Allied planners seemed to be on getting troops into the area of operations and sustaining their supply lines rather than moving out of the landing areas and pushing deeper into France. While the location of the invasion surprised the Germans, thanks in part to the Allied deception efforts, they were able to quickly contain the Allied forces and establish an effective defensive perimeter.

The German defenders were greatly aided by the terrain and lack of roads in the Normandy area of operations. For centuries, French farmers had plowed their small fields and pushed the tailings away to the edges of their plots. These man-made features, known as hedgerows or *bocage*, gave the German defenders a series of ready-made defensive positions to fight behind. While these terrain features were clearly visible on Allied maps and aerial reconnaissance photos, they apparently surprised every senior Allied planner other than Patton. Bradley admitted, "I hadn't visualized it all that much as I had studied photographs and maps before I went in." Similarly, General Bedell Smith confessed, "You cannot imagine it when you have not seen it."[1]

Despite Patton's warnings about the hedgerow terrain in Normandy, the Allies chose to begin their invasion of Europe in this exact region and were forced to cross between the hedgerows into exposed killing zones where the

Germans had prepositioned mortars, machine guns, and artillery to make maximum use of these trench-like positions.[2] American planners had hoped to overcome these obstacles with tanks and superior firepower, but they fundamentally overestimated the ability of armored vehicles to operate in this terrain as well as the ability of their artillery to inflict damage on the German troops positioned on the reverse slope of the hedgerows.[3] Despite great personal courage and sacrifice, the Allied infantry paid an extremely high cost as they moved through this terrain, and daily progress was often measured in yards, not miles. While improvised equipment such as the rhinoceros tank and improvements in close air support helped the Allied efforts, the grim reality was that the Allied drive into France was stalled and there was no obvious way to break the stalemate and restore movement to the front.[4]

While Third Army was not yet active, Patton again attempted to insert himself into the ongoing Allied operations. In late June, he spent one night and part of two days with his longtime friend General Eisenhower. The two generals discussed the current operations, and Patton attempted to convince Eisenhower of the possibility of executing a pivoting maneuver that would allow the First Army to strike into the unprotected German rear. He felt so strongly about his "reverse Schlieffen plan" that he wrote a short memo outlining it in detail and had their mutual friend General Everett Hughes add it to Eisenhower's daily reading.[5] Despite the fact that he "dressed my paper up with the names of Scharnhorst, Clausewitz and Moltke so as to catch Ike's eye," the plan was ignored.[6]

This ambitious planning revealed significant foresight, yet it still did not solve the immediate challenges of extracting the Allies from the confining territory in Normandy. Indeed, when the Third Army commander and his staff flew to France on July 6 to meet with General Bradley and prepare for a more active role in combat operations, the ultimate outcome of the campaign was still very much in doubt. General Bradley grimly admitted, "By July 10, we faced a real danger of a World War I–type stalemate."[7]

Patton's Thirty Years of Foresight

Although Patton's Third Army would not become operational until August 1, 1944, and was serving as a strategic reserve during the initial attacks of Operation Cobra, the general was indispensable even in this limited capacity. He was made the unofficial commander of First Army and consistently prodded Bradley and Eisenhower to act more aggressively in the upcoming assault.[8] He was seemingly everywhere, visiting frontline units and solving many of the operational challenges that faced the Allied armies. The result was an attack and breakout that bore many of Patton's fingerprints, even though he was not in command.[9]

Despite Patton's efforts, the Allies were significantly hindered by the poor intelligence regarding the area of operations. In fact, much of the Allied intelligence on the region and planning for the campaign was based on commercially available Michelin automobile-club maps, which provided inadequate detail about the region's roads.[10] The Germans did an excellent job of blocking the main roads out of the region, and the Allied planners desperately needed a military appraisal of the local secondary road network.[11] Remembering his work from the summer of 1913, Patton contacted the War Department and asked that he be given a copy of the study he prepared following his "honeymoon" to France. The detail of this study proved invaluable, as it greatly surpassed the quality of the existing maps and made clear and straightforward assessments of the available routes out of the Normandy *bocage*. Based on this study, he even prepared his own plan for the Allied breakout, although there is no record that he ever presented this plan to Bradley or Eisenhower.[12]

In an undated series of observations, probably written in late July or early August, Patton attempted to reflect on the history of the regions and the opportunities before him:

> This is my fourth trip to France. . . . The road into Brittany is full of reminders of William the Conqueror and of his unwilling guest Harold, for in their campaign against Dinan they passed through Coutances where even yet the most striking cathedral I have ever seen in France stands as evidence of the uneasy conscience of William's successors.
>
> The bridge south of Avranches undoubtedly had its predecessor in William's time, and from there the road leading to Dol and Dinan is undoubtedly the same one traversed by William and Harold, hawk on fist. . . . Nearly everyone [*sic*] of these towns has all or part of a castle, and these are more eloquent than anything else . . . which has occurred in the last 900 years. One air bomb or salvo from our 240's would breach any castle which in those days sustained sieges measured in years. . . .
>
> . . . [T]he people are exactly as they were when I saw them last in 1913.[13]

In the weeks that followed, Patton would be actively involved in making history in the region of castles and people that he had so fondly remembered from his previous trips.

A Lost Opportunity at Falaise

Following the initial breakout, Patton's Third Army was activated on August 1, 1944, and released into open country.[14] Fighting alongside the US First Army, Patton's Third Army achieved unprecedented successes as it began its legendary drive across Europe.[15] In fact, the Third Army moved so quickly that they had the opportunity to surround a large portion of the German Army in what became known as the Falaise Pocket. By August 12, 1944, parts of twenty Nazi divisions were facing encirclement by British, Canadian, and American forces.[16] Sensing an unprecedented opportunity, Patton insisted on a bold but risky plan. Rather than protect his flanks against a possible counterattack, he wanted to close the trap before any German units could escape. To this end, on August 13 he ordered his subordinate Major General Wade Hampton Haislip, "Hell go to the English Channel if you have to. Just bag those Germans."[17]

While Patton had a clearly articulated vision of warfare that prized initiative and pursuit over protecting the flanks, this bold plan worried other Allied leaders, who feared that it could lead to disaster. A crisis quickly ensued in the Allied High Command, as the British forces under General Montgomery were particularly worried about the logistics of the operation and potential for fratricide as the Allied armies moved to close the gap.[18] Patton lobbied General Bradley for aggressive action, demanding that he ignore the British objections: "Let me go on to Falaise and we'll drive the British into the sea for another Dunkirk," a clear indication that he did not care about the safety of the coalition forces in the region and was already blaming others for blocking his grand plan.[19]

Despite Patton's insistence on closing the Falaise Pocket, the Allies acted conservatively out of fear of fratricide and the very real consideration that much of the operational area had been heavily mined. Poor weather also aided the Germans, by restricting Allied airpower and allowing them to evacuate without being harassed from above.[20] The result was a hollow victory, where the Allies were able to capture approximately fifty thousand Germans, while as many as fifty to one hundred thousand escaped to fight another day. While historians remain divided as to the exact number of Germans who escaped the pocket, this missed opportunity remains one of

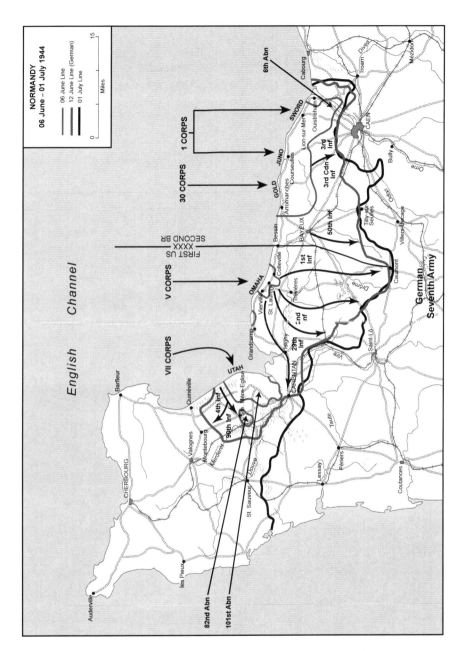

Map 6: Normandy breakout. While the initial Allied landings in Normandy were an overwhelming success, the drive inland quickly slowed down as the Germans consolidated their positions and made excellent use of the hedgerows in the region. Prior to Third Army's activation as a combat unit on August 1, 1944, Patton made himself indispensable to the Allies by sharing his knowledge of the region's road network and helping plan for the breakout phase of the campaign. Map by Chris Robinson.

the most intriguing "what ifs" of the European campaign. Patton's plan had the potential for destroying a much larger percentage of the German Army and may have led to a collapse of the German defenses in the West, thus significantly shortening the war.[21] Regardless of these historical debates, the Battle of Falaise was a massive defeat for the German Army and significantly limited their combat power for the coming months, yet Patton saw it as a lost opportunity to significantly shorten the war.[22] In fact, many of the units that escaped the trap at Falaise would be resupplied and sent back into the fight at Arnhem, the Saar, and the Bulge, a point that embittered Patton.[23]

With a keen eye to preserving his place in history, Patton documented his frustrations in his diary entry of August 13, noting, "I am sure that this halt is a great mistake, as I am certain the British will not close on Falaise." Three days later, he expanded on his belief that British timidity was impeding the campaign as a result of "jealousy of the Americans or to utter ignorance of the situation, or to a combination of the two."[24] Patton vented his frustrations to his friends General Hugh Gaffey and Colonel Robert Allen and directed Allen to place a stenographic record of their conversation into the historical files of the Third Army.[25]

While the failure of the Allies to exploit their successes at Falaise clearly angered Patton, it did not alter the fact that his mastery of history and the operational arts was critical to the Allied success in the Normandy campaign. On August 14, he wrote in his diary of his triumphs, "In exactly two weeks the Third Army has advanced further and faster than any Army in the history of war."[26] True to his prediction made more than thirty years before, Patton *did* fight a decisive battle in the unlikely setting of Normandy. When the moment of decision came, Patton was prepared: after all, he had already studied the problem years before, on his honeymoon. Perhaps more than any other moment, this episode underscores the tangible dividends that a lifetime of historical engagement paid for the general and his men.

Metz: A Bloody Prelude to the Bulge

As the Allied forces approached the German border in the fall of 1944, it appeared as if Nazi resistance was collapsing and the war was entering its final days. Noting the success of Patton's forces in the Normandy breakout, the Allied Supreme Headquarters Allied Expeditionary Forces (SHAEF) intelligence section claimed, "The August battles have done it, and the enemy in the west has had it." Based on these overly sanguine assessments, the US War Production Board began canceling a wide range of contracts, including

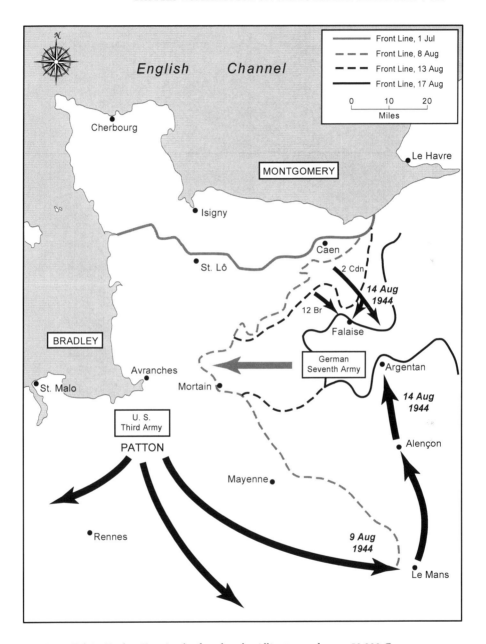

Map 7: Falaise Pocket. Despite the fact that the Allies trapped some 50,000 German troops in the Falaise Pocket, between 50,000-100,000 escaped to fight another day. Patton was frustrated with the timidity of his senior commanders as he believed their caution significantly lengthened the war. Map by Chris Robinson.

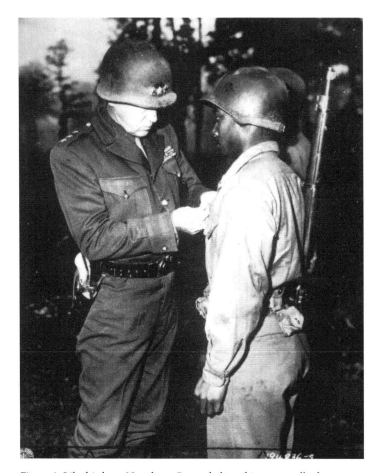

Figure 8. Like his hero Napoleon, Patton believed in personally decorating his troops for valor. Here, he pins the Silver Star on Private Ernest A. Jenkins of New York City for conspicuous gallantry in the liberation of Châteaudun, France. National Archives.

those for the production of artillery shells, and the British War Cabinet set December 31 as the final day for planning hostilities in Europe.[27] This optimism was also common among frontline-combat veterans who believed that the enemy was finished and the war would soon be over. Captain Richard "Dick" Winters of the 101st Airborne expressed the hopes of many frontline soldiers when he said, "Things are going pretty very well. . . . [A]s I see it . . . we could be in Berlin by Christmas."[28]

Victory fever permeated the Allied ranks, and the working assumption was that the German Army was incapable of conducting anything other than holding actions or limited-objective attacks.[29] With the notable exceptions of Winston Churchill and George Patton, few senior leaders even questioned the assessments that the German Army was a spent force. Despite their experiences fighting the Germans in both world wars, these two leaders were largely dismissed as overly pessimistic. While Patton insisted that the war could have been won in 1944 if he had been allowed the freedom of action to close the Falaise gap and drive forward into Germany, he recognized that the moment had passed and the Germans had reconstituted much of their combat power as they executed a brilliant fighting retreat.[30]

An inhospitable combination of rain, mud, rough terrain, logistical challenges, and German defenders stalled the Third Army around Metz and the Saar from September to early December.[31] In contrast to the previous month of fast-moving mechanized warfare, this phase of the war was characterized by a lack of maneuver and grim, frustrating battles of attrition.[32] During this period of relative inaction, Patton read Erwin Rommel's memoir of the First World War, *Infantry Attacks*.[33] He found some comfort in the fact that Rommel's offensive operations in September 1914 had also been hindered by foul weather and noted that this helped him sleep better, knowing that he was dealing with the age-old issue of natural forces imparting friction on military operations.[34]

Despite this comfort from the past Third Army's campaigns, Loraine and Metz were extremely frustrating for Patton. Third Army surrounded Metz, yet was unable to force a decisive battle through movement and superior firepower.[35] He openly criticized the Allied High Command, complaining to his staff, "We roll across France in less time than it takes Monty to say 'Regroup' and we are stuck here in the mud of Loraine. . . . Because somewhere up the line some so-and-so who never heard a shot fired in anger or missed a meal believes in higher priorities for pianos and ping-pong sets than for ammunition and gas." In his diary, Patton further blamed his failure to quickly take Metz on the timidity of the Allied leaders, particularly Omar Bradley, whom he called a "tent maker" and "too conservative," concluding, "I wish he had a little more daring."[36]

Attempting to take comfort from history, Patton claimed in a November 19, 1944, letter to Beatrice that "only Attila [the Hun] and Third Army has ever taken Metz by assault."[37] In fact, this claim was both premature and inaccurate. The battle for Metz was by no means finished, and Third Army would need almost another month to neutralize the last pockets of resistance in the city. More interestingly, Patton got his history wrong. In fact, Metz had fallen to the French in 1552 and the Germans in 1870.[38] Despite this uncharacteristic error, it was clear that the general was trying to understand and defend his place in history while finding comfort during a time of stress and uncertainty.[39]

To bring an end to the war, Patton believed that the German Army, not enemy territory, was the true prize. This was a correct understanding of the German center of gravity, but it did not alter the fact that Patton himself had spent several months stuck trying to capture German defensive positions and cities around Metz. He blamed the lack of decisive action on other Allied leaders who focused on gaining territory, not destroying the enemy ground forces, an observation that he shared with Beatrice on December 9: "There is no purpose in capturing these manure-filled water logged villages. The purpose of our operations is to kill or capture the German personnel and vehicles . . . so that they cannot retreat and repeat their opposition."[40] These frustrations were compounded by the perception that Allied failures during Operation Market Garden had placed further strain on Third Army's supplies and forced them to remain in a supporting role.[41] Rather than strike decisively at the enemy's center of gravity, Patton's forces continued to plod along with severe logistical restrictions and did not conclude their operations around Metz and in the Saar until early December.[42]

Privately, Patton would admit to his trusted aide Colonel Paul Harkins that he should have bypassed Metz rather than directly assaulting it, but he never made this claim in writing or admitted his error in public.[43] Rather, he blamed others, the inhospitable weather, and his tenuous supply situation for his failure to achieve decisive victory. While his shortcomings in this campaign were quickly eclipsed by his heroic actions during the Battle of the Bulge, the failure to achieve decisive results clearly bothered the general, as indicated by his selective portrayal of the campaign in his writings and memoirs as well as his unusually candid comments to Colonel Harkins.[44]

Anticipating the German Attack

After the fall of Metz, Patton finally had the supplies and opportunity to strike into German territory, and he craved the opportunity for glory and redemption that another major campaign could provide. On December 10, 1944, as he prepared to strike into Germany, Patton's intelligence reports noted a large concentration of German armored units to the north of their positions. The general and his staff remained convinced that the Germans were still capable of fierce resistance and could be massing for a counterattack into Belgium and Luxembourg.[45] Patton inferred that the Germans were planning a major operation or else they were "using a hell of a lot of gasoline doing nothing."[46]

As he prepared to strike deep into the Saar, Patton reiterated his belief that the Germans would offer fanatical resistance in a December 12 letter to the entire Third Army, titled "Relations with the German People." Here he elucidated his belief that the enemy would continue to resist: "The friendship and cooperation of the French people will be replaced in Germany by universal hostility, which will require that we regard all Germans, soldiers and civilians, men, women, and even children, as active enemies. It is expected that we shall encounter sniping, guerilla warfare, sabotage, and treachery." Far from believing that the Nazi regime was about to collapse, the general was preparing himself and his men for some of the most brutal and bloody fighting of the war. In his words, the war would be decided not in France by the end of 1944, but "east of the Rhine" in 1945.[47] Unlike much of the Allied High Command, Patton had not made the age-old mistake of underestimating the enemy.

On December 16, 1944, Patton and his staff were preparing for their advance into Germany, which was scheduled to begin on December 19.[48] During the morning briefing, Colonel Oscar Koch, the Third Army's head of intelligence, reported that the Germans had been massing their forces and supplies in the Ardennes sector. In this region, the Germans had achieved a two-to-one numerical advantage over the Americans, who were resting their forces in this "quiet" sector of the front after the costly fighting in Hürtgen Forest.[49] In addition to this buildup, the German forces had enforced strict radio silence for their frontline units. In the US Army, radio silence meant only one thing: a major attack was about to begin.[50] Based on this intelligence, Patton and his staff predicted that "the Germans are going to launch an attack, probably at Luxembourg."[51] With the help of his intelligence chief and a mastery of military strategy, Patton had anticipated the German intentions for a major offensive.[52]

On that same day, the Germans began their last desperate bid for victory in the West as they attacked and overwhelmed the thinly held American positions in the Ardennes Forest. Although the battle was taking place outside of Patton's area of operations, his suspicions were confirmed later that evening when he received a telephone call from General Bradley ordering him to transfer his 10th Armored Division to VIII Corps and to assume temporary command of this unit.[53] While he protested the order and argued that the

Americans should exploit the opportunity to make an attack of their own, Bradley cut his protests off with the curt response, "I can't discuss this matter over the phone."[54] Reasoning that "he probably knows more of the situation that he can say over the phone," he complied with the order and reinforced Middleton, even though it would upset his plans for a drive into Germany.[55]

Even though he was not formally briefed on the Allied situation until December 18, Patton was already analyzing the unfolding campaign through the lens of historical analogy. On December 17, he wrote his old mentor Major General Fox Conner that the German offensive "reminds me very much of March 25, 1918 and I think it will have the same results."[56] Here, Patton was referring to the German spring offensives during World War I, where the Germans made a final desperate attempt to attack the Allies and win victory in the West.

Even though this assessment was based on limited information of the operational situation, it turned out to be surprisingly accurate. Much as they would in World War II, in 1918 the Germans achieved surprise and gained significant ground in their initial assaults, pushing a large bulge into the Allied lines. Much like in 1918, however, the Germans ultimately paid an unacceptably high cost for their gains, left their flanks exposed, and destroyed much of their remaining combat power in the process.[57] In both cases, once the Allies responded to the shock of the initial assaults, they were able to stabilize the front and ultimately attack into the flanks of the exposed German positions.[58] In classic Patton form, he anticipated that the Germans had overextended themselves, and this was the ideal moment to attack, but despite his insistence his pleas to launch a major counteroffensive aimed at encircling hundreds of thousands of German troops were ultimately ignored.

On December 18, Patton and his staff drove to General Bradley's headquarters to be briefed on the unfolding situation. The news was grim, as the Germans had driven deep into the American lines and threatened to divide the Allied forces and capture the critical port of Antwerp. Chaos and confusion reigned, but Patton reacted with coolness and dispatch. Acting on Bradley's orders, he telephoned General Hobart Gay, the Third Army chief of staff, and halted the movements of the 4th Armored and 80th Infantry Divisions and alerted the 26th Infantry Division to be ready to move in twenty-four hours. He returned to his headquarters after dark and had another phone call with Bradley at approximately 2000. Bradley advised him that the strategic situation had worsened since they had last spoken and ordered Patton and his staff to attend a meeting with Eisenhower and other senior leaders at Verdun, scheduled for 1100 the next morning.[59]

Despite his incomplete understanding of the unfolding operational situation, Patton did his best to develop an actionable plan prior to the meeting the next morning with Eisenhower.[60] At approximately 2015, the general and his staff began to develop contingency plans based on the situation, "insofar as it was known." The staff worked throughout the night and reconvened for a formal meeting at 0700:

> I started the meeting by saying that plans had been changed, and, while we were all accustomed to rapid movement, we would now have to prove that we can operate even faster. We then made a rough plan of operation based on the assumption that I could use the VIII Corps, First Army (Middleton), and the III Corps, Third Army (Millikin), on any two of three possible axes. From the left, the axes of attack were in order of priority as follows: From the general vicinity of Diekirch, due north; from the general vicinity of Arlon, on Bastogne, which was still held by our troops; and finally, from the general vicinity of Neufchateau, against the left nose of the enemy salient.[61]
>
> When it is considered that Harkins, Codman, and I left for Verdun at 0915 and that between 0800 and that hour we had had a staff meeting, planned three possible lines of attack, and made a simple code in which I could telephone General Gay which two of the three lines we were to use, it is evident that war is not so difficult as people think.[62]

Patton's comments were self-serving, yet they provide a key insight into his formula for success. In the moment of crisis, he remained calm and was able to think rationally through the military challenges that he and his men faced. Working with an impressive knowledge of the operational environment, the capabilities of his forces, and the decisive points on the battlefield, he was able to get into the minds of his foes and anticipate their movements. Based on this understanding, he was able to begin the planning process of reversing the tables on his opponents, prior to the formal briefing with Eisenhower.[63] Although he would imply in his memoirs that this was a simple task, it was an impressive synthesis of a lifetime of preparation and study that required much more than natural talent and efficient staff work.[64]

Meeting at Verdun

When Patton arrived at Eisenhower's headquarters for the 1100 briefing, the mood was "far from happy."[65] Senior Allied commanders who had been predicting the collapse of Nazi Germany just days before now worried that the German offensive could split the Allied forces and threaten their vital base of Antwerp. Eisenhower insisted, "The present situation is to be regarded as one of opportunity for us not a disaster. There will only be cheerful faces at this conference table," yet few shared the supreme commander's confidence. "True to his impulsive nature," Patton interjected that he agreed that this was a unique opportunity to overextend the Germans and cut them off in the process: "Hell let's have the guts to let the _____ __ _____ go all the way to Paris. Then we'll really cut 'em off and chew 'em up."[66] This display of pique lightened the heavy mood, but despite Patton's bravado his plan was a nonstarter with the rest of the Allied High Command, who feared a collapse of their entire position and were unwilling to accept this level of risk.[67]

Of particular concern was the fate of the 101st Airborne Division that had been deployed to stand in the path of the Nazi advance and defend the critical road junction of Bastogne, Belgium.[68] By the morning of the nineteenth, the Germans had already made contact with the 101st and had begun to encircle the badly outnumbered and outgunned defenders.[69] Both Allied and German generals understood that this otherwise insignificant village was critical to the outcome of the campaign. If the Germans could quickly seize the town and neutralize the American defenders, they would be free to continue their drive westward. If the Americans could hold the town, they could disrupt the timetable for the German advance, tie up key units, and continue to pose a threat to the enemy's flanks and rear.[70] Patton summarized the importance of holding the position thusly: "We decided to hang on to Bastogne, because it is a very important road net, and I do not believe that the enemy would dare pass without reducing it."[71]

Eisenhower wanted to know what the Third Army could do to help relieve the 101st Airborne and impede the Nazi advance. After a moment's pause, Patton responded coolly that he could "make a strong attack with three divisions, namely, the 4th Armored, and the 26th and 80th Infantry Divisions, by the twenty-second."[72] Many in the room dismissed this claim as typical Patton braggadocio. "When I said I could attack on the 22nd, it created quite a commotion—some people seemed surprised and others pleased—however, I believe it can be done."[73]

Given the technical complexity of pulling these units out of the front, changing their axis of advance, and moving them into position to attack in two days, Eisenhower had his doubts as to the feasibility of Patton's plan. He believed that if Third Army could move that quickly, it would lack coordination and striking power. Rather than attack piecemeal, Eisenhower suggested that it would be preferable to take more time so that he could attack with six divisions. Patton responded that it would take significantly more time to bring six divisions to bear and that "if I waited, I would lose surprise."[74] In his typical dramatic fashion, Patton then lit a cigar and declared to General Bradley, "Brad, this time the Kraut's stuck his head in a meat-grinder." He then cranked his hand in a circular motion and added, "and this time I've got hold of the handle."[75]

This plan was bold, and since Eisenhower had few other options, he approved. As the meeting was breaking up, Eisenhower, newly promoted to the five-star rank of general of the US Army, said to Patton, "Funny thing, George, every time I get a new star, I get attacked [a reference to his promotion prior to the American disaster at Kasserine Pass in North Africa]." Without a moment's hesitation, Patton retorted, "And every time you get attacked, Ike, I pull you out."[76] With his typical flair, Patton had set the stage for what would be the greatest moment of his military career.

Winning the Battle of the Bulge

Immediately after his meeting with Eisenhower, Patton set his plan in motion with a telephone call to his chief of staff, General Gay. "As soon as these various decisions were made, I telephoned Gay to start the 26th Division and the 4th Armored on Arlon via Longway, and the 80th Division on Luxembourg via Thionville."[77] Using the code word *nickel* that he had devised that morning, he quickly communicated which of the three contingencies was in effect, and the Third Army began to move.[78] "The 4th Armored had actually pulled out the previous night, December 18. The 80th started next morning, the nineteenth, and the 26th started on receiving orders."[79]

The Third Army began to move at an astonishing speed. Time was of the essence if they were to reach Bastogne soon enough to relieve the 101st and stop the German drive. Patton worked relentlessly during this period in an attempt to motivate his men and lead them to victory. According to one observer, "After daylight came, the general was very visible weaving up and down the column, giving . . . the thumbs up. . . . He radioed instructions from his jeep, rode alongside to shout directions . . . and at tricky intersections, he dismounted to personally point the way."[80] In a December 21 letter to Beatrice, he described his frenetic pace: "Though this is the shortest day of the year, to me it seems interminable. . . . I am very confident that a great success is possible. . . . Yesterday I again earned my pay. I visited seven divisions and regrouped an Army alone. It was quite a day and I enjoyed it."[81] Patton's forces moved throughout the night to get into position for an attack, but thanks to the extraordinary efforts of their commanding officer and his men, Third Army was ready to strike the Germans on the morning of December 22.[82] While the American commanders were tired and "full of doubt," the night before Patton exuded confidence and optimism, noting, "I seemed always to be a ray of sunshine, and by God, I always am."[83]

Third Army attacked the Germans at along a twenty-mile front at 0600 on the morning of December 22. Despite heavy snow and the Germans' demolition of roads and bridges, the attacking forces penetrated to a distance

Map 8: The Battle of the Bulge. Patton's finest moment was at the Battle of the Bulge. By anticipating the German attack, he was able to pull his units out of a winter battle, pivot, attack into the German flank, and relieve the 101st Airborne Division. Map by Chris Robinson.

of approximately five miles on the first day.[84] While Patton had "hoped for more [progress]," he could barely contain his pride at having made good on his promise to Eisenhower three days earlier. While he was still engaged in fierce fighting to reach Bastogne, he reflected on his place in history in a December 22 letter to his wife: "I think the move of the Third Army is the fastest in history. We moved over a hundred miles starting on the 19th and attacked to day [sic] all ship shape and Bristol fashion." In the same letter, he revealed his plans to "put on a more daring operation just after Xmas" to relieve Bastogne but noted that "replacements are the bottle neck" and detailed his use of eight thousand rear-echelon troops as replacements for losses in rifle companies.[85]

The weather cleared on the twenty-third, and Patton's attacks continued without letup. While the Third Army's attacks were somewhat disorganized, they continued to make progress, advancing between two and five miles over the next twenty-four hours. The improved weather allowed Allied air forces to provide much-needed support to the American ground units and suppress the Germans' ability to move and fight during the daylight hours.[86] On "a very bad Christmas Eve," the Germans counterattacked and pushed "the 4th Armored back some miles with the loss of ten tanks." Reflecting on the lessons of the day's battle, Patton wrote, "This was probably my fault, because I had been insisting on day and night attacks. . . . [T]he men get too tired." In an attempt to understand the German perspective on the unfolding campaign, he continued, "I believe that the German General Staff is running this attack and has staked all on this offense to regain the initiative. They are far behind schedule and I believe beaten. . . . On the other hand, in 1940 they attacked as at present. . . . They may repeat—but with what?"[87]

To strengthen the spirits of the 101st Airborne, Patton relayed a message that read simply, "Xmas Eve present coming up. Hold On," and he continued his unceasing attack on the German lines.[88] As Christmas Eve drew to a close, Patton attended a candlelight service at an Episcopal church in Luxembourg. US Army chaplain Frdrick McDonald told his commanding officer that Kaiser Wilhelm II attended the church during the First World War and inquired, "Would you, sir, like to sit in the Kaiser's pew?" Without a pause, Patton replied, "Lead me to it." This brush with history must have made a powerful impression on the general since he mentioned the incident in his diary on Christmas Day.[89]

Christmas 1944 was "clear cold . . . lovely weather for killing Germans, which seems a bit queer, seeing Whose [sic] birthday it is."[90] Patton was up early to visit the frontline divisions and issued a decree: "To each officer and soldier in the Third United States Army, I wish a Merry Christmas. I have full confidence in your courage, devotion to duty, and skill in battle. We march in our might to complete victory. May God's blessing rest on each of you this Christmas Day."[91]

While the spirits of the men were high and they greatly appreciated the special turkey sandwiches that they had been provided, their commanding officer brooded "because we are not going fast enough" to relieve Bastogne. Patton was on the precipice of achieving his greatest accomplishment, yet he still feared that he would fail to reach the defenders of Bastogne in time. On December 26, he expressed his frustrations in his diary: "Today has been rather trying as in spite of our effort, we have failed to make contact with the defenders of Bastogne." Sometime later, he returned to his diary to note his improved fortunes: "At 1400 Gaffey phoned to say that if I authorized the risk . . . Colonel Wendell Blanchard could break through to Bastogne by a rapid advance. I told him to try it. At 1845 they made contact and Bastogne was liberated. It was a daring thing and well done. . . . The speed of our movements is amazing even to me, and must be a constant source of surprise to the Germans."[92] Patton wrote Beatrice about the breakthrough: "Ever since the 22nd, we have been trying to relieve Bastogne. . . . [W]e did it." This success must have been a major relief, as he then told her, "I have some boxes [containing Christmas presents] from you that I will open after supper."[93]

In reaching Bastogne and breaking the German advance on this key position, Patton had won a remarkable victory. Despite this accomplishment, he believed that the Allies were yet again missing an opportunity to shorten the war. By the evening of December 26 (the same night he relieved Bastogne), he was already arguing for an ambitious counteroffensive. Based on both his historical appreciation of the German failures in 1918 as well as the recent Allied failures at Falaise, he argued that the Americans should strike boldly at the exposed enemy flanks and cut off a large portion of their forces that remained exposed in the bulge they had driven into the American lines.[94] Much like he had argued at Verdun on the nineteenth, Patton hoped to conduct a bold counterstrike that would cut off the German advance at the base of the bulge and trap the enemy forces between the Allied pincers. Yet again, his aggressive instincts were restrained by Generals Bradley and Eisenhower, who claimed that the poor weather and lack of Allied forces in the region made the attack impractical. While it is impossible to know if the general's plan would have worked, he clearly believed that bold action would have avoided the battles of attrition that would ultimately follow.[95] He bluntly stated in his December 27 diary entry, "I could win this war now," if he had been given three additional divisions to spearhead his attack. On December 30, he further vented his frustrations in his diary: "Eyeryone [*sic*] of the generals involved urged me to postpone the attack." He then reflected on his broader successes: "Some people call it luck, some genius. I call it determination."[96]

Despite Patton's frustrations with the Allied timidity, he was effusive in his praise in his New Year's message to the Third Army and complimented his men by way of historical analogy to the Mexican War, stating, "I can find no fitter expression for my feelings than to apply to you the immortal words spoken by General Scott at Chapultepec when he said 'Brave rifles, veterans, you have been baptized in fire and blood and have come out steel.'"[97] Not content to rest on the laurels of his victory, Patton continued to drive his men forward, urging them to continue to attack the retreating Nazi formations.[98] Once again, he was practicing his belief that constant pressure on the German lines would keep them from re-forming and launching coordinated counterattacks and thus shortening the war. As he grimly noted, "We have to push people beyond their endurance in order to bring this war to an end."[99]

He explained this desire to keep attacking despite the high costs in a letter to Henry Stimson and again deferring to an historical analogy: "In my opinion, this present battle is a replica of Grant's 'Wilderness Campaign,' and we will have to fight it out on these lines if it takes all winter and all next summer. Naturally, things would be facilitated if we had more divisions, but so far as I know, there are no more, so we will have to get by with what we have."[100] Here again, Patton's analogy was apt. Much hard fighting was needed to reverse the German gains and end the war, but the Allies now dictated the pace of the battle and eventually exhausted their enemy through a combination of greater numbers and logistical superiority.[101]

Patton's victory at the Bulge was the greatest achievement in his five-decade military career and was a perfect synthesis of his approach to war. The famously tough and disciplined general had prepared his men for the rigors of the campaign and built loyalty and esprit de corps by insisting on hard training, excellent personal care, and strict attention to minor details. Prior to committing his forces to battle, he was prepared to act because he understood the geography of the region, recognized the key vulnerabilities of the Allied position, and studied German operational doctrine to anticipate how they would structure their attack. Once the Germans attacked, he immediately readied his forces for battle by planning for multiple contingencies with his staff prior to meeting with senior Allied commanders. When he met with Eisenhower and his staff, he was able to remain calm when others panicked. Once he was given the order to proceed with an attack, he used a prearranged code to implement an ambitious drive to Bastogne that he had already planned with his staff. During the operations during the next few days, his energy and personal leadership inspired those around him to move forward, push the limits of human endurance, and maintain a frenetic pace of combat operations.

Patton was able to master the moment because his obsessive personal drive and professionalism were combined with an understanding of historical principles of warfare. The preparation, planning, understanding of the enemy, mastery of his own emotions, speed, and hands-on leadership all reflected his beliefs that certain historical principles were enduring and transferable across time. In an interview with journalist Leland Stowe conducted a few days after the relief of Bastogne, the general referred to himself in the third person and revealed the role history had played in his generalship: "I've studied military history all my life. George Patton knows more about military history than any living person in the United States Army today. With due conceit—and I've got no end of that—I can say that's true."[102] Indeed, there is no better example in Patton's career to demonstrate that he was able to achieve victory through an understanding of the past than the Battle of the Bulge.

For the remainder of his life, he would highlight the importance of these insights in his public and private writings and would do his best to pass on these insights to future generations of military leaders. In summing up his victory in his memoirs, Patton could say confidently, "During this operation the Third Army moved further and faster and engaged more divisions in less time than any other army in the history of the United States—possibly the history of the world." In an attempt to share credit with the men he trained and inspired, he continued, "The results were made possible only by the superlative quality of American officers, American men, and American equipment." Perhaps with an eye toward the Soviets, he concluded, "No country can stand against such an Army."[103]

The price of victory was high. It had cost Patton's Third Army some 50,630 casualties, the largest single share of the nearly 80,000 Allied soldiers killed, wounded, or missing in the campaign. Despite these grim figures, it was a masterpiece of leadership and forever cemented Patton's legacy as one of the boldest and most successful commanders in modern history.[104] Perhaps

Field Marshal Gerd Von Rundstedt, the overall commander on the German side of the battle, paid Patton the best compliment after the war when he told his captors simply, "Patton, he is your best."[105]

Drive to the Rhine

After consolidating the Allied positions after the Battle of the Bulge, Third Army prepared to move into Germany. In addition to the accolades that this campaign would bring, Patton relished this opportunity for historical reasons as well. He craved the opportunity to follow in the footsteps of Caesar and Napoleon, whose campaigns in this area had inspired him since he was a boy. Indeed, one of the few books that he always carried with him on campaign was a copy of Caesar's *Commentaries on the Gallic Wars*, and he often referred to the Roman general as his guide in times of trouble and uncertainty.[106]

Despite his desire to advance along a narrow front, quickly cross the Rhine River, and drive deep into the German homeland, Patton was blocked by General Eisenhower, who acted cautiously in the weeks after the Battle of the Bulge. Eisenhower decided to push forward across a broad front and keep a substantial force in reserve to avoid exposing American forces as he had at the Ardennes.[107] This strategy confounded Patton. He wanted to win greater fame for crossing the Rhine first, and he also believed that this approach was unduly cautious.[108] In his diary, he vented his frustration about this reserve strategy: "Reserve against what? This seemed like locking the barn door after the horse was stolen. . . . [N]o reserve was needed—simply violent attacks everywhere with everything. . . . [T]he Germans do not have the resources to stop it."[109]

Despite his generally cautious attitude, General Bradley fully supported Patton's assessment of the situation, and both generals threatened to resign if they were not provided more latitude to conduct operations as they saw fit in order to exploit the German weaknesses.[110] While Eisenhower eventually allowed his subordinates some additional freedom of action, the Allies continued to advance along a 450-mile-wide front that diluted their striking power. These restrictions were compounded by a combination of foul weather and fanatical Nazi resistance that further slowed the Allied advance into Germany.[111]

Although he had several of his best divisions transferred to General Simpson's Ninth Army in early February, Patton continued to attack toward the Rhine. In his diary, he compared his mode of advance to that of Napoleon, stating, "The current operation for the encirclement of Trier is the result of the ability to change plans to meet opportunities developed by combat or as Napoleon said, 'I attack and then I look.'"[112] While he still did not have the freedom of action that he desired, he directed his advance along the ancient Roman roads toward Trier, a clear expression of his desire to follow in the footsteps of Caesar as well as his belief that this remained the key piece of ground in the region. His diary entries during this period are littered with references to the Romans, as if he was keenly aware that he was writing for future historians. In his diary he stated that the inspiration for the campaign occurred to him as part of a dream, where it "popped into my head like Minerva," a clear attempt to suggest that he was a natural and atavistic warrior guided by divine inspiration.[113] With a rhetorical flourish, he later said that he could still "smell the coppery sweat of the legions" and that "I'm going to be an awful irritation to the military historians, because I do things by sixth sense. They won't understand."[114]

Frustrated by the limitations placed on his advance, Patton traveled to Saarburg on February 28 and remarked in a letter to Beatrice, "It was the home of John the blind [sic] king of Bohemia and [the] Duke of Luxembourg who was killed at Crecy. The Prince of Wailes [sic] uses his crest."[115] While the general did not mention the incident from his childhood, this was the same John the Blind that he had once claimed to have fought alongside after he had destroyed his family chicken coop by driving an armored wagon into the unsuspecting flock.[116] This diversion boosted the general's spirits and also provided excitement, as "while I was sight seeing [sic], a shell came quite close. Also they shelled the hell out of the town at the time I was supposed to be there—I was late—I think that they tap our [telephone] wires."[117]

Ultimately, despite his frustrations, Patton's understrength forces liberated Trier on March 2, much to the surprise of Bradley and his superiors. Shortly after capturing the city, he was instructed to bypass it, prompting his famously defiant response: "Have captured Trier with two divisions. Do you want me to give it back?"[118] After the fall of Trier, Patton took a short leave to visit Paris and conduct a short hunt at the old royal game preserve used for centuries by the French monarchy. He traveled on what had previously been Hermann Göring's private train, a small personal triumph that was not lost on the general and his staff.[119] On the urging of the manager of the world-famous cabaret Folies Bergère, he even considered a postwar retirement to the pleasures of Paris but rejected this life of leisure, noting in his diary, "I can imagine no more restless place than the Follies, full of about one hundred practically naked women."[120] While the general drank and met with friends, Third Army consolidated its positions and prepared to resume its drive into Germany. This visit restored Patton's spirits and allowed him to refocus his efforts on the final campaigns in Europe.[121]

While the honor of being the first Allied army to cross the Rhine went to General Courtney Hodges's First Army, which crossed the still intact Ludendorff Bridge at Remagen on March 7, Patton continued to push forward at a frantic pace.[122] Taking little time to regroup his forces, he continued to employ his limited resources to press the two outnumbered and disorganized German armies defending the Saar-Palatine Triangle. Although he was not able to move as quickly as he had hoped, he was able to defeat these German units through maneuver and initiative.[123] In comments aimed at both the defeated foe and his own high command, he noted, "Now I *know* the Germans are crazy. No more crazy, however than our own directive from on high to maintain an 'active defense.' There are times when I'm sorry the word 'defense' was ever invented. From the Great Wall of China to the Maginot Line, *nothing, anywhere, ever*, has been successfully defended."[124]

Patton's aggressive plans had the support of his immediate superior, General Bradley, but they worried the still cautious Eisenhower, who chided him, "George, you are not only a good general, you are a lucky general, and, as you remember . . . Napoleon prized luck above skill." Undeterred by this backhanded compliment, Patton retorted, "Well, that is the first compliment you have paid me since we served together."[125] Although disguised as friendly banter, these churlish comments to his longtime friend reveal a deep insecurity about his place in the pantheon of Allied generals. Patton feared that other generals had surpassed him in the eyes of his commanding officer and was privately extremely hurt that Eisenhower rarely praised him to his face.[126]

Whether it was Napoleonic luck or Patton's vision of war that won the day, the results were indisputable. From March 11 to March 25, Third Army surrounded large portions of the German forces in the region and even cut off and bypassed a portion of the Seventh US Army that was stuck in defensive positions adjacent to Third Army. This led to the famous cable from General Leonard Gerow, who congratulated Patton "ON YOUR BRILLIANT SURROUNDING AND CAPTURE OF THREE ARMIES, ONE OF THEM AMERICAN."[127]

Crossing the Rhine

As Patton's forces approached the Rhine River, he took a short trip to the recently liberated city of Trier to inspect both the recent battlefields and the Roman ruins. He reflected on the visit in his March 14 diary entry: "Visited

Trier. . . . So did Caesar . . . whose Gallic wars I am now reading. It is interesting to view in imagination the Roman legions marching down the same road. One of the few things undestroyed in Trier is the amphitheater which still stands in its sturdy magnificence."[128] Despite this rhetorical flourish, Patton's imagination appears to have admittedly gotten the better of him. While Caesar did fight several campaigns in the area between 58 and 50 BC, the city was founded during the reign of Emperor Augustus more than a half century later. The Roman amphitheater dates from approximately AD 100, some century and a half after the Roman general fought in Gaul. Similarly, much of the remains of ancient Trier date from its heyday during the third and fourth centuries AD, and it is improbable that Caesar or his legions ever marched down any of the roads mentioned in this diary entry.[129] In this context, Patton's writings are best seen as an attempt to gain comfort in the past and project an image of an atavistic warrior during his ongoing drive to the Rhine, not a serious attempt at scholarship.

The 5th Infantry Division of the Third Army crossed the Rhine River under cover of darkness on the night of March 22. Consistent with Patton's belief that speed, surprise, and maintaining the intuitive were key to keeping the retreating Germans from consolidating their positions, the crossing was conducted without artillery or air support. In fact, the operation was so hastily prepared that the 5th Infantry's commanding officer, Major General S. LeRoy Irwin, had less than twenty-four hours' notice that his unit had been picked to lead the Third Army across the Rhine. While Irwin and his staff were surprised by the boldness of their mission and had to work without rest to implement these orders on such short notice, the 5th Infantry had specialized in river crossings and the Rhine would be its twenty-third and most famous crossing of the war. The Germans did not anticipate that an attack in the region could be conducted so quickly and had only token forces guarding the banks on the Rhine in this sector of the front. As a result of Patton's boldness, the Americans maintained the initiative and were able to cross the Rhine River with the cost of only twenty casualties on the first night.[130]

Despite his desire for glory, Patton insisted on secrecy so as not to expose the small force that had made the river crossing and was potentially exposed to a German counterattack. On the morning of the twenty-third, he telephoned General Bradley, exclaiming, "Brad, don't tell anyone, but I am across." An incredulous Bradley replied, "Well, I'll be dammed. You mean the Rhine?" to which a delighted Third Army commander explained, "Sure am. I sneaked a division over last night. But there are so few Krauts around there they don't know it yet so don't make any announcement—we'll keep it a secret until we see how it goes." News of Patton's coup quickly spread, and that evening he again telephoned Bradley, exclaiming, "Brad . . . for God's sake tell the world we're across. . . . I want the world to know Third Army made it [across] before Monty."[131]

When the Germans finally learned about the extent of Third Army's advance across the Rhine, they responded with a massive aerial bombardment designed to destroy the pontoon bridges and halt the advance. Despite repeated attacks on March 23, the Luftwaffe was unable to destroy these bridgeheads and lost a staggering thirty-three aircraft to Third Army's antiaircraft units. On the twenty-third, Bradley's headquarters released a glowing statement that highlighted Third Army's accomplishments, which were done "without the benefit of aerial bombardment, ground smoke, artillery preparation or airborne assistance," a stirring testament to the courage of the men and the boldness of their commanding officer.[132]

With the news out, Patton began to act out his historical fantasies as a means of maximizing his moment of glory and projecting himself as a commander in the same spirit of great generals from the past. On March 24, 1945, he invited the press to witness his crossing of the Rhine River. Flanked by General Eddy and his personal bodyguard, Major Alex Stiller, he began to walk across the pontoon bridge at Nierstein. Approximately halfway across, he stopped and pronounced, "Time out for a short halt." He then unzipped his fly and urinated into the river that was the traditional border of Germany and said, "I have been looking forward to this for a long time."[133] The assembled press took photos of the incident and forever documented this crude but memorable display of Patton bravado.

Once on the German side of the river, Patton acted as if he tripped, fell to one knee, grabbed two handfuls of dirt, let them dramatically fall to the ground, and stated defiantly, "Thus, William the Conqueror!" Here, Patton was directly referencing the legendary actions of William the Conqueror, who landed on the shores of England, pretended to fall, and said, "I have taken England with both hands."[134] The general's diary entry was surprisingly modest on this accomplishment, noting simply, "Drove to the river and went across on the pontoon bridge, stopping in the middle to take a piss in the Rhine, and then to pick up some dirt on the far side . . . in emulation of William the Conqueror."[135]

Interestingly, Patton knew that Napoleon had made a Rhine crossing in this very region, but could not remember the exact location. In October 1945, he received a letter from his son, George, then a cadet at West Point,

Figure 9. Patton crossing the Rhine in the footsteps of Caesar and Napoleon. Courtesy the General George Patton Museum of Leadership, Fort Knox, Kentucky.

which claimed that he had just learned that Napoleon had crossed the river at nearly the exact same spot.[136] Patton responded to his son, "I did not know until you told me that Napoleon crossed near Oppenheim. I picked this when I was still in England as the place to cross the Rhine because the terrain on my side dominated the other side . . . and because . . . there was a barge harbor there from which we could launch boats unseen."[137] Clearly, even after the moment had passed, Patton enjoyed comparing his decisions to those of Napoleon, and despite being ignorant of this historical fact he believed that great military minds had thought alike.

For the remainder of his life, Patton would highlight the Rhine crossing and the Palatine campaign as two of his greatest accomplishments. Despite this triumph, he was already anticipating an uncomfortable peace with the Soviets and was still unsure of the fate of his son-in-law Lieutenant Colonel John Waters. On March 13, prior to the victorious Rhine crossing, he took the unusual step of writing General George Marshall, requesting a transfer to a combat command in the Pacific. In the weeks that followed, he began to write with growing fatalism that this would be "my last war."[138] This sense that the war was ending and with it his opportunity to win glory appears to have been the motivation to take enormous risks in the coming weeks that would ultimately jeopardize his place in history. For the moment, he savored the opportunity to build his reputation as a bold and decisive fighter guided by a supernatural sense of history.

· ·

NOTES

1. Carlo D'Este, *Decision in Normandy*, 341; Morningstar, *Patton's Way*, 169.

2. "After Action Report: Third US Army, 1 August 1944–9 May 1945, Volume I, 'The Operations," 12–13.

3. *The United States Army in World War II: The War against Germany: Europe and Adjacent Areas*, 137; Robert S. Allen, *Forward with Patton: The World War II Diary of Colonel Robert S. Allen*, 53; Mansoor, *GI Offensive in Europe*, 148–49.

4. On the point of ingenuity and improvisation in the Normandy campaign, James Jay Carafano, *GI Ingenuity: Improvisation, Technology, and Winning World War II*, esp. 87–164; "After Action Report: Third US Army, 1 August 1944–9 May 1945," 11.

5. Morningstar, *Patton's Way*, 5.

6. Diaries, 1910–45, George S. Patton Papers, Manuscript Division, Library of Congress, Washington, DC.

7. Bradley quoted in D'Este, *Patton*, 615. For a similar appraisal predicting a World War I–style stalemate, see Allen, *Forward with Patton*, 53.

8. *CSI Battlebook 21: Operation Cobra: 4th Armored Division: Deliberate Attack Exploitation*, 4-2.

9. Dennis E. Showalter, *Patton and Rommel: Men of War in the Twentieth Century*, 365.

10. Koch and Hayes, *G-2: Intelligence for Patton*, 53, 59.

11. Third Army's official after-action report makes numerous references to overcrowded roads hindering movements during the Normandy campaign. "After Action Report: Third US Army, 1 August 1944–9 May 1945," 10–11, 13, 20–22, 40, 47.

12. D'Este, *Patton*, 620; Diaries, 1910–45, Patton Papers.

13. Blumenson, *The Patton Papers*, 2:500. It is worth noting that the Bayeux Tapestry contains similar imagery of William and Harold riding with hawk on fist.

14. It was only in the first days of August that the Germans began to reevaluate their assessment that Patton was planning on invading France via Calais. The

Germans recognized their mistake when units that had been assigned to the fictitious army began to appear in Normandy as part of the actual Allied order of battle. By this time, however, the Allied deception had already achieved its goal of pinning down the German forces farther to the north and allowing the invasion to encounter weaker resistance in the critical opening weeks of the campaign. Joachim Ludewig, *Rückzug: The German Retreat from France, 1944*, 89.

15. Mansoor, *GI Offensive in Europe*, 167–71.

16. Anthony Tucker-Jones, *Falaise—the Flawed Victory: The Destruction of Panzergruppe West, August, 1944.*

17. Jordan, *Brothers, Rivals, Victory*, 379.

18. Martin Blumenson, *The Battle of the Generals: The Untold Story of the Falaise Pocket—the Campaign That Should Have Won World War II.*

19. Essame, *Patton as Military Commander*, 167; Ludewig, *Rückzug*, 100.

20. *CSI Battlebook 21*, 3-3.

21. Martin Blumenson, *Breakout and Pursuit*; Blumenson, *Battle of the Generals*; Jordan, *Brothers, Rivals, Victory*, 379–80; Ludewig, *Rückzug*, 99-100; Chester Wilmot, *The Struggle for Europe: An Account of the War in Europe, 1940–45*, 410–20.

22. This view was shared by many in the German High Command, including prominent staff officer Major General F. W. von Mellenthin, who noted the sense of crisis among Hitler and his inner circle in his postwar memoir. F. W. von Mellenthin, *Panzer Battles: A Study of Employment of Armor in the Second World War*, 343–44.

23. Citino, *Wehrmacht's Last Stand*, 266–71. This frustration clearly affected Patton's staff during the Battle of the Bulge. On December 28, 1944, a frustrated Colonel Robert Allen wondered in his diary, "Why Patton was not allowed to close the Falaise pocket[?]" Allen, *Forward with Patton*, 139.

24. Diaries, 1910–45, Patton Papers.

25. Blumenson, *Battle of the Generals*, 210; Jordan, *Brothers, Rivals, Victory*, 380.

26. A careful reader will note the very similar language to his statement after the campaign in Sicily and his comments after the Battle of the Bulge. Clearly, this entry was written to document what he believed to be an impressive personal accomplishment that placed him in the highest echelon of military commanders. Diaries, 1910–45, Patton Papers. Patton made a similar point to his staff on August 15, but added, "In the weeks to come it is my intention to advance further and faster still." Codman, *Drive*, 162.

27. Antony Beevor, *Ardennes 1944: The Battle of the Bulge*, 5.

28. Stephen E. Ambrose, *Band of Brothers: E Company, 506th Regiment, 101st Airborne from Normandy to Hitler's Eagle's Nest*, 106–7.

29. "After Action Report: Third US Army, 1 August 1944–9 May 1945," 153, 157.

30. Citino, *Wehrmacht's Last Stand*, 268.

31. Atkinson, *Guns at Last Light*, 342–43; Mansoor, *GI Offensive in Europe*, 202–4.

32. For the definitive overview of Patton's role in the Loraine and Metz campaigns, see John Nelson Rickard, *Patton at Bay: The Lorraine Campaign, September to December, 1944.*

33. Rickard, *Patton at Bay*, 175.

34. Atkinson, *Guns at Last Light*, 346; Essame, *Patton as Military Commander*, 213. For an excellent overview of the weather during the campaign, see Rickard, *Patton at Bay*, 173.

35. For series of complaints on weather, supply shortages, and Allied cooperation, Patton diaries November 6 1944–December 14, 1944. Diaries, 1910–45, Patton Papers.

36. Codman, *Drive*, 203; Atkinson, *Guns at Last Light*, 343; Citino, *Wehrmacht's Last Stand*, 349.

37. Family Papers, 1857–1979, Patton Papers.

38. Blumenson, *The Patton Papers*, 2:576; Groom, *The Generals*, 370. Interestingly, Patton's aide Charles Codman also repeated this factual error in his memoirs, a clear indication that he had discussed this point with his commanding officer. Codman, *Drive*, 219.

39. Rickard, *Patton at Bay*, 235–36. According to Rickard, Patton's sense of history may have encouraged him to directly assault Metz rather than maneuver around it and reduce it by siege. While this is impossible to definitively prove, Patton's subsequent refusal to admit that he failed to make the proper command decision and his selective treatment in his private writings lend some credence to this interpretation.

40. Blumenson, *The Patton Papers*, 2:589.

41. Roberts, *Storm of War*, 502.

42. Anthony Kemp, *The Unknown Battle: Metz, 1944*. For an overview of the immense difficulties of keeping Third Army supplied with fuel, see Irzyk, *Gasoline to Patton*.

43. Rickard, *Patton at Bay*, 235–36.

44. Paul D. Harkins, *When the Third Cracked Europe: The Story of Patton's Incredible Army*, 57; Rickard, *Patton at Bay*, 239.

45. Barron, *Patton at the Battle of the Bulge*, 36–39.

46. Allen, *Forward with Patton*, 108.

47. Blumenson, *The Patton Papers*, 2:590, 596.

48. Cole, *United States Army in World War II*, 485.

49. Robert S. Rush, *Hell in Hürtgen Forest: The Ordeal and Triumph of an American Infantry Regiment*.

50. Rickard, *Advance and Destroy*, 82.

51. Koch and Hayes, *G-2: Intelligence for Patton*, 86–87.

52. Rickard, *Advance and Destroy*, 80–81.

53. Cole, *United States Army in World War II*, 255; "After Action Report: Third US Army, 1 August 1944–9 May 1945," 167.

54. D'Este, *Patton*, 673.

55. Blumenson, *The Patton Papers*, 2:595.

56. Blumenson, *The Patton Papers*, 2:596.

57. The Germans were well aware that they were leaving their flanks exposed to a potential counterattack, but at this point in the war did not have sufficient forces available to protect their flanks. Instead, they gambled that they could rapidly achieve victory before the Allies could launch an effective counter attack. Citino,

Wehrmacht's Last Stand, 383; Rickard, *Advance and Destroy*, 30; Yeide, *Fighting Patton*, 359.

58. On the successes and failures of the German spring offensives, see Stephen Biddle, *Military Power: Explaining Victory and Defeat in Modern Battle*, 78–107; and David T. Zabecki, *The German 1918 Offensives: A Case Study in the Operational Level of War.*

59. Blumenson, *The Patton Papers*, 2:596–98.

60. Rickard, *Advance and Destroy*, 94–95.

61. Patton, *War as I Knew It*, 190.

62. In *War as I Knew It*, Patton says the meeting began at 0800, but most other sources suggest the meeting began at 0700. While it is possible that Patton was attempting to alter history to make it appear that he and his staff did the same work in less time, the most likely explanation is that Patton either misremembered the exact time or incorrectly transcribed it into his memoir. Blumenson, *The Patton Papers*, 2:598.

63. Barron, *Patton at the Battle of the Bulge*, 58; Rickard, *Advance and Destroy*, 99.

64. Patton would often compliment his staff using the historically based compliment, "You know, Julius Caesar would have had a tough time being a brigadier general in this army!" Koch and Hayes, *G-2: Intelligence for Patton*, 156.

65. Patton, *War as I Knew It*, 190.

66. D. Eisenhower, *Crusade in Europe*, 350.

67. Blumenson and Hymel, *Patton*, 72–73.

68. Although Patton would eventually send his forces to relieve the 101st, he never agreed with the Allied strategy of leaving this highly trained but lightly armed unit in the path of the Nazi advance. Rickard, *Advance and Destroy*, 122.

69. Citino, *Wehrmacht's Last Stand*, 395–96.

70. For an excellent overview of the timetable for the German advance and the little-known history of the 28th Infantry Division and elements of the 9th and 10th Armored Divisions who delayed the Nazis and made the defense of Bastogne possible, see John C. McManus, *Alamo in the Ardennes: The Untold Story of the American Soldiers Who Made the Defense of Bastogne Possible.*

71. Blumenson, *The Patton Papers*, 2:602.

72. Patton, *War as I Knew It*, 191.

73. Blumenson, *The Patton Papers*, 2:599–600. There is some confusion as to the exact time frame Patton promised Eisenhower. In his memoirs and letters, Patton mentioned December 22, a time more than forty-eight but less than seventy-two hours in the future. However, it their postwar writings, both Bradley and Eisenhower indicate the time frame as forty-eight hours. Rickard, *Advance and Destroy*, 106; Barron, *Patton at the Battle of the Bulge,* 59.

74. Patton, *War as I Knew It*, 191.

75. Rickard, *Advance and Destroy*, 107.

76. Codman, *Drive*, 232; Blumenson, *The Patton Papers*, 2:600.

77. Patton, *War as I Knew It*, 192. .

78. "After Action Report: Third US Army, 1 August 1944–9 May 1945," 171; Barron, *Patton at the Battle of the Bulge*, 60; Codman, *Drive*, 230–32.

79. Patton, *War as I Knew It*, 192.

80. Major (later Brigadier General) Albin Irzyk quoted in Rickard, *Advance and Destroy*, 118.

81. Blumenson, *The Patton Papers*, 2:603.

82. During World War II, it was extremely unusual for American armored forces to move at night. However, the men of the 4th Armored Division sensed the importance of their mission and understood that they were acting on orders from Patton himself. Barron, *Patton at the Battle of the Bulge*, 3.

83. Diaries, 1910–45, Patton Papers.

84. "After Action Report: Third US Army, 1 August 1944–9 May 1945," 174.

85. Blumenson, *The Patton Papers*, 2:604; Allen, *Forward with Patton*, 139–40.

86. "After Action Report: Third US Army, 1 August 1944–9 May 1945," 177.

87. Diaries, 1910–45, Patton Papers.

88. Cole, *United States Army in World War II*, 475.

89. Beevor, *Ardennes 1944*, 278. In his diary, Patton incorrectly claims that the pew was once occupied by Wilhelm I. Diaries, 1910–45, Patton Papers. For a similar version of the event, Codman, *Drive*, 235.

90. Diaries, 1910–45, Patton Papers.

91. "After Action Report: Third US Army, 1 August 1944–9 May 1945," 180.

92. Diaries, 1910–45, Patton Papers.

93. Blumenson, *The Patton Papers*, 2:607.

94. Cole, *United States Army in World War II*, 611.

95. Rickard, *Advance and Destroy*, 181–225.

96. Diaries, 1910–45, Patton Papers.

97. Blumenson, *The Patton Papers*, 2:610.

98. Barron, *Patton at the Battle of the Bulge*, 324–25.

99. Blumenson, *The Patton Papers*, 2:702.

100. Blumenson, *The Patton Papers*, 2:620.

101. Note the similarity of Patton's words to Grant's actual quote from his May 11, 1864, letter to Major General Henry Halleck, including his request for reinforcements: "We have now ended the 6th day of very heavy fighting. The result up to this time is much in our favor. But our losses have been heavy as well as those of the enemy. . . . I am now sending back to Belle Plain all my wagons for a fresh supply of provisions and ammunition, and propose to fight it out on this line if it takes all summer. The arrival of reinforcements here will be very encouraging to the men, and I hope they will be sent as fast as possible, and in as great [of] numbers." Ulysses S. Grant, *The Personal Memoirs of Ulysses S. Grant: The Complete Annotated Edition*, 544. To win support of the Northern people, President Abraham Lincoln popularized the Grant quote, "I am going through on this line if it takes all summer," but would add his own statement of determination, "I say we are going through on this line if it takes three years more." Chernow, *Grant*, 392. For an excellent overview of the Battle of the Wilderness, see Gordon C. Rhea, *The Battle of the Wilderness, May 5–6, 1864*.

102. Leland Stowe, "Old Blood-and-Guts Off the Record"; D'Este, *Patton*, 690.

103. Patton, *War as I Knew It*, 228.

104. Despite the significant scholarly attention paid to the battle, there is no exact number of American or German casualties. Patton arrived at the 50,630 in his memoir based on after-action reports from the Third Army. Patton, *War as I Knew It*, 228. For a representative overview of the casualty debate, see Beevor, *Ardennes 1944*, 367; Cole, *United States Army in World War II*, 674; and Rickard, *Advance and Destroy*, 316.

105. Von Rundstedt interviewed in *Stars and Stripes* magazine. D'Este, *Patton*, 701.

106. B. Patton, "A Soldier's Reading."

107. Rickard, *Advance and Destroy*, 55.

108. Codman, *Drive*, 252.

109. Diaries, 1910–45, Patton Papers.

110. Beevor, *Ardennes 1944*, 358.

111. According to Patton biographer Carlo D'Este, "Bradley's biggest ally was none other than Patton. This incident marked the pinnacle of their solidarity." D'Este, *Patton*, 706.

112. Patton used the same analogy to calm his nerves in the days before the Torch landings.

113. Diaries, 1910–45, Patton Papers.

114. D'Este, *Patton*, 708.

115. Blumenson, *The Patton Papers*, 2:649.

116. R. Patton, *The Pattons*, 94–95.

117. Blumenson, *The Patton Papers*, 2:649.

118. D'Este, *Patton*, 708.

119. Codman, *Drive*, 252.

120. Diaries, 1910–45, Patton Papers.

121. Codman, *Drive*, 252–57.

122. Ken Hechler, *The Bridge at Remagen: A Story of World War II.*

123. After the war, German major general F. W. Von Mellenthin would praise Bradley and Patton's initiative and pushing their retreating foe during the first weeks of March. Mellenthin, *Panzer Battles*, 415–18.

124. Codman, *Drive*, 260 (emphasis in the original).

125. Codman, *Drive*, 264.

126. D'Este, *Patton*, 701.

127. D'Este, *Patton*, 713; Codman, *Drive*, 265.

128. Diaries, 1910–45, Patton Papers; Blumenson, *The Patton Papers*, 2:655.

129. Edith Mary Wightman, *Roman Trier and the Treveri*, 71–123.

130. Mansoor, *GI Offensive in Europe*, 244.

131. Codman, *Drive*, 268–69; Roberts, *Storm of War*, 514.

132. D'Este, *Patton*, 712.

133. Diaries, 1910–45, Patton Papers.; Codman, *Drive*, 269.

134. Codman, *Drive*, 252 Interestingly, Winston Churchill had already urinated in the Rhine on March 3, but unlike Patton insisted that the press not take photos, stating, "This is one of those operations conducted with this great war which must

not be reproduced graphically." Churchill quoted in D'Este, *Patton*, 713; and Allen, *Forward with Patton*, 203.

135. Diaries, 1910–45, Patton Papers.

136. For an excellent overview of this father-son relationship, see Brian M. Sobel, *The Fighting Pattons*.

137. Blumenson, *The Patton Papers*, 2:660.

138. Diaries, 1910–45, Patton Papers.

CHAPTER FIVE

BATTLES WITH HISTORY DURING UNCERTAIN TIMES

Racing the Soviets in the War's Final Days

DURING THE FINAL days of World War II, Third Army moved virtually unopposed, gobbling up territory in Bavaria, Austria, and Czechoslovakia. Patton pushed his troops forward in part because of his desire for personal glory and love of combat, but also for geopolitical reasons. Since the end of World War I, he had harbored a deep personal animosity toward communist movements in general and the Soviet regime in particular. This fear of communism was so deeply held that he frequently expressed concerns in his private writings that the Roosevelt administration was leading the United States toward socialism. The politics of workers' rights, collectivization, centralization, five-year plans, and the denial of religious autonomy appalled Patton, who fervently believed in capitalism, free markets, and religious values. These political biases were confirmed by the brutal revenge the Soviet Army enacted on the peoples of Eastern Europe during their drive into Germany. These atrocities reinforced the general's preconception that the Soviet regime was composed of barbarous savages who ruled with violence and intimidation and were no better than the Nazis they replaced. He romanticized the aristocratic values of the Romanovs and believed that the communists had irresponsibly destroyed their old-fashioned, refined way of life in the name of revolution and unleashed unmitigated savagery on Europe.[1]

These political biases were further reinforced by Patton's understanding of history. For centuries, Russia had attempted to expand into Western Europe, and only the dedicated effort of European powers had stopped these aggressive actions. According to this view, the Russian thirst for power and

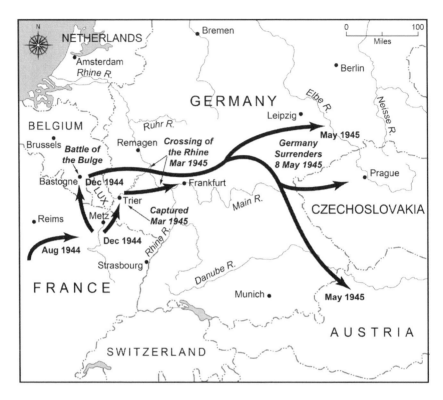

Map 9: Patton's drive across the Rhine River and drive into Austria and Czechoslovakia. After crossing the Rhine River, Patton's forces moved at an incredible speed through Germany and into Austria and Czechoslovakia. Not only did these campaigns show the power and efficiency of the Third Army, but they also prevented vast swaths of territory, millions of people, priceless art treasures, and the world famous Lipizzaners from falling into Soviet hands. Map by Chris Robinson.

influence would naturally repeat itself, much as it had in the eighteenth century under Peter and Catherine the Great, in the nineteenth century after the fall of Napoleon, and in the early twentieth century after the Russian Revolution. The Soviets were no longer a critical ally but a potential threat to the peace and security of Europe. The prospect that Europe might again be threatened by an aggressive Russia disgusted Patton and drove his actions for the remainder of his life.

Despite his sense of foreboding, Patton believed that he had a unique opportunity to limit Soviet aggression during the war's final weeks. His plan was to drive the Third Army as deep into German-held territory as possible in an effort to deny these areas to the Soviets. By physically occupying key population and industrial centers, he hoped to provide the Western Allies with a superior geopolitical position for confronting the Soviets after the end of hostilities. The sense of relief expressed by the local populations that they were being occupied by the Americans, not the Russians, seemed to confirm Patton's view that the Americans were protecting these peoples from the ravages of the Red Army.[2]

Although the Germans were still at war with the Americans, they chose to play into this strategy by focusing their efforts on fighting the Russians, leaving the approaches to key cities such as Munich and Prague virtually undefended.[3] Eisenhower recognized that the Americans had an opportunity to exploit the German weakness and ordered all of his armies to move as quickly as possible along a broad front. While he wanted to avoid fratricide or inadvertently antagonizing Soviet troops, Eisenhower believed that capturing these cities would strengthen the American postwar position while sparing German civilians from the ravages of the Red Army.[4] Patton chafed at Eisenhower's broad-front approach and frequently complained in his diary and private letters that he could move faster if he was not tied down to other American units.[5]

Task Force Baum

Despite the fact that the Third Army was moving rapidly, Patton was bored and frustrated. He already anticipated that the war would soon be over and was upset that General Douglas MacArthur had dominated the recent news headlines with his daring raid to rescue more than five hundred American prisoners at Cabanatuan in the Philippines.[6] On March 25, 1945, he would make one of the most controversial decisions of the war. After hearing a rumor that his son-in-law Lieutenant Colonel John Waters was among those interned a German prison outside Hammelburg, he ordered a small task force under command of Captain Abraham Baum to liberate the camp.

Interestingly, Baum was not Patton's first choice to command the task force. The mission was originally going to be led by Lieutenant Colonel Harold "Hal" Cohen, but he was suffering from a severe case of bleeding hemorrhoids. When Patton learned of the malady, he instantly thought of history and said, "I don't want any dammed hemorrhoids lousing up an important mission, Napoleon's hemorrhoids defeated him at Waterloo. He couldn't sit [on] a horse for long and had to direct the battle from his tent. If Cohen's ass is hurting, I don't want him going." To settle the matter, Patton then ordered Cohen to drop his pants so that he could personally inspect the hemorrhoids. The tough-minded general then noted, "That is some sorry ass, my God, they're the size of golf balls," and the mission was then assigned to Baum.[7]

Since Waters's capture in North Africa in early 1943, the fate of his son-in-law was never far from the general's mind, and this constant strain, combined with his broader frustration, prompted him to take an unnecessary gamble to save his loved one.[8] Despite the fact that German resistance was crumbling, the mission was extremely risky and ignored basic military principles. The raid was premised on the ability to maintain speed and surprise, but it lacked proper intelligence, was hastily planned, and was significantly undermanned. Furthermore, the mission was ordered by Patton over the objections of General William Hoge and the unit's battalion commander, Lieutenant Colonel (later General) Creighton Abrams.[9] Had Patton thought about his own theories of warfare, it is unlikely that he would have taken such an extreme risk. While Patton had long advocated audacity and boldness, he typically applied maximum pressure on the enemy. Task Force Baum, on the other hand, was such a small force that it did not have the combat power to apply significant pressure on the Germans and would have to avoid contact with hostile forces in order to survive. Rather than acting boldly, it would appear that in this case, he allowed personal emotions to cloud his judgment and took an unacceptable risk.

Task Force Baum embarked on its mission on the evening of March 26 with a skeleton force of sixteen tanks, twenty-seven half-tracks, three 105mm self-propelled guns, and a mere 294 officers and men. Patton's aide Major Alex Stiller was attached to Task Force Baum as well for the express purpose of identifying Waters, a clear indication of the general's true motives.[10] While rumors buzzed around Patton's headquarters, the officers did their best to quiet speculation and maintain a "shush-shush" atmosphere. Despite these attempts, "Patton [was] very concerned about it," and his staff planned multiple reconnaissance missions to provide information regarding the status of Task Force Baum.[11]

Initially, the task force ran into minimal opposition, the audacity of the mission apparently taking the Germans by surprise. En route to the Hammelburg camp, the task force liberated a prison camp containing 700 Russian prisoners of war, who quickly began to seize Nazi weapons and loot and to create chaos, thus alerting the Germans to their presence. The small American force pushed on to Hammelburg and crashed their tanks through the gates of the Nazi prison camp, temporarily liberating 5,000 POWs, including 1,291 Americans. Lieutenant Colonel Waters was among the Americans held there, but he was seriously wounded in the resulting firefight. The camp's Serbian doctor saved Waters's life by treating him with a kitchen knife and bandages made of paper, but he was unable to be evacuated as a result of his life-threatening wound.[12]

Task Force Baum was unprepared for the unexpectedly high number of Allied prisoners and could transport only about 250 of them at a time back to American lines. Baum's men took as many Americans as they could, but left the remaining prisoners behind, including the gravely wounded Waters. The task force attempted to fight its way back out to safety, but was surrounded by German reinforcements and captured.[13] The fate of Task Force Baum was not learned until the Americans liberated Hammelburg on April 5, when most of its members, along with the original prisoners, were freed.

Upon hearing the news that Waters was alive but in serious condition, Patton rushed his personal surgeon, Dr. Charles Odom, and two light aircraft to Hammelburg. This decision cemented many people's belief that the general had ordered the raid specifically to rescue his son-in-law and that his judgment had been dangerously clouded by his personal sentiments. In press conferences after the failed raid, Patton categorically denied that he knew of Waters's presence at the camp and explained his decision to raid the camp was "because we were afraid that the American prisoners might be murdered by the retreating Germans."[14] In fact, there was no direct evidence that the Germans were planning on eliminating prisoners prior to retreating, and such large-scale executions of Americans were quite uncommon. The failed raid resulted in the deaths of 25 American soldiers and is unquestionably one of Patton's greatest failures.[15]

Patton was lucky that the press did not learn about the failed raid until ten days later, when public attention was fixated on the death of President Franklin Roosevelt. The few papers that did pick up the story dismissed this failure as "Army Blundering," and he escaped with little more than a tongue-lashing from Eisenhower, who claimed he "took Patton's hide off" for his recklessness.[16] Noting his uncommon luck with the press, the general bemused, "What the hell! With the President's death you could execute buggery in the streets and get no further than the fourth page."[17] Despite these wry remarks, the failure of the Hammelburg raid clearly weighed on his conscience, and he understood that his recklessness and nepotism could threaten his place in history. In the months following the end of World War

II, Patton would make extraordinary efforts to cover up his involvement in the failed raid and would purposely distort the historical record to suit his own ends.

Saving Europe's Cultural and Historical Legacy
During their drive, the Third Army was also able to help preserve some of the cultural treasures of Europe. On April 2, 1945, the 90th Infantry attacked the Germans outside of the salt-mining town of Merkers-Kieselbach. They expected light resistance, but instead encountered a regiment of Germans who had been ordered to hold the town at all costs. "Ignorant of the German determination to hold at all costs, however, the 90th advanced, smashed the line and moved forward." As the 90th Infantry entered the city, two German midwives who were rushing to deliver a baby were stopped and interrogated. Desperate to get to their patient, they quickly revealed to their captors that "below the local salt mine was hidden a vast supply of gold."[18]

The midwives were soon released, and their claims were immediately investigated. While the mine was soon found and surrounded with an armed guard, it contained a vast network of tunnels. Word was immediately sent to Patton about the discovery. Sensing the need for caution, the general imposed strict censorship on the news and detailed a regiment of the 90th Infantry to stay behind and guard the mine while the remainder of the unit pushed on toward the Czech border.[19] Despite the insistence on secrecy, word of the find quickly leaked out, much to the displeasure of Patton, who fired the censor who leaked the news.

After two days of searching the complex, soldiers found the promised treasure behind a locked metal door. Patton instructed his men to "blow open that fuckin' vault and see what's in it."[20] According to the official history of the 90th Infantry Division:

> An inventory of the mine revealed that it contained: 100 tons of gold bullion, 5,000,000,000 German marks, 2,000,000 American dollars, 4,000,000 Norwegian pounds, 100,000,000 French francs, 110,000 English pounds, plus Spanish, Italian, Turkish and Portuguese currency. In addition there were 1,000 cases of paintings and statutes, priceless art works of inestimable value. Included were the works of Raphael, Rembrandt, Van Dyck, Durer and Renoir. Invaluable tapestries and engravings looted from the art centers of Europe were found hidden in the underground chambers of the unassuming salt mine at Merkers.[21]

Eisenhower and Bradley traveled to Merkers to inspect the find.[22] Patton traveled down into the mine shaft with the two generals on a rickety elevator suspended by a single cable and could not resist an opportunity for gallows humor, noting that "promotions in the United States Army would be considerably stimulated" if the cable suddenly broke. This joke angered Eisenhower, who promptly told Patton to refrain from such jokes "until we are above the ground again."[23]

Figure 10. General Dwight D. Eisenhower, accompanied by General Omar Bradley and Lieutenant General George Patton, inspects art treasures stolen by Germans and hidden in a salt mine. National Archives.

After exiting the mine, the generals shared lunch, and Eisenhower asked Patton what he would do with the treasure if he was allowed to choose. Without batting an eye, he claimed that half should go to the men of the Third Army and half should provide funding for new weapons after the war. Eisenhower was amused by this impossible request and ended the discussion by remarking, "He's always got an answer."[24] While the Allies did their best to return the art treasures to their rightful owners, the fate of the captured gold would not be resolved until December 1997, when the US government formally renounced its claim on the assets. The gold was donated to the Nazi Persecution Relief Fund and was officially transferred to the Tripartite Gold Commission in a ceremony held in Paris in September 1998.[25]

Sensing the crumbling German resistance, Patton met with Eisenhower on April 11 and begged him to allow Third Army to take Berlin. Eisenhower believed that this was an overly ambitious operation and reasoned:

> From a tactical point of view, it was highly inadvisable for the American Army to take Berlin. . . . [I]it had no tactical or strategic value, and would place upon the American forces the burden for caring for thousands and thousands of Germans, displaced persons, Allied prisoners of war, etc.
>
> General Patton replied, "Ike, I don't see how you figure that one. We had better take Berlin and quick and on to the Oder."[26]

Despite Patton's insistence, he was overruled and ordered to continue his drive into Austria.

On April 13, 1945, Patton and his staff visited the recently liberated Nazi prison camp of Buchenwald and came face-to-face with the horrors of the Nazi regime. The notoriously tough general was sickened and stated that "words are inadequate to express the horror of these institutions." The general invited Eisenhower and representatives of the press to view the camp in order to "build up another page of the necessary evidence as to the brutality of the Germans." The two generals visited the camp, and, according to Eisenhower: "The visual evidence and the verbal testimony of starvation, cruelty, and bestiality were so overpowering as to leave me sick. In one room where there were piled up twenty or thirty naked men, killed by starvation, George Patton would not enter. He said he would get sick if he did so."[27] This incident seemed to harden Patton's resolve to end the war as rapidly as possible, and he redoubled his drive toward Linz, Austria, in the coming days.[28]

Figure 11. Generals Eisenhower, Bradley, and Patton watch grimly while occupants of a German concentration camp demonstrate Nazi torture techniques. In contrast to his "blood-and-guts" persona, Patton was physically sickened by his tour of the camp. National Archives.

On the evening of April 17, Patton received the news that he had been officially nominated by President Truman to receive his fourth star. He was "glad to be a full General" but believed that he was an "also-ran" because Generals Bradley, Devers, and Clark had already been promoted in early April and were thus more senior.[29] Despite his wounded pride, he quickly had his aide Charles Codman secure "for me the last two 4-star pins in existence in Paris and also a 4-star flag," an important symbol of Patton's professional achievement.[30]

The glow of the promotion had not worn off on April 28 when Patton triumphantly crossed the Danube near Regensburg. He remarked that "we French stormed Ratisbon: a mile or so away . . . on a little mound, Napoleon stood on our storming-day." After making this improbable claim of reincarnation, he then further built up his own present-day accomplishment by noting, "Which only goes to show that in those days Supreme Commanders were even less anxious to get up front than they are today."[31]

In early May, Patton received the good news that his old friend General Jean Houdemon had been liberated from a German prisoner-of-war camp. The general traveled to meet his friend and was accompanied by two Mexican generals. This unusual assembly of military figures ate and drank late into the evening, rekindling old friendships and making new ones. The Mexican generals made it a point to express their goodwill to Patton and insisted that they would not fight against the United States, as "we Mexicans are too intelligent to attempt to spit upwards." Houdemon then took the general's private aircraft on a trip back to his home in France, and the two made plans to visit further after the war.[32]

While the rescue of his friend lifted the general's spirits, he soon learned of another opportunity to preserve part of Europe's cultural history. As the Third Army entered Czechoslovakia, American intelligence began to report rumors that the world-famous Lipizzaner stallions had fled the bombing of Vienna and were hidden somewhere in the area. These rumors were confirmed when the director of the Spanish Riding School, Alois Podhajsky, secretly contacted a major from the XX Corps and asked for help. Podhajsky told the Americans that he believed that advancing Soviets would capture the stallions and either send them back to Russia as trophies of war or slaughter them on the spot for their meat. His pleas for assistance were forwarded up the Third Army chain of command, first to XX Corps commanding officer General Walton Walker and then to Patton himself.[33]

To highlight the importance of the mission to the Americans, Podhajsky arranged for a short dressage show for Patton, Walker, and other American officers on May 7. Podhajsky had served in the Austrian Army, rising to the rank of colonel and, like Patton, had represented his nation as an Olympic athlete.[34] He and the horses were nervous because they believed that their fate depended on this performance. After a brilliant routine, Podhajsky rode directly to Patton and said, "We ask [for] your protection." The general stared at the Austrian colonel and replied, "Magnificent! These horses will be wards of the U.S. Army until they can be returned to the new Austria."[35] In a dramatic display of thanks, each of the riders slowly removed their hats and bowed to the general.

This relatively minor incident would be made into a 1963 Disney film, *The Miracle of the White Stallions*, starring Robert Taylor, and would be a much-lauded example of the general's cultural sensitivity.[36] Despite the favorable press, Patton had divided emotions regarding his role in rescuing the Lipizzans. In his diary, he wrote, "Originally the gyrations taught the horses were of military importance . . . for the purpose of letting the horse come down at the same time that the sword was swung, so as to give more force," but then confessed:

> It struck me as strange that, in the midst of a world war, some twenty young and middle-age men in great physical condition . . . had spent their entire time teaching a group of horses to wiggle their butts and raise their feet. . . . Much as I like horses, this seemed to me wasted energy. On the other hand, it is probably wrong to permit any highly developed art, no matter how fatuous, to perish from the earth. . . . To me the high-schooling of horses is certainly more interesting than either painting or music.[37]

Whatever his private feelings, Patton's understanding of history and culture, combined with his distrust of the Soviets, motivated him to save this fragment of Old Europe for future generations.[38]

Figure 12. Patton riding one of the Lipizzaner stallions he helped save during the final days of World War II in Europe. Courtesy the General George Patton Museum of Leadership, Fort Knox, Kentucky.

Patton was able to prevent these horses from falling into Soviet hands, yet he was unable to convince the Allied High Command to allow him to capture Prague in the war's final days. The general took a particular interest in the city because it was the last major landmark in his operational area and because he had received radio communications from the Czech resistance fighters begging for assistance. Sensing a final opportunity to be a hero, he pleaded with General Bradley on May 5, "For God's sake, Brad, those patriots in the city need our help we have no time to lose." Patton even suggested a ploy to absolve Bradley from responsibility by pretending to be out of contact until his forces had captured the city and then presenting the capture as a fait accompli (as he had done with Trier several months before), but this plan was quickly rejected by Bradley.[39]

While Patton ultimately obeyed his orders and stopped his troops short of the city, the failure of the Western Allies to come to the aid of the Czech resistance led to four additional days of bloody fighting and countless deaths before the German Army finally evacuated from the city on May 9. During this period, the Soviet Army held back their forces and allowed the Nazis to exact a terrifying toll on Czech insurgents and civilians. Patton witnessed this and took a bitter view of the decision in his diary: "It seems to me that as great a nation as America is, it should let other people worry about complications. . . . I would like to go to the line of the Moldau River and tell the Russians that is where I intend to stop."[40]

The Uneasy Peace

Patton's postwar troubles began the day before the war in Europe officially ended. During a May 8 press conference, reporters questioned the general regarding Allied occupation policy, stories of captured Nazi gold, and the terms of the German surrender. He inadvertently created a scandal when he was asked, "Are SS troops to be handled any differently [than other German prisoners of war]?" Without fully considering the implications of his answer, he replied: "No. SS means no more in Germany than being a Democrat in America—that is not to be quoted. I mean by that that initially the SS people were special sons-of-bitches, but as the war progressed, they ran out of sons-of-bitches and then they put anybody in there. Some of the top SS men will be treated as criminals, but there is no reason for trying someone who was drafted into this outfit."[41] While Patton was technically correct about the historical evolution of the SS from an elite all-volunteer group to a conscript force, he missed the point and clearly did not comprehend the severity of these statements.[42] These ill-considered remarks were the first of many that would follow in the coming months and severely damage the general's reputation.

World War II in Europe ended on May 9, 1945. General George S. Patton Jr. stood at the pinnacle of his career, yet he seemed to lack a purpose now that the fighting in Europe was finished. He described himself to his staff as "lower than . . . [a] whale's arse" and openly talked about his desire to fight in China.[43] This lack of purpose would set into motion a series of events that would ultimately disgrace the general and cause him to lose command of his beloved Third Army. In a letter to Beatrice, Patton was reflective, noting, "Two and a half years ago to day [sic] we landed in Africa and now it is all over." Patton described what he hoped was a temporary assignment to Bavaria: "We will move . . . near Munich soon and take up governing of this part of Germany. I hope I don't stay there long. I want to go home for a while on my way to China."[44]

Although he had been promised a combat command in the Pacific theater by President Roosevelt, his hopes for a reassignment faded after the president's death on April 12, 1945. Without the blessing of FDR, Patton knew his transfer would likely be blocked by General Douglas MacArthur, who jealously protected his reputation and did not wish to share his glory with another high-profile general. Although Patton realized his efforts to obtain a Pacific command were probably in vain, he had been lobbying friends, family, and his chain of command for a transfer for several months and clung to this slim hope for more action.

In addition to wanting to see further action, Patton desired a transfer to the Pacific because he dreaded the herculean task of rebuilding a war-torn Germany. He detested politics and knew that he was ill-suited for the job of governing Bavaria and had fundamental reservations about the denazification mission. On the broadest level, he believed that the Allied time frame for achieving their goals was unrealistic. In his own family, he had witnessed the romanticism for the Confederacy and understood that memories of the Nazi regime would endure for generations. He believed that Abraham Lincoln's plan to rebuild the South after the Civil War was the ideal model for building peace, not a harsh and punitive settlement like that enacted by the Radical Republicans. To forget this lesson of history would make it harder to eradicate sympathy for the Nazi regime and build a sustainable and lasting peace in Europe.[45]

On a more pragmatic level, Patton feared that the American efforts, although well intended, risked creating an international power vacuum.[46] He had observed in the American withdrawal from global politics after World

War I, watching the US Army shrink to a pitiful size and state of readiness during the interwar period.[47] Like many others, this had a profound impact on Patton's view of geopolitics, and he concluded that the rise of Hitler was a direct consequence of American isolationism. In this moment of triumph, it would be dangerous to forget these lessons of history and waste the sacrifices of his brave men by allowing the Soviets to dominate the postwar peace.

For Patton, the United States faced two choices: retreat from Central Europe and accept Soviet domination by default or maintain a military presence strong enough to deter communist aggression. The choice seemed obvious—stand up to the Soviet Union at all costs. This would require a significant military and financial commitment to Europe and would necessitate at least partially rehabilitating the defeated German foe. These views would eventually gain broad support and form the basis of the strategy of containment, but they were unwelcome and potentially dangerous in 1945.

Forced Celebration with the Russian Allies

Despite his dislike of the Soviets, Patton was obligated to celebrate Germany's defeat with the Eastern allies on numerous occasions in the weeks following the end of the war. Patton put on a happy public face for these meetings, but his actions behind the scenes indicated a clear animosity and distrust of the Soviets. Prior to each of these meetings, Patton and his staff were mindful not to display fancy pistols or mementos, as Soviet officers would invariably ask to trade them for weapons and medals of inferior quality.[48] Similarly, he knew of the Russian proclivity to drink to excess and devised a scheme to avoid undue inebriation and reverse the tables on their allies. To avoid intoxication, Patton and his staff chose to water down their whiskey and to drink copious amounts of mineral oil prior to their meetings.[49] The result was that he and his men remained sober, whereas according to his diary entry of May 12, "I unquestionably drank the Russian commander under the table and walked out under my own steam. We are going to pay back a call on the 14th prior to that date I will drink quite a lot of mineral oil, as they will unquestionably try to get us drunk."[50] In a letter to his wife on May 13, Patton recounted the incident, but added his personal view that "[the Russians] are a scurvy race and simply savages. We could beat [the] hell out of them."[51]

Two days later when Patton and his staff were the guests of the Russians, they again made good on their plans to avoid drunkenness. The general reiterated his dislike of his Soviet hosts in his diary, noting, "They certainly put on a tremendous show," and highlighted their underlying harshness: "I have never in any army at any time, including the German Imperial Army of 1912, seen as severe discipline as exists in the Russian army. The officers with few exceptions give the appearance of recently civilized Mongolian bandits. The men passed in review with a very good imitation of the goose step. They give me the impression of something that is to be feared in future world political reorganization."[52]

Third Army did experience some excitement, though, as Yugoslav communist leader Marshal Josip Tito's forces continued to wage internal conflicts along the Allies' southeastern flank.[53] While Patton correctly predicted that these actions would not provoke a broader war, he had to guard against the possibility that Tito was intentionally creating a distraction for the Western Allies as a prelude to a Soviet invasion of Western Germany. In a May 18 diary entry, he noted, "The situation should clarify itself within a few days. . . . In my opinion, the American Army as it now exists could beat the Russians with the greatest ease, because while the Russians have good infantry, they are lacking in artillery, air, tanks, and in the knowledge of the use of combined arms; whereas we excel in all three of these. . . . I believe that by taking a strong attitude, the Russians will back down. So far we have yielded too much to their Mongolian nature."[54] Sensing that this was simply a test of American resolve, Patton and his staff acted carefully not to provoke Tito or the Russians, and the crisis quickly subsided.[55]

While Patton was showered with accolades and temporarily resided in the lavish villa of the former Nazi publisher Max Amann, he seemed more focused on obtaining a transfer to the Pacific than enjoying the laurels of victory or managing Bavaria.[56] He wrote his friend Lieutenant General Robert Eichelberger, now preparing for the invasion of Japan as commander of the US Eighth Army, "You have certainly been doing a great job, and I should think by now you practically have webbed feet. In my limited experience with amphibious attacks, I found them the most dangerous form of sport yet devised. I would like nothing better than to have a chance of fighting somewhere in the East against the Japanese. If I should be so fortunate, I am going to sit at your feet and learn how to do it." The general revisited his desire for a transfer in June 2 letters to Generals Geoffrey Keyes and Thomas Handy. He wrote to Handy, "I am naturally somewhat interested in my own future and hate to see all these other Armies going to the Pacific and me staying here. I am not asking any favors, but I am curious to know the reason, so if it is a proper question please tell me."[57]

A Final Trip Home

Although Patton was unable to secure his transfer to the Pacific, he was able to contribute to the war effort as a keynote speaker at a series of war-bond rallies in the United States. The general appreciated the opportunity to escape the drudgery of his occupation duties, and the adoring crowds that greeted him soothed his ego. On June 4, in his adopted hometown of Boston, Patton traveled along a twenty-five-mile parade route, where he was greeted by an estimated one million people. In front of approximately twenty thousand people at Boston's Hatch Shell, he inadvertently created a controversy when he implied that men killed in action were not necessarily heroes. The general's poorly chosen words reflected his genuine warrior mentality, yet they created an unintended controversy at a time when he needed to show discretion. Patton's old friend and secretary of war Henry Stimson publicly defended the general, and despite unflattering newspaper editorials and letters of complaints from relatives of fallen veterans, the controversy quickly blew over.

Patton continued his tour of the United States with stops in Hamilton, Massachusetts; Denver; Los Angeles; Fort Riley, Kansas; and Washington, DC. While his fiery speech in front of one hundred thousand spectators at the Los Angeles Coliseum made headlines, his more private visit to Walter Reed Hospital in Washington, DC, was far more revealing of his mental state. Patton had defiantly played the role of a conquering hero in front of crowds, yet he was reduced to tears when he visited the double-amputation ward where his daughter Ellen worked as a volunteer. Unable to control his emotions, he candidly told these men, "God damn it, if I had been a better general, most of you wouldn't be here."[58]

While visiting his daughters in Washington, Patton also had a strange premonition of death. When Beatrice stepped out of the room, he matter-of-factly told them, "Well goodbye girls. I won't be seeing you again. Take care of Georgie [Patton's son]. I'll be seeing your mother, but I won't be seeing you." When he was reminded that the war in Europe was over, Patton persisted: "No I mean it. I have a feeling that my luck has run out at last."[59] This prediction would prove eerily true—Patton would not see his daughters again after he departed Washington, but he would see Beatrice as she rushed to visit him as he clung to life after an unlikely traffic accident.

During his time in the nation's capital, Patton finally received word regarding his long-anticipated transfer to the Pacific. While visiting the newly constructed Pentagon, he was informed that his only paths to a command in

Asia were if China opened a major port to bring additional supplies into the theater or if General Douglas MacArthur was killed or incapacitated. He recognized that both of these contingencies were unlikely and that his dreams of glory in Asia were effectively finished, but he still clung to a desperate hope that he would fight in the Pacific war, writing to his friend Colonel Charles Odom, "As you know, I was disappointed in not going to the Orient, but I believe that my luck or destiny, or whatever it is, will get me there if there is need for my services. Personally, I do not concur with the rumors current in Washington that the Japs are about to quit. I certainly hope they don't because I think they should be utterly destroyed."[60]

An Uneasy Return to Europe

When Patton returned to Bavaria in July, he was again struck by the enormity of the task at hand and depressed by his inability to utilize his talents as a warrior. In what was to be his final fitness report, dated July 5, 1945, Patton's dedication as a fighter was confirmed by his commanding officer, Omar Bradley. Bradley rated his fighting abilities as "Superior," ranking him first out of ten generals under his authority and noting that Patton was "colorful, courageous, energetic, pleasing personality, impetuous. Possesses high degree of leadership, bold in operations, has fine sense of feeling of enemy and own capabilities. An outstanding combat leader." Despite these accolades, Bradley ranked Patton only fifth out of ten generals at his seniority level in "experience for all around duty," a clear indication that he recognized his old friend's limitations and liabilities off the battlefield.[61]

Patton watched in nervous anticipation as the top Allied leaders convened for the Potsdam Conference from July 17 to August 2, 1945. The purpose of the meeting was to map out a postwar order for Europe and to ensure Soviet cooperation in the ongoing war with Japan. While the general was not a participant in the Potsdam negations, he traveled to the Berlin suburb and met with old friends such as George Marshall and Henry "Harry" Stimson. He was troubled by what he believed to be the Western Allies' failure to acknowledge and adapt to the Soviet threat. As he wrote Beatrice, "At Potsdam I was just a visitor but later had long talks with George and Harry. Hap Arnold is the only one who understands the Mongols except me. But the rest are waking up."[62]

The general invited controversy while at Potsdam when his off-the-cuff remarks to Undersecretary of War Robert Patterson were overheard by reporters and printed. Patton ranted: "Let's keep our boots polished, bayonets

Figure 13. *Left to right*: Major General Floyd Parks, US commanding general, Berlin area; General George S. Patton Jr., commanding general, US Third Army; Colonel W. H. Kyle, aide to Secretary of War Stimson; J. J. McCloy, assistant secretary of war; H. H. Bundy; and Secretary of War Henry Stimson. Reviewing the 2nd Armored Division in Berlin during the Potsdam Conference. National Archives.

sharpened, and present a picture of force and strength to these people [the Soviets]. This is the only language they understand and respect. If you fail to do this, then I would like to say to you that we have had a victory over the Germans and have disarmed them, but have lost the war."[63] While Patton firmly believed that the rapid demobilization and redeployment from Europe was a repeat of the mistakes made by US policy makers after World War I, he was clearly out of step with the foreign policy elite. Fortunately, these comments were quickly forgotten and, for the moment, did not impact the general's career.

Patton further elaborated his thoughts in a July 21 letter to Beatrice:

Drove to Potsdam and saw the palace you, Nita, my self [*sic*], and the family visited in 1912. . . . [A]ll the furniture and rugs have been taken by the Mongols. . . . The Mongols are a bad lot. . . . Berlin gave me the blues. We have destroyed what could have been a good race and we [are] about to replace them with Mongolian savages. And all Europe will be communist. It's said that for the first week after they took it [Berlin] all women who ran were shot and those who did not were raped. I could have taken it had I been allowed. Harry looks tired. . . . George [Marshall] was most friendly, almost gushing. I also saw the President [Truman] who was nice.[64]

Patton reiterated these concerns in two other letters also dated July 21, 1945. To his sister, Nita, he wrote, "I am very much afraid that Europe is going to go Bolshevik, which, if it does, may eventually spread to our country."[65] On the same day, he wrote to Codman, "One cannot help but feel that Berlin marks the final epitaph of what should have been a great race. I really do not see how they can recover, particularly in view of the activities of some of our Allies, and I am not at all sure that we are not stepping out of the frying pan into the fire by concurring in what is going on. However, this is a personal opinion which probably nobody else shares." On August 6, he reflected on the lessons of history and predicted, "If ever there was a war breeder, it is Europe today. Russia is just like the French Republic in 1870. Germany is out. The Checks [sic] hate every one. The French are communistic. The British fools. And we, God knows."[66]

On a more tactical level, he also believed that the combat experience of the Allies would also soon be forgotten, as he confided to his diary on August 8:

Having studied war since I was about sixteen years old, I have only come across some twelve books which deal with fighting, although there are many hundreds which deal with war. This is because the people who fight either are killed or are inarticulate. . . . Of course, the horrid thought obdurate itself that, in spite of my efforts—which will probably be filed and forgotten—the tactics of the next war will be written by someone who never fought and who acquired his knowledge by a meticulous study of the regulations of this and the last World War, none of which were ever put into practice in battle. . . . In this war we were also unfortunate in that our high command in the main consisted of staff officers who, like Marshall, Eisenhower, and McNarney, had practically never exercised command.[67]

Patton continued his entry with criticisms of what he believed to be the myopic Allied denazification policies: "Under our rules, which demand total denazification of Germany, we have to remove everyone who has ever expressed himself in any way as a Nazi or has paid party dues. It is very evident that anybody who was in business, irrespective of his real sentiments, had to say he was a Nazi and pay dues. The only young people who were not Nazis came out of the internment camps and are therefore either Jews or

Communists. We are certainly in a hard position as far as procuring civil servants is concerned."[68] These private musings reveal a man deeply conflicted about his role in the Allied occupation of Europe, tortured by a belief that history was tragically repeating itself, uncertain regarding his own future, yet still clinging to the slim hope of reassignment.

When news reached Europe of the unconditional Japanese surrender, Patton was one of the few people who regretted the end of the war, writing to Beatrice on August 10:

> Well the war is over. We just heard that Japan had quit. Now the horrors of peace, pacifism, and unions will have unlimited sway. I wish I were young enough to fight in the next one . . . killing Mongols. I suppose poor George [his son] is all broken up. I would be in his case. Tell him that if I am here in June I will get a special dispensation and have you and he over for ten days and we will drive all over the campaigns. It would be fun. . . . Last time a war stopped I wrote a poem. . . . Now I feel too low. It is hell to be old and passé and know it.[69]

Patton expanded on these points in his diary entry on the same day, noting, "Another war has ended and with it my usefulness to the world. It is for me personally a very sad thought. Now all that is left to do is to sit around and await the arrival of the undertaker and post-humous [*sic*] immortality."[70]

The euphoria surrounding the atomic bombs also deepened Patton's sense of gloom, as he worried that policy makers would draw the wrong conclusions about the value of the American nuclear monopoly:

> The use of the atomic bomb against Japan was most unfortunate because it gives a lot of vocal but ill-informed people—mostly fascists, communists, and s.o.b.'s assorted—an opportunity to state that the Army, Navy, and Air Forces are no longer necessary as this bomb will either prevent war or destroy the human race. Actually the bomb is no more revolutionary than the first throwing-stick or javelin or the first cannon or the first submarine. It is simply, as I have often written, a new instrument added to the orchestra of death which is war.[71]

For the remaining months of his life, Patton would reiterate his belief that atomic weapons had altered little regarding the actual conduct of war or politics, arguing that the United States should not succumb to the temptation of cutting their military or relaxing their guard on the assumption that world politics had been transformed. While these comments convinced many of his contemporaries that Patton was out of touch with the times, his views were ultimately proved correct, as the American military suffered from unpreparedness and atrophy in its conventional forces just five years later, with the outbreak of the Korean War.[72]

Patton continued his diary entry on a more upbeat note, attempting to focus on and explain the ongoing task of governing Bavaria:

> Fortunately, I also have to occupy myself with the de-Nazification and government of Bavaria. . . . I have arranged to have wood cut by the Germans and by prisoners of war so that all the cities of Bavaria will have sufficient wood to heat at least one room for every family. This project is proceeding quite well except in the case of the Displaced Persons who are too worthless to even cut wood to keep themselves warm. We have also started, by the use of German prisoner of war Signal personnel to restore German commercial telephone lines. In addition to this, we are working to re-establish railway, canal, and road communications—primarily as a means of redeploying our own troops.[73]

Bored by his administrative responsibilities, Patton busied himself with the task of inspecting approximately three divisions per week, prioritizing those who were returning to the United States. Patton described his self-imposed schedule of inspecting his troops in a letter to his top aide, Colonel Charles Codman, "I am more occupied than during combat, as I have to, or feel that I have to, visit all the divisions, inspect them administratively and tactically, and also again visit them when they leave, to say goodbye. The result is that I spend a great deal of time flying. . . . There is no probability, although there is always a possibility, of a flare-up on the continent."[74] Despite his love and admiration of his men, Patton's heart was no longer in this task he once so enjoyed. His speeches to the men were profane yet formulaic and clearly lacked the energy and focus that they once had. He felt as if he were trapped in a moment of history where he clearly saw the future and was powerless to act.

In an August 11, 1945, letter to Eisenhower, he again demonstrated that he was out of step with the Allied denazification efforts when he complained that "too many trained administrators were being removed and too many inexperienced and inefficient officials were being put into office." This problem was exacerbated by the policy of finding workers without Nazi affiliations because party membership had often been a prerequisite for the civil service, and thus, "it is no more possible for a man to be a civil servant in Germany and not have paid lip service to Naziism than for a man to be a postmaster in America and not have paid at least lip service to the Democratic Party or the Republican Party when it is in power."[75]

Rather than simply a moral distinction between good and evil, Patton saw the practical need to provide for the welfare of the millions of German civilians under his control. In a letter to Beatrice, he confided that his first priority was practical, not political: "I am raising the devil to get enough wood cut to keep the people from freezing this winter."[76] Despite his good intentions, Patton was unwittingly courting disaster.

Patton was so frustrated by the task of governing Bavaria that he even requested a transfer to the noncombat assignment of commandant of the Army War College. He argued that it would utilize his love of history while allowing him to pass on his experience and mentor a new generation of army officers. Despite the fact that this position would have better utilized the general's talents, he was denied this position, as it was technically beneath his rank. Patton vented his frustration in his diary: "In a letter from Beatrice today she stated that Gerow is to get the War College. This is too bad, as he was one of the leading mediocre corps commanders in Europe and only got the Fifteenth Army because he was General Eisenhower's personal friend. With the War College gone, there is nothing open to me so far as now seems available. However, things have looked gloomy before and something has always turned up."[77] Here, Patton was simply being petty and giving voice to his anger at the expense of his friend. In fact, he had enjoyed an excellent relationship with Leonard Gerow and had frequently praised the dedication and skill of his fellow warrior both in public and in his private writings.

Rebuilding Bavaria

Despite the personal misgivings of its commanding officer, the Third Army made significant initial progress in eradicating remnants of the Nazi regime. By mid-July all clergymen in the American-controlled zones had been screened for potential collaboration with the Nazis. Most Nazi street and building names had been changed and fascist memorials and monuments removed from public spaces. By early August, Nazi businessmen had been removed from most key posts, and the vast majority of telephone, telegraph, and radio workers had been checked for party affiliations. While the task of auditing financial institutions for illicit funds and removing Nazis from key government positions was only just beginning, Patton could take comfort in the words of Henry Stimson, that the American-controlled zones of

Germany had been "purged of Nazi membership or influence" by the early fall of 1945.[78]

On August 22, General Bedell Smith telephoned Patton's headquarters to congratulate Third Army on their progress denazifying Bavaria. Despite the official approval from Eisenhower's staff, trouble was brewing. That very same day, Patton's chief of staff, General Hobart Gay, issued an ambiguously worded memorandum regarding borderline cases where critical administrators with Nazi affiliations could be provided leniency. Aware of the potentially explosive ramifications of this message, General Eisenhower personally warned Patton in writing on the twenty-third of August that the goal of the Allies was the "obliteration" of fascism from Europe and that denazification was "a most delicate subject both here and at home" and that "our governmental representatives as well as newspapers have been quick to seize upon" any deviation from strict enforcement of denazification policies.[79] While Eisenhower's warning should have convinced Patton that he should act with care and dispatch regarding the purge of Nazis from the Bavarian government, he had other things on his mind and did not see the need to more carefully tailor his public messaging.

In private, Patton was already using his understanding of history to predict another war and unabashedly making the case that the former Soviet allies were the new enemy. In an August 23 letter to his close friend Colonel Hugh H. McGee, Patton outlined his desire to fight the Soviets:

> In my opinion and strictly for your private ear, we never had a better chance of producing another war than we have in Europe now. I have never seen so much vitriolic hatred, mistrust, and avarice as exists here today. Furthermore, as you know, a certain proportion of the people with whom we are dealing do not have Occidental minds [that is, the Soviets] which makes it even more difficult if not impossible to come to an understanding with them. I doubt if the top blows off very soon, but unless something very radical happens and happens within a reasonable time, the top will blow off, probably after we have redeployed our army.[80]

Patton's private comments are an interesting view into his priorities as well as his increasingly warped application of history. After the Japanese surrender, he appeared to be more willing to consider, at least in private, a war with the Soviets. To this end, maintaining an aggressive posture to deter the Soviets took precedence over strict denazification. This led to a doubly dangerous combination—Patton became increasingly willing to voice his anti-Soviet beliefs, while at the same he appeared to be neglecting his duties to eradicate the Nazi regime.

On August 26, Third Army's staff officially requested permission to release the lowest classification of Nazi Party members without trial and to stop further arrests of lower-ranking party members who had not been accused of specific crimes. Though the proposal was pragmatic, it was promptly rejected by Eisenhower. Patton saw Eisenhower at a meeting in Frankfurt the next day and recorded his thoughts in his diary: "There were a number of speeches by General Eisenhower and his various assistants, all of which were unrealistic and in every case the chief interest of the speaker was to say nothing which could be used against him. . . . What the Military Government is trying to do is undemocratic and follows practically Gestapo methods."[81]

Patton also disagreed with the so-called Morgenthau Plan to deindustrialize Germany and to return it to an agriculture-based economy.[82] For Patton, this was not only unwise but impossible: "It is patently impossible for Germany to be an agricultural state. First, because there is not enough in Germany for the country to feed itself on such a basis, and second, because if Germany has not purchasing power, we will not be able to sell our goods to her and, therefore, our markets will be very considerably restricted." Patton believed that Germany should be rebuilt, but his views were considerably ahead of their time and fell on unsympathetic ears. "I stated that in my opinion Germany was so completely blacked out that so far as military resistance was concerned they were not a menace and that what we had to look out for was Russia. This caused considerable furore [sic]."[83]

Chafing under the denazification policies, Patton wrote Beatrice on August 31, reiterating his views that the Germans were preferable to the Russians, even suggesting that he would quit the army if he could not obtain a command that better suited his talents. While Patton was obviously displeased with the job of administering Bavaria, it is important not to infer too much from this letter. In his typical fashion, he was privately voicing his frustrations and had no immediate plans to resign in protest over Allied policies. However, his letter to Beatrice on September 2 is similarly bitter, noting, "I had never heard that we fought to de-nazify Germany—live and learn. What we are doing is to utterly destroy the only semi-modern state in Europe so that Russia can swallow it whole."[84]

On September 6, Patton traveled to Berlin to represent General Eisenhower at an Allied military parade. What should have been a simple affair to highlight Allied unity verged on disaster, as Patton appeared determined to insult Soviet marshal Georgy Zhukov. An unabashed Patton described the encounter in a September 11 letter to his wife:

> On the 7th there was an inter-allied review to celebrate V-J day. U.S., English, French, and Russians each had 1,000 men and 50 vehicles in the parade. Marshal Sukov [*sic*] was senior, I was next. He was in full dress uniform much like comic opera and covered with medals. He is short, rather fat and has a prehensile chin like an ape but good blue eyes. . . . Our troops looked the best, the Russians next. The R's [Russians] had a lot of new heavy tanks of which they were very proud. The Marshal asked me how I liked them. I said I did not, and we had quite an argument. Apparently I was the first person ever to disagree with him.[85]

As part of this argument, Marshal Zhukov said, "My dear General Patton, you see that tank, it carries a cannon which can throw a shell seven miles." Unimpressed, Patton retorted, "Well, my dear Marshall Zhukov, let me tell you this, if any of my gunners started firing at your people before they had closed to less than seven hundred yards I'd have them court-marshaled for cowardice." This ended the terse exchange, and, according to Patton's aide Major Van S. Merle-Smith, "It was the first time I saw a Russian commander stunned into silence."[86]

Figure 14. Patton and Zhukov share a tense moment at a military parade in Berlin. Courtesy National Archives.

Trouble with Eisenhower

While this minor international incident was quickly forgotten, a much larger and ultimately damaging scandal was brewing for Patton: his continued refusal to fully implement Allied denazification policies regarding former Nazi Party members. General Eisenhower was particularly sensitive to these political issues, and on September 11 he penned a private letter to his old friend, warning him of the need to fully comply with these policies:

> As you know, I have announced a firm policy of uprooting the whole Nazi organization regardless of the fact that we may sometimes suffer from local administrative inefficiency. Reduced to its fundamentals, the United States entered this war as a foe of Naziism; victory is not complete until we have eliminated from positions of responsibility, and in appropriate cases properly punished, every active adherent to the Nazi party.
>
> I know that certain field commanders have felt that some modifications to this policy should be made. That question has long since been decided. We will not compromise with Naziism in any way.
>
> I wish you would make sure that all your subordinate commanders realize that the discussional stage of this question is long past and any expressed opposition to the faithful execution of this order cannot be regarded leniently by me. I expect just as loyal service in execution of this and other policies applying to the German occupation as I received during the war.[87]

Eisenhower's letter is unusual for two reasons. First, he had to reiterate that fascism was the motivating factor for the war and that the Nazis must be destroyed. Second, Eisenhower felt compelled to remind Patton, who had served in the military for more than four decades, of the chain of command and the consequences of insubordination. Had Eisenhower doubted that Patton lacked an understanding of either of these two points, it would have been entirely appropriate to relieve Patton of command.

While it is impossible to know exactly what Eisenhower was thinking when he wrote this letter, it is worth noting that Patton and Eisenhower had been close friends for three decades, and Eisenhower continued to have mutual respect for his friend's abilities, despite the recent strains on their relationship.[88] Like he had done so many times in the past, it appeared as if Eisenhower wanted to retain Patton's skills as a combat commander and was willing to provide yet another opportunity for him to moderate his behavior. Despite his admiration for his friend, Eisenhower was a keen political operator. He did not want to appear soft on the defeated Nazis, but recognized that punishing Patton would also incur significant political costs. This letter was clear and unequivocal, yet it allowed Patton the opportunity to correct his actions and remain in his commanding officer's good graces.

Despite Eisenhower's best efforts, Patton seemed unwilling to change his behavior. The stage was set between a final showdown between these two old friends, one that would permanently damage their friendship and tarnish Patton's legacy. Acting proactively on the denazification issue, Eisenhower began to personally inspect his subordinate's progress. The two met on September 15 and spent the next few days together. For a brief period, it was like the good old days. Patton noted in his diary on September 16:

> [Eisenhower] arrived at 2000, and we had supper and spent the evening talking over the situation. In fact we talked until 3.00 o'clock in the morning. . . . He asked me, in view of that situation, what I wanted to do. . . . I stated there were only two jobs in the United States which I felt I could take. One was President of the Army War College, which I believed was taken, and the other was Commanding General of the Army Ground Forces. . . . Therefore, at the present writing, it would seem the only thing I can do is to go home and retire. However, Eisenhower asked me to remain at least three months after he left so as to get things running quietly. I tentatively agreed to this.[89]

The next day, Patton and Eisenhower drove to Munich to inspect some camps for displaced persons. While the camp for refugees of Baltic descent was "extremely clean in all respects," the camp for Jewish displaced persons was "in a bad state of repair when we arrived."[90] Both generals were appalled by the overcrowding and existence of human waste throughout the camp. To relieve the overcrowding, Eisenhower ordered that the German residents living in the surrounding houses be evicted so the camp could be expanded. Eisenhower was furious at the condition of the Jewish camp, yet he chose to retain Patton, trusting that he would act on his orders and quickly remedy the situation. Patton acted rapidly to clean up this camp, yet the fact that he was unaware of this disgusting situation in his own area of responsibility indicates that he was careless to the point of negligence in his management of Bavaria.

The Fatal Press Conferences

Patton exacerbated an already tense situation on September 22. After the routine Saturday-morning briefing, he appeared frustrated and tried to leave, yet he agreed to answer a few questions from the assembled press.

No notes were officially made regarding Patton's comments, but according to General Gay, his chief of staff, the general insisted that denazification was proceeding as fast as possible and that no known Nazi currently held a position in the German government. Patton then made a critical mistake by stating that in many ways the Nazis were little different from the Republicans and Democrats and that he was trying to restore the German economy as quickly as possible.

While these comments were little different from many of the other statements he had made in private, he lost his composure in a tense public setting. Hungry for controversy, the press seized upon his comments and were quick to portray these statements in an unflattering light. Patton noted this changed relationship with the press in his diary:

> Always had them on my side. Today there was an very apparent hostility. . . . They were evidently quite shocked when I told them I would kick nobody out without the successful proof of guilt before a court of law. . . . I am inclined to think that I made a great mistake in serving them [the American people] for nearly forty years, although I had a very good time doing it. . . . [T]he fall of Germany for Communism will write the epitaph of Democracy in the United States. The more I see of people I regret that I survived the war.[91]

Controversy erupted when the *New York Times* printed their version of Patton's remarks at length, quoting him as saying:

> The Nazi thing is just like a Democrat-Republican election fight. To get things done in Bavaria, after the complete disorganization and disruption of four years of war, we had to compromise with the devil a little. We had no alternative but to turn to the people who knew what to do and how to do it. . . . I don't like the Nazis any more than you do. I despise them. In the past three years I did my utmost to kill as many of them as possible. Now we are using them for lack of anyone better until we can get better people.[92]

This quote was accompanied by the news that Patton had released more than eight thousand Nazi Party members and that several leaders of the newly installed Bavarian government, most notably Friedrich Schaeffer, the head of the government, had ties to the Nazi Party.

While initially buried in the back pages of the *Times*, the story quickly took on a life of its own, and Patton's career was again threatened by a scandal of his own making. The public perception was that the general was not complying with Allied policies or was at best halfhearted in his enforcement efforts. Perhaps even more damaging was the suggestion by some newspaper editorials that he was unfit to command because he fundamentally misunderstood the moral purpose behind the Allied war against Nazi Germany. While there is no evidence that he actually sympathized with the Nazis, he had clearly lost control of the message. His genuine efforts and successes in rebuilding Bavaria were overshadowed by the controversial statements, and despite his good intentions he was in serious trouble.

Eisenhower telegraphed to demand an explanation, issuing orders to halt the practice of releasing Nazis until further notice. Patton claimed that he had been misquoted, but agreed to halt further prisoner releases. However, he stopped short of ordering the rearrests of lower-level Nazis who had already been granted their freedom. Eisenhower accepted his old friend's claims that the issue was simply a misunderstanding, but demanded that he clarify his remarks with another press conference on September 25.

Patton began his press conference by reading a prepared statement designed to emphasize his support of Allied denazification policies and to avoid any potential misunderstanding. To this end, the prepared comments are worth excerpting at length:

> I am sorry that I haven't got anything exciting for you this afternoon. Owing to some difficulties which we sometimes incur, I am going to become extremely like most other generals and read a statement. . . . As the direct result of our last talk together, apparently some startling headlines appeared in the home paper. . . . [S]ome of these things alleged to have been said by me might possibly reflect on my commanding officer, General Eisenhower. That would be very unjust. His policy and orders exactly reflect the terms of the Potsdam Conference. . . . General Eisenhower reiterated these instructions in a personal letter to both District Commanders; that is, to both myself and General Keyes. . . . I am carrying out these directives with the same vigor and loyalty as I carried out those with resulted in the victories at Casablanca, El Guettar, Sicily, and here. I am convinced that as the result of my efforts I shall be just as successful here as I was in those other places. God knows, I was pretty successful. However, you must remember that results cannot be obtained overnight. . . . It will certainly take a reasonable amount of time to de-Nazify and reorganize our portion of Germany. Unquestionably when I made the comparison of so vile a thing as Nazism with political parties, I was unfortunate in the selection of analogies. The point I was and am trying to bring out is that in Germany practically all or at least a very large percentage of tradespeople, small businessmen, and

even professional men such as doctors and lawyers were beholden to the Nazi party, particularly for the patronage which permitted them to carry on their businesses and professions, and that therefore many of them had to give lip service, but lip service only, and I would extend this to mean paying dues was nothing but a form of black mail and holding their jobs. If we kick them out, all this bunch, we will so retard the reorganization of Bavaria . . . that we will certainly be guilty of the death by starvation or freezing of women, children, and old men this winter.[93]

Patton's well-intended statement was designed to calm tensions by clarifying his position and stating that he was acting in accordance with Eisenhower's orders. Furthermore, by reminding the audience of his significant military accomplishments, he was hoping that his ability as a warrior would again protect him against a scandal of his own making.

Had Patton simply ended his comments after reading this statement, he may have defused the controversy. However, when the press asked him for additional comments, he indicated that he would answer questions for seven minutes. When asked, "General, if you recall, what was the direct quote about political parties?" Patton reopened the controversy by attempting to answer the question as forthrightly as possible, stating, "I said that Naziism might well be compared to any of the parties at home, either Republican or Democrat. I also referred to my cousin who remained a postmaster for years by judicious flip-flops, and I don't consider him a son of a gun either."[94]

Then Patton exacerbated this situation by denying that he had any specific knowledge of former Nazis in the Bavarian government, suggesting that if he *did*, they would be treated according to the American principle of assuming innocence until proved guilty. When asked directly about the head of the Bavarian government, Friedrich Schaeffer, Patton badly mishandled the questions, stating, "He was in an internment camp *and* so far as I know has not been proved to be a Nazi. . . . Schaeffer was, as a matter of fact, picked out before I got here. So far, we have not definitely proved he is a misfit, but we have no brief for him or against him. What we are trying to do is to provide a governing body for Bavaria."[95] Although pragmatic, Patton's legalistic and defensive comments did not help him and instead made it appear that he was attempting to hide Nazis behind the shroud of due process under law. While the prepared comments at Patton's press conference could have aided the besieged general's cause, his off-the-cuff answers to the reporters' questions certainly did not.

The same evening, Patton received a telegram from Eisenhower:

> Press reports make it appear that you and I are of opposite conviction concerning method to be pursued in denazification of Germany and that in spite of repeated orders, you have given public expression to your own views on the matter. I simply cannot believe that these reports are accurate, and [General Bedell] Smith tells me that in a telephone conversation with you he understood, in spite of the poor connection, that you stated that you were incorrectly quoted. He tells me that you are holding a press conference immediately to straighten out the matter. I hope that you are completely successful because this question is a very serious one. . . . Please take the first opportunity to fly up here on a good weather day and see me for an hour.[96]

Patton sensed that his career was in serious jeopardy, as reflected by his diary entry on September 25: "After supper I received a telegram from General Eisenhower stating that I had been accused of differing with him in the conduct of the de-Nazification of Bavaria and asking me to fly up . . . whenever the weather permitted. It may well be that the Philistines have at last got me. On the other hand, every time I have been in serious trouble or thought I was, it has turned out to my advantage. At last, this time I do not have to go on the defensive."[97] In a letter to his aide Charles Codman, who was with his ailing wife in Boston, Patton candidly noted, "I am again at one of those critical periods when I may be sent home in a hurry at any moment. You certainly aren't missing much by not being here."[98]

The best hope for Patton was that a war would break out soon and that his abilities as a field commander would once again make him indispensable. He wrote to Beatrice of this hope and made reference to an attached article about recent tensions: "If the Devil and Mars had gotten together to plan for an early and certain resumption of hostilities, they could not have produced a finer document than the attached. As always among allies, it is a compromise but Russia did the least compromising since Russia knows what she wants (world conquest) and the rest don't. George [Patton's son who missed World War II as a cadet at West Point] need not worry about missing a war. The next is on the way."[99]

Still upset by the brewing controversy, Patton wrote Beatrice again on September 26: "It may be that I will get home as soon as this [letter]. You are even now probably being bothered by reporters." Shifting blame for the incident, Patton continued, "The whole thing is a deliberate mis-quote with the intent of getting me in trouble because I am not pink."[100] Because of bad weather and a previously planned hunting trip, Patton did not travel to see Eisenhower on September 26.

In an attempt to calm the press, Eisenhower ordered his deputy General Bedell Smith to further clarify Patton's remarks. Smith told the press that "General Patton will carry out his orders" and assured them that "Patton will be up here sometime next week to give an account of his stewardship with General Eisenhower."[101] While Smith's comments were carefully worded, they were intended primarily to help protect his boss, not Patton. For his part, Patton was doing his best to ignore the issue; his diary entry of September 27 focused primarily on his hunting expedition, noting simply, "The assault on me in the papers is still going on but is losing its steam."[102] In fact, he could not have been more wrong, and the continued controversy in the press and the perception that he was not complying with Allied policy had severely jeopardized his career.

Patton's Relief and Transfer

Continued bad weather made flying impossible, so Patton rode seven and a half hours to see Eisenhower on September 28. Sensing the need to be humble and flatter his commanding officer, the embattled general chose to dress in his ordinary uniform and left his pistols and swagger stick behind. He entered the former I. G. Farben Building for what he expected to be simply a tongue-lashing. Eisenhower flashed his trademark grin as a means of easing the tension, yet he appeared tired and it was apparent that this situation had weighed heavily on his mind.[103]

Despite Eisenhower's attempts at formality and kindness, it was clear that he was going to relieve his old friend. "Ike was quite friendly and gave me a long oration on my inability to keep my mouth shut." Patton countered that he had been misquoted and suggested that "perhaps my greatest virtue and my greatest fault was my honesty and lack of ulterior motive. Ike said my greatest virtue and my greatest fault was my audacity." Eisenhower continued by saying, "He was certainly at fault as much as I was in that, knowing my strength and weakness as he did, he should not have put me in as Military Governor." Patton attempted to argue that Bavaria was the best-run sector in occupied Germany, but he was finished as commander of the Third Army. According to Patton's diary:

> Ike said that had he possessed any adequate command for me at the time, he would have given it to me rather than have me act as Military Governor

of Bavaria. He then was apparently struck with an idea, which was probably acting on his part, that since Gerow was going home, it might be a good idea to transfer me to the Fifteenth Army whose mission it is to write the account of the history and tactics of the war. . . . I told him in my opinion I should simply be relieved, but he said he did not intend to do that and had had no pressure from the States to that effect. I said then I thought I should be allowed to continue the command of the Third Army and the government of Bavaria. He said he felt on mature thought I should certainly continue for ten days or two weeks and then he thought I should take command of the Fifteenth Army.[104]

Despite Eisenhower's diplomatic nature, the message was very clear: Patton was going to be relieved from command of Third Army and transferred to the Fifteenth. This was a tense moment for both men that would mark the end of their close friendship.

Patton noted the changed relationship in his diary: "Ike was apparently very anxious that he should not seem too friendly with me because almost the first word he said was, 'If you are spending the night, of course you will stay with me, but since I feel you should get back to Bad Tölz as rapidly as possible, I have my train set up to take you, and it leaves at 7.00 o'clock.' It was then 6.30. I took the train."[105] The famously stoic Eisenhower was also deeply hurt. According to his confidante and rumored mistress, Kay Summersby, Ike "aged ten years in reaching the decision." Eisenhower confessed his feelings in a letter to his wife, Mamie: "That man [Patton] is yet going to drive me to drink. He misses more good opportunities to keep his mouth shut than almost anyone I ever knew."[106] Patton noted simply, "During the whole of the proceeding interview Eisenhower was more excited than I have ever seen him."[107]

Patton was similarly distraught by his transfer. He loved Third Army and, despite the difficulties of rebuilding an occupied Germany, wished to remain in his current position. The Fifteenth Army seemed to be a demotion for the general. However, in his more candid moments, he realized that his transfer provided unique opportunities for engaging with history and avoiding further controversy. He described his internal conflict in the pages of his diary:

At the present moment I am of two minds. If I am kicked upstairs to the Fifteenth Army, should I accept or should I ask for relief and put in my resignation? By adopting the later course, I would save my self-respect at the expense of my reputation but, on the other hand, would become a martyr too soon. It is my belief that when the catchword "de-Nazification" has worn itself out and when people see it merely a form of stimulating Bolshevism, there will be a flop of the pendulum in the opposite direction.

When that occurs, I can state that I accepted the job with the Fifteenth Army because I was reluctant, in fact unwilling, to be a party to the destruction of Germany under the pretense of de-Nazification.[108]

Patton cast his transfer in a similar manner to his wife: "This august lady [the Fifteenth Army] . . . has the job of reviewing the strategy and tactics of the war to see how the former conformed to the unit plans and how the tactics changed. Were it not for the fact that it will be, so far as I am concerned, a kick up stairs [sic], I would like it much better than being a sort of executioner to the best race in Europe. Am I weak and a coward? Am I putting my posthumous reputation above my present honor? God how I wish I knew."[109]

On September 29, Eisenhower wrote Patton and officially informed him of his transfer to Fifteenth Army. Attempting to soften the blow and reassure his old friend, Eisenhower wrote: "As I have told you before, this change in no way reflects upon your loyalty, your administrative ability, nor does it indicate any lessening of my admiration for your soldierly qualifications. It results merely from my belief that your particular talents will be better employed in the new job and that the planned arrangement visualizes the best possible utilization of available personnel."[110] Patton could not accept that he was not the best general to command Third Army, yet took some satisfaction in the fact that his former subordinate Lucian Truscott was designated to replace him, noting, "I am sure [Truscott] will do as good a job as he can in an impossible situation."[111]

Over the next few days, Patton attempted to keep a low profile, avoiding both public attention and the duties of governing Bavaria, which had so vexed him. He did, however, remove the controversial Schaeffer on September 29 and did his best to ensure a smooth transition for General Truscott. During this period, Patton also sat for a now famous oil-painting portrait (reproduced on the cover of this book) and awarded his driver Master Sergeant John L. Mims a Silver Star for his years of faithful service prior to rotating home.[112]

In an attempt to make the most out of a bad situation, Patton wrote his old mentor General Thomas T. Handy on October 2, 1945, "From a personal standpoint the new assignment is more in keeping with my natural academic tendencies than is that of governing Bavaria, but I naturally regret being relieved, however graciously, under circumstances that will be detrimental to my reputation."[113] While still defiant, this note indicated that Patton was warming up to the idea of his new assignment and happy to be done with the tasks of administration and governance.

Although Eisenhower had planned to announce Patton's transfer on October 8 as a means of allowing the controversy to subside and saving face, the press got word of his decision, and controversy quickly ensued. Papers such as the *New York Daily News* ran stories suggesting that Patton's removal was part of a plot by Eisenhower and others to silence and disgrace the general. The *Daily News* even editorialized that he should "ASK A TRIAL" to clear his name, while the more sober-minded *New York Times* noted, "He was obviously in a post which he was unsuited by temperament, training or experience to fill. It was a mistake to suppose a free-swinging fighter could acquire overnight the capacities of a wise administrator. His removal by General Eisenhower was an acknowledgement of that mistake."[114]

Given this new wave of negative press, Eisenhower felt compelled to announce Patton's transfer sooner than planned. He called his old friend to inform him of this decision, to which Patton replied with a combination of resignation and gallows humor: "I could not see that it made any difference."[115] In private he was less gracious, claiming that "Eisenhower is scared to death" and that his transfer "will be beneficial to him." Despite his misgivings, the general stated that his "head is bloody but unbowed" and spent his time "helping Lucian [Truscott] to get the hang of the show. . . . I was terribly hurt for a few days but am normal again."[116]

Because of heavy rains, the change-of-command ceremony was moved from the parade ground to a gymnasium. At noon on October 7, 1945, Patton gave the following speech:

General Truscott, Officers, Men: All good things must come to an end. The best thing that has ever come to me thus far is the honor and privilege of having commanded Third Army.

The great successes we have achieved together have been due primarily to the fighting heart of America, but without the coordinating and supply activities of the General and Special Staffs, even American valor would have been impotent.

You officers and men here represent the fighting, administrative, and the supply elements of the Army. Please accept my heartfelt congratulations on your valor and devotion to duty, and my fervent gratitude for your unwavering loyalty.

When I said that all good things come to an end, I was referring to myself and not to you because you will find in General Truscott every characteristic which will inspire in you the same loyalty and devotion which you have so generously afforded me.

A man of General Truscott's achievements needs no introduction. His deeds speak for themselves. I know that you will not fail him.

Goodbye and God bless you.[117]

Patton then handed the Third Army flag to General Truscott, who made a short speech that he "could not hear as he was very emotional and shouted into the machine."[118] The band then played the Third Army March, and the two generals exited the gymnasium to the chorus of "For He's a Jolly Good Fellow." After cocktails, lunch, and more speeches, Truscott escorted Patton to a waiting train at 1430. The train promptly departed at 1500, taking Patton away from his beloved Third Army and to his new command.

As the train carried Patton through the rain, the famous general was at a personal and professional low point. Although good things had come to an end, he realized that this new assignment was an opportunity. Now it was his duty to do what he always loved: study history, write, and reflect on the enduring lessons of the ages. He would fight this last battle with his trademark tenacity and ultimately win an underappreciated victory.

· ·

NOTES

1. Michael Jones, *After Hitler: The Last Ten Days of World War II in Europe*, 53, 156–60.

2. Atkinson, *Guns at Last Light*, 617.

3. Ian Kershaw, *The End: The Defiance and Destruction of Hitler's Germany, 1944–1945*, 369–70; Yeide, *Fighting Patton*, 382.

4. Antony Beevor, *The Fall of Berlin, 1945*.

5. For example, see the April 5 letter to Beatrice. Family Papers, 1857–1979, George S. Patton Papers, Manuscript Division, Library of Congress, Washington, DC.

6. Duane Schultz, *Patton's Last Gamble: The Disastrous Raid on POW Camp Hammelburg in World War II*, 25. For additional support for the thesis that Patton felt a need to compete for fame and glory with MacArthur, see Allen, *Forward with Patton*, 192.

7. Schultz, *Patton's Last Gamble*, 35.

8. Schultz, *Patton's Last Gamble*, 8–23. In addition to these motivations, Patton biographer Duane Schultz also claims that Patton had been spoiled his entire life

and believed that the rules did not apply to him. This interpretation may help explain why the general chose to order the mission, despite the fact that it ignored military logic, was opposed by his subordinates, and was obviously self-serving.

9. Lewis Sorley, *Thunderbolt: General Creighton Abrams and the Army of His Times*, 92–93.

10. Codman, *Drive*, 270; Jordan, *Brothers, Rivals, Victory*, 495; Schultz, *Patton's Last Gamble*, 30–31, 41–42, 52, 104, 115.

11. Allen, *Forward with Patton*, 203.

12. Schultz, *Patton's Last Gamble*, 89–90, 107–9.

13. Richard Baron, Abe Baum, and Richard Goldhurst, *Raid! The Untold Story of Patton's Secret Mission*; D'Este, *Patton*, 714–17.

14. Schultz, *Patton's Last Gamble*, 164, 179.

15. The official casualty list contains nine killed in action and another sixteen "presumed dead" who were never found. Baron, Baum, and Goldhurst, *Raid!*; D'Este, *Patton*, 714–17.

16. Eisenhower quoted in Blumenson, *The Patton Papers*, 2:689.

17. D'Este, *Patton*, 717; Schultz, *Patton's Last Gamble*.

18. "History of the 90th Division in World War II," 78–79.

19. "History of the 90th Division," 78–79.

20. Ladislas Farago, *The Last Days of Patton*, 45.

21. "History of the 90th Division in World War II," 78–79.

22. Atkinson, *Guns at Last Light*, 587–88.

23. Codman, *Drive*, 281; D'Este, *Patton*, 719.

24. D'Este, *Patton*, 720.

25. Greg Bradsher, "Nazi Gold: The Merkers Mine Treasure."

26. Blumenson, *The Patton Papers*, 2:685.

27. Blumenson, *The Patton Papers*, 2:686, 688.

28. For a similar account of Patton and Eisenhower's visit to the camp and the impact it had on their desire to rapidly end the war, see Codman, *Drive*, 282–83.

29. Diaries, 1910–45, Patton Papers; Blumenson, *The Patton Papers*, 2:690.

30. Diaries, 1910–45, Patton Papers. For Codman's account, see Codman, *Drive*, 291.

31. Codman, *Drive*, 294. This comment from Codman is interesting, as it is one of the only examples of him uncritically recording one of Patton's claims of reincarnation.

32. Codman, *Drive*, 296–97.

33. D'Este, *Patton*, 742.

34. Letts, *Perfect Horse*, 1–11, 211–20, 234.

35. D'Este, *Patton*, 742.

36. Arthur Hiller, dir., *The Miracle of the White Stallions*.

37. Diaries, 1910–45, Patton Papers; Codman, *Drive*, 298–99.

38. Letts, *Perfect Horse*, 222, 266.

39. Jones, *After Hitler*, 160.

40. Diaries, 1910–45, Patton Papers; Jones, *After Hitler*, 160–61.

41. Blumenson, *The Patton Papers*, 2:700–701.

42. On the evolution of the SS, see George S. Stein, *The Waffen SS: Hitler's Elite Guard at War, 1939–1945*, esp. 137–96.

43. Codman, *Drive*, 301.

44. Blumenson, *The Patton Papers*, 2:699.

45. Blumenson and Hymel, *Patton*, 84.

46. Earl F. Ziemke, *The U.S. Army Occupation of Germany, 1944–1946*, 131–32.

47. Johnson, *Fast Tanks and Heavy Bombers*, 107–10.

48. Patton, *War as I Knew It*, 326. For his part, Patton was awarded the Order of Kutuzov (First Class), a fancy decoration that was anything but inferior quality. In a humorous episode, his aide Charles Codman left his medal on the dinner table after their meeting with the Soviet generals. It was quickly returned to Patton, but not before Codman crossed Soviet lines to retrieve his award. After much confusion, Codman returned with a replacement, only to find that the Soviets already returned the general's original award. Patton remarked, "Oh good. That will make a spare set." Codman, *Drive*, 306–15 (quote on 315).

49. Codman, *Drive*, 303.

50. Diaries, 1910–45, Patton Papers.

51. Chronological File, 1901–77, Patton Papers.

52. Diaries, 1910–45, Patton Papers.

53. Codman, *Drive*, 316.

54. Diaries, 1910–45, Patton Papers.

55. On May 22 the Third Army found two-and-a-half-ton truckloads of German intelligence reports on the Soviet armies. Patton's staff worked to survey these contents of these documents, but given the drawdown in staff, the ongoing crisis over Yugoslavia, and the massive trove of documents, it is not known how deeply Patton or his staff investigated their contents. No doubt, Patton would have found them interesting, but he did not read German and would have had to have the documents translated or summarized for him to make use of this potentially useful intelligence source. Allen, *Forward with Patton*, 215.

56. Codman, *Drive*, 317.

57. Blumenson, *The Patton Papers*, 2:707, 720.

58. Blumenson, *The Patton Papers*, 2:721.

59. Blumenson, *The Patton Papers*, 2:723.

60. Blumenson, *The Patton Papers*, 2:728–29.

61. Blumenson, *The Patton Papers*, 2:725.

62. Chronological File, 1901–77, Patton Papers.

63. Michael Neiberg, *Potsdam: The End of World War II and the Remaking of Europe*, 55.

64. Chronological File, 1901–77, Patton Papers.

65. Blumenson, *The Patton Papers*, 2:731.

66. Correspondence, 1903–45, Patton Papers.

67. Diaries, 1910–45, Patton Papers.

68. Diaries, 1910–45, Patton Papers.

69. Chronological File, 1901–77, Patton Papers.

70. Diaries, 1910–45, Patton Papers.

71. Diaries, 1910–45, Patton Papers. On Patton's views that war was filled with technical moves and countermoves, see George S. Patton Jr., "The Effects of Weapons of War."

72. Chronological File, 1901–77, Patton Papers.

73. Diaries, 1910–45, Patton Papers.

74. Correspondence, 1903–45, Patton Papers.

75. Chronological File, 1901–77, Patton Papers.

76. Chronological File, 1901–77, Patton Papers.

77. Diaries, 1910–45, Patton Papers.

78. Blumenson, *The Patton Papers*, 2:738. Despite Stimson's optimistic tone, the process of denazification would take decades. On this point, see Tony Junt, *Postwar: A History of Europe since 1945*.

79. Chronological File, 1901–77, Patton Papers.

80. Blumenson, *The Patton Papers*, 2:741.

81. Diaries, 1910–45, Patton Papers.

82. On the Morgenthau Plan to permanently deindustrialize Germany, see Henry Morgenthau Jr., *Germany Is Our Problem*.

83. Diaries, 1910–45, Patton Papers.

84. Chronological File, 1901–77, Patton Papers.

85. Chronological File, 1901–77, Patton Papers. In his memoir, *On to Berlin*, American general James M. Gavin recounted the scene, noting that Patton was "resplendent with twenty stars and his ivory-handled pistols," and also commented on the almost comic number of Zhukov's medals, "down his chest to his waist on both sides of his tunic." According to Gavin, he and Patton made it a point to ride parallel to the Soviet general as a means of showing their equal standing and avoiding a secondary position. James M. Gavin, *On to Berlin: Battles of an Airborne Commander, 1943–1946*, 295.

86. Merle-Smith quoted in D'Este, *Patton*, 739.

87. Chronological File, 1901–77, Patton Papers.

88. M. Holland, *Eisenhower between the Wars*, 14, 16–17, 77–80.

89. Diaries, 1910–45, Patton Papers.

90. Blumenson, *The Patton Papers*, 2:753.

91. Blumenson, *The Patton Papers*, 2:762–66.

92. D'Este, *Patton*, 766; Farago, *Last Days of Patton*, 178.

93. Blumenson, *The Patton Papers*, 2:770–71.

94. Blumenson, *The Patton Papers*, 2:771–72.

95. Blumenson, *The Patton Papers*, 2:771–72.

96. Blumenson, *The Patton Papers*, 2:773.

97. Diaries, 1910–45, Patton Papers.

98. Blumenson, *The Patton Papers*, 2:772.

99. Chronological File, 1901–77, Patton Papers.

100. Chronological File, 1901–77, Patton Papers.

101. Blumenson, *The Patton Papers*, 2:775.
102. Diaries, 1910–45, Patton Papers.
103. D'Este, *Patton*, 770.
104. Diaries, 1910–45, Patton Papers.
105. Diaries, 1910–45, Patton Papers.
106. D'Este, *Patton*, 770.
107. Diaries, 1910–45, Patton Papers.
108. Diaries, 1910–45, Patton Papers.
109. Chronological File, 1901–77, Patton Papers.
110. Chronological File, 1901–77, Patton Papers.
111. Diaries, 1910–45, Patton Papers.
112. D'Este, *Patton*, 776.
113. Blumenson, *The Patton Papers*, 2:789.
114. D'Este, *Patton*, 775.
115. Diaries, 1910–45, Patton Papers.
116. Chronological File, 1901–77, Patton Papers.
117. Chronological File, 1901–77, Patton Papers.
118. Blumenson, *The Patton Papers*, 2:789.

CHAPTER SIX

BATTLES WITH HISTORY IN THE SHADOWS

A Brief History of the US Fifteenth Army

FROM A MILITARY standpoint, Patton's new command was less than impressive. In contrast to Patton's beloved Third Army, which enjoyed a storied reputation after its legendary drive across Europe, the US Fifteenth Army was the last Allied army to enter the fight against Germany in December 1944. In the final months of the war, the Fifteenth Army had been assigned a series of lesser roles that, while critical to Allied success, did not match the exploits of other Allied armies. During its brief time in the European theater, Fifteenth Army was tasked with rehabilitating, reequipping, and training units from the Twelfth Army Group, managing the arrival schedules of American units landing in northern French ports, and acting as a holding force tasked with containing German units in Lorient and Saint-Nazaire, as well as in the Ruhr Pocket. In addition to these missions, the Fifteenth Army conducted a series of humanitarian operations designed to feed displaced people and helped prevent the spread of typhoid fever in its area of operations.[1]

After the war, the Fifteenth Army shifted its mission to occupation duties: transferring additional personnel to civil defense, public health, and law enforcement missions. During this period, special attention was given both to protecting displaced persons and to preserving the remains of German industry. The Fifteenth Army's area of operations contained approximately 310,000 displaced persons, many of whom were Russian prisoners serving as slave labor for the Nazi regime. To help with the repatriation process, the Fifteenth Army established eighty-three camps for displaced persons. At these "displaced persons assembly centers," these people were documented, interrogated by counterintelligence personnel, and provided with food, water, and basic medical care.[2]

In addition to managing this vast number of displaced persons, the Fifteenth Army was also tasked with surveying the remains of German industry and conducted studies on 2,473 sites before control of the region was transferred to the British and French. These surveys were vital in helping restart the German economy after the war, although some, including US secretary of the treasury Henry Morgenthau Jr., had opposed rebuilding German industry and advocated for the destruction of the German economy. While prominent Allied leaders like Churchill and Roosevelt found Morgenthau's views attractive, they ultimately decided not to implement the secretary's plan, and the rebuilding of German industry was greatly expedited by the surveys conducted by the Fifteenth Army.[3]

During the Fifteenth Army's period of occupation, the civilian population of the region was described by the official history as "generally quiet."[4] German civilian resistance was limited to a few minor incidences of sabotage, but they were neither well organized nor widespread. During the first week of June, seventeen Werewolf insurgents were arrested at their covert training schools in Mettmann and Langenberg, but their specific targets were unclear. The Werewolf movement stoked fears among Allied planners of a protracted German insurgency, yet it was generally ineffective and was quashed by the end of 1945 due to a lack of popular support and vigorous Allied counterintelligence efforts. While the Werewolf movement resulted in the deaths of three to five thousand people throughout Germany, the arrest of these seventeen Werewolf members was the only confirmed insurgent activity in the Fifteenth Army's zone of control.

Clearly, this was a quiet region, and the US efforts at providing for the welfare and security of the local population were generally effective.[5] An official report titled "German Attitude toward Occupation" summed up the feelings of the average German citizen: "In general the German nationals in the area surveyed were not hostile to American Military Government; were agreeably surprised by the good conduct of our troops; considered requisitioning of their property for military needs as a rightful price of defeat; blamed the Nazis for their misfortunes; held their own army in high esteem; and were as yet too apathetic to even consider political action towards reconstruction of a German government acceptable to the Allies." While major challenges remained, the average German citizen was more concerned about the potential for a communist takeover of the country than resisting American authority and made great efforts to prove that they were "good Germans," not Nazi ideologues.[6]

The greatest obstacle for the occupation forces was not organized resistance by Nazi fighters but displaced persons. In the days following the liberation, newly freed slave laborers roamed the countryside, stealing food and supplies, looting, and inflicting reprisals on their former oppressors. While separating these foreigners from the local population was a difficult and unpopular task, it was critical for restoring order to the region and beginning the process of repatriating these displaced persons to their native lands.[7]

On April 24, Fifteenth Army established the War Crimes Branch of the Judge Advocate Section to investigate German crimes against American personnel that had occurred in the Fifteenth Army's area of occupation. The most prominent case involved an American airman who had parachuted safely, only to be killed by enraged German civilians. In two separate trials, four German men were found guilty of murder and were sentenced to death. Three of these men were hanged by order of General Gerow on June 29, 1945, while the other's sentence was commuted to life imprisonment. While a minor footnote in the larger series of war-crimes trials, this case was notably the first prosecution of a civilian for war crimes held in occupied Germany and the last major act conducted by the Fifteenth Army as an occupying force. By July 8, the Fifteenth Army officially ended its occupation mission.[8]

Relieved of its occupation duties, the Fifteenth Army began to redeploy its troops to the United States. Some units were to be deactivated, but others, such as the 26th Infantry Division, were assigned to the staging areas for the anticipated invasion of Japan. While the men of the 26th and other units could not know it at the time, they would forgo deploying to Asia because of the atomic bombs and the Japanese surrender.[9] With the defeat of Japan, the Fifteenth Army's mission shifted from redeploying combat units to the Pacific to sending them home for deactivation.[10]

From Occupying Army to Official Historians
While the majority of the Fifteenth Army's units were returned to the United States for demobilization, it retained a small headquarters in the spa town of Bad Nauheim, Germany. The Fifteenth's new headquarters, located in the Grand Hotel, was described by a young John Eisenhower, who was newly assigned to the unit, as "pleasant indeed. . . . [A]thletic facilities abounded. The officers were of high caliber and the junior mess was convivial." The future author of several notable books on military and diplomatic history was less sanguine on the Fifteenth Army itself, describing it as having "no troops assigned to it; it was simply an organization whose sole mission was

to study the European campaign and to determine objectively what had been done right and what had been done wrong."[11]

In this luxurious setting, the skeletal remains of the Fifteenth Army remained to oversee the work of the European Theater General Board. The General Board, as it was known, was tasked with collecting the tactical lessons learned from the war in Europe.[12] While writing the lessons learned from the recent war in Europe was an important task, it was not a high priority for the US Army. Since it was generally assumed that these lessons would be neglected, priority was given to completeness rather than speed. These reports covered a vast range of 131 topics, including the organizational structure of tactical formations, personnel policies, military music, medical care, psychological operations, and logistics. Indeed, prior to Patton's arrival, the pace of the General Board's work was relatively leisurely, with a target of getting the reports finished by early to mid-1946. The academic pace of operations would continue until October 1945, when George Patton became the Fifteenth Army's commanding officer and demanded the work be accelerated for fear of losing its relevance.

By the time Patton was given command, the Fifteenth had been reduced to a small "paper army." The limited role of this "army" was reflected by its size, a mere 367 officers and 3,090 enlisted men.[13] This force was dwarfed by the awesome combat power of the Third Army, which had 540,000 men spread over eighteen combat divisions on V-E Day in May 1945, a disparity that was not lost on the new commanding officer.[14] While Patton would ultimately come to see his reassignment as an opportunity to rehabilitate his personal and professional reputation, he was initially disappointed by both the combat record and the scope of his new command.

Despite its diminutive size and less than glamorous combat history, the Fifteenth Army was an ideal assignment for the disgraced general. If Patton could avoid further controversy, he would have the opportunity to remain in the army, institutionalize the lessons learned from World War II, rehabilitate his reputation, *and* study history. While maintaining a low profile was never easy for Patton, the Fifteenth Army, stationed in Bad Nauheim, was about as far from the public eye as he could expect. As such, the press paid little attention to his daily routines, and he was able to avoid the incidents or ill-considered statements that had previously threatened his career. He came to enjoy this anonymity and settled into a routine that provided him ample time to work on his own memoirs as well as reconnect with friends and colleagues. By staying out of trouble and writing history, Patton hoped to revitalize his reputation, and the Fifteenth Army was the ideal place to do so.

Patton Takes Command of the Fifteenth Army

Patton's first day as commander of the US Fifteenth Army began early. He arrived by train in Bad Nauheim at 0530 on October 8 and was met by Major General Leven Allen, the acting commander of Fifteenth Army. Patton attempted to relieve Allen's tense mood at receiving his new commanding officer by interjecting, "Well you know damn well that I didn't ask for this job, don't you?"[15] The two generals enjoyed a quick breakfast, and Allen drove Patton to Fifteenth Army headquarters.

Like he had done so many times in the past, Patton wanted to make a strong first impression on his new command. He was greeted by the assembled staff, who were standing at attention with an air of trepidation. The general broke the silence with the self-deprecating humor that he had used ever since the slapping incidents in Sicily: "There are occasions when I can truthfully say that I am not as much of a son of a bitch as I may think I am. This is one of them."[16] Patton continued, "'I have been here and studied your work today.' Then, raising his voice a pitch higher, he shouted, 'I have been SHOCKED'—and then in a lower tone—'by the excellence of your work.'"[17] This broke the tension, yet sent a clear message that Patton was already taking a keen interest in his new mission.

Patton briefly met with each of the officers and pulled First Lieutenant John Eisenhower, General Eisenhower's son, aside for a "brief and congenial chat," relieving his fears that Patton may have harbored personal animosity toward him because of the recent friction with his father.[18] According to Patton's diary, "Allen gave me a good orientation. . . . I spoke to the Chiefs of the various sections telling them I proposed to make no changes for one week and that the best is the enemy of the good, by which I mean that something now will be better than perfection when it is too late to have any influence."[19]

While Patton was reviewing his new command, a reporter from the Associated Press, Mr. McDermott, called and asked for an interview. Patton agreed. Since he had recently lost command of Third Army because of his ill-considered comments to the press, this was a potentially risky decision. To protect himself from being misquoted, Patton conducted the interview in the presence of several members of his staff and had a stenographic record kept of the meeting. During the interview, Patton was careful to avoid controversial statements, indicating new wisdom and a desire to rehabilitate his reputation. Patton told the reporter:

> My friend, I know nothing in a big way. . . . I got here this morning . . . and at present I am completely bemused. There is an awful lot to be read. I have got to get some eyedrops. It is the most essential piece of equipment. This is right down my alley because I have been a student of war since I was about seven years old. . . . I believe that it will be proven that Bavaria is more de-Nazified and more reorganized than any section of Germany. . . . [On his thoughts about leaving the Third Army] I had the same sentimental attachment to the I Armored Corps and the Seventh Army. . . . If a man has done his best, what the hell is there? I consider that I have done my best. . . . [My] conscience is clear. . . . Anyone who says there won't be a future war is a God damned fool.[20]

Despite repeated attempts to probe Patton's views about the US-Soviet tensions, he categorically refused to take the bait, stating explicitly, "I won't discuss American-Russian relations."[21] Patton had not only survived his first press encounter as Fifteenth Army commander without incident, but also provided several interesting clues about his mind-set. He acknowledged that his new command was primarily academic in nature and that eyedrops, not bullets, were his primary tool.

The historiographic task that the new commander of the Fifteenth Army faced was daunting. Seemingly no topic, whether it was military music, medical care, or the role of female-support units, was exempt from thorough study. While the broad outlines of these subjects were drawn prior to Patton's arrival at Fifteenth Army and would continue after his death, he and his staff had an overwhelming array of subjects to contemplate and master. A September 30 document titled "Report of Studies Assigned for Committee Study Report and Recommendation" outlined the scope of the task. According to the report, the majority of the studies assigned to the Fifteenth Army were 25 percent or less complete.[22] Given the incompleteness of the work, many of these studies risked falling behind schedule, being truncated, or getting canceled altogether.

While Patton privately doubted that anyone would ever read the Fifteenth Army's work, he knew that to have any relevance, these lessons learned must be completed in a timely manner. True to the maxim he repeated throughout his life, "*Don't Delay*: The best is the enemy of the good. . . . [A] good plan violently executed *now* is better than a perfect plan next week," he drove the writing process forward at an ambitious pace.[23] The effect was immediate: "On Patton's arrival . . . the atmosphere among the previously calm, studious staff immediately became electric. One of his first announcements was that he wanted to go home by March. And we were by God going to have all our reports finished by that time! Everyone became frantic."[24]

While Patton's role was primarily one of delegating and overseeing work-loads, he pushed himself to work at a prodigious rate. Consistent with his command philosophy of leading by example, he insisted on reading interim drafts of the reports and providing suggestions for their improvement. Patton frequently expressed frustration with the scope of the General Board's mission, but he used hunting trips as well as an increased appetite for smoking cigars and eating to sustain his work.

Patton would generally begin his day early and work late into the evening, reading drafts from his staff while simultaneously editing his own diaries and papers. This schedule was nothing compared to the stress of his campaigns during World War II, but it required an impressive dedication to the study of history and the military profession. While he was upset that "people don't work here on Sundays," he chose not to alter their schedule, as he had plenty of work and professional obligations to keep him busy.[25] He wrote Beatrice on October 30, claiming that he had read so many theater reports that "I am almost nuts."[26]

Thanks to Patton's leadership, the Fifteenth Army began to work more efficiently. John Eisenhower described the pace of the writing: "It turned out the studies of the Theater General Board had been accelerated even faster than General Patton had foreseen. By early January 1946 the Fifteenth Army was being deactivated, and its former members were in the process of seeking new assignments."[27] The speed that Fifteenth Army completed its work is even more impressive when compared to other official histories, such as the *United States Army in World War II*. This official history, known by historians as "Green Books" for the color of their covers, was not completed until 1998, more than five decades after the war ended.[28] In comparison, the 131-volume work of the General Board, while smaller in total pages, was completed in an astonishing seven months. Yet again, the general pushed his men to their limits to achieve success, this time in the field of scholarship.

Despite his high standards, Patton was not optimistic as to the impact of the Fifteenth Army's work on the larger US Army. To this end, he wrote Beatrice on October 10, "This was very much like the old Historical section in Washington. We are writing a lot of stuff that no one will ever read."[29] In spite of his private doubts, he dedicated himself to the task, recognizing an opportunity to revive his reputation while making a positive contribution to the army and to history.

Mentoring the Young Eisenhower
Although Patton pushed his staff to produce results, he made a special effort to develop a closer relationship with John Eisenhower, Dwight's son. Despite their age differences, both officers respected and admired each other. On a more self-serving level, Patton may have thought that his mentorship of John was a means for repairing his strained relationship with General Eisenhower and also influencing a new generation of younger officers. The general had known John since he was a boy, tracking his growth as a man and supporting his decision to enter the army as a cadet at West Point. John happily recounted that since his early childhood,

> I always held the Pattons in considerable awe, because of their obvious wealth and the fact that Patton was a lieutenant colonel while Dad was a major. . . . Patton was a good-humored man who loved to joke. His language was full of the purple expressions for which he later became famous. I was astonished that he not only swore profusely around ladies but also encouraged all three of his children to do the same. When young George . . . would come out with an appropriate piece of blasphemy, Patton would roar with pleasure.[30]

When John Eisenhower graduated from West Point on June 6, 1944 (the same day as the Normandy landings), he had the makings of a promising military career. Eisenhower was assigned to the 71st Infantry Division and was scheduled to ship to Europe as a rifle-platoon leader. Despite his desire to lead his men into battle, John was removed from frontline service on the recommendations of Generals Bradley and Patton. Both generals feared that John's death, injury, or capture could compromise the mental fortitude of his father, the supreme Allied commander, and that "the future of one second lieutenant was not worth the burden that Dad would bear by having me as a rifle platoon leader." The young Eisenhower was "given no choice in the matter" and was embarrassed by the entire situation. Both Bradley and Patton offered to take John on as their personal aides, but he refused to accept their offers.[31]

This lack of combat experience likely hurt the young Eisenhower's career and opened him up to rumors of favoritism, yet it did provide him with a unique view of the war in Europe. John was first assigned to assist his father, helping to lessen the personal stress on the supreme Allied commander. To this end, he was generally successful, as his father was able to share his innermost thoughts with his son and took pleasure in providing advice to a young and eager junior officer. One of the more humorous moments of the father-son interaction occurred when John inquired regarding the proper protocol for saluting an officer that was "above me but below you. . . . Should I salute first and when they return my salute, do you return theirs?" According to John, "Dad's annoyed reaction was short: 'John there isn't an officer in this theatre who doesn't rank above you and below me.'" John's status was a bit ambiguous, and he soon realized, "Certainly SHAEF on a permanent basis was no place for me," and he sought opportunities for assignments elsewhere.[32]

John Eisenhower was "delighted" when he "was offered the chance to join Fifteenth Army," as it gave him an opportunity to escape his father's shadow. Indeed, he enjoyed not only the independence and relative anonymity, but also the opportunity to indulge his own love of history. By the time Patton arrived, John was serving as a first lieutenant in the intelligence section, "little realizing that this assignment would be only the first of several intelligence jobs I would hold."[33] Eisenhower described his service in the Fifteenth Army as "pleasant indeed" and had many accolades and insights about his commanding officer, General Patton. While the young Eisenhower was "personally a little apprehensive when Patton came to his new command," his fears were soon relieved, as the general's "generous nature showed through."[34]

On October 12, General Eisenhower briefly met with Patton during a dinner party. Patton described him as "full of friendship" but did not elaborate further in his letter to Beatrice.[35] In his October 13 diary entry, Patton provided a bit more detail about his interaction with his old friend and their mutual relationship with John, noting, "John Eisenhower told his father yesterday that since I had taken over the Fifteenth Army, people had begun to work. . . . Eisenhower was also quite anxious for me to run for Congress—I presume in the belief that I might help him."[36]

The suggestion that he should run for Congress was very curious. Patton had neither the patience nor the inclination to serve as an elected official and had repeatedly refused overtures from politicians. More than any other person, Eisenhower should have known that his old friend was ill-suited for political office, as his recent tenure as military governor of Bavaria so clearly demonstrated. Perhaps he was simply flattering his old

friend or projecting his own political ambitions. More cynically, he may
have thought Patton would resign or retire from the army to run for office,
and if he won a seat, he could prove an asset for Eisenhower's own political
career. Whatever Eisenhower's motivations, it was clear that Patton had no
political ambitions and that for the immediate future he wanted to shape
his legacy through the production of the written word. However, reports
persisted that he was preparing to run for office. To help silence these repeated rumors and to avoid phone calls from reporters, Patton cleared a
statement with Eisenhower for public release. It read simply, "I am a soldier,
have always been a soldier, belong to no political party, and have never even
voted. I am not interested."[37]

Patton's last meeting with his old friend Dwight Eisenhower occurred at
a football game in Frankfurt on October 14. According to Patton's letter to
Beatrice, which he wrote the next day, an awkward situation resulted: "Ike
was there and they put me right next to him." Both generals were apparently
uncomfortable but were determined to present a unified public front:

> As usual a lot of soldiers with cameras, several hundreds, came and wanted to
> take pictures but the MP's would not let them get close, so Hughes suggested
> that Ike let them come up. Instead he decided to go down in front near them.
> He waved his hand and "grinned" and they took a few pictures and he came
> back but the soldiers did not leave and presently they began to shout we want
> Patton, so I went down and there was really an ovation. Lot of film was used up.
> Then Ike came down and we posed together.[38]

While Eisenhower and Patton put on a brave face for the official photos,
the sternness of their expressions speaks to an underlying tension. As John
Eisenhower wrote decades later, "Both are smiling but pensive. I took great
pleasure in seeing that photo, thinking that the feelings on Patton's part were
not hard. In fact, he was devastated, and the friendship of a lifetime was over.
That was the last time, to the best of my knowledge, that Ike and Patton ever
saw each other."[39]

Patton clearly felt a deep hurt surrounding his relief from command,
and he vented his frustrations concerning Eisenhower's budding political
ambitions in his October 15 letter to Beatrice: "Ike is bitten by the presidential bug and is also yellow. He has convinced him self [sic] that he did
me a favor by getting me out of the realy [sic] grave risks entailed by being a
governor. . . . He will never be president!"[40] While Patton was incorrect in his

Figure 15. The last known photographs of Patton and Eisenhower together were taken at an army football game near Frankfurt a few days after Patton's transfer to Fifteenth Army. While the two generals were polite and put on a brave public face, their friendship had been severely strained. Courtesy National Archives, the Dwight D. Eisenhower Presidential Library and Museum.

prediction, these statements indicate that he still thought his treatment had been politically motivated and harbored resentment toward his old friend, despite the warm relationship he enjoyed with Eisenhower's son.

The Path Forward?

In the same October 15 letter to Beatrice, Patton wrote, "I will resign when I have finished this job which will not be later than Dec. 26. I hate to do it but I have been gagged all my life, and whether they are appreciated or not, America needs some honest men who dare to say what they think, not what they think people want them to think." While the public Patton was carefully rebuilding and guarding his image, privately he was implying that Eisenhower was no longer an honest public servant and relishing the opportunity to speak his mind. He reiterated his desire to retire and speak the truth in an October 18 letter to his former aide Charles Codman: "My present plan is to finish this job, which is a purely academic one, about the first of the year and then submit my resignation after which I can do all the talking I feel like. . . . My private opinion is that practically everybody but myself is a pusillanimous son of a bitch and that by continued association with them I may develop the same attributes."[41]

Patton expanded on this desire speak truth to power in an October 22 letter to retired General J. G. Harbord: "It is my present thought . . . that when I finish this job, which will be around the first of the year, I shall resign, not retire, because if I retire I will still have a gag in my mouth. . . . I should not start a limited counter-attack, which would be contrary to my military theories, but should wait until I can start an all out offensive." Patton then reversed course and returned to his work with Fifteenth, noting with satisfaction, "The study was progressing with remarkable exactitude and no speed until I assumed charge. . . . I am convinced we should avoid the error we made at the end of the last war of taking this war as an approved solution for future unpleasantness. We must use this factual account simply as a datum plane from which to annually build a new set of jigs and dies."[42]

Again, it is difficult to separate Patton's true intentions from the deep pain he had experienced at Eisenhower's hands and his apprehensions about the future of Europe. Like a jilted lover, Patton was lashing out, talking in extravagant terms in the heat of the moment, but then referring with satisfaction to his historical work with the Fifteenth Army. Ultimately, it is unclear exactly how much of this talk was private bluster and how much of it was Patton's true feelings. Since he died before he had an opportunity to carry out his threats to resign and tell the truth, it is impossible to definitively know. Publicly, the general was careful to avoid expressing these doubts, but privately he verged on insubordination. He summed up his feelings in an October 20 letter to Beatrice in his own unique blend of bluster, pique, and humor, claiming, "I know I am right and the rest can go to Hell or I hope they can but it is going to be very crowded."[43]

On October 24, Patton took a break from his work to fly to Paris. There, he had lunch with French general Charles de Gaulle and received a medal for his contribution to the liberation of France. Basking in the glory, he forgot his troubles for a moment. "[De Gaulle] compared me to everybody from Napoleon up and down. I replied . . . that the history of France's great leaders had always been an inspiration to American soldiers. . . . After lunch we went to the Invalides and . . . to the tomb of Napoleon, and . . . downstairs where people are not normally allowed. It was very impressive, and we all enjoyed it." Patton was free the next day, and he traveled to Notre Dame, Saint-Chapelle, and Versailles. On his "quick look around" of Louis XIV's palace, Patton reflected that "I had not been there since 1912, but it has not changed."[44]

Patton traveled to Rennes on the twenty-seventh, where he indulged in a champagne-filled luncheon in his honor. This event ended when "a very fat and sweaty young girl presented me with a large bouquet of flowers . . . [and] demanded that I kiss her, and I found that she had certainly bathed recently because she tasted soapy."[45] The general then reviewed some French troops, was made an honorary citizen of several towns he had liberated, and then rewarded the audience with a short speech expressing his gratitude. He then briefly met Madame Becourt Foch, the daughter of his old friend from the French cavalry school General Houdemon. Patton mistakenly apologized to the young widow for killing her husband whom he believed had died fighting his forces in North Africa. In fact, Madame Foch's husband had died in an airplane crash in 1944 while serving with the Free French, but she did not make an effort to highlight the general's mistake and gracefully accepted his apology.

Patton continued his tour the next day in the historic city of Chartres. Again, he was revered by an adoring French population, who displayed signs and ignored decorum by shouting and cheering in the famous cathedral. After lunch and a parade in his honor, Patton returned to Paris and concluded his tour of France. This outpouring of love combined with good food and tours of historical and religious sites made Patton the happiest and most good-humored he had been since his relief from Third Army and caused him to note, with self-deprecating humor, that "I collected ten Citizen of Honor certificates, two plaques, and a tremendous case of indigestion."[46]

Although his mood was temporarily improved, Patton remained frustrated by a lack of action and his continued belief that the Soviets were poised to dominate Europe. As he approached his sixtieth birthday, he became increasingly morose about his own mortality, hoping for either death or action. About this time, Beatrice had a dream that Patton would soon die. This thought weighed on the general's mind, as he became convinced that his time on earth was short. Indeed, Patton was in a minor traffic accident but escaped uninjured and wrote Beatrice that the wreck "was nothing but a bent fender, so your dream did not work."[47]

To combat his feelings of despair and irrelevance, Patton continued to distract himself with paperwork, reading theater reports, and planning hunting trips with General Gay and other friends. On November 2, he wrote that he was having his "trick tooth glued back," that he was getting a new pair of glasses, and that "the staff is having a big party for me on the eleventh [Patton's birthday]—what a sad day." Indeed, Patton did not like birthdays and would shift attention away from his own birthday by noting, "I think the 11th of November should not any more be celebrated as my birthday but rather as the anniversary of the first victory in Europe."[48]

In his writings, Patton focused on institutionalizing the lessons of war that he believed were a story of remarkable continuity. By distilling his insights into a short set of maxims like Napoleon, he believed he could guide warriors for generations to come. He explained his desire to create Napoleonic maxims in a November 3 letter to his son, George: "It is quite natural that my speeches should sound like Napoleon's because, as you know, I have studied him all my life. You are wrong in saying he fought a different type of war—he and I fought the same way but by means of progress [mine] were better than his."[49]

Building on this desire to contribute to the understanding of war, Patton issued his final in a long series of "Notes on Combat" on November 4, 1945. Like his previous "Notes on Combat," these observations were produced on the general's own initiative and designed to have practical value for the war fighter. In this final installment, the general focused on division-level leadership, organization, and tactics and imparted his trademark aggressiveness and audacity to the topic:

> Violent and rapid attack with the marching fire is the surest means of success in the use of armor. . . .
>
> The length of a command is measured in time not miles. . . .
>
> In considering the forgoing of any other organizational scheme we must remember that it is simply the datum plane from which new ideas and new formations must be developed. The primary function of war has not within historic time been mutually changed by the advent of new weapons. The unchanging principle of combat is to inflict on the enemy the maximum amount of wounds and death in the minimum amount of time and as cheaply as possible. If future leaders will remember that nothing is impossible, that casualties received from enemy action in battle are a function of time and effective enemy fire, and that any type of troops can fight in any place, they will not go wrong.[50]

Patton wrote the former commanding officer of the Fifteenth Army General Leonard Gerow on November 6, enclosing a copy of his "Notes on Combat" and noting that the Fifteenth Army's progress was experiencing a "rapid reduction of personnel due to redeployment" but that its reports "probably will be completed by 1 January [1946]." After previewing his and the Fifteenth Army's studies to Gerow, who was then serving as the commandant of the Command and General Staff College, Patton then suggested that these studies should be incorporated into the military's professional military education curriculum, "with the idea of keeping our fighting techniques and equipment up to date."[51] Even at this personal and professional low point, the general remained committed to studying the lessons of war and boldly trying to convince others of his military genius.

Despite his misgivings, Patton's sixtieth birthday was a surprisingly pleasant affair. In a letter to Beatrice, Patton hinted at a more positive outlook on the occasion, noting, "For a man of my advanced age I feel fine and every one [sic] says I look the same way."[52] Sensing the need to cheer up their boss, the general's staff, led by Colonel Paul Harkins, planned an elegant celebration to mark the occasion. While the affair has been incorrectly described as a surprise party, the transformation of the ballroom at the Grand Hotel in Bad Nauheim was stunning nevertheless. Friends from far and near came to celebrate the festivities. Cigars, alcohol, and good food were in abundance, and for a moment the general forgot his worries. Despite his claims of humility, Patton greatly appreciated the attention and admiration provided and was able to enjoy the evening.[53]

Acting Commander of US Forces Europe

As the most senior general officer remaining in Europe, Patton was briefly promoted to acting commander of US Forces European Theater (USFET) after General Eisenhower returned to the United States on leave on November 11.[54] While Eisenhower would soon be named the chief of staff of the US Army and would not return to Europe, Patton believed that his old friend would return and was careful not to create a disturbance in the interim. Despite the temporary nature of the assignment, Patton traveled to the USFET Headquarters on November 13 to inspect the headquarters, attend a staff conference, and see to other administrative matters.

The primary item of business for the staff meeting was the planned relocation of Jewish refugees from Poland to Bavaria. This presented a series of logistical challenges, but also upset Patton's political sensibilities. After briefly noting his concerns, Patton decided to do nothing, explaining, "Since I am simply pinch-hitting during the brief absence of General Eisenhower, I do not conceive it to be my duty to make any radical changes." He then "signed a number of court-martial cases and discovered that it is the policy of the Theater commander not to give death sentences to any American soldier accused of raping a German woman."[55] The general had a long history of recommending capital punishment for convicted rapists, going back to his days in North Africa, but again chose to do nothing, despite his belief that anything short of the death sentence "seemed somewhat at variance with Anglo-Saxon customs."[56]

Complaining to Beatrice about the lack of real authority in his temporary position, the general noted, "I am not being much worse than a rubber stamp. If I had the job permanently—which God forbid—I would certainly drive things. It is not a Headquarters, just a chatequa [sic]. I go down there about three times a week mostly to sign court martial sentences."[57] His only major changes in American policy were temporarily halting the destruction of German factories and then ordering a study on the feasibility of using these factory buildings to house German citizens and other displaced persons during the winter months. While the orders halting the destruction of German factories would soon be overturned, the general maintained a genuine desire to restore his defeated foe, based on pragmatic as well as humanitarian grounds.[58]

Depression and thoughts of mortality still haunted Patton. Increasingly, the general began to ponder his historical legacy and consider the possibility of a postmilitary life. The fact of the matter is that the general known for his decisiveness and drive on the field of battle was stuck at a personal and professional crossroads. Patton pondered retirement to a life of leisure, but he had promised Eisenhower that he would complete his job with the Fifteenth Army and had a genuine interest in completing this task. Moreover, Patton was concerned about his historical legacy and held on to the slim hope for the resumption of hostilities or an appointment to the Army War College or the newly formed National War College.[59] Either of these positions would have allowed him to continue shaping the institutional memory of the army through writing the history of World War II while also mentoring a new generation of officers—two tasks Patton would have excelled at and enjoyed. For the immediate future, the general knew he must remain in the army and avoid controversy to have any prospect of attaining these coveted positions.

In a letter to Major George Murnane Jr., who had served as a top aide to General Hobart Gay, Patton summarized this mixed sense of frustration and loyalty:

I do not consider the episode leading to my transfer to Fifteenth Army so much an attack on me as a lack of intestinal fortitude on the part of others. However, I feel that I have obligations to my profession which, for the time being at least, outweigh personal emotions and I therefore do not propose to take any personal action because I am convinced that just as in the case of the slapping incident and the Knutsford affair, the final reaction is more favorable to me than to the other parties.

Furthermore, and this is very frank and personal, there is one job which would cause me to contemplate remaining in the Army. This job would be President of the War College. . . . Therefore, it would be inexpedient for me to start throwing my weight around until I find out.

I trust this does not shock your opinions of my high motives which, after all, are not too high.[60]

Institutionalizing Lessons Learned

Despite the continuing uncertainty regarding his future in the army, Patton worked diligently on the Fifteenth Army's task of compiling lessons learned from World War II. He was actively involved in the process and continued to fill his time with reading, writing, and thinking about the implications of the recent conflict. On November 17, he described his contribution in his diary:

> To day [sic] I have been working on my thoughts as to how to reduce the human expense of war by a judicious increase in mechanization. Americans, as a race, are adept in the use of machines and also in the construction of machines. The people whom they will have to fight will be the Russians and Japanese, neither of whom are adept . . . but both have a large manpower which they are willing to expend recklessly. It therefore behooves us to devise military formations which will exploit our national aptitude for machines and at the same time save our somewhat limited and very valuable manpower.[61]

Since his first experiments with mechanized warfare in Mexico and World War I, Patton took a particular interest in these types of tactical and operational questions. He feared that the United States would again neglect its military preparedness, and he worked to ensure that the US Army would be ready for the next war.

On November 20, 1945, Patton chaired the Conference on the Infantry Division at the Grand Hotel, in Bad Nauheim, Germany. The resulting

General Board Report, "Organization, Equipment, and Tactical Employment of Infantry Divisions," bore many Patton fingerprints. It made the case for a lighter, faster, and more lethal infantry division based on Patton's theories of mobile warfare. Contributing to this and other studies provided Patton with a sense of accomplishment, sustaining him when his career prospects seemed dim.

On November 23, Patton was informed that General Eisenhower was not returning to command USFET because of illness and that General Joseph McNarney would soon be arriving to take his place. Patton was not disappointed by the news but noted that Eisenhower's confidante and rumored mistress, Kay Summersby, "was in a high state of nerves as a result of hearing that General Eisenhower is not returning."[62] Patton would die without ever seeing his old friend again, and it is only a matter of speculation if the two could have repaired their relationship. For the moment, he appeared content to let time and distance heal their strained friendship and took no direct action to make amends.

Reunions with Old Friends

While Patton's relationship with Eisenhower remained damaged, he continued to cultivate his personal and professional contacts. In late November, members of the 1912 Swedish pentathlon team invited their old rival to join them in Stockholm as a guest of honor at the team reunion. Seeing an opportunity to escape the academic routine of headquarters, he gladly accepted the offer and made arrangements to combine this excursion with a visit to France.

Patton first traveled to Metz, where he toured the famous cathedral and enjoyed many gastronomic indulgences. As part of a four-hour luncheon celebration filled "with much oratory," Patton was then made a citizen of honor of Metz, Toul, Reims, Luxembourg, Chateau, Thierry, Sarreguemines, Thionville, Eperney, and Verdun.[63] After the festivities, the general spent time with his old friend Jean Houdemon, renewing the bond they first formed at the French cavalry school on the eve of World War I. While the exact content of the two generals' conversation is lost, it was likely little different from the hours of discussion and debate that they had enjoyed as young lieutenants decades before. He noted in his diary, "After the luncheon I drove him back to Pont-a-Mousson, where I met his wife and was presented by them with two much treasured porcelain figurines of the Grenadiers of Napoleon's Army, in which Houdemon's grandfather was a general. I tried to persuade them not to give them to me, but had no success."[64]

Such friendships helped sustain Patton and to moderate his impulses during these periods of uncertainty. In addition to having his spirits lifted by Houdemon, he also received good advice from his old friend General Harbord, who urged him not to resign from the army in order to "tell the truth," take revenge on Ike, or otherwise settle old scores with past rivals. Recognizing Harbord's wisdom, he wrote to express his thanks: "Your advice is very good and, having gotten over my rage, I had almost reached the same conclusion myself." Noting the next stage of his trip, he added, "This afternoon I am leaving for Copenhagen and then Stockholm and then probably to a coffin as a result of acute indigestion from overeating."[65]

Patton traveled in grand style as he departed in a special six-car train from Frankfurt to Copenhagen and then to Stockholm. The train cars were opulently appointed and extremely spacious, "quite unnecessary for four people." Patton's historical interest was piqued when he learned that two of the train cars that carried his small party had once been owned by the legendary German field marshal and politician Paul von Hindenburg.[66]

Patton immediately felt at home in Sweden. Upon his arrival, he was greeted by an entourage of officials and VIPs, including the chief of staff of the Swedish Army and eight surviving members of the 1912 pentathlon team. Much like his visit four decades before, Patton was immediately accepted into the elite strata of Swedish society. He began his visit with a lavish breakfast at the Grand Hotel with Count Folke Bernadotte and met with King Gustavus Adolphus V the following morning. He relaxed by touring various museums, cathedrals, and universities, many of which he had visited years before with his family. The general also addressed a crowd of about five hundred members of the Swedish-American Society, expressing his love and admiration for the American and Swedish peoples, whom he believed were natural friends and comrades. True to his prediction to General Harbord, Patton happily indulged in drinking, eating, and socializing, reflecting in his diary with a mixture of braggadocio and disgust that he "ate and drank steadily for some two hours."[67]

The highlight of Patton's trip to Sweden was his reunion with the 1912 pentathlon team. The old athletes enjoyed recounting their past glories and rekindling their friendships over many rounds of drinks. As part of the reunion, a reenactment of the pistol competition from the Olympic Pentathlon was staged in a cave specially built for the occasion. This was a welcome opportunity for Patton, who had narrowly missed a medal in 1912 because of an unexpectedly poor showing in the event. This time, he achieved redemption by shooting thirteen points better than he had in 1912, placing an impressive second. He was also the guest of honor at a special ice carnival and hockey game held at the Olympic Stadium for him and the 1912 team.[68]

Despite the leisurely nature of the trip, Patton did not neglect his study of the military arts. He inspected several military units and met with members of the Swedish military staff. The general took a particular interest in studying Swedish military equipment, which was significantly different from Allied or Axis material in several key respects. He was impressed with the Swedish submachine guns, an 81mm mortar, and a field stove that could serve as a heating device by replacing a tent's central support pole with the stove's chimney. Building on his recent initiative to improve the equipment and organization of the infantry division, Patton would recommend that the Ordnance Department look into adopting these innovations.[69]

This trip was a welcome diversion that allowed Patton to relax and forget his troubles while indulging his tastes for the finer things in life. He enjoyed the break from his official duties as well as the attention from the Swedish people, with whom he had enjoyed a powerful bond for more than thirty-three years. While Patton was provided intelligence briefings from Baltic and German sources expressing their fears of Russian domination, he chose not to act or speak out about these developments, taking grim solace in the fact that "I could do nothing about this." The general left Stockholm contented, returning through Denmark, where he met the aging monarch King Christian X. From there, he flew to Frankfurt to return to his normal duties. In his diary he summed up the trip with wry humor, noting, "It is my considered opinion that anyone who can survive a trip to Metz and one to Sweden within a week is apt to live forever or die of a stroke."[70]

A Return to the Uneasy Routine and Uncertain Future

The general's good spirits did not last long, as he almost immediately resumed worrying about his historical legacy and the politics of post–World War II Europe. In a letter to Frederick Ayer, dated December 3, Patton expressed his desire to avoid these worries and retire in grand style, writing, "The main thing is that I wish to have sufficient money to be very extravagant for the next fifteen years because, as I told you [in his letter of November 17], it is my intention to do that."[71]

Patton's frustration was exacerbated by his lack of respect for the new commanding officer for the European theater, General Joseph McNarney. He noted his dislike of McNarney and the new set of senior officers in his diary on December 3. Patton could not have known it at the time, but this bitter discourse would be his final entry:

> General Smith gave a luncheon for General McNarney. . . . With the exception of Generals Keyes, Truscott, Allen, Gay, and myself, and a limited number of others, I have rarely seen assembled a greater bunch of sons-of-bitches. . . . [T] he Deputy Theater Commander, General Clay, and the Theater Commander, General McNarncy, have never commanded anything, including their own self-respect, or if that, certainly not the respect of anyone else. The whole luncheon party reminded me of a meeting of the Rotary Club in Hawaii where everyone slaps every one [sic] else's back while looking for an appropriate place to thrust a knife. I admit I was guilty of this practice, although at the moment I have no appropriate weapon.[72]

By referencing his time in Hawaii during the interwar period, Patton was recalling one of the most troubled periods of his professional and personal life. Throughout his two deployments to the islands, he had been fearful that his chance for glory was slipping away and had struggled with depression. These private demons caused him to be reckless in his personal behavior, yet he had found temporary comfort in writing history during the interwar period. Given Patton's cyclical view of history, it seems likely that the general was telling himself that he had experienced similar lows before and would rise to greatness again, even if the path forward was unclear.

It was clear to both Patton and his staff that he was restless. After receiving an early Christmas present from his old friend Colonel Harry Whitfield, Patton resumed smoking cigars, a habit he had quit and restarted numerous times during his life. Thanking his friend, Patton reflected on his vice, writing on December 5, "Your munificent present of cigars which I have stopped smoking arrived a few moments ago with the result that I have resumed smoking." Patton then stated his desire to hunt with his friend in Virginia, imploring him to "look up a few reliable foxes because I expect to go hunting around the first of January."[73]

On December 5, in what would be his last letter to Beatrice, Patton wrote both to communicate his travel plans and to complain about his career uncertainty and frustrations:

> I leave South Hampton [sic] on the USS New York, 45,000 ton battle ship on December 14 and should arrive where ever [sic] it lands on December 19. I have a months [sic] leave but don't intend to go back to Europe. If I get a really

good job [a reference to the Army War College positions] I will stay in [the army], otherwise I will retire. . . . I hate to think of leaving the Army but what is there? We can get a chance at the visiting foxes any how [*sic*]. . . . I was going to shoot pigs to day but it was too snowy. . . . I may see you before you see this.[74]

Indeed, hunting and planning for his upcoming leave to the United States dominated Patton's thoughts during these early days of December. Patton's chief of staff, Hobart Gay, was particularly concerned about Patton's dark mood and decided that hunting was the ideal diversion for the general. As Patton described in the letter to Beatrice, he had tried to go boar hunting in early December, but severe storms had canceled the trip, leaving him snowbound and frustrated.

With Patton rescheduled for a December 10 departure, Gay believed that a final hunting trip would be the ideal way to spend his last day prior to his planned leave. On the evening of December 8, Gay suggested to Patton that they should hunt pheasant the next day in Rhine Palatinate, west of Speyer, Germany. Gay implored his boss, "You haven't done any hunting for quite a while," and noted that the general "could stand a little relaxation before you take off for home. . . . I know exactly where to go for some good hunting." Patton's mood seemed to brighten at the thought of one last hunt prior to his departure, as he responded, "You've got something there, Hap. Doing a little bird-shooting would be good. . . . Yes, let's do it. You arrange to have the car and guns on hand early tomorrow and we'll see how many birds we can bag."[75] With that, General Gay began making the arrangements for a final festive hunt.

The General's Anticlimactic Death

The morning of December 9, 1945, was clear and very cold. At approximately 0700, Patton's orderly, Master Sergeant George Meeks, called Patton's personal driver, Private First Class Horace Woodring, to ready the general's 1939 Model 75 Cadillac limousine. The nineteen-year-old Woodring had attracted Patton's attention for his ability to drive quickly and for his repeated infractions of Allied policies prohibiting fraternization with local women. The general ignored the young private's sexual escapades and instead focused on his aggressive driving, which stood in stark contrast to his wartime driver Master Sergeant Mims's conservative but accident-free style.[76] Using a play on General Nathan Bedford Forrest's maxim, he bragged that Woodring "is the fastest and the mostest. He's better than the best Piper Cub to get you there *ahead* of time," referring to a recent trip to Liege, Belgium, a distance of 150 miles covered in less than two hours. While Woodring's driving record and personal indiscretions would later attract scrutiny, Patton was proud of his driver and overlooked these flaws. Indeed, all seemed well when Patton and Gay boarded the Cadillac and headed toward the hunting grounds west of Speyer.[77]

The hunting party departed Bad Nauheim at approximately 0900. Generals Patton and Gay rode in the Cadillac driven by Woodring and were followed by Technical Sergeant Joe Spruce, driving a jeep carrying a hunting dog and guns. The convoy made good time as it proceeded down the autobahn toward Mannheim. Ever the lover of history, Patton insisted upon a detour to inspect the ancient Roman military outpost at the base of the Taunus Mountains. He inspected the ruins and relieved himself during the short stop, and the hunting party continued on National Route 38 sometime between 1100 and 1130.

On Route 38, they encountered a checkpoint manned by a single shivering MP. Following orders, the MP would not let the general's car pass without checking the passengers' identification, despite the prominent four-star pennant on the front bumper of the Cadillac. Patton, who had been cold and wet ever since his diversion to the Roman fort, jumped out of the car and approached the MP. Anticipating the mixture of fear and duty in the young soldier, he "patted him on the back and told him in a pleased paternal voice: 'You are a good soldier, son. I'll see to it that your C.O. is told what a fine MP you make.'"[78]

After checking the general's ID, the MP allowed the convoy to pass, and Patton walked back to his limousine. Sensing that the hunting dog was freezing in the open air of the "Goddamn truck," Patton moved the canine into the front seat of his own car.[79] The general returned to the rear of the Cadillac and sat on the edge of the right backseat as the convoy resumed its drive to the hunting grounds near Mannheim. In this part of Germany, the secondary roads were still littered with wreckage from the war. The general leaned forward in his seat so that he could better observe the countryside and the devastation inflicted by the recent conflict.

As the limousine entered the northern Mannheim suburb of Käfertal, it stopped briefly at a railroad crossing to allow a train to pass. As the gates went up, Woodring crossed the tracks and allowed Spruce to pass in the jeep to lead the way to the hunting site. Patton's vehicle increased speed to approximately thirty miles per hour, and the general began to comment on the devastation he saw on the roadway, saying, "Look at all the derelict vehicles! How awful war is. Think of the waste." Woodring was momentarily distracted by the general's comment and took his eyes off the road for a fraction of a second. In this critical moment, a two-and-a-half-ton truck driven by Robert L. Thompson suddenly turned left across the road to enter a quartermaster's depot, directly into the path of the general's car. Recognizing the danger a moment too late, Woodring slammed on the breaks and turned the steering wheel hard to the left. Gay anticipated the crash and exclaimed, "Sit tight." The vehicles collided at approximately a ninety-degree angle, smashing the right front bumper of the truck into the right front side of the Cadillac. Because of the relatively low speed of the collision, only the radiator and front fender of the Cadillac were damaged, and neither the drivers nor General Gay was seriously hurt.[80] Patton, however, who had been sitting on the side of the car closest to the impact point, was grievously injured. According to Gay's account:

> [The general] apparently was thrown forward and then backward, because at my next recollection of the accident (I was unhurt except for slight bruises) I was sitting in the back seat on the left side, half-faced to the right with my right arm around General Patton's shoulders. His head was to the left and I was practically supporting him on my right shoulder in a semi-upright position. He was bleeding profusely from wounds of the forehead and scalp. He was conscious.[81]

Despite the shock of his injuries, Patton's first thoughts were for his fellow passengers. He asked Gay and Woodring if they were injured. After both men replied that they were unhurt, the general said, "I believe that I am paralyzed. I am having trouble breathing. Work my fingers for me. Take and rub my arms and shoulders and rub them hard." Gay did as he was asked, attempting to restore sensation to the general's extremities, but Patton could feel nothing. After a few moments, he insisted, "Damn it, rub them," not knowing that Gay was doing exactly as told.[82] It became immediately clear that the general was in grave danger. Gay understood that it would be unwise to move the general and told him that they must await help. Patton responded fatalistically to the news, "This is a helluva way to die."[83]

Approximately five minutes later, an MP, Lieutenant Peter K. Babalas, arrived on the scene to find Gay holding Patton in the rear of the car. Gay told Babalas that the general had been injured and directed him to summon a doctor and an ambulance as soon as possible.[84] Shortly thereafter, two medics arrived and bandaged the general's scalp, which had been lacerated after colliding with the partition in the limousine or a clock mounted in the rear of the car. About fifteen minutes later, two doctors arrived in an ambulance. They carefully transferred Patton to a stretcher and into the rear of the ambulance. While there was a military hospital nearby in Mannheim, both doctors agreed that due to the severity of Patton's injuries, he should be transferred to the larger and better-staffed 130th US Army Station in Heidelberg, twenty-five miles away.

Patton remained conscious but silent during the entire drive and arrived in Heidelberg at 1245. He was immediately taken into the emergency room and placed on the operating table. The hospital's commanding officer, Colonel Lawrence Ball, and the hospital's chief surgeon, Lieutenant Colonel Paul Hill, took charge of the chaotic scene. Patton was clearly suffering from severe shock, as evidenced by cold extremities, an ashen complexion, a pulse of forty-five, and barely measurable 86/60 blood pressure. The immediate priority was to stabilize the general's vitals and to control for shock. When a corpsman informed the general that they needed to cut off his uniform, he replied, "Hell, yes. Sergeant. Cut Away. It's been done before." With this, the general's clothing was removed and blood and plasma transfusions were administered. Patton's pistols were placed in a locker for safekeeping, but his bloodstained clothing, shoes, and badges of rank were taken by hospital personnel hungry for souvenirs.[85]

As the blood and plasma infusions stabilized Patton, he became more talkative. True to his trademark style, he mixed gallows humor with defiance, apparently enjoying his interactions with the hospital staff. He spoke directly to the doctors and said, "If there's any doubt in any of your Goddamn minds that I'm going to be paralyzed the rest of my life, let's cut out all this horse-shit right now and let me die," but then broke the tension by laughing at himself and saying, "Relax, gentlemen, I'm in no condition to be a terror now," and then, "Jesus Christ, what a way to start a leave." Patton was intrigued when the doctor indicated that he had put seventy-two stitches in his scalp. He began to recount his other injuries sustained during his long career, noting that the scar on his right buttock "may be symbolic for something or another. . . . [T]he only permanent memento of my historic service in the First World War is this goddamn scar on my ass." Patton, a deeply religious man, was also comforted by the hospital chaplain, who said a few prayers at the general's side, prompting him to remark, "I guess I need it."[86]

Because the hospital did not have an elevator, a six-hundred-pound X-ray machine was dragged down the stairs and into the operating room so that doctors could examine the extent of the general's internal injuries. The X-rays confirmed the doctors' worst fears. Patton had a broken third vertebra as well as a damaged spinal column and was paralyzed from the neck down. While the general was not in immediate danger, his long-term prognosis was grave. These injuries ensured that the famous general would never regain the use of his arms and legs and would live indefinitely as a paraplegic. With Patton's condition stabilized, he was moved to a small private room on the first floor of the hospital. On the evening of December 9, he was placed in skeletal traction in an effort to immobilize and straighten his spinal column. These devices were painful and had to be repositioned several times after they slipped out of position.[87]

Despite the grim prognosis, Patton's longtime friend and the top surgeon for the European theater, Major General Albert Kenner, began to assemble a team of top neurosurgeons to care for the stricken general. Dr. Kenner telephoned the US Army surgeon general in Washington, DC, who suggested that he contact the British neurosurgeon and Oxford University professor Brigadier Hugh Cairns. Cairns agreed to fly to Heidelberg and arrived with his assistant on the morning of December 10.[88] Though he was satisfied with the steps taken thus far, Dr. Cairns decided to increase the intensity of the general's spinal traction by placing additional weight on the traction device and securing the device by inserting fish hooks into the tissue under the patient's eyes. This increased traction was extremely painful, but Patton stoically endured this new procedure for nine days until the hooks were removed and his neck was encased in a plaster cast.[89]

Dr. Kenner was also able to obtain the assistance of the top US Army neurosurgeon, Colonel R. Glen Spurling. Dr. Spurling was scheduled to leave the army and resume his civilian career starting on December 20 and was on a train to Cincinnati when he was ordered to fly to Washington, DC. Spurling initially thought that the emergency involved his family, but when he arrived at the airport in DC, he was met by a member of General Marshall's staff as well as Beatrice Patton. Beatrice explained the situation, and the two quickly boarded a waiting C-47 to fly to Europe via Newfoundland and the Azores. The plane was diverted to Marseilles due to bad weather, and the party continued to Mannheim on General J. C. H. Lee's personal airplane.[90]

Beatrice and Dr. Spurling arrived at the general's bedside on the afternoon of December 11. Beatrice's presence had a striking effect on Patton's spirits, as he was now accompanied by his most trusted and intimate companion. Mrs. Patton quickly took charge of the situation, presenting a stoic yet optimistic face, despite the dire circumstances. Addressing a large group of reporters, she said, "Well, I have seen Georgie in these scrapes before and he always came out all right," a reference to his numerous accidents suffered from horseback riding, accidents, and battle. Privately, Patton confided to Beatrice his fears: "I am afraid, Bea, this may be the last time we see each other." Throughout the following days, Beatrice would remain a constant source of support and encouragement, recounting old times and reading from his favorite books on military strategy.[91]

Dr. Spurling's examination of the general gave little cause for optimism. The doctor confirmed that Patton suffered from complete paralysis and noted that the general's internal organs were similarly incapacitated. He explained that Patton's "prognosis for recovery [was] increasingly grave" and concluded that surgery to relieve pressure or repair the general's spinal cord was impossible. After conferring with the medical team, Spurling concluded that Patton would not recover from these injuries and decided that they should break the news to the general and his wife.[92]

Patton awoke from a nap to find himself surrounded by Drs. Kenner, Cairns, and Spurling. According to Spurling's memoirs, Patton "was fully conscious, in fact almost jovial," as the two men exchanged pleasantries. Patton apologized "for getting you out on this wild goose chase, and I am particularly sorry since it probably means that you won't be home with your family for Christmas. This is an ironical thing to have happened to me—after the best of the Germans have shot at me, then to get hurt in an automobile accident going pheasant hunting." Patton then summoned Spurling to his bedside. After a bit more small talk, the general got to the point. "Now, Colonel, we've known each other during the fighting and I want you to talk to me as man to man. What chance have I to recover?" Spurling was evasive and suggested that it depended on his progress over the next few days. Sensing that his doctor was avoiding his question, Patton asked, "What chance have I to ride a horse again?" Spurling replied simply, "None." Patton replied, "In other words, the best I could hope for would be semi-invalidism." Spurling replied yes. The general thought for a moment and replied, "Thank you, Colonel, for being honest."[93]

In spite of this news, Patton attempted to maintain an upbeat mood. Noting that "you're surrounded by an awful lot of brass around here," he insisted that Spurling was "the boss—whatever you say goes." The two then discussed visitors, and Patton quickly agreed that they should be limited to Beatrice, General Keyes, and the medical staff, noting, "It's kind of hard for me to see my old friends when I'm lying here paralyzed all over." Spurling insisted that he conserve his strength, and Patton promised, "I'll try to be a good patient."[94]

True to his promise, the general would be a model patient. Contrary to his "son of a bitch" persona, he rarely complained and was gracious to his doctors and nurses. Rather than focus on his injuries and his deteriorating medical condition, he preferred to chat with his doctors about the Allied victory in World War II; daydreaming about returning to sail his yacht, the *When and If*; and making plans for the publication of his memoirs.

In addition to recounting his past glories and daydreaming about the future, Patton was also comforted by engaging with history. While he could not hold a book or move his head to read, Beatrice read to him for hours at a time and even made arrangements for several of Patton's books to be sent to him in the hospital. She read primarily from the memoirs of Napoleon's foreign minister and general, Armand de Caulaincourt.[95] The general had long admired Napoleon and made many observations to Beatrice about the famous general's strategies, tactics, and sense of destiny.[96] While Beatrice's reading tales of past military glories helped maintain the general's spirits, his physical condition gradually deteriorated.

Despite attempts to maintain the general's privacy, the press, army brass, and numerous well-wishers and gawkers descended upon the hospital. Press conferences were held daily at 1100 to provide updates on the general's condition.[97] These press briefings were purposely vague and overly optimistic and had the unintentional effect of fueling wild speculation and rumors regarding Patton's true condition. Some reports even suggested that Patton had fully recovered and was walking just days after the accident. Such reports would later fuel rumors that Patton was murdered as he recovered in the hospital.

In truth, Beatrice and the doctors were worried that the general would develop pneumonia or a pulmonary embolism like the one that had nearly killed him in 1937. Such maladies were common with immobile patients and could be exacerbated by pressure from a dislocated spinal column. These fears proved accurate, and by December 19 Patton was unable to expel mucus from his lungs and began suffering from violent coughing fits. On December 20, while Beatrice was at his side reading, Patton interrupted stating, "I feel like I can't get my breath." The general was given oxygen, but X-rays the next morning confirmed that he had suffered a small pulmonary embolism in his right lung. While the general did his best to act cheerful, by the morning of December 21 Patton's doctors concluded that he would probably only live another forty-eight hours.[98] Beatrice spent most of the twenty-first by her husband's side reading to him as he took short naps between his coughing fits.

Patton was asleep at 1715 when Beatrice and Dr. Spurling went for dinner at the hospital mess. They were summoned at 1800 with the news that Patton had died in his sleep. The official cause of death was listed as "pulmonary edema and congestive heart failure." His last words to Beatrice that morning had reportedly been, "It's too dark. . . . I mean too late."[99]

Patton, a man who had been fascinated with death and reincarnation, had passed into history. In an attempt to retain the general's dignity, Beatrice refused a request by Dr. Spurling for a formal autopsy, a decision that would later fuel rumors of foul play and cover-up.[100] Respecting the precedent to bury fallen soldiers in European soil and consistent with Patton's demand, "In God's name don't bring my body home," the general was laid to rest in the American cemetery in Hamm, Luxemburg.[101] While Patton had been denied the death in battle that he so passionately desired, his wishes for a simple military burial were fulfilled. He was buried on December 24, 1945, among 5,076 of his fellow Americans, many of whom paid the ultimate price while serving in Patton's Third Army.[102]

At the time of his death, the general was nearing completion on two projects that would aid him in the battle for history—the reports of the General Board and his memoirs that would be published posthumously in 1947 as *War as I Knew It*. Patton's approach to these works reveals that he was not finished fighting his battles with history.

. . . .

NOTES

1. "History of the Fifteenth United States Army, 21 August 1944 to 11 July 1945."

2. The repatriation process proceeded with astonishing speed, by July 10, when the Fifteenth ceased operations, only twenty-one thousand displaced persons remained. Of these, eighteen thousand were of Polish citizens awaiting a political settlement with the Soviets, and the remaining three thousand were classified as either various Eastern European or "stateless persons" who waited in a similarly uneasy geopolitical limbo. "History of the Fifteenth United States Army, 21 August 1944 to 11 July 1945," 60–61.

3. "History of the Fifteenth United States Army, 21 August 1944 to 11 July 1945," 60–61. On the so-called Morgenthau Plan, see Morgenthau, *Germany Is Our Problem*.

4. "History of the Fifteenth United States Army, 21 August 1944 to 11 July 1945," 72.

5. Perry Biddiscombe, *Werwolf! The History of the National Socialist Guerrilla Movement, 1944–1946*.

6. Appendix 4, "History of the Fifteenth United States Army," 108–10.

7. Appendix 4, "History of the Fifteenth United States Army," 72.

8. Appendix 4, "History of the Fifteenth United States Army," 77–78.

9. D. M. Giangreco, *Hell to Pay: Operation Downfall and the Invasion of Japan, 1945–1947*, 30.

10. "History of the Fifteenth United States Army," 78.

11. John S. D. Eisenhower, *Strictly Personal*, 113, 112. For a representative sample of John Eisenhower's excellent later work as a historian, see *The Bitter Woods: The Battle of the Bulge*, *So Far from God: The U.S. War with Mexico, 1846–1848*, and *Soldiers and Statesmen: Reflections on Leadership*.

12. "The First Year of the Occupation—Special Text 41-10-63," Office of the Chief Historian, European Command, 1947, 48.

13. In addition to these personnel, the Fifteenth Army also had a temporary attachment of a light brigade consisting of an additional 323 officers, 22 warrant officers, and 5,616 enlisted personnel. October 6 report, "Strength of Fifteenth US Army and Attached Units," Military Papers, 1903–76, George S. Patton Papers, Manuscript Division, Library of Congress, Washington, DC.

14. To put this figure in perspective, the Third Army was roughly comparable to the entire American military force deployed to Vietnam at this height of the war. On this point, see Rick Atkinson, introduction to *War as I Knew It*, by Patton, xi.

15. D'Este, *Patton*, 778.

16. D'Este, *Patton*, 778.

17. J. Eisenhower, *Strictly Personal*, 114.

18. J. Eisenhower, *Strictly Personal*, 114.

19. Diaries, 1910–45, Patton Papers.

20. Blumenson, *The Patton Papers*, 2:795–96.

21. Blumenson, *The Patton Papers*, 2:796.

22. Military Papers, 1903–76, Patton Papers.

23. Patton, *War as I Knew It*, 354. Alternatively, this quote has been given as "an imperfect decision executed at once was worth more than a perfect solution later." Blumenson, *Patton*, 123.

24. J. Eisenhower, *Strictly Personal*, 115.

25. Blumenson, *The Patton Papers*, 2:797.

26. Chronological File, 1901–77, Patton Papers.

27. J. Eisenhower, *Strictly Personal*, 115–16.

28. Mary Ellen Condon-Rall and Albert E. Cowdrey, *The Medical Department: Medical Service in the War against Japan*.

29. Chronological File, 1901–77, Patton Papers.

30. J. Eisenhower, *Strictly Personal*, 8–9.

31. J. Eisenhower, *Strictly Personal*, 78.

32. J. Eisenhower, *Strictly Personal*, 63, 112.

33. J. Eisenhower, *Strictly Personal*, 112, 113; Theatre General Board, Headquarters Fifteenth US Army Roster of Officers, October 4, 1945.

34. J. Eisenhower, *Strictly Personal*, 113, 114.

35. Chronological File, 1901–77, Patton Papers.

36. Diaries, 1910–45, Patton Papers.

37. Blumenson, *The Patton Papers*, 2:797.

38. Chronological File, 1901–77, Patton Papers.

39. John S. D. Eisenhower, *General Ike: A Personal Reminiscence*, 72. On this point, see D'Este, *Patton*, 772.

40. Chronological File, 1901–77, Patton Papers.

41. Chronological File, 1901–77, Patton Papers.

42. Correspondence, 1903–45, Patton Papers.

43. Chronological File, 1901–77, Patton Papers.

44. Diaries, 1910–45, Patton Papers.

45. Diaries, 1910–45, Patton Papers.

46. Diaries, 1910–45, Patton Papers.

47. Chronological File, 1901–77, Patton Papers.

48. Chronological File, 1901–77, Patton Papers.

49. Correspondence, 1903–45, Patton Papers.

50. Blumenson, *The Patton Papers*, 2:803–4.

51. Correspondence, 1903–45, Patton Papers.

52. Chronological File, 1901–77, Patton Papers.

53. Even Patton's best and most detailed biographer, Carlo D'Este, mistakenly calls this party a "total surprise" for Patton (*Patton*, 779). While it is tempting, perhaps romantic, to believe that the event was a surprise, Patton clearly knew about the basics of the party, as he indicated in his November 2 letter to Beatrice.

54. "First Year of the Occupation," 62.

55. Diaries, 1910–45, Patton Papers.

56. Blumenson, *The Patton Papers*, 2:802. During his occupation of Morocco, Patton was quick to use the death penalty on American soldiers convicted of rape. He even credited this decision as a major success in building rapport with the local Arab leaders. Patton, *War as I Knew It*, 22–24.

57. Chronological File, 1901–77, Patton Papers.

58. On the factory issue, see Patton's diary entry of November 16, 1945. Diaries, 1910–45, Patton Papers.

59. On this point, see Patton's November 23 letter to General Handy hinting about his desire for a position at the war colleges and discussing retirement or resignation in Blumenson, *The Patton Papers*, 2:809.

60. Correspondence, 1903–45, Patton Papers.

61. Diaries, 1910–45, Patton Papers.

62. Patton diary entry of November 23, 1945, Diaries, 1910–45, Patton Papers. Indeed, after the war, Eisenhower saw Summersby as a potential political and personal liability and sought to distance himself from her. This occurred in stages, as

Ike edited her out of official photos, dropped her from travel lists, and ended all communications. The general's failure to return to his post in Europe effectively signaled the end of the relationship. Hugh A. Mulligan, "War's End Made Non-Person of Eisenhower's Devoted 'Shadow,'" *Los Angeles Times*, May 28, 1995.

63. Blumenson, *The Patton Papers*, 2:810.

64. Diaries, 1910–45, Patton Papers. In addition to their long friendship, General Houdemon's generosity may have been motivated by the fact that Patton had personally interceded to compensate the French general for personal property that was stolen and damaged during the recent fighting. Patton wrote a series of official requests to General Keyes and others asking for help restoring his friend's property. Of particular concern was a rug valued at 390,000 francs!

65. Correspondence, 1903–45, Patton Papers.

66. D'Este, *Patton*, 781; Blumenson, *The Patton Papers*, 2:811.

67. Diaries, 1910–45, Patton Papers.

68. D'Este, *Patton*, 781.

69. Blumenson, *The Patton Papers*, 2:811.

70. Diaries, 1910–45, Patton Papers.

71. Correspondence, 1903–45, Patton Papers.

72. Diaries, 1910–45, Patton Papers.

73. Blumenson, *The Patton Papers*, 2:813.

74. While Patton wrote Beatrice that he was going to travel to the United States via the battleship *New York*, Patton's plans quickly changed, as he was ordered to travel to Paris and then fly home to the United States. Correspondence, 1903–45, Patton Papers.

75. D'Este, *Patton*, 782.

76. Farago, *Last Days of Patton*, 239–40. On Patton's love of driving and riding at high speed, see Codman, *Drive*, 155.

77. D'Este, *Patton*, 783–84.

78. Farago, *Last Days of Patton*, 242.

79. Farago, *Last Days of Patton*, 241–42.

80. Farago, *Last Days of Patton*, 244.

81. D'Este, *Patton*, 785.

82. Farago, *Last Days of Patton*, 246.

83. D'Este, *Patton*, 785.

84. Farago, *Last Days of Patton*, 245–46.

85. D'Este, *Patton*, 788.

86. Farago, *Last Days of Patton*, 253, 252; D'Este, *Patton*, 788.

87. D'Este, *Patton*, 789.

88. Farago, *Last Days of Patton*, 261–62.

89. D'Este, *Patton*, 789.

90. General Lee had been a West Point classmate and rival of Patton's but willingly lent his aircraft to assist the famous general. D'Este, *Patton*, 790.

91. Totten, *Button Box*.

92. Farago, *Last Days of Patton*, 273–74.

93. Farago, *Last Days of Patton*, 278–79.

94. D'Este, *Patton*, 791.

95. Farago, *Last Days of Patton*, 276.

96. D'Este, *Patton*, 792.

97. Chronological File, 1901–77, Patton Papers.

98. Farago, *Last Days of Patton*, 290–91.

99. Farago, *Last Days of Patton*, 291.

100. In the years since Patton's death, conspiracy theories have become something of a cottage industry. Despite the fact that there is no credible evidence of a conspiracy to kill the famous general, dozens of articles and books have been published on the subject as well as a major Hollywood motion picture and several documentary films produced. For a representative sample of this vast conspiracy literature, see Bill O'Reilly and Martin Dugard, *Killing Patton: The Strange Death of World War II's Most Audacious General*; Robert K. Wilcox, *Target Patton: The Plot to Assassinate General George S. Patton*; Fredrick Nolan, *The Algonquin Project*; Ferdie Pacheco, *Who Killed Patton?*; Robert Orlando, *Silence Patton: The First Victim of the Cold War*; and John Hough, *Brass Target*. A close reading of many of these proconspiracy accounts reveals the troubling fact that they are often based on a series of interviews by former OSS agent Douglas Bazata. Bazata's claims first appeared in the fringe-right publication *Spotlight* in 1979. The now defunct paper was popular with white supremacists and anti-Semitic elements and frequently published a wide range of antigovernment and antiglobalist conspiracy theories. When taken in this context, these wild claims are all the more troubling, yet, despite their shady provenance, these interviews continue to be cited as evidence and fuel irresponsible claims to the present day. Martin Price, "I Was Paid to Kill Patton: Exclusive Interview with OSS 'Hitman'" and "Who Killed Patton? Super Spy Says He Was Paid $10,000 to Murder World War II Hero."

101. Correspondence, 1903–45, Patton Papers.

102. Farago, *Last Days of Patton*, 306.

.

CHAPTER SEVEN

UNFINISHED BATTLES WITH HISTORY

GEORGE S. PATTON JR. understood the power of words to project ideas. Before he was able to read, his family indoctrinated him with stories from Homer, Julius Caesar, and their own Confederate ancestors.[1] These idealized histories had the effect of pushing the youth toward a military career and seeking out his own opportunities for military glory. From his early days as a cadet at West Point, he believed that he had a duty to learn as much as possible about history and the military arts. While Patton initially viewed history as a means for simply improving his own martial skills, as he matured he realized that the written word also provided him an outlet for advancing his own views. Then, as now, military history was a common topic of discussion and debate among professional officers, and Patton realized that it was a potentially powerful tool to win his fellow officers over to his way of thinking.

Patton's first experiments with using history to shape army doctrine came while he was still a lieutenant. Recognizing that the current cavalry saber was not optimized for lethality, the young officer wrote a series of articles advocating for a new model that had a lighter, straighter blade. By making arguments rooted in history as well as theory, he was successful in changing more than a half century of orthodoxy on the design and use of the cavalry saber, no small accomplishment for a junior officer in the notoriously conservative army of the period. These initial successes made Patton more confident in his abilities, and for the remainder of his career he used historical examples and analogies to support his theories of warfare and to influence others.

Early Examples of (Mis)shaping History
While the young Patton's early writings were typically on technical topics such as swords and cavalry tactics, he was not above manipulating the historical record for his own self-serving ends. An early example of this purposeful disregard for facts came in his official report on the 1912 Stockholm Olympic Games. While he finished an impressive fifth in the modern pentathlon, he narrowly missed winning a medal because of his unexpectedly poor showing in the pistol-shooting portion of the competition. In what should have been one of his best events, he apparently missed the target twice, placing him a disappointing twenty-first after the first day of competition.

For the remainder of his life, Patton claimed that he did not actually miss the target and was denied an Olympic medal. According to his retelling of the story, his shooting was so precise that his two "missing" bullets in fact passed through the same hole and were scored misses when they were actually spectacularly impressive hits. While it is impossible to test this claim, it is in all probably untrue. With a keen eye toward history, he appears to have manipulated his official report to the army as a means of saving face with his fellow officers and to appear better than he truly was. A closer inspection of the official Olympic scoring and Patton's report to the army reveals multiple instances where the young officer appears to have falsified his record.[2] Although Patton should have been extremely proud of his fifth-place finish in the pentathlon, this minor incident indicates that he was in fact terribly insecure about his place in history and was not above misreporting facts to serve his own ends.

Another early example of Patton's slippery relationship with the truth occurred during the 1916 campaign in Mexico. In a swirling gun battle with General Cárdenas and two of his bandits, he came face-to-face with a bandit who was attempting to flee on horseback. The young officer recalled the advice from the lawman Dave Allison to shoot at the horse of a mounted opponent rather than the man himself and was able to break the hip of the bandit's horse and send the fighter tumbling to the ground. In his official report, Patton claimed that he wasted no time in dispatching the bandit, firing before he could regain his footing: "We all hit him. He crumpled up."[3]

This story won Patton instant fame with General Pershing and the press, and for the remainder of his life he would recount it with considerable glee. Despite the fact that the story was heroic enough, there is ample evidence that it evolved and was embellished over time. In 1928 he wrote another account of the fight, claiming that he allowed the fallen rider the opportunity to stand and reenter the fray before killing him. According to this account, he was "impelled by misplaced notions of chivalry" and "did not fire until on the Mexican who was down until he had disentangled himself and rose to fire."[4] On a similarly self-serving level, Patton's 1928 version de-emphasizes the role of his fellow American in the battle, and by leaving them out of the action implies that Patton was solely responsible for the death of this hardened bandit. Although it is possible that the passage of time had caused Patton to misremember key elements of this story, these inconsistencies are troubling. In every case, the 1928 version of events is more flattering to Patton, an embellishment of the truth that served to emphasize his role as a warrior.

These two incidents clearly indicate that, from an early age, Patton understood the potential to use history to serve his own ends. While it is impossible to know his exact motive, it was most likely that, as a young officer, he desperately wanted to distinguish himself in order to climb the notoriously slow promotion ladder of the "old army." For a man who so loved history, this may have been a difficult choice, but it was one that the young officer did make. Ultimately, Patton would be given the opportunities to win fame and glory and his many achievements would stand on their own merits, but it does not alter the fact that he could be a biased source.

The Historian's Task

This pattern of Patton manipulating history for his own aggrandizement during his early years presents a problem for students of his later writings. Just as he feared that he would not be allowed the opportunity for advancement during the early stages of his career, toward the end of his life he also believed that he was being forgotten and ignored. This powerful desire to rehabilitate his reputation combined with his prodigious output and untimely death make the historian's task extremely difficult.

A close inspection of Patton's writings during his final months reveals two general approaches to the facts, both of which are consistent to the type of writing he was undertaking. On the official task of supervising the work of the US Fifteenth Army, Patton attempted to advance his own theories of war without overtly manipulating historical facts. In the General Board reports, he makes the case for firepower and mobility being keys to winning future conflicts and spends significant time discussing the value of training and leadership, but makes no purposeful distortion of the facts. While he had significant power to frame issues as he saw fit, he was part of a larger editorial team and his work had to have the appearance of an official document devoid of an explicit agenda or personal bias.

In his private memoirs, however, Patton went to great lengths to emphasize his own role in winning World War II while simultaneously defending himself against his critics. He achieved this by colorfully emphasizing his successes and exposure to the same dangers of his men while simultaneously choosing to de-emphasize and distort his involvement in more controversial incidents, such as the slappings in Sicily and the failed Hammelburg raid. Posthumous editors would censor much of Patton's foul language and soften his ad hominem attacks, but in this unofficial capacity the general was free to provide his own version of events. The result was a much more distorted and self-serving work of history than that produced by the Fifteenth Army.

An analysis of Patton's work is further complicated by the fact that both of his major projects were unfinished at the time of his death. Despite the fact that they were completed by others, both the official history and his posthumous memoir reflect his deep beliefs about the value of history in mastering the military profession. Similarly, both were written to be timely and readable to ensure their maximum impact on future historians and military thinkers. The incompleteness of these two works presents two key questions for historians: How did General Patton influence these two posthumous publications, and what did he hope to achieve with his writings?

The first question is difficult to answer. In an attempt to trace Patton's influence on these works, this chapter analyzes the *process* the general used to produce the General Board's reports and his memoirs, paying particular attention to portions of these works he is known to have written and edited. Based on these known pieces of writing, it is possible to understand how the general sought to influence history.

This task is more difficult for the General Board reports than the memoirs because they involved many more contributors. However, drawing on the four reports to which Patton contributed as a principal consultant and the three others containing memos and notes from the commanding officer, it is possible to reach some interesting conclusions about his views on the enduring lessons of war that he desired to be passed on to future generations of warriors.

For Patton's memoirs, this task is comparatively simple, as he left behind both his unedited journals and his edited chapter drafts. This task is made easier still by the fact that his wife, Beatrice, also donated several working versions of these chapters to the Library of Congress. In these drafts, Beatrice and Patton's deputy chief of staff, Colonel (later General) Paul Harkins, edited the general's work to make it more suitable for publication. These edited manuscripts, combined with letters to the publisher, Houghton Mifflin, and correspondence with military historian Douglas Southall Freeman make tracing the evolution of Patton's posthumous book a much simpler and richer enterprise.

The answer to the second question—what did Patton hope to achieve with his writings?—is simple. Consistent with his lifelong relationship with history, Patton sought a combination of understanding, glory, and lasting influence. The surest means of achieving these goals was through writing history, both in his official capacity as commander of the Fifteenth Army and by editing his diaries into a memoir.

Both of these tasks would put Patton's talents and energies to excellent use while allowing him to highlight his exploits and pass his military insights along to future generations. In addition to examining the process that Patton used to write these two histories, this chapter will also analyze how Patton used history to shape his own legacy. Understanding his intimate relationship with the past is key to unraveling both the true man and his place in history.

Patton's Twin Historical Tasks

While Patton had deep personal misgivings about leaving the Third Army, he quickly warmed to his new command because he saw that it provided him with a unique opportunity to rehabilitate his reputation. Freed from the responsibilities of overseeing the occupation and rebuilding of Bavaria, he escaped the public spotlight to return to his engagement with history. Indeed, the official duty of the Fifteenth Army was to study the lessons of World War II, and there was no general officer who more thoroughly understood the need for codifying this experience or who was as knowledgeable about military history as Patton.

At the same time, Patton began to prepare his memoir for publication. While Patton had kept a detailed diary since August 1942, he recognized that it was unpublishable in its unedited form. Moreover, his diary contained language and material that would taint his historical legacy. If the contents were made public, his private reactions to scandals such as the Hammelburg raid would prove that he had lied about key decisions. With the help of trusted staff members including Codman, Gay, and Harkins, he began the process of editing his diary, cutting out foul language, omitting unflattering portrayals of the Allied High Command, eliminating military jargon, standardizing place-names and terms, and altering certain uncomfortable facts.

During this period, Patton wrote to friends, family members, generals, and politicians to seek their editorial and promotional advice. While he solicited their critiques, he was careful to ensure that they kept a close hold on the unpublished drafts, numbering copies and explicitly asking that these reviewers not distribute these manuscripts. This secrecy was critical, as the task of editing and publishing his memoir was beyond his official duties and may have been a violation of censorship rules had he chosen to publish it while on active duty. Nevertheless, he persisted in working on his side of the story during this period and was nearing completion of a manuscript at the time of his death.

These parallel projects suited Patton, as they provided purpose and the promise of redemption during this otherwise uncertain period. The writing of history was more than an official duty or a pleasant diversion; it was an opportunity to remain relevant and to ensure that his insights on warfare were passed on to future generations.

The Work of the Fifteenth Army

Patton set a new tone for the Fifteenth Army on his very first day. By applying his trademark leadership style, he jarred the staff out of their academic malaise and encouraged them to work faster at completing their massive historiographic task. He did this primarily because he wanted them to publish their findings while these lessons were still fresh and could be studied before the next war occurred. While he was pessimistic as to the impact these studies would have on the bureaucratic culture of the army, he realized that time was working against his efforts and that the sooner they could present the findings, the better chance they would have in shaping history. Despite the Allied victory, he saw much room for improvement and believed that the Fifteenth Army could potentially fix problems and save lives. Although it would have been easy to ignore American failures and instead focus on the ultimate victory, these reports made an honest effort to report not only American successes but also numerous failures.

Prominent examples of such candor include reports on the composition of American infantry division, and the report on the personnel rotation and replacement system. In both of these cases, the US Army was successful, despite bureaucratic deficiencies that weakened combat proficiency.[5] After American failures were exposed by the audit of battle, Patton noted them in his after-action reports and as commanding officer of the Fifteenth Army, he took great efforts to return to these shortcomings and to make constructive criticisms.

Patton took a particularly active role in assessing the composition of the American infantry divisions, as he believed that this was not only one of the most critical needs but also a subject in which his understanding of history could have the greatest impact. Because of his personal interest, he dedicated significant time and attention to the report titled "Organization, Equipment, and Tactical Employment of Infantry Divisions," editing drafts, providing extensive comments, and soliciting feedback from his army colleagues. More than any other product of the Fifteenth Army, this report bears most of the commanding officer's trademarks, as it is one of only four of the Fifteenth Army's studies that lists Patton as an author.

To spur the work forward, Patton personally chaired the Conference on the Infantry Division at the Grand Hotel in Bad Nauheim, Germany, on November 20, 1945. The purpose of the meeting was to "consider the Organization, Equipment, and Tactical Employment of the Infantry Division and to make such recommendations as are deemed necessary."[6] The general was listed on the conference agenda as providing both the opening and the closing remarks, and he was actively engaged throughout the proceedings. The general's opening statement set the tone for the conference. After a few perfunctory remarks, he jumped directly into his views on the task. His first goal for the conference was to promote his idea of increasing the effectiveness of American infantry divisions by improving both their lethality and their survivability in combat:

> There are two points which I would personally like to call to your attention. The first one is this: we must figure what we do to the enemy on the basis of what the enemy does to us, remembering that the casualty figures are based on wounded not dead because we have no way of finding out how the dead were killed. The infantry component of the division, which is 65.9% of the total personnel, inflicts on the enemy by means of small arms, automatic weapons, mortars and hand grenades approximately 37% of the casualties. In order to inflict 37% of the casualties the infantry sustains 92% of the casualties of the division. . . . This is one phase of the subject which I arrived at independently.[7]

Patton then moved on to his second goal for the conference, improving infantry mobility through increased mechanization:

> My second point is: Americans as a race are the most adept in the use of machinery of any people on earth and they are the most adept in the construction of machines on a mass production basis. This suggests to my mind the fact that

we should exploit to the utmost of our ability in the use of mechanical aids both on the ground and in the air. But we must remember that if the next war is delayed, as we all hope it will be for several years, perhaps 25, it is probable that very few of the weapons on this chart will be used. So this division on which we are working is only the datum plane from which further developments must be carried on.[8]

This opening statement thus quickly established the goal of the conference: to compile timely and practical lessons learned to leverage American strengths for use in future wars.

The general was particularly involved in the roundtable discussion portion of the conference—seeing it as the ideal venue to promote his many theories on the tactical lessons of World War II. The minutes of the discussion showcase how Patton passionately expressed his views that infantry divisions should be increasingly mechanized and equipped with lighter weapons to help facilitate movement. While he did not want to simply turn the infantry into an armored force, he believed that adding more tanks and self-propelled guns to the infantry units would give them the mobility, protection, and firepower to win the battles of the future.[9]

With the goal of keeping the infantryman's equipment load as light as possible, Patton also sought to minimize unused items, such as heavy machine guns and towed artillery, and even discussed eliminating the rifle sling and adjustable sights to save cost and weight.[10] Here the general was attempting to impart his own experience and theories of war, namely, that speed, firepower, and armored protection were the keys to decisive victory, and to subtly influence future doctrine and strategic thought.[11]

One of the most consistent points Patton made during this conference was the need to minimize infantry casualties. While the general was extremely sensitive to losses within his units, this concern provides a stark contrast to the popular "blood-and-guts" stereotype that has dominated his popular legacy. For Patton, saving his soldiers' lives was the principal concern: "Money is not [the] object. I wish that war could be less bloody. It costs about $40,000 for a man to get killed. If we can keep him from getting killed by a few extra dollars, it is a cheap expenditure." When the discussion turned to the fact that many soldiers were wounded or killed trying to move their weapons forward into the battle space, he reasserted the need to find solutions to this problem, noting, "Personally, I'm in favor of trying to find less bloody ways of fighting." The general also stated several times that he wanted overhead protection for weapons such as artillery pieces that "sits to fight" as a means of reducing losses. On the controversial topic of better integrating replacements into frontline combat units, Patton was unequivocal that the existing system was not only unfair and ineffective but "murder."[12]

While he recognized there was still much work to be done, Patton was pleased by the conference and was brief but gracious in his closing remarks, freely sharing credit and praise: "I would like to thank both the visiting officers and members of The Board for the remarkable intelligence shown. Also for the very hard work which has been put into the study and I wish to reiterate that this study is not a result of The Board, but the result of a large number of people mentioned on these pages."[13]

All told, the conference was a major success for Patton and the Fifteenth Army. The general was able to ensure that his ideas were clearly represented in the discussion and would serve as the basis for the official recommendations for the future of the infantry division. The resulting General Board report, "Organization, Equipment, and Tactical Employment of Infantry Divisions," bore many Patton fingerprints. That report and two of the other studies to which Patton served as a principal contributor ("Organization, Equipment and Tactical Employment of the Airborne Division" and "Types of Divisions—Post-war Army") each made the case for a lighter, faster, and more lethal infantry division based on Patton's theories of mobile operational-level warfare. Among the chief findings of this study were that American infantry units needed significant improvement in multiple areas to meet the demands of future warfare:

> The service units are deficient in men and equipment for adequate support of the combat elements; the ordnance and quartermaster units should be increased to battalion size and the other units considerably augmented. . . . The present cannon is unsatisfactory and should be replaced by the 105mm howitzer mounted on the medium tank (assault gun) pending development of a lighter, smaller, self-propelled cannon, having equivalent ballistic qualities. . . . The present anti-tank company weapon . . . is unsatisfactory and should be eliminated. . . . Infantry weapons should be lighter and more maneuverable; the automatic rifle is preferable to the light machine gun in the rifle squad. . . . The rank of the infantry regimental commanders should be raised to brigadier general. . . . The division artillery is deficient. . . . [A]ll batteries . . . should be increased to six guns. . . . An anti-aircraft artillery battalion should be an organic part of the infantry battalion. . . . Armored units should be organic in

the infantry battalion. . . . The reconnaissance troop should be replaced by a mechanized cavalry squadron. . . . The engineer battalion should be increased to a two battalion regiment. . . . A reinforcement (replacement) cadre, consisting of six officers and 30 men, should be made an organic part of the infantry division. . . . Every effort should be made to improve our present weapons and equipment and at the same time continue research for new and better weapons and equipment. While preliminary tests of recoilless weapons are favorable, more extensive tests should be conducted. . . . Tactical doctrines, methods and techniques of the various arms and of the combined arms must be continuously reviewed in the light of new developments.[14]

Though Patton's future in the army was uncertain, he took a personal interest in sharing his expertise on tactical and operational-level subjects, such as the composition, equipment, and employment of combat forces. Thanks to his attention, this report was one of the more useful documents produced by the Fifteenth Army: it made candid assessments of American strengths and weaknesses while providing actionable recommendations for addressing these deficiencies.

Patton took great interest in addressing the army's replacement policy for frontline troops. Throughout the war, he and other American commanders lamented the inefficient process by which new troops were incorporated into existing units. He first mentioned this issue in his diary on September 17, 1943: "Replacements are the thing. I am convinced that some day [sic] a serious investigation will take place with respect to the culpable negligence shown by the staff of AFHQ [Allied Forces Headquarters] in failing to keep General Eisenhower informed of shortages, and in failing to supply those shortages."[15] Although it was generally acknowledged that the army's personnel policies were flawed, the scope of the issue surprised many of the top American commanders.[16] As a result, these disastrous policies were not seriously studied during the war, and little was done to ease the burden on green troops or their commanding officers.[17]

Now that he had to opportunity to study this issue in an official capacity, Patton wasted no time in addressing this problem. To this end, the resulting report was painfully objective in its assessment of US shortcomings and made a series of constructive suggestions for improving these policies before the next war. This report, titled "Reinforcement System and Reinforcement Procedures in the European Theater of Operations," assessed the entire process of reinforcement, from training in the continental United States to shipping to Europe and integrating replacements into the ranks of frontline units. While it noted the great efforts of US servicemen and highlighted massive Allied logistical advantages, it was extremely critical of reinforcement as a process and recommended wholesale changes.

Perhaps the most damning portion of the report was the appraisal of new replacements' combat readiness, written by Colonel John Albright on the orders of the commanding officer of the 36th Infantry Division, Major General John Dahlquist. This report noted that new members of the unit were inadequately incorporated into their new units and were a dangerous liability to the unit as a whole. The report brutally underscored the consequences of green troops in its concluding section:

6. Common reinforcement faults which must be overcome are:
   a. Every artillery shell makes him jump, stop, and hit the dirt.
   b. He is slow to shoot. He has been told to hold his fire, until he has a definite target and not to give away his position. This is wrong. If you see or suspect an enemy, shoot him whether you give away your position or not.
   c. His physical condition is not good.
   d. He lacks pride. Do not let him feel like a bastard at a family reunion.
   e. He is a buncher. Insist on proper dispersion.
   f. He will not move forward.
   g. He will not take care of his equipment.
   h. He has no knowledge of combat sanitation.
   i. Has a poor idea of what constitutes adequate protection in Field Fortification.
   j. Doesn't know what to do when fired upon except to hit the dirt.[18]

Like the rest of the "Reinforcement System and Reinforcement Procedures in the European Theater of Operations," this document was written to save lives, not egos. To this end, the report was highly critical of US Army policies and provides an alternative and sometimes unflattering view of the "citizen soldiers" and "America's Greatest Generation."[19]

This concern for the mental toughness of untested troops was in fact nothing new. During his famous speech to the Third Army that was adapted as the basis for the opening scene to the 1970 film, Patton repeatedly hammered on the themes that it is normal to be scared, but that real heroes are able to overcome their fear and become effective soldiers. While the general did his best to bolster the fighting spirit of his men throughout the war, he clearly believed that the mental preparation of American troops demanded further attention.[20] Here, in his official capacity, Patton attempted to solve problems and save lives by thoroughly documenting deficiencies and building upon hard-won experiences. In the context of writing official lessons learned, this insistence on objectivity was a strong virtue. Rather than be defensive and deny that his troops exhibited deficiencies, Patton sought to document their failures with an eye toward improving their prospects for survival in future wars.

In his official capacity, Patton actually passed on the opportunity to push his own views on the issues of battle fatigue and the failure to adequately supply Third Army's drive toward the German frontier in the fall of 1944. On the issue of battle fatigue, Patton chose to avoid promoting his belief that it was a haven for cowards, and instead the reports deal with the issue in quite clinical and detached terms. Similarly, he skirted controversies regarding the prioritization of supplies for Third Army during their drive toward Germany, preferring to focus on the broader issues of resupply. While he would provide his own particular interpretations of these issues in his memoirs, he chose to keep them out of the official history. Perhaps he concluded that his views were unpopular and that forcing them into the official history would appear too self-serving and draw unwanted attention to his own failures to contain his temper in Sicily and to win decisively in the battles around Metz. In the one known case where he openly disagreed with the General Board (regarding the utility of the Army Tactical Information Service), he made a short note expressing his reservations, but did not otherwise attempt to alter the board's findings.[21]

Patton wrote only a small percentage of the total words of the vast historical corpus, yet he should be given ample credit for his efforts. In his short time in command of the Fifteenth Army, he adroitly managed a team of writers, encouraged them to work quickly and objectively, avoided the temptation to promote his own particular views on divisive issues, and made timely recommendations designed to benefit the United States military in the coming decades. As a result of this evenhanded approach, the reports of the General Board were surprisingly candid and direct. While the army would have a mixed record of implementing these recommendations in the postwar period, this was more a result of larger malaise, rapid demobilization, and a mistaken belief in the transformative effects of the American nuclear monopoly rather than a failure of the Fifteenth Army to objectively study and discuss the past.

Charges of Bias in the General Board Reports

Despite the fact that the reports of the General Board are generally well regarded for their lack of bias, some have claimed that they contain a systematic overemphasis of the role Patton's Third Army played in World War II. The most notable critic of these reports was John Eisenhower, the son of the famous general and a member of the Fifteenth Army's staff during the general's tenure. While generally positive regarding his commanding officer's intentions and historical process, Eisenhower claimed that Patton's presence caused the Fifteenth Army to alter its approach to historiography.

John Eisenhower, who would later become a noted historian in his own right, remarked on this subtle influence, stating, "I am certain that substantial revisions in the studies were made [after Patton assumed command of Fifteenth Army]. For the final report, 'The Strategy of the Campaign,' as I read it, showed the fine hand of the new commander. Even though I felt that First Army had contributed more to victory than had the Third, I noticed that Patton's army was mentioned about three times as often as any other [army] in the theater."[22]

While John Eisenhower makes no specific claims about Patton directly influencing the writing process, his statement that his commanding officer's "fine hand" influenced the Fifteenth Army's view of the war should be taken seriously. Not only did he serve in the Fifteenth Army under Patton, but he worked as a dedicated public servant for more than four decades, earning a reputation for kindness, good judgment, and selflessness. Indeed, because Eisenhower was generally positive in his comments on Patton and his time with the Fifteenth Army, this claim stands out in that it does not fit his broader narrative.

Upon closer inspection, John Eisenhower's claims regarding the overemphasis of Patton's Third Army do not stand on their own merits. A textual analysis of the report, "The Strategy of the Campaign in Western Europe, 1944–1945," does support Eisenhower's general claim that the role of the Third Army was mentioned more than the First Army, but nowhere near the "three times as often" as claimed. In fact, Third Army was mentioned 87 times in the report, while First Army was mentioned 78 times.[23] Moreover, the report makes numerous references to these two armies working in conjunction with each other, sharing divisions as needed, protecting each other's flanks, and holding the Germans in place so that the other army could gain the freedom of movement necessary to capture key positions. Cooperation between units such as the First and Third Armies is a consistent theme throughout the report, and their shared place in the history is entirely consistent with the fact that both armies were under the command of General Omar Bradley's 12th Army Group and fought on adjacent sections of the front for much of the European campaign. Far from portraying the European theater of operations as the exclusive domain of Third Army or other American ground units, this document shares credit with the US Air Corps as well as other members of the Allied coalition that played a vital part in winning victory over the Nazis.[24]

Other American armies are mentioned in this document with a frequency that roughly matches their relative contribution to the Allied victory in Europe, with the Ninth Army mentioned 35 times, the Seventh Army 19, and the Fifteenth a mere 2 times.[25] While greater attention could have been given to each of these units and the sacrifices of their officers and men, the editorial priority appears to have been to provide balance based on their combat record, not equal attention for the sake of inclusiveness.

When broadened to include other Allied general officers, John Eisenhower's claim appears weaker still. While Patton was mentioned twice in the report (once in the narrative and one more time in the appendix), he does not overshadow other prominent Allied commanders. Dwight Eisenhower was mentioned 15 times, Omar Bradley 6, and Bernard Montgomery 2 times. This greater emphasis on these other commanders reflects that they, not Patton, were making operational-level decisions, and the report assigns due credit for their actions.

In fact, the Fifteenth Army was less effusive in its praise of their commanding officer than later official histories would be. The "Green Book" official history of the Allied High Command, *The United States Army in World War II European Theater of Operations: The Supreme Command*, by Forrest C. Pogue, was extremely pro-Patton. In this volume, Patton who was mentioned 154 times compared to First Army's commander General Hodges who is mentioned a mere 60. Patton is portrayed as one of the true heroes of the war, and his memoir, *War as I Knew It*, is frequently cited as an authoritative source on the campaign in Europe.

Ultimately, Patton did not have to bias the General Board reports because, as he predicted, they were not widely read by future historians. The Green Book official history and later generations of scholars accepted the version of events Patton presented in his memoir and diaries, and this, combined with his flamboyant personality, ensured that his famous deeds would endure. There is no evidence that the work of the Fifteenth Army and the General Board contributed in any meaningful way to *The United States Army in World War II European Theater of Operations: The Supreme Command.* In fact, the General Board's work is cited only once in the entire 639-page official history and was used to document shortages of ammunition during the fighting around Brest, France, a campaign in which Patton's forces did not participate.[26]

If anything, the Fifteenth Army was not critical enough of the British failures during the Falaise Pocket campaign and Operation Market Garden.[27] Given Patton's and others' well-documented distaste for Montgomery and other senior British leaders as well as a belief that their plodding ground operations lengthened the war, this is an interesting editorial choice. Indeed, it would have been easy to focus on these failures and make the American successes appear greater by comparison. It is unclear why the Fifteenth Army did not do more to hold the British accountable for these and other operational shortcomings. Perhaps the decision was made to focus on American actions, or possibly a spirit of comradeship made it unpalatable to emphasize the failures of the British allies. Whatever the reason, this omission was the exception that proved the rule: the reports were balanced, candid, and careful to provide constructive lessons learned from the campaign in Europe.

While it is impossible to understand the private thoughts of John Eisenhower when he made his claim of bias, a closer inspection of this and other reports provides no basis for this accusation. Eisenhower is also not listed as a contributor to the report he cites, and there is no evidence he ever directly worked on this specific project. This claim first appeared in his 1974 memoir, *Strictly Personal*, written nearly thirty years after his assignment to Fifteenth Army.[28] He most likely *believed* Patton was using the work of the Fifteenth Army to rehabilitate his tarnished reputation and made such an accusation without going back to the report and fact-checking his own claim. Had he done so, he certainly would not have made the claim that Patton's Third Army was mentioned three times as frequently as the First Army, and this minor controversy could have been avoided.

Despite Eisenhower's incorrect memory of the specific details, the fact that he *believed* that Patton was interested in preserving his place in history and avidly boasted of his beloved Third Army's reputation is unquestionably true. Patton was a self-promoter who took every opportunity to claim glory for himself and his men, but this did not appear to have overtly biased the work of the Fifteenth Army. In his official capacity as commander of the Fifteenth Army, Patton put his ego aside and faithfully provided objective lessons for future historians and war fighters —a very "fine hand" indeed.

In sum, the work of the Fifteenth Army in compiling the reports of the General Board was impressive, and Patton deserves ample credit for his efforts. Rather than push his own agenda, Patton dutifully used this official mandate to evaluate the army's standard operating procedures and to make official recommendations for improving them. To the extent that the general's views were directly incorporated into the work, they were arguing for greater speed, firepower, lethality, and survivability, not settling old grudges with the British or pushing particular theories on topics such as psychological casualties.

While many of these suggestions would be ignored, just as the general had predicted, these reports made a good-faith effort to identify problems and suggest solutions; this legacy reflects highly on the integrity of the Fifteenth Army and its commanding officer. While the reports of the General Board and the Fifteenth Army are now largely forgotten, their final product remains an impressive example of a complete, timely, and objective piece of historical analysis. They serve as a tribute to Patton's love of history and his final, unfinished, attempt to lead the army in an official capacity.

Patton's Own Story: "War as I Knew It"

Patton had once told his wife, Beatrice, that he would never write a memoir, insisting that the true version of history was not known until one hundred years after the events had taken place and all the participants were dead.[29] Despite this fervent renunciation, the general worked feverishly during the final months of his life on just such a project, editing his diaries and notes into a publishable memoir. What caused the notoriously stubborn general to change his mind? The most obvious answer is that Patton saw the crafting of history as a means of both preserving his military insights while simultaneously rebuilding and protecting his reputation—one-hundred years of historical perspective be damned!

The resulting book, *War as I Knew It*, was published posthumously in 1947. Since it was incomplete at the time of his death, the book has been a tantalizing "what if" for historians ever since. The general consensus among Patton's friends and biographers is that the book would have been significantly different had the general lived and that readers were cheated by the general's untimely end. As the general's longtime friend General Geoffrey Keyes noted, "The accident that killed General Patton destroyed what could have been the best book to come out of World War II."[30]

Even in its edited and posthumous form, *War as I Knew It* is an impressive book. Thanks to the diligent efforts of Patton's editors, the book was a commercial success that cemented the general's reputation as one of the most daring and successful commanders in American history, while minimizing some of his less admirable traits. Indeed, had he lived to see the work to completion, the text would have probably incorporated more of his salty language and may have been considerably more critical of top Allied commanders. Beyond these generalities, it is impossible to know exactly what the book would have contained had Patton lived.

The final form of the book displays many legendary Patton trademarks, including his vivid descriptions of combat; his views about the necessity of personal leadership, initiative, and movement in modern war; and a section detailing lessons learned from his four decades of military service. True to its title, the book recounts his firsthand experiences as a commander, describing how his decision making impacted his campaigns and battles during World War II. This mix of personal detail and an operational-level history of the war is well paced and contextualizes Patton's view of the war. Throughout the work, the general stresses the importance of history and culture in understanding the operational environment, while also highlighting the courage and sacrifice of his fellow officers and soldiers. As such, even in its edited form, the text imparts many of Patton's key insights on the military arts.

Patton began the process of editing his diary entries into a memoir sometime after the end of World War II. While the exact date that the general began this project is uncertain, he had completed a large amount of work on this task prior to losing command of the Third Army. By late summer 1945, he had completed his initial edits on what would become the first eight chapters of *War as I Knew It*. These chapters covered the general's wartime experiences and served as the basis for the final work.

At this stage of the process, Patton's own edits appear to have been primarily for length and readability.[31] The majority of these cuts related to his diary's extensive discourses on history and geography as well as lengthy accounts of private conversations with senior leaders. For example, he cut an entire section from the opening chapter that detailed his December 23–24, 1942, visit to Marrakech and Ouarzazate, Morocco. While Patton's descriptions of the architecture, horticulture, and history of the region were artfully rendered, he decided that his personal observations distracted from the focus and pace of the wartime narrative. To this end, Patton boldly struck through this entire passage and wrote "OMIT."[32]

After completing these initial edits, Patton begun to circulate these first eight chapters among a small circle of family and military contacts. The general was worried about these drafts becoming public and potentially embarrassing him, so he carefully detailed who received these chapters in a private memo dated September 26, 1945. The list totaled eighteen people, including Generals Hughes, Summerall, Harbord, Handy, Cook, Henry, Weyland, and Gay, plus Colonel Harkins, as well as family members Beatrice, George Patton IV, and Frederick Ayer.[33] In his private correspondence with each of the recipients, Patton further impressed the need for privacy and discretion, as he did in a September 21 letter to Major General O. P. "Opie" Weyland: "For goodness sake do not let anyone else see it, because I am sure it would get me in a great deal of trouble. I merely sent it to you and a few others for whom I have real affection and great confidence."[34]

While Patton appears to have received little in the way of editorial guidance from these friends and family members, they were quite supportive of these initial efforts and encouraged him to work toward the book's completion. A short message from General Charles P. Summerall, then president of the Citadel, dated November 4, 1945, is representative of these responses:

> Let me thank you most gratefully for the eight chapters of "War as I Knew It" and for the charts of the operations of the Third Army. I have read and studied them with absorbing interest. They give a vivid and stirring picture of a new epic in warfare and fill me with wonder and admiration. Not the least of your masterful leadership was the psychology that you employed so skillfully. You have made history that will live always to inspire and guide leaders and men in future wars. Your gift of writing graphically and humanly makes your present assignment most fortunate for the history of the war. You have been most kind to me. When one has seen his last war, the thought and loyalty of others have a priceless value.[35]

With a keen eye toward the practical application of history, Patton wanted his memoir to be more than simply an account of his experiences during World War II. To this end, he began thinking about the lessons he would impart in the final two chapters of his book around the time he was transferred to Fifteenth Army. These last chapters, which were published under the titles "Reflections and Suggestions" and "Earning My Pay," were significantly different from the previous eight. These chapters were not directly adapted from his diary and did not provide a chronological narrative of the war. The original title for these sections, "Helpful Hints for Hopeful Heroes," gives a clear indication that he wanted to provide useful maxims for future leaders. By distilling his military philosophy into these aphorisms, Patton sought to conclude his book on a positive note and provide pithy aphorisms and insights in the tradition of his heroes Napoleon and Frederick the Great.

These chapters were composed at about the same time as his final "Notes on Combat," which he completed on November 4.[36] This paper focused on division-level problems, including organization, leadership, and tactics. Like his previous efforts, Patton wrote this report entirely on his own initiative, with the goal of creating another set of practical lessons for future use. Here the general focused on providing lessons learned that were narrower than the General Board reports, yet broader than the more personal observations in the final chapters of his memoir. Patton conducted these efforts in parallel: reading widely, editing the work of the Fifteenth Army, and distilling his views on warfare. To aid in this effort, the general obtained many unit histories and outside reports, incorporating their findings into both projects.[37]

Although Patton had been ruminating on these lessons for many months, he wrote these final chapters surprisingly quickly during late November 1945. He described his inspired pace of writing in a series of letters to Beatrice, noting on November 21: "People certainly have periods of mental laziness and mental activity. To day [sic] I was active as hell and wrote nearly all of Chapter nine 'Helpful Hints to Hopeful Heros' [sic] or rather I dictated it to my machine six cylinders at a stretch of course they have to be corrected and rewritten but one gets the thoughts down on time."[38] Patton finished chapter 9 on November 22 and immediately began dictating the final chapter on the same day. In a November 24, 1945, letter to Beatrice, Patton previewed his forthcoming "great eating tour" to Metz, Copenhagen, and Stockholm and bragged about his continued progress on the final chapter of the book, noting, "I have finished Chapter X and also 'Earning My Pay' a new extravaganza describing the few times I did things which materially affected the issue."[39]

Patton completed the initial draft of these final chapters just days before he was scheduled to return to the United States for leave, working with Hobart Gay to transcribe and edit his dictations and notes. Despite this personal triumph, the general's mood remained fatalistic and dark. After helping Patton complete these drafts prior to his planned leave, Gay suggested they should embark on the hunting trip on December 9—the expedition that resulted in the tragic automobile accident and Patton's death.

Acting on the general's instructions, General Gay forwarded copies of the final two chapters to a select group of friends for review on December 18.[40] While Gay's cover letters do not insist on the same tight security, it was understood that these chapters should remain closely held. To this end, his staff compiled a master list of recipients dated December 19, which detailed the means of delivery as well as the number of copies outstanding.[41] Even as he was lying on his deathbed, Patton's staff knew that the memoir was a sensitive matter and worked to carefully guard the general's reputation.

Posthumous Edits to "War As I Knew It"

Patton died on the evening of December 21 with an impressive range of military and personal accomplishments, yet his work as a writer remained unfinished. The general's friends and family knew that even in its incomplete form, this book had the potential to be a commercial success that would solidify Patton's legacy. In her husband's absence, Beatrice took the lead in shepherding the book to publication.

Recognizing the work needed significant edits for readability and tone, she approached Patton's deputy chief of staff, Colonel Paul Harkins, to assist with the task. Harkins was an excellent choice, as he was a loyal confidant who was familiar with the manuscript's litany of military terms and proper names. Harkins, who would later rise to general and lead the Military Assistance Command in Vietnam from 1962 through 1964, provided multiple rounds of edits, standardizing language, cutting military jargon, and softening Patton's criticisms of Allied leaders. Harkins exchanged these drafts with Beatrice, and they both made extensive corrections and comments to each other's work. Beatrice was so indebted to Harkins that she chose him to write the preface to the book's first edition. For the remainder of his life, Harkins would remain dedicated to preserving Patton's memory, serving as a historical consultant to the 1970 film and writing a flattering account of his operations in Europe titled *When the Third Cracked Europe: The Story of Patton's Incredible Army.*[42]

Sensing that Patton's memoirs needed the support of an established historian, Beatrice approached the eminent military biographer Douglas Southall Freeman. Freeman had been famous for decades for his biographies on Robert E. Lee and his subordinates and was, in Patton's view, "the greatest military biographer of our time."[43] Beatrice asked Freeman to serve as the general's official biographer, but he was already busy writing a multivolume history of George Washington and died without committing to the project.

Ultimately, Freeman would provide Beatrice some advice regarding editing and marketing of the book and write a short introduction to the first edition, but he contributed little to prepare the manuscript for publication.

Martin Blumenson: Patton's Official Biographer
Failing to secure this prominent historian, the Patton family would eventually select Martin Blumenson, who had served under Patton as a historian in the Seventh and Third Armies, to become the general's official biographer and editor of his papers. Though Blumenson was not as prominent as Freeman, he nevertheless proved to be an excellent choice for building and promoting Patton's historical legacy. He had already attracted attention for his history of the Normandy campaign, *Breakout and Pursuit*, published in 1961, which highlighted Patton's aggressiveness and initiative, as well as his 1969 official history of American operations in Italy, titled *Salerno to Cassino*.[44]

Blumenson agreed to serve as the general's official biographer in the late 1960s after retiring from a career as a historian in the United States Army. Despite being left off the memoirs, he would diligently serve Patton and his family for the remainder of his life. As part of his agreement with the Patton family, he was given exclusive access of the Library of Congress's collection of Patton's papers, until their public release in 1974. In effect, this allowed Blumenson to corner the market on Patton scholarship and set him up as the leading authority on the general's life and career. Over the next four decades, the Patton family would cultivate a close friendship with Blumenson and would add their own color and personal perspectives to his research.[45]

In his role as an official biographer, Blumenson dedicated himself completely to the task of researching, writing, and promoting George S. Patton Jr. In addition to his copious writings, he lectured extensively on Patton and held academic appointment at the Army and Navy War Colleges, the Citadel, the University of North Texas, Bucknell University, the University of Texas–Austin, and George Washington University. He had a generational impact on Patton scholarship, as he befriended hundreds of military officers and scholars and took the time to personally answer countless inquiries regarding the general and his role in World War II. Even at the time of his death in 2005, he was nearing the completion of a second Patton biography that would be published posthumously.[46]

Blumenson's greatest contribution to the Patton historiography was the editing and publication of the two-volume collection *The Patton Papers* (1972, 1974). These two books were much more than simply a chronological collection of his writings, but instead an annotated guide to the development of Patton's views on warfare. By providing significant biographical and operational-level context, Blumenson meticulously documents how Patton approached the study of the military arts and how these efforts impacted his impressive career. While these documents are almost all available in public archives and the Library of Congress collection, *The Patton Papers* have provided countless scholars a quick and comprehensive guide to the primary source literature.[47]

As a biographer, he also dedicated himself to the study of Patton, publishing dozens of articles about a wide range of the general's exploits, ranging from his days as a student at the Army War College to his military campaigns in Mexico and Europe. In 1985 he wrote a biography titled *Patton: The Man behind the Legend, 1885–1945* that portrayed Patton as a military genius and smoothed over some of his more caustic personality traits, including his anti-Semitism. This is surprising, since Blumenson had access to Patton's personal papers, which are littered with derogatory comments regarding Jews and denazification policies.

This omission is even more interesting given that Blumenson did discuss Patton's other personal foibles in great detail, including his temper, vanity, and his extramarital affairs with his niece Jean Gordon. Unfortunately, it is impossible to definitively know why Blumenson downplayed Patton's anti-Jewish sentiments. It has been speculated that since Blumenson was Jewish, he was unwilling to make an issue of Patton's anti-Semitism or was able to understand it in the broader context of ignorance and bigotry all too common in both the army and "polite society" of the period. Interestingly, Patton's two other Jewish biographers, Ladislas Farago and Oscar Koch, similarly downplay the general's caustic anti-Semitism and instead venerate their subject rather than explore this lesser-known flaw in his character.[48]

Blumenson's relationship with the Patton family may have also shaped his views on the general and caused him to forgo the opportunity to make charges of anti-Semitism. The family was extremely generous and supportive of Blumenson's efforts and made a point to remain in contact with the author for the remainder of his life. This friendship was genuine, and, according to Patton's grandson Benjamin, "he thought my grandfather was one of the greatest military geniuses of all time. . . . Blumenson obviously adored my grandfather."[49] While there is no evidence to suggest that the Patton family ever pressured Blumenson to censor his opinions, the very fact that he was a trusted member of their inner circle may have shaped his interpretations of his subject. Whatever the motivations for Blumenson's decision, it has had a profound influence on contemporary historiography and has helped protect Patton's legacy to the present day.

In addition to these biographical works, Blumenson also wrote several histories of World War II campaigns, including *Duel for France, 1944* (1963), *Kasserine* (1967), and *The Battle of the Generals* (1993), which portray Patton as the most effective Allied commander of the war. In particular, *The Battle of the Generals* explicitly endorses Patton's claim that he could have short-ened the war had he been given the opportunity to close the Falaise Pocket in the summer of 1944 and implicitly endorses Patton's views that he was surrounded by more cautious and conservative commanders who did not benefit from his unique strategic insights.[50]

This was a considerably more critical interpretation of the Allied fail-ures during the Normandy campaign than the one Blumenson had made three decades prior when he wrote *Breakout and Pursuit*. In that work, he claimed, "Why Bradley did not allow Patton to try to close the gap and seal the Argentan-Falaise pocket later became the subject of a considerable polemic," but then he went to great lengths to explain that the area had been heavily mined and noted the difficulty of coordinating the meet-up between American and Canadian forces in the region. After assessing these risks, he concluded that "these reasons were sufficient to justify Bradley's decision." Blumenson quotes General Eisenhower's assessment that Falaise "might have won us a complete battle of annihilation" but ultimately concludes that "where the assumption of risk was involved, finesse, good manners, and the subtleties of coalition warfare required the responsible commander to make the responsible decision."[51]

Three decades later, Blumenson's portrayal of the Falaise campaign re-versed course. In *The Battle of the Generals*, the failure of the Allies to destroy the Nazi forces was now portrayed in much starker terms: "The fact was, the Allies had had the Germans on the ropes in Normandy and had been unable to deliver a knockout blow. . . . Hitler needed only a short respite to recon-stitute his combat forces" and would employ these same troops at Market Garden and the Ardennes. The problem was that while "Patton opted for audacity . . . Montgomery, like Bradley, preferred to be safe." Blumenson quotes from *War as I Knew It* that this was "a monumental error" on the part of the Allies that significantly lengthened the war. According to *The Battle of the Generals*: "But they [the Allies] had failed to grasp the more important opportunity of eliminating the Germans in Normandy. Dislodging from the region was hardly enough. The German continuing combat efficiency in post-Overlord operations on the approaches to Germany and beyond ensured the endurance of the struggle. The fighting in Europe would last for eight more months." According to Blumenson, "From the first, he [Patton] understood the need for dispatch. . . . [W]illing to take chances in order to terminate the warfare, he was the single commander who grasped what needed to be done and had the know how to do it," but he was unfortunately "bound to execute the plans formulated by his superiors."[52]

What made Blumenson change his mind? The most logical explanation was that he was writing *Breakout and Pursuit* in an official capacity and needed to be sensitive to the politics and egos within the army, whereas he wrote *The Battle of the Generals* as a private citizen who did not operate under these editorial sensitivities and was free to interpret history as he saw fit. More cynically, he could have also thought this new and controversial version of events would help sell books or was necessary to attract a publisher, but this seems unlikely for a historian as seasoned and respected as Blumenson.

The most intriguing possibility is that Blumenson's position as Patton's official biographer and his friendship with the Patton family colored his understanding of history and portrayal of the man. In the intervening period, he had extensive access to Patton's personal papers, had written a generally flattering biography of the man, and had formally endorsed the view that Patton was a military genius. In sum, Blumenson's role as the official biographer made him committed to promoting the general's historical legacy, and it would appear he ultimately accepted Patton's claims that he could have shortened the war had he been given greater control over the Falaise campaign.

Much like the issue regarding Patton's well-documented anti-Semitism, it would appear that Blumenson may have become infatuated with his subject, despite his efforts at impartiality. Patton's own force of personality, his use of the written word, and the social graces of his family had the effect of securing the venerated place in history he so desperately craved. Even in death, Patton won battles with history by convincing his official biographer that he was an authentic genius.[53]

Patton's Version of History
When it was released by Houghton Mifflin in 1947, *War as I Knew It* was an instant commercial success. Thousands of readers were enthralled by Patton's descriptions of battle and eagerly read his accounts, as if "the froth and

emotion of battle still were upon him."[54] Although the memoir focuses on the general's vision of war and the larger triumphs of the Allied war effort, it was particularly critical of several key aspects of the war. Patton claimed that the failures to close the Falaise Pocket, Eisenhower's broad-front strategy, and the American timidity after the relief of Bastogne lengthened the war and cost needless deaths, three controversies that were relatively unknown to the general public at the time.[55] Despite these criticisms, Patton's book did not provoke the widespread public backlash that some feared. At this time, few professional historians focused on the failures of American strategy during the war, and these critiques were softened by the broader triumphalism of the work. In more recent years, a new generation of historians has explored these "what ifs" regarding American operations during the Second World War and have been generally supportive of the claims that the Allies could have shortened the war by acting more aggressively in their drive toward Germany.[56]

On the whole, the editors served the deceased general well, casting him as one of the boldest and most daring leaders of the war, while shielding the public from the more caustic elements of his character. Freed from the controversy that would have inevitably arose from explicit language and personal attacks, the final form of War as I Knew It allowed Patton's vivid descriptions of battle and personal triumphs to stand on their own merits rather than miring his legacy in contention. However, there are some who still long for the "true Patton." As the Pulitzer Prize–winning journalist and longtime Patton admirer Leland Stowe lamented, "Looking back, there's one thing that seems a great and everlasting pity. There will never be a completely unexpurgated version of the vocal Blood-and-Guts. . . . It's too bad, Georgie. The history books will never do right by you."[57]

While Patton was remarkably evenhanded in his approach to the official history, he used his memoirs in a much more self-serving manner—the most prominent example being his treatment of the ill-fated Task Force Baum. A closer examination of the historical record exposes Patton's true motives and misgivings regarding the failed mission. On March 27, shortly after Task Force Baum went missing, Patton confided to his diary, "I was quite nervous all morning over the 'task force' I sent to rescue the prisoners, we could get no information concerning them. I do not believe there is anything in that part of Germany heavy enough to hurt them, but for some reason I was nervous—probably I had indigestion."[58]

The same night, John Eisenhower reported that Patton knew that Waters was wounded in the failed rescue attempt. Patton confided to Eisenhower that "Waters had gotten his ass shot up," broke into tears, and "told me how much he owed my father [General Dwight Eisenhower]."[59] On April 5, prior to receiving news of the camp's liberation, Patton wrote Beatrice in an apologetic mood: "I feel terribly, I tried hard to save him and may be the cause of his death. . . . I don't know what you and B [Patton's daughter Beatrice, wife of John Waters] will think. Don't tell her yet. . . . We have liberated a lot of PW camps but not the one I wanted."[60] Patton's writings indicate that he knew that Waters had been in the camp, while also casting doubt on his cover story that the raid was simply a show-of-force mission. Clearly, the private Patton was worried about his professional reputation and was sensitive to charges of favoritism regarding Waters.

Interestingly, the general would use his writings to defend himself against charges of nepotism in an October 1945 press conference. When he was asked if he thought that his son-in-law might be held in Hammelburg, the general defiantly held up what he claimed to be his diaries as a prop. He insisted that his diaries proved that he did not know that Waters was held in the camp until nine days after he ordered the raid. He then claimed that he ordered the raid out of fear of the Germans killing the prisoners and defiantly challenged the reports to dispute his version of events. Despite the assertion that the diaries exonerated him, he did not allow the reporters to inspect their contents, an indication that either they were a prop or he feared what the reporter might find. This gambit apparently satisfied the assembled press, and there were no further investigations at the time into Patton's writings or claims of impartiality.[61]

While Patton was lucky to have defused controversy in the short term, he knew that his memoirs needed to present a carefully worded version of the events to protect his place in history. To this end, in his chapter drafts, he thoroughly edited out his expressions of doubt and misgivings from his diary and replaced them with excuses and misleading half-truths. Indeed, the brief mention of Task Force Baum in *War as I Knew It* places blame on everybody but the general and purposely distorts the historical record.

Patton begins his description of the ill-fated Hammelburg raid first by emphasizing his crossing of the Rhine River, then producing a self-serving post hoc rationalization for the mission: "On March 26, I crossed the Rhine with Codman and directed [General Manton S.] Eddy to send an expedition across the Main River to Hammelburg. There were two purposes to this expedition: first, to impress the Germans with the idea that we were moving due east, whereas we intended to move due north, and second to release some nine hundred American prisoners of war who were at Hammelburg."[62] The claim that Task Force Baum was designed to serve as a diversion is simply unbelievable. Indeed, the lightly armed raiding party departed on the evening of March 26 and moved under cover of darkness, attempting to use speed and surprise to accomplish its mission. Had this been a diversionary show of force, the operation probably would have been larger or would have moved more conspicuously to alert the Germans to its presence. Furthermore, the idea that this was a show of force appears to directly contradict his diary entry stating that he did not believe that there were any large German units in the area. It would have been illogical to send a small unit deep into enemy territory under cover of darkness when there were no units to observe or react to this deception.

Patton also covered up the true purpose of the mission, the rescue of his son-in-law, John Waters. While his memoirs do state that he intended to liberate the American prisoners, nowhere in his justification of the mission does he mention the goal of freeing Lieutenant Colonel Waters. This stands in stark contrast to two private letters Patton wrote to Beatrice detailing his motives. On March 23, 1945, he stated, "We are headed right for John's place and may get there before he is moved," and on March 25, he added, "Hope to send an expedition tomorrow to get John."[63] When combined with the unconvincing claim of a diversionary movement, this purposeful omission seems little more than an attempt to conceal the general's private motives under the guise of sound military practice and a heroic rescue mission.

Next Patton continues to distort the historical record by attempting to cast blame on his subordinates for failing to provide adequate resources to this mission: "I intended to send one combat command of the 4th Armored, but, unfortunately, was talked out of it by [Manton S.] Eddy and [William M.] Hoge, commanding the 4th Armored Division, so I compromised by sending one armored company and one company of armored infantry."[64] In fact, Patton ordered the mission over the objection of his subordinates, not that they refused to dedicate proper resources to the raid. As the commanding officer of the Third Army, he could have ordered a larger force be sent, but he instead ignored his generals' advice and proceeded with the mission.

The combined failure of the Hammelburg raid and the stresses of serving as Patton's subordinate ultimately took a toll on General Eddy. By mid-April, he developed dangerously high blood pressure and was ordered home to recuperate on April 19. While Eddy was a loyal subordinate who would accept much of the blame for the failed mission, the true responsibility lies with none other than the Third Army's commanding general. While Eddy would ultimately recover from his hypertension and serve with distinction until 1953, reaching the rank of lieutenant general, the man Patton dubbed the "Prince of the Rhine" for his bold actions in March 1945 would be an all too convenient scapegoat in the months that followed.[65]

In the margins of his draft chapter of *War as I Knew It*, Patton explicitly acknowledged that he needed to be careful in his description of this event: "This will be rewritten when I have new information."[66] However, despite his notes and significant access to more information, the general never altered this section, as he was apparently content to allow this incorrect version of events to remain in his manuscript. Instead, the next few paragraphs provide an account of the larger successes of Third Army, even noting that they captured the command post of the 107th German Infantry Division, where they found a "tremendous carved eagle which we sent to the United States Military Academy as a gift from the Third Army."[67]

When the memoirs return to the fate of Task Force Baum, the tone is dismissive and purposely avoids accepting responsibility: "On the other hand, we were very much disturbed because we could get no information at all as to what had happened to the task force sent east from the 4th Armored Division." After two more pages highlighting the exploits of Third Army, Patton returns to the fate of Task Force Baum: "On the thirtieth, the German radio announced that the American armored division attacking Hammelburg had been attacked and destroyed," but even here he uses a footnote to dismiss the German report by writing that the "actual composition" of the force was only one company of armor and one company of infantry.[68]

After further describing the rapid movements of Third Army, Patton returns to the story of Task Force Baum, noting that on March 31: "I made arrangements to reconstitute the two companies of the 4th Armored Division, which we now definitely knew had been captured. After forcing a crossing over the Main east of Frankfurt, in which the Captain in command was slightly wounded, they continued the attack and reached the outskirts of Hammelburg. There they ran into elements of three German divisions which, as we hoped, had been drawn by their attack."[69] Here, Patton attempts to cover his mistake by again claiming that the true mission of Task Force Baum was to divert German forces from the Third Army's main thrust north.

The general's account ignores the fact that the mission was conducted under cover of darkness, but also fails to accept responsibility for two companies of Americans who had been vastly overmatched by three German divisions.

Had the general truly "hoped" to distract these large German formations, military logic would have dictated sending a considerably larger force. Again in the margins of this section, Patton writes, "This will be rewritten/new information," but with the exception of minor rewording, the main claims were allowed to remain unaltered, a purposeful falsification of the general's motivations.[70]

Patton continues his memoir with an embellished account of the fighting around Hammelburg, claiming:

> While some of the tanks and some of the armored infantry engaged the divisions, other tanks went to the prison camp, some six miles to the north, and released the prisoners. These tanks, accompanied by some twelve hundred prisoners, rejoined the rest of the force in the vicinity of Hammelburg and started back over the road they had taken. The following report was made by my Aide, Major Stiller, who was with them but not in command. He suggested that, instead of returning over the road already used, the column strike north. The officer in charge declined that advice and the column stopped to refuel. While engaged in this refueling, they were attacked by three regiments of German infantry from three different directions, and scattered. When the confusion had cleared, Major Stiller, the Captain in command of the force, and five enlisted men continued to fight until they had used up all their ammunition and had their vehicles destroyed, when they surrendered.[71]

Once more, Patton's version of history is distorted and self-serving. He fails to mention that Task Force Baum did not have sufficient transportation to extract the majority of American prisoners and instead suggests that all twelve hundred were temporarily saved by Baum's force. Similarly, while he highlighted Major Stiller's heroics, he neglected to mention that he was included on the mission because he knew Lieutenant Colonel Waters and had personally told Patton, "I'll recognize Johnny."[72] The memoir also implies that a combination of the unnamed Baum's poor judgment and the need to refuel resulted in the force being surrounded and that these men fought to the last man in a heroic gesture reminiscent of Custer's Last Stand.

The simple fact of the matter is that the two companies of Americans were vastly outnumbered and deep behind enemy lines when they were surrounded and captured. Regardless of the road they took, they were unlikely to have avoided encirclement and capture. The need to refuel sealed the fate of Task Force Baum, but this logistical limitation was not simply bad luck; rather, it was because the mission was ill equipped to move so deep into hostile territory. Finally, while the men of Task Force Baum fought bravely, they did not literally "fight until they had used up all their ammunition and had their vehicles destroyed," but instead surrendered when it became obvious that their military situation was untenable and that further resistance would result only in needless deaths.[73]

Only after hiding his true intention for the raid and distorting the reasons for its failure did Patton mention the fate of the American prisoners. Yet, even here, he took great care to avoid the appearance of favoritism for Waters. According to Patton, "That evening [April 4, 1945] two lieutenants, who had been liberated from Hammelburg and made their way across country to our lines, paid me a visit." He does not describe in detail his conversation with the two junior officers, but added in his footnote, "These two lieutenants reported that General Patton's son-in-law, Colonel J. K. Waters, was a prisoner in the camp at Hammelburg and had been shot during the melee at the camp when the American troops arrived."[74]

In his margin notes, below this footnote, the general further distorts the facts in an attempt to hide his intentions, stating, "This was the first word received that Waters was in the camp."[75] While this note was not included in the final version of his memoirs, it is demonstrably false when compared to Patton's previous letters and diary entries.

The memoir continues, "Late that evening, Patch called up to say that three other officers from Hammelburg had reached his Headquarters and told him that Colonel Waters had been badly wounded. Patch said he would do everything in his power to capture the camp on the fifth." Here, the memoir conveniently misreports the fact that Patton had known for more than a week that Waters was in the Hammelburg prison and had "gotten his ass shot up" in the failed rescue mission. Again he shifts blame to a subordinate by claiming that the Allied efforts to recapture the camp had been the prerogative of the commanding officer of the Seventh Army, General Alexander "Sandy" Patch. Technically, Patton did not lie, but the purposeful omission of what he knew about Waters's location and condition combined with his suggestion that Patch was the motivating force behind the successful rescue lead readers to conclude that Patton's motives were purely professional. In his memoir, Patton recounted the liberation of the prison as follows: "The 13 Armored Division started to close as Army Reserve in the rear area of XX Corps. Late in the evening, Patch telephoned that the 14th Armored Division (commanded by Major General A. C. Smith) had recaptured

Hammelburg and that only about seventy American prisoners remained, among whom was Colonel Waters, critically wounded."[76] Careful to avoid the appearance of favoritism, Patton omitted the fact that he had sent his personal physician to assist Waters and instead highlights his first meeting with his newly freed son-in-law: "I returned to the hospital and pinned the Silver Star and Oak Leaf Cluster on Waters. He did not know that he had been awarded either decoration, having not lived, in an historical sense, for more than two years, since his capture in Tunisia."[77] Here the general plays the part of the concerned relative but minimizes his own role in Waters's ordeal by shifting the focus to his decorations and personal sacrifices, not the circumstances of his rescue.

Immediately after the description of their meeting in the hospital, Patton had actually written a margin note in his draft of the memoirs where he began to describe Waters's capture in Tunisia in greater detail. However, the general marked through this note, and it was not included in the final version of the book, quite possibly to avoid the appearance of nepotism.[78] While Waters is mentioned several times in the remainder of his book, it was only in reference to his improved health and the heroic decision to stand by his comrades rather than attempt escape from imprisonment.[79] While the ordeal of John Waters is part of Patton's larger narrative, it serves primarily to absolve Patton from responsibility and to mislead the reader by emphasizing his son-in-law's bravery and sacrifice.

The same cannot be said of the task force commander, Captain Abraham Baum. In fact, the memoir never mentions Baum by name and instead chooses to refer to him as "the Captain in command."[80] This editorial choice appears purposeful, as Patton met with Baum after the raid and personally decorated him with the Distinguished Service Cross for his actions, telling him, "You did one helluva a job. I always knew you were one of my best." Baum greatly admired Patton and asked him naively, "You know sir, it's difficult for me to believe that you would have sent us on that mission just to rescue one man [Waters]." An uneasy Patton reportedly replied, "That's right, Abe, I wouldn't."[81]

Baum claimed that Patton's aide instructed him that the mission was top secret and that he should not discuss it in the future. This struck Baum as a purposeful cover-up and led him to conclude that he had been "screwed again," as the army would never allow his heroic actions to become public knowledge.[82] For the remainder of his life, Baum believed that he and his men deserved the Medal of Honor for their actions but that Patton had intervened to quash the decoration, knowing this award would require a formal report that may have exposed the general's true motives.[83]

With luck, censorship, and a careful crafting of narrative, Patton was able to present a version of history that suited his purposes. Had his true motives for the raid been known at the time, it is possible that he would have been removed from command and his legacy permanently tarnished. Instead, thanks in part to Patton's historiographic efforts, this controversy remains relatively unknown. Even among those who have knowledge of the incident, there is a general sense that this type of action was not a liability, but rather an example of the boldness and initiative that distinguished Patton from other less active Allied generals. Indeed, Patton himself attempted to explain the failed Hammelburg raid as an example of his boldness: "I can say this, that throughout the campaign in Europe I know of no error I made except that of failing to send a Combat Command to take Hammelburg. Otherwise, my operations were, to me, strictly satisfactory. . . . I was under wraps from the Higher Command. This may have been a good thing, as perhaps I am too impetuous. However, I do not believe I was, and feel that had I been permitted to go all out, the war would have ended sooner and more lives would have been saved."[84]

Despite the fact that most of the recent scholarship on the Hammelburg raid has been extremely critical, several prominent historians have defended Patton's decisions as part of his bold approach to war.[85] Prior to serving as the general's official biographer, Martin Blumenson argued in a 1955 edition of *Military Review* that "despite failure, the Hammelburg mission had accomplished much. It had disrupted the entire Aschaffenburg-Hammelburg sector . . . and provoked general uncertainty and confusion. . . . [T]he task force caused the Germans to draw additional forces to the Hammelburg area—thereby making Patton's feint successful. . . . As a typical Patton maneuver—a cavalry action combining audacity and a willingness to gamble—it deserves to be remembered."[86] Similarly, Pulitzer Prize–winning historian John Toland made a case for the second-order effects of the raid, claiming, "The mission to Hammelburg was a complete failure, but the gallant force had accomplished something quite different, and even more important than Patton intended. Task Force Baum had left a path of destruction in its wake. Every town it had passed through was in a state of confusion and hysteria. The German Seventh Army still did not know what had happened."[87] In both of these examples, historians who were aware of the controversy chose to focus on the boldness of Patton's actions and provide an account that defended the general's legacy. While it is impossible to know how Blumenson reached his conclusions, as his article contains neither notes nor citations, Toland used Patton's memoirs as a key source in his book. At least in this case, it would appear that Patton's memoir protected his legacy years after his death and perpetuated the notion that boldness and rapid action were key elements of his command style.

Throughout his memoirs, Patton exercised tight control on how he presented his contributions to history. While his manipulation of the history surrounding Task Force Baum was by far the most prominent example of this control, the general was also careful to present other controversies such as the slapping of two soldiers in Sicily in a manner that suited his purposes. Indeed, Patton barely mentioned the famous slapping incidents in his book, framing them as the fault of subordinate officers who failed to enforce discipline and esprit de corps, noting, "Had other officers had the courage to do likewise, the shameful use of 'battle fatigue' as an excuse for cowardice would have been infinity reduced."[88] In his memoirs, Patton's unapologetic and defiant defense of his actions is cast as a virtue, but has not aged well. Indeed, the shell-shocked soldiers whom he assaulted are generally viewed with sympathy by modern readers, and many have concluded that the general was likely suffering from his own post-traumatic stress when he lost his temper and recklessly jeopardized his career.

Patton's memoirs are completely silent on another famous controversy—his comments at Knutsford, England, where he inadvertently insulted the Russians. At the time, Patton was deeply concerned that his loose tongue would cost him command of Third Army, confiding to Beatrice, "I get in a cold sweat when the phone rings." The general was even more upset in the pages of his diary, writing, "I feel like death. . . . [T]his last incident was so trivial in its nature, but so terrible in its effect, that it is not the result of an accident, but the work of God."[89] Ultimately, Patton avoided being sent home in disgrace only because the upcoming invasion of Europe required able combat leaders. He used this opportunity to great effect, and the incident was quickly overshadowed by his military exploits. In his memoirs, the general purposely forgoes the opportunity to present his side of the Knutsford incident and instead jumps straight into his campaign in Europe.

Much like his more extensive treatment of Task Force Baum, Patton's motives with the slappings and the Knutsford incident are quite simple. He saw this control of history as the best means of protecting his legacy. For a casual reader, or Patton admirer, it is possible to read the general's memoirs and accept that the slappings were justified or to simply forget the general's impolitic remarks to a group of English ladies.

War as I Knew It was remarkably successful in manipulating the historical record: it focused on the general's successes as a leader, downplayed the more controversial elements of his character, and perpetuated the myth of a pure warrior. The book has remained in print for more than sixty years and continues to portray Patton as a bold and decisive commander, instinctively in command of both the battlefield and his place in history.

An Unfinished Historical Legacy?

While Patton died before he could complete his memoirs, there is no reason to believe that this would have been his final attempt at writing history. Throughout his life, he wrote history with an eye toward provoking debate and influencing others. As long as the general was alive, he would have had ideas, and it is fair to conclude that he would have continued to publish, promote, and defend them.

On November 18, 1945, he wrote Beatrice, "I hope to leave here by boat around the 1st of the year." Expanding on his rationale, he continued, "I am going by boat so I can keep my numerous boxes of papers with me in my state room and not have them lost in transit."[90] Patton had a lifelong tendency to collect historical memorabilia and to save even the most trivial family or personal mementos, but these documents were critical to save because they recorded his glorious past and also contained potentially damaging information as well. This desire to personally travel with his documents indicates that Patton valued these papers highly enough to travel via a less efficient means in order to ensure that they reached their destination. It is tantalizing to consider what additional writing projects the general had in mind once his tour as commanding officer of the Fifteenth Army was completed—he never said.

On December 8, 1945, Patton wrote what would be his last letters. While he wrote to several American fans to thank them for their "constant support" and for Christmas packages, one letter stands out from the rest. Despite his impending departure, he wrote a brief letter of thanks to Emil Ludwig, an acquaintance of Patton's and a noted military historian and biographer of Napoleon. Ludwig and Patton had met in April of that year, and the general was eager to maintain this growing friendship with a noted military author. Despite his busy schedule, the general took time from his day to engage with the historian and thank him for sending him an article about his exploits during World War II. Even in small things, he cared about remembering the past and shaping his legacy for generations to come.[91]

Had Patton lived to see their publication, the reports of the General Board and *War as I Knew It* would have been truer reflections of Patton's own views and possibly more controversial. However, they probably would not have been the last chapter in Patton's battle with history. As long as Patton was able to engage with a public audience, he would have remained a controversial figure. If given the opportunity, it seems unlikely that he would have withheld his opinions on the military debates of the day, surrendered silently to criticism, or been content to recede anonymously into the past.

• •

NOTES

1. For an excellent account of Caesar's manipulation of history, see Andrew Riggsby, *Caesar In Gaul and Rome: War In Words*.

2. Bergvall, "Fifth Olympiad," 647; D'Este, *Patton*, 132–33; George S. Patton Jr., "Report on the Olympic Games," September 19, 1912, Chronological File, 1901–77, George S. Patton Papers, Manuscript Division, Library of Congress, Washington, DC; Harold E. Wilson Jr., "A Legend in His Own Mind: The Olympic Experience of General George S. Patton Jr.," 99–114.

3. "Report on the Death of Col. Cardenas," Military Papers, 1903–76, Patton Papers.

4. D'Este, *Patton*, 174.

5. For an excellent work on the US Army overwhelming problems with its dominant industrial, logistical, and population base, see John Ellis, *Brute Force: Allied Strategy and Tactics in The Second World War*. Contrast this with the proficiency of the German Army despite logistical and material hardships. See Martin Van Creveld, *Fighting Power: German and US Army Performance, 1939–1945*.

6. General Board, United States Forces, European Theater, Study No. 15, "Organization, Equipment, and Tactical Employment of Infantry Divisions."

7. General Board, United States Forces, European Theater, Study No. 15, "Organization, Equipment, and Tactical Employment."

8. General Board, United States Forces, European Theater, Study No. 15, "Organization, Equipment, and Tactical Employment." A careful reader will note the striking similarities between these comments regarding the American comparative advantage in mechanization with the general's 1932 Army War College thesis, his diary entry from November 17, as well as Patton's description of the mission of the Fifteenth Army to create a "datum plane" for future study and refinement of warfare from his October 22 letter to General J. G. Harbord (see chapter 4). See Blumenson, *The Patton Papers*, 2:800, 809.

9. Rickard, *Advance and Destroy*, 49, 318.

10. General Board, United States Forces, European Theater, Study No. 15, "Organization, Equipment, and Tactical Employment."

11. Patton frequently expressed his belief that the infantry needed better and newer equipment to help provide an advantage in combat. Codman, *Drive*, 215.

12. General Board, United States Forces, European Theater, Study No. 15, "Organization, Equipment, and Tactical Employment."

13. General Board, United States Forces, European Theater, Study No. 15, "Organization, Equipment, and Tactical Employment."

14. General Board, United States Forces, European Theater, Study No. 15, "Organization, Equipment, and Tactical Employment."

15. Diaries, 1910–45, Patton Papers.

16. In Patton's own Third Army, both the number and the quality of replacements were significantly lacking. For data on this problem, see "After Action Report: Third US Army, 1 August 1944–9 May 1945," 145, 190, 238, 281.

17. "Training in the Ground Army, 1942–1945, Study No. 11," Army Historical Section, 1948, 55.

18. General Board, United States Forces, European Theater, Study No. 3, "Reinforcement System and Reinforcement Procedures in the European Theater of Operations," appx. 19, 4–5.

19. Stephen E. Ambrose, *Citizen Soldiers: The U.S. Army from the Normandy Beaches to the Bulge to the Surrender of Germany—June 7, 1944–May 7, 1945*; Tom Brokaw, *The Greatest Generation*.

20. Patton's insistence on talking directly to his men about the stress of combat was very clear. He said, "You are not all going to die. Only two percent of you right here today would die in a major battle. Death must not be feared. Death, in time, comes to all men. Yes, every man is scared in his first battle. If he says he's not, he's a liar." Brighton, *Patton, Montgomery, Rommel*, 260–68.

21. The text of Patton's note reads: "This report represents the opinion of a majority of the Board. However, from my point of view gained from no inconsiderable experience as an Army Commander, I feel that there is no need for a Tactical Information Service of this nature between Army Headquarters and subordinate units." General Board, United States Forces, European Theater, Study No. 18, "Army Tactical Information Service," 6.

22. J. Eisenhower, *Strictly Personal*, 115.

23. General Board, United States Forces, European Theater, Study No. 1, "The Strategy of the Campaign in Western Europe, 1944–1945."

24. Throughout his career, Patton was an advocate for airpower and worked closely with Air Corps generals such as Jimmy Doolittle and Pete Quesada. See generally David N. Spires, *Air Power for Patton's Army: The XIX Tactical Air Command in the Second World War*; John J. Sullivan, *Air Support for Patton's Third Army*.

25. General Board, United States Forces, European Theater, Study No. 1, "Strategy of the Campaign in Western Europe."

26. Forrest C. Pogue, *CMH Publication 7-1, United States Army in World War II European Theater of Operations: The Supreme Command*, 268n19.

27. On the Operation Market Garden campaign's numerous failures, see David Bennett, *Magnificent Disaster: The Failure of Market Garden, the Arnhem Operation, September 1944*; Cornelius Ryan, *A Bridge Too Far*.

28. J. Eisenhower, *Strictly Personal*.

29. Totten, *Button Box*, 350.

30. Farago, *Last Days of Patton*, 13.

31. The one major exception to this general rule is Patton's self-serving treatment of the failed Hammelburg raid, which will be discussed in detail below.

32. Speeches and Writings File, 1900–1947, Patton Papers.

33. Speeches and Writings File, 1900–1947, Patton Papers.

34. Correspondence, 1903–45, Patton Papers.

35. Correspondence, 1903–45, Patton Papers.

36. Blumenson, *The Patton Papers*, 2:803–4.

37. Patton to George Marshall, October 10, 1945; Patton to Walton Walker, November 6, 1945; and Patton to Geoffrey Keyes, November 17, 1945, Correspondence, 1903–45, Patton Papers.

38. In this same letter, Patton notes the receipt of the letter from General Summerall: "Just had a nice letter from Charles P. Summerall which I answered at some length. He is a fine old man." Chronological File, 1901–77, Patton Papers.

39. Chronological File, 1901–77, Patton Papers.

40. Correspondence, 1903–45, Patton Papers.

41. Speeches and Writings File, 1900–1947, Patton Papers.

42. Sarantakes, *Making "Patton,"* 36, 50, 84, 96–97, 115, 118, 174; Harkins, *When the Third Cracked Europe*.

43. Patton, *War as I Knew It*, Front Matter.

44. Blumenson, *Breakout and Pursuit*; Martin Blumenson, *The United States Army in World War II: The Mediterranean Theater of Operations, Salerno to Cassino*.

45. R. Patton, *The Pattons*, 295–96; Benjamin Patton and Jennifer Scruby, *Growing Up Patton: Reflections on Heroes, History, and Family Wisdom*, 16, 20.

46. Blumenson and Hymel, *Patton*.

47. Indeed, *The Patton Papers* were the motivation for a young Carlo D'Este, among others. While stationed in Burtonwood Army Depot, England D'Este fortuitously found a copy of volume 1 in a military library and was immediately entranced. This led him to purchase the second volume, decide on becoming a military historian after he retired from the army, begin a long friendship with Blumenson, and ultimately become the leading authority on George S. Patton. Carlo D'Este, "Martin Blumenson: My Remembrances of a Friend," January 2, 2008, http://armchairgeneral.com/martin-blumenson-my-remembrance-of-a-friend.htm.

48. On Patton's relationships with Jewish staff members and his treatment by Jewish biographers, see D'Este, *Patton*, 171–72; Groom, *The Generals*, 447; and Victor Davis Hanson, *The Soul of Battle: From Ancient Times to the Present Day, How Three Great Liberators Vanquished Tyranny*, 280–81.

49. B. Patton and Scruby, *Growing Up Patton*, 16.

50. Blumenson, *Battle of the Generals*.

51. Blumenson, *Breakout and Pursuit*, 506–9.

52. Blumenson, *Battle of the Generals*, 22, 206, 264, 260, 217.

53. While meticulously researched, Blumenson's books are consistently more positive about Patton and his accomplishments than those of other major biographers. For example, Carlo D'Este noted that Operation Torch "was hardly Patton's finest hour." Ladislas Farago similarly noted, "The battle for Morocco lasted exactly 74 hours, but they were not George Patton's finest hours." In contrast, Blumenson stated, "The invasion of Morocco confirmed Patton's military brilliance. His zeal and unerring intuition had assured victory in the landings. His quick organization of a major attack on Casablanca was masterful." Quotes and discussion in Yeide, *Fighting Patton*, 146.

54. Freeman quoted in Patton, *War as I Knew It*, front matter.

55. Essame, *Patton as Military Commander*, 171; Rickard, *Advance and Destroy*, 309.

56. For example, see Ellis, *Brute Force*; Norman Gelb, *Ike and Monty: Generals at War*; Blumenson, *Battle of the Generals*; and Charles Dick, *Victory to Stalemate: The Western Front, Summer 1944 Decisive and Indecisive Military Operations*.

57. D'Este, *Patton*, 818.

58. Diaries, 1910–45, Patton Papers. Patton's aide Charles Codman expressed similar misgivings and uncertainties in his memoir entries dated March 28, April 4, and April 7, 1945. Codman, *Drive*, 277–79.

59. D'Este, *Patton*, 716.

60. Chronological File, 1901–77, Patton Papers.

61. Schultz, *Patton's Last Gamble*, 179–80.

62. Patton, *War as I Knew It*, 275.

63. Chronological File, 1901–77, Patton Papers; Atkinson, *Guns at Last Light*, 570.

64. Patton, *War as I Knew It*, 275.

65. Harold R. Winton, *Corps Commanders of the Bulge: Six American Generals and Victory in the Ardennes*, 356–57.

66. Speeches and Writings File, 1900–1947, Patton Papers.

67. Patton, *War as I Knew It*, 277.

68. Patton, *War as I Knew It*, 277.

69. Patton, *War as I Knew It*, 280.

70. Speeches and Writings File, 1900–1947, Patton Papers.

71. Patton, *War as I Knew It*, 281.

72. Jordan, *Brothers, Rivals, Victory*, 495.

73. Patton, *War as I Knew It*, 281.

74. Patton, *War as I Knew It*, 285.

75. Speeches and Writings File, 1900–1947, Patton Papers.

76. Patton, *War as I Knew It*, 285, 286.

77. Patton, *War as I Knew It*, 289.

78. Speeches and Writings File, 1900–1947, Patton Papers.

79. Patton, *War as I Knew It*, 303, 319.

80. Patton, *War as I Knew It*, 280–81.

81. Baron, Baum, and Goldhurst, *Raid!*, 250; D'Este, *Patton*, 718.

82. Baron, Baum, and Goldhurst, *Raid!*, 250; D'Este, *Patton*, 718.

83. Interestingly, despite the controversy, Baum became close friends with John Waters. He also befriended numerous German soldiers, exchanged yearly holiday cards with the German commandant of the Hammelburg prison, and returned to Hammelburg in 2005 to reenact his mission. He worked in the garment industry after the war, wrote a book about the raid, and retired to Southern California. Baum died in 2013 and was buried with full military honors in Arlington National Cemetery.

84. Patton, *War as I Knew It*, 332.

85. Schultz, *Patton's Last Gamble*, 200–202.

86. Martin Blumenson, "The Hammelburg Mission."

87. John Toland, *The Last 100 Days: The Tumultuous and Controversial Story of the Final Days of the War in Europe*, 296.

88. Toland, *Last 100 Days*, 382.

89. Diaries, 1910–45, Patton Papers; D'Este, *Patton*, 583–600.

90. Chronological File, 1901–77, Patton Papers.

91. Blumenson, *The Patton Papers*, 2:813.

CONCLUSION

BATTLING WITH THE MYTH OF A NATURAL WARRIOR

PERHAPS THE BIGGEST reason the Patton mythos has been so enduring is the most obvious—his life seems to have a perfect story arc. He prepared himself for decades, overcame scandal and frustrations, gained increasing fame and confidence in his own abilities, played a pivotal role in some of the biggest battles in World War II, and died soon after the war was over.

In many ways, Patton's contradictory personality makes him an alluring modern-day Don Quixote archetype. This Don Quixote allusion was particularly strong in the 1970 biopic that purposely exaggerated Patton's sense of fate and the supernatural and had the general walk into the distance past a windmill in the final scene while a voice-over discussed the fleeting nature of glory.[1] Indeed, there is something fascinating about a flawed warrior trapped between the past and the future.[2]

Due to the success of the film and other popular works, the prevailing interpretation is that Patton was a perfect warrior who was unable to cope with the drudgery of peace. War was necessary for him because it sustained his passions and gave him the perfect outlet for his energies. Removing him from war would thus be his undoing because it would deprive him of purpose. Exactly eight months before the fateful traffic accident, Patton told his friend and confidant Colonel Robert S. Allen, "The best end for an old campaigner is a bullet at the last minute of the last battle," a claim that has been used to support the notion that even the famous general believed his life was finished.[3]

Popular myths suggest that Patton died a bitter failure who was out of place and had been denied the soldier's death he so desperately craved. Yet, in truth, the general was already working to restore his image and ego through writing history. The auto accident that abruptly took Patton's life ended his attempt at personal and professional rehabilitation. Nevertheless, he was actively engaged in a purposeful attempt to continue making history on his own terms. While Patton's last chapter was unfinished, his last battle with history was fought with his legendary tenacity and passion.

Reassessing Patton's Battles with History

The key to Patton's success was his unique combination of historical knowledge and a fanatical drive to succeed. Much like his hero Napoleon, he was able to do more than others because of his absolute dedication to achieving mastery in all aspects of warfare.[4] Whether it was physical conditioning, proficiency with weapons, soldierly bearing, or knowledge of obscure facets of history such as the Norman road network, he believed that every aspect of the military profession was worth his attention.

While it is often obscured by the more colorful elements of his personality, a deep engagement with history was essential to Patton's success. He studied history to better understand the uncertainty and chaos of battle and learn from the successes and failures of those who had gone before. He wrote history to advance his career, promote his ideas, and protect his legacy. He made history because, like Napoleon, he achieved coup d'oeil and had the confidence to vigorously implement his vision of warfare.

This extraordinary motivation came at a price. Patton was easily frustrated, often expected too much of his subordinates, and did not suffer fools gladly. During times of inaction, this drive often overshadowed his skills as a warrior, as it convinced many that he was an unstable anachronism who could not adapt to the political realities of peace. Even during war, this fanatical drive could be a major liability. During World War II, he exacerbated tensions within the Allied High Command, lost control of his temper with the two shell-shocked soldiers in Sicily, strained numerous friendships, and gambled with the lives of his men during the Hammelburg raid.

Despite these deep character flaws, he was saved by friends and superiors who understood that his unique talents were invaluable during times of war. Patton made the most of these opportunities, and his many battlefield victories have guaranteed him a place among history's greatest military leaders. It is worth studying this complex man's battles with history and to reflect on its lessons.

Lessons for Contemporary Scholars and Practitioners
INSTITUTIONALIZE A PRACTICAL APPROACH TO MILITARY HISTORY

For many, history is not a priority. Rather than being a key to victory, it falls into the category of a "nice to have." Unlike technical skills, physical training, suicide prevention, substance-abuse classes, and other administrative tasks that have a clear and immediate benefit for an officer's career and the mission, history is often seen as having little relevance or connection to the present. This is understandable, but a mistake. Rather than being seen as an ancillary skill, modern warriors should be taught that a personal *and* relevant approach to the past is an indispensable skill for the military profession.

While Patton loved history for its own sake, he firmly believed that it had a practical application. In his view, history was far more than a chronology of names, dates, and places, but also contained lessons for the present. To understand these lessons, Patton purposely analyzed the complex interaction of geography, technology, human factors, information, and culture that had combined to shape events. To this end, he purposely sought out primary sources, after-action reports, memoirs, and veterans of past wars to better understand how leaders in the past grappled with their own circumstances. In addition to this reading and interviewing, Patton often traveled to battlefields to conduct his own staff rides of the terrain. While conducting these studies, he did his best to put himself in the position of the soldiers and their commanders and to try to understand the challenges they faced. Expanding on this sympathetic understanding, he worked through multiple courses of action in his own mind to determine how he would have reacted if he were faced with a similar situation.

Rather than ask *what* happened, Patton took the additional steps of critically analyzing *why* events happened as they did and how they might have gone differently if circumstances had been different. He formalized these studies by making a series of notes and reports summarizing his views for both private study and public release. While these notes could at times be self-serving, they reveal a mind that was critically analyzing the past and was not satisfied with knowing the simple textbook answer. By conducting his own self-directed decision analysis, Patton hoped to be ready when his moment came to make history by understanding and engaging with the past. His future ability to react almost instantly to unfolding events was a synthesis of this practical approach to understanding military history.

Modern historians and practitioners would do well to adopt this same approach. In addition to expanding practical teaching exercises such as staff rides, they should look to the famous general for inspiration and guidance.[5] By analyzing how Patton prepared himself, students could move beyond the triumphalism that surrounds his career and develop a more nuanced and useful understanding of the famous general. As this book has argued, Patton's victories were not preordained but rather based on a purposeful approach to understanding others who came before him. While Patton would undoubtedly enjoy his fame, he would certainly want his life and work analyzed and applied for the future. To neglect this insight is to perpetuate the view that Patton was a natural warrior and to miss one of his most powerful contributions to the study of war.

ACADEMIC CURIOSITY IS A RARE GIFT THAT CAN PAY UNEXPECTED DIVIDENDS

Despite the vast amounts of time and money dedicated to predicting the future, strategic planners are often wrong. In fact, one recent analysis boldly claimed that famous groundhog Punxsutawney Phil's record of predicting the onset of spring with a 40 percent success rate would be a vast improvement over the Department of Defense's record at predicting future contingencies.[6] If it is true that it is almost impossible to correctly predict the time, place, and nature of future wars, then a study of the past would seem like a fool's errand.

While Patton's understanding of the evolving nature of warfare was better than most, he was also imperfect. For every correct prediction, such as his study of the Norman road network on his honeymoon, he had another, such as his insistence in the continued relevance of the horse cavalry, that was incorrect. Like so many others, the general had a decidedly mixed record at predicting the future, a fact that should be encouraging for practitioners and scholars alike!

Where Patton was successful was not in his rate of prediction but in the wide range of subjects that he studied in detail and his flexibility of mind that allowed him to adapt to unanticipated circumstances, adjust his approach, and apply his studies to the problem of the moment. He was wrong about the horse cavalry, but he could easily drop the matter once it became clear that mechanization was the way of the future. On the other hand, he could fall back on his study of the Norman roads when it became clear that the Allies needed a plan to break the stalemate they encountered in the *bocage*. This broad intellectual tool kit allowed Patton to draw from a wide range of knowledge and apply it in way that he and others did not fully anticipate.

This impressive knowledge base and his flexibility of mind were made possible by Patton's uncommon intellectual curiosity and desire to learn. Seemingly no element of the military art was beyond his study. To take just another example, consider Patton's reading of the Koran on his voyage to Morocco. On his trip across the Atlantic, the general took the time to learn about the culture of the Muslim population in the region, confident in the belief that this study would prove beneficial. While the Allies would have probably still won the campaign in North Africa without their commander's academic initiative, Patton was able to use this new cultural knowledge to quickly build a rapport with the local power brokers and avoid a mass insurgency in his rear areas.

This intellectual curiosity and his desire to be a lifelong learner were rare gifts indeed and paid unexpected dividends on battlefields across three continents. Given the uncertain nature of warfare, it is imperative to develop future leaders with this same open-mindedness and willingness to study the complex world around them. Such an approach will not produce a crystal ball for perfectly divining the unknowable, but it may provide critical perspectives to mastering the battlefields of the future.

HISTORY DOES NOT REPEAT ITSELF, BUT THERE ARE COMMON THEMES
Modern scholars are quick to say that history does not repeat itself. Instead, they argue that every case is in fact different. Despite these warnings, there is always a temptation to compare cases across time and look for similarities. One can always take two historical cases and create a post hoc explanation for why they are in fact similar. While this may create the illusion of history repeating itself, such analysis is often oversimplistic and deterministic and strips actors of their agency—so say the experts.

Patton's view of history was in many ways more arcane than those types practiced today. Although he did not believe that history literally repeated itself, he believed that through careful study of the past he could gain insight into the present. By studying great leaders and their campaigns, Patton hoped that he could understand what drove these men and why they made the choices that they did. This study reinforced in the general's mind the value of personal leadership, discipline, initiative, fighting spirit, terrain, and countless other factors on the battlefield. While the specific circumstances might change, Patton believed that these factors were enduring elements to success, and he made them a central part of his leadership philosophy.

Through such an understanding of the past, Patton could also reason by analogy. This not only allowed him to respond to an unfolding situation on the battlefield more rapidly, but also allowed him to effectively and quickly communicate his ideas to his fellow officers who had also studied these bat-tles. For example, while the II Corps' positions in North Africa appeared uncertain, even tenuous, Patton's quick and confident analogy to the Battle of Second Manassas could put his subordinates' minds at ease, while giving them a better way to conceptualize the unfolding battle and plan to turn the tables on the overextended Germans. As discussed in the previous chap-ters, the fighting in North Africa was not the same as the fighting around Manassas, yet it allowed the general and his subordinates to have a theory of the case to guide their planning.

Given the modern interpretation of history, Patton's views may seem quaint, simplistic, or even dangerous. Yet he clearly believed that there was a tangible value to his studies, and he worked diligently to improve upon his own knowledge of the past. When his time came, he used history to support his theories of leadership, act quickly, buoy his own confidence, and portray a mastery of the battlefield.

Future leaders would do well to adopt this approach to the past, especially because the future is uncertain. Given this uncertainty, it is critical to be able to understand why factors such as concentration of force, technology, initiative, geography, and leadership have mattered in the past. Such an understanding is not a guarantee of victory, but it can be a powerful tool and source of comfort in the chaos and confusion of battle. Through a careful study of the past, it is possible for future leaders to develop a similar sense of coup d'oeil and decisiveness that led Patton to victory on three continents.

TAKE TIME TO REFLECT ON THE LESSONS OF THE PAST

Being a military officer is one of the most demanding tasks on the planet. Rather than simply being masters of combat arms, officers are busy with a wide range of responsibilities, including counselor, career manager, bureau-crat, babysitter, and countless other roles. Given this daunting range of jobs, how could any officer, no matter how intellectually curious and motivated, possibly hope to dedicate a significant portion of his or her time to a deep study of history, culture, and strategy?

In many ways, Patton was lucky. He benefited from a family that indulged his love of history and provided him with the financial means to travel, purchase books, and enjoy the finer things of life. He also had a first-rate military education, which included six years of undergraduate study at VMI and West Point, the opportunity to attend the French Cavalry School for two summers, as well as assignments to various army schools.

Patton also benefited from a slower pace of military life prior to the outbreak of World War I and during the interwar period. During these periods of calm, he was dedicated to improving his mind and took the time to read, lecture, and reflect about the changing nature of war. While he craved action, the young officer quickly developed a work ethic and dedication to improving himself even during times of peace. Rather than simply enjoy the good life, he traveled to battlefields, interviewed soldiers, read and wrote extensively, and made personal connections that would benefit his career.

This is a credit to Patton, but it is not entirely of his own doing. Had he come from a humbler background or served in a different era, it is highly unlikely that he would have had the opportunities to develop his thinking on such a wide range of military subjects, despite his dedication to learning and self-improvement. Without the twin benefits of wealth and spare time, he may have been more like his friends Eisenhower and Bradley, dedicated professionals, but not a polished scholar of history and the military arts. It is fortunate for the US Army that Patton had these opportunities and made the most of them, but it does not alter the fact that his case was the exception, not the rule for modern officers.

Unfortunately, there is not a simple solution to the time demands on contemporary leaders. Given the pace of deployments and their myriad other responsibilities, it seems unlikely that a significant portion of the modern officer corps could be given the time to develop this deep appreciation for culture and history. Moreover, combat roles and promotions are typically given to leaders with significant combat experience, not those with academic training. Patton had both, but this does not alter the fact that for many these career opportunities are mutually exclusive.

Like Patton, leaders such as David Petraeus, James Mattis, and H. R. McMaster were able to showcase their impressive intellectual gifts only because they were excellent combat leaders first and foremost. Moreover, each of these recent generals came of age as junior officers prior to the increased pace of operations necessitated by the wars in Iraq and Afghanistan. In their formative years, these future generals had the time to do more thinking and reflecting on broader issues of strategy, opportunities that may have been denied to them had they entered the service a decade later.

While the American military has made efforts to encourage deeper engagement with academia and encourage reading and self-study, it is unclear if it has taken adequate steps to address its own shortcomings. Reading lists and assignments to various war colleges and staff colleges help, but they are only part of the solution. Unfortunately, many excellent officers struggle to develop their own human capital because they lack both the time to read and reflect on the lessons of the past and the organizational support for their efforts. Providing time and support for more academic endeavors would not make officers' jobs any easier. Rather, it would nurture a different part of their diverse skill set and encourage them to think more as strategists and historians and less as technocrats and managers.

DO NOT ACCEPT MYTHS AND LEGENDS AT FACE VALUE

One of the overarching themes of this book is that myths and legends are intriguing but imperfect. By their very nature, myths capture our imagination through exaggerating both strengths and weaknesses of human beings and placing them into a compelling and often selective narrative of history.

George Patton was in many ways the perfect person for such hagiography because he had a strong personality, he achieved excellence in a wide range of endeavors, and he died while his fame was still fresh in the minds of the American public. Indeed, if you want an American Achilles or Don Quixote, look no further than Old Blood 'n' Guts! He captured the American spirit, defeated the Nazis, and was quickly swept from the scene.

Like much of the popular mythos, this interpretation contains an element of truth yet obscures a more complex reality. The truth is that Patton did enjoy the challenge of battle, but he was painfully aware that his usefulness as an officer extended far beyond the battlefield. During moments of frustration and uncertainty, he took comfort from his love of history and institutionalized lessons learned in his public and private writings. While neither of these tasks could compare to the challenge and intensity of battle, the general believed that he was contributing to the mission of the army while also promoting and defending his place in history. Failing to recognize these purposeful engagements with the past risks perpetuating the caricatured view that the general was nothing more than a lover of war.

To properly understand this flawed genius, it is imperative to peel back the mythology that distorts his true character. George S. Patton Jr. was not the natural warrior of legend. He was not reincarnated. He was not psychic. He was brave and flamboyant, to be sure, but he was also an incredibly driven lifelong learner. Patton achieved greatness by understanding, writing, and applying history, and he ultimately achieved the lasting fame he so passionately craved.

If the myth is right and Patton was a natural warrior, there would be little left to learn from his life's work. The truth is more subtle and complex and deserves continued study.

. . . .

NOTES

1. According to the authoritative source on the film, Nicholas Sarantakes, many scenes were purposely written to evoke memories of this literary classic. Sarantakes, *Making "Patton,"* 84, 141–45.

2. Alan Axelrod, *Patton's Drive: The Making of America's Greatest General*; Hanson, *Soul of Battle*; Keane, *Patton*; Sarantakes, *Making "Patton."*

3. Robert S. Allen, *Lucky Forward: The History of Patton's Third Army*, 402.

4. Alistair Horne, *The Age of Napoleon*, 48, 75.

5. For an excellent overview of how the US Army conducts staff rides, see William G. Robertson, *The Staff Ride*.

6. Joseph J. Collins, "Of Groundhogs and Ground Combat."

BIBLIOGRAPHY

Archival Material

Dwight D. Eisenhower Presidential Library and Museum. Photo Collection, Abilene, KS.

General George Patton Museum of Leadership. Photo Collection, Fort Knox, KY.

Ike Skelton Combined Arms Research Library. Digital Library, Fort Leavenworth, KS.

National Archives. Photo Collection, Washington, DC.

Patton, George S., Papers. 1807–1979, Manuscript Division, Library of Congress, Washington, DC.

Published Sources

"After Action Report: Third US Army, 1 August 1944–9 May 1945, Volume I, 'The Operations.'" 652nd Engineer Battalion, Co. B, and 942nd Engineer Aviation, Battalion, May 1945.

Allen, Robert S. *Forward with Patton: The World War II Diary of Colonel Robert S. Allen*. Edited by John Nelson Rickard. Lexington: University Press of Kentucky, 2017.

———. *Lucky Forward: The History of Patton's Third Army*. New York: Vanguard Press, 1947.

Ambrose, Stephen E. *Band of Brothers: E Company, 506th Regiment, 101st Airborne from Normandy to Hitler's Eagle's Nest*. New York: Simon and Schuster, 1998.

———. *Citizen Soldiers: The U.S. Army from the Normandy Beaches to the Bulge to the Surrender of Germany—June 7, 1944–May 7, 1945*. New York: Simon and Schuster, 1992.

Anderson, Charles R. *Tunisia, 17 November 1942 to 13 May 1943*. CMH Pub 72-12. Washington, DC: US Army Center of Military History, 1993.

Astor, Gerald. *Terrible Terry Allen, Combat General of World War II: The Life of an American Soldier*. New York: Ballantine Books, 2003.

Atkinson, Rick. *An Army at Dawn: The War in North Africa, 1942–1943*. New York: Henry Holt, 2002.

———. *The Day of Battle: The War in Sicily and Italy, 1943–1944*. New York: Henry Holt, 2007.

———. *The Guns at Last Light: The War in Western Europe, 1944–1945*. New York: Henry Holt, 2013.

Axelrod, Alan. *Patton on Leadership: Strategic Lessons for Corporate Warfare*. Paramus, NJ: Prentice Hall, 1999.

———. *Patton's Drive: The Making of America's Greatest General*. Guilford, CT: Lyons Press, 2009.

Ayer, Fred, Jr. *Before the Colors Fade: A Portrait of a Soldier, George S. Patton, Jr.* Boston: Houghton Mifflin, 1964.

Baron, Richard, Abe Baum, and Richard Goldhurst. *Raid! The Untold Story of Patton's Secret Mission*. New York: G. P. Putnam's Sons, 1981.

Barron, Leo. *Patton at the Battle of the Bulge: How the General's Tanks Turned the Tide at Bastogne*. New York: Penguin Group, 2014.

———. *Patton's First Victory: How General George Patton Turned the Tide in North Africa and Defeated the Afrika Korps at El Guettar*. Guilford, CT: Stackpole Books, 2018.

Barry, Steven Thomas. *Battalion Commanders at War: U.S. Army Tactical Leadership in the Mediterranean Theater, 1942–1943*. Lawrence: University Press of Kansas, 2013.

Beevor, Antony. *Ardennes 1944: The Battle of the Bulge*. New York: Viking, 2015.

———. *D-Day: The Battle for Normandy*. New York: Viking, 2009.

———. *The Fall of Berlin, 1945*. New York: Viking, 2002.

Bennett, David. *Magnificent Disaster: The Failure of Market Garden, the Arnhem Operation, September 1944*. Drexel Hill, PA: Casemate, 2008.

Bergvall, Erik, ed. "The Fifth Olympiad: The Official Report of the Olympic Games of Stockholm, 1912." Stockholm: Wahlstrom & Widstrand, 1913.

Bezdek, Richard H. *American Swords and Sword Makers*. Vol. 1. Boulder, CO: Paladin Press, 1994.

Biddiscombe, Perry. *Werwolf! The History of the National Socialist Guerrilla Movement, 1944–1946*. Toronto: University of Toronto Press, 1998.

Biddle, Stephen. *Military Power: Explaining Victory and Defeat in Modern Battle*. Princeton, NJ: Princeton University Press, 2004.

Bielakowski, Alexander M. "The Role of the Horse in Modern Warfare as Viewed in the Interwar U.S. Army's *Cavalry Journal*." *Army History* (Summer–Fall 2000): 20–25.

Birtle, Andrew J. *Sicily 1943, the U.S. Army WWII Campaigns. Washington, DC: US Army Center of Military History, 1993.*

Bixel, C. P. "Memorandum for All Ground General and Special Staff, Headquarters Army Ground Forces, Subject: Lessons Derived from Operations at Casablanca and Oran." Washington, DC: Army War College, February 25, 1943.

Black, Robert W. *Cavalry Raids of the Civil War*. Mechanicsburg, PA: Stackpole Books, 2004.

Blumenson, Martin. *The Battle of the Generals: The Untold Story of the Falaise Pocket—the Campaign That Should Have Won World War II*. New York: William Morrow, 1995.

———. *Breakout and Pursuit*. Washington: Office of the Chief of Military History, US Army, 1961.

———. "George S. Patton's Student Days at the Army War College." *Parameters* 5, no. 2 (1976): 25–32.

———. "The Hammelburg Mission." *Military Review* 35 (May 1955): 24–31.

———. *Kasserine Pass*. Boston: Houghton Mifflin, 1967.

———. *Patton: The Man behind the Legend, 1885–1945*. New York: William Morrow, 1985.

———, ed. *The Patton Papers*. Vol. 1, *1885–1940*. Boston: Houghton Mifflin, 1972.

———, ed. *The Patton Papers*. Vol. 2, *1940–1945*. Boston: Houghton Mifflin, 1974.

———. *The United States Army in World War II: The Mediterranean Theater of Operations, Salerno to Cassino*. Washington, DC: Government Printing Office, 1969.

Blumenson, Martin, and Kevin M. Hymel. *Patton: Legendary World War II Commander*. Washington, DC: Potomac Books, 2008.

Bradley, Omar N., and Clay Blair. *A General's Life*. New York: Simon and Schuster, 1983.

Bradsher, Greg. "Nazi Gold: The Merkers Mine Treasure." *Prologue Magazine* 31, no. 1 (Spring 1999): 7–21.

Brassford, Christopher. *Clausewitz in English: The Reception of Clausewitz in Britain and America, 1815–1945*. Oxford: Oxford University Press, 1994.

Brighton, Terry. *Patton, Montgomery, Rommel: Masters of War*. New York: Crown, 2009.

Brokaw, Tom. *The Greatest Generation*. New York: Random House, 1998.

Brown, Anthony Cave. *Bodyguard of Lies: The Extraordinary True Story behind D-Day*. Guilford, CT: Lyons Press, 2002.

Carafano, James Jay. *GI Ingenuity: Improvisation, Technology, and Winning World War II*. Mechanicsburg, PA: Stackpole Books, 2006.

Chandler, David G. *The Campaigns of Napoleon*. New York: Scribner, 1966.

Chernow, Ron. *Grant*. New York: Penguin, 2017.

Churchill, Winston S. *My Early Life: 1874–1904*. New York: Charles Scribner and Sons, 1930.

———. *The Second World War*. Vol. 6, *Triumph and Tragedy*. Boston: Houghton Mifflin, 1953.

Citino, Robert M. *The Wehrmacht's Last Stand: The German Campaigns of 1944–1945*. Lawrence: University Press of Kansas, 2017.

Clark, J. P. *Preparing for War: The Emergence of the Modern U.S. Army, 1815–1917*. Cambridge, MA: Harvard University Press, 2017.

Clausewitz, Carl von. *On War*. Translated by Michael Howard and Peter Paret. Princeton, NJ: Princeton University Press, 1976.

Codman, Charles R. *Drive*. Boston: Little, Brown, 1957.

Coffman, Edward M. *The Regulars: The American Army, 1898–1941*. Cambridge, MA: Belknap Press, 2004.

Cohen, Richard. *By the Sword: A History of Gladiators, Musketeers, Samurai, Swashbucklers, and Olympic Champions*. New York: Random House, 2007.

Cole, Hugh M. *United States Army in World War II, the European Theater of Operations, the Ardennes: Battle of the Bulge*. Washington, DC: US Army Center of Military History, 1965.

Collins, Joseph J. "Of Groundhogs and Ground Combat." *Small Wars Journal* (April 11, 2013). https://smallwarsjournal.com/jrnl/art/of-groundhogs-and-ground-combat.

Condon-Rall, Mary Ellen, and Albert E. Cowdrey. *The Medical Department: Medical Service in the War against Japan*. Washington, DC: US Army Center of Military History, 1998.

Corum, James S. *The Roots of Blitzkrieg: Hans von Seeckt and German Military Reform*. Lawrence: University Press of Kansas, 1992.

Cox, Edward. *Grey Imminence: Fox Conner and the Art of Mentorship*. Stillwater, OK: New Forums Press, 2010.

CSI Battlebook 21: Operation Cobra: 4th Armored Division: Deliberate Attack Exploitation. Fort Leavenworth, KS: Combat Studies Institute, 1968.

Daniel, J. Furman, III. "Patton as a Counterinsurgent? Lessons from an Unlikely COIN-Danista." *Small Wars Journal* (January 1–14, 2014).

———, ed. *21st Century Patton: Strategic Insights for the Modern Era*. Annapolis, MD: Naval Institute Press, 2016.

Daniel, J. Furman, III, and Paul Musgrave. "Synthetic Experiences: How Popular Culture Matters for Images of International Relations." *International Studies Quarterly* 61, no. 3 (September 2017): 503–16.

Daniel, J. Furman, III, and Brian A. Smith. "Burke and Clausewitz on the Limitation of War." *Journal of International Political Theory* 11, no. 3 (2015): 313–30.

D'Este, Carlo. *Decision in Normandy*. Reprint. 1983. Reprint, New York: Konecky and Konecky, 2000.

——— ———. *Patton: A Genius for War*. New York: HarperCollins, 1995.

Dick, Charles J. *Victory to Stalemate: The Western Front, Summer 1944 Decisive and Indecisive Military Operations*. Vol. 1. Lawrence: University Press of Kansas, 2016.

Dietrich, Steve E. "The Professional Reading of General George S. Patton, Jr." *Journal of Military History* 53, no. 4 (1998): 387–418.

DiNardo, Richard L. *Mechanized Juggernaut or Military Anachronism? Horses and the German Army of World War II*. Westport, CT: Praeger, 1991.

Duggan, William. *Napoleon's Glance: The Secret of Strategy*. New York: Nation Books, 2002.

Eisenhower, Dwight D. *Crusade in Europe*. New York: Doubleday, 1948.

———. "Report of the Commander-in-Chief Allied Forces to the Combined Chiefs of Staff on Operations in North Africa."

Eisenhower, John S. D. *The Bitter Woods: The Battle of the Bulge*. New York: G. P. Putnam's Sons, 1969.

———. *General Ike: A Personal Reminiscence*. New York: Free Press, 2003.

———. *So Far from God: The U.S. War with Mexico, 1846–1848*. New York: Random House, 1989.

———. *Soldiers and Statesmen: Reflections on Leadership*. Columbia: University of Missouri Press, 2012.

———. *Strictly Personal*. New York: Doubleday, 1974.

Ellis, John. *Brute Force: Allied Strategy and Tactics in the Second World War*. New York: Viking, 1990.

Essame, H. *Patton as Military Commander*. Conshohocken, PA: Combined, 1998.

Farago, Ladislas. *The Last Days of Patton*. New York: McGraw-Hill, 1981.

———. *Patton: Ordeal and Triumph*. Yardley, PA: Westholme, 2005.

Faulkner, Richard S. *Pershing's Crusaders: The American Soldier in World War I*. Lawrence: University Press of Kansas, 2017.

Ferrell, Robert H. *America's Deadliest Battle: Meuse-Argonne, 1918*. Lawrence: University Press of Kansas, 2007.

"The First Year of the Occupation—Special Text 41-10-63." Office of the Chief Historian, European Command, 1947.

Frieser, Karl-Heinz. *The Blitzkrieg Legend: The 1940 Campaign in the West*. Translated by John T. Greenwood. Annapolis, MD: Naval Institute Press, 2005.

Fuller, J. F. C. *Tanks in the Great War, 1914–1918*. New York: E. P. Dutton, 1920.

Funk, Arthur L. *The Politics of Torch: The Allied Landings and the Algiers Putsch, 1942*. Lawrence: University Press of Kansas, 1974.

Gabel, Christopher R. "The 1941 Maneuvers: What Did They Really Accomplish?" *Army History* 14 (April 1990): 5–7.

Gavin, James M. *On to Berlin: Battles of an Airborne Commander, 1943–1946*. New York: Viking, 1978.

Gelb, Norman. *Ike and Monty: Generals at War*. New York: William Morrow, 1994.

General Board, United States Forces, European Theater, Study No. 1. "Strategy of the Campaign in Western Europe, 1944–1945." n.d.

General Board, United States Forces, European Theater, Study No. 3. "Reinforcement System and Reinforcement Procedures in the European Theater of Operations." n.d.

General Board, United States Forces, European Theater, Study No. 15. "Organization, Equipment, and Tactical Employment of Infantry Divisions." n.d.

General Board, United States Forces, European Theater, Study No. 18. "Army Tactical Information Service." n.d.

Giangreco, D. M. *Hell to Pay: Operation Downfall and the Invasion of Japan, 1945–1947*. Annapolis, MD: Naval Institute Press, 2009.

Gilbert, Daniel T., Romin W. Tafarodi, and Patrick S. Malone. "You Can't Not Believe Everything You Read." *Journal of Personality and Social Psychology* 65, no. 2 (1993): 221–33.

Grant, Ulysses S. *The Personal Memoirs of Ulysses S. Grant: The Complete Annotated Edition*. Edited by John F. Marszalek, with David S. Nolen and Louie P. Gallo. Cambridge, MA: Harvard University Press, 2017.

Greenfield, Kent Roberts. *American Strategy in World War II: A Reconsideration*. Baltimore: Johns Hopkins University Press, 1963.

Groom, Winston. *The Generals: Patton, MacArthur, Marshall, and the Winning of World War II*. Washington, DC: National Geographic, 2015.

Hanson, Victor Davis. *The Soul of Battle: From Ancient Times to the Present Day, How Three Great Liberators Vanquished Tyranny*. New York: Free Press, 1999.

Harkins, Paul D. *When the Third Cracked Europe: The Story of Patton's Incredible Army*. Harrisburg, PA: Stackpole Books, 1969.

Hechler, Ken. *The Bridge at Remagen: A Story of World War II*. New York: Ballantine Books, 1957.

Heller, Charles E., and William A. Stofft, eds. *America's First Battles, 1776–1965*. Lawrence: University Press of Kansas, 1986.

Henley, David C. *The Land That God Forgot: The Saga of Gen. George Patton's Desert Training Camps*. N.p.: Western Military History Association, 1989.

Hennessy, John J. *Return to Bull Run: The Campaign and Battle of Second Manassas*. Norman: University of Oklahoma Press, 1993.

Hess, Earl J. *In the Trenches at Petersburg: Field Fortifications and Confederate Defeat*. Chapel Hill: University of North Carolina Press, 2009.

Hiller, Arthur, dir. *The Miracle of the White Stallions*. Burbank, CA: Walt Disney, 1963.

Hirshon, Stanley. *General Patton: A Soldier's Life*. New York: HarperCollins, 2002.

"History of the Fifteenth United States Army, 21 August 1944 to 11 July 1945." N.d.

"History of the 90th Division in World War II." N.d.

Holland, Matthew F. *Eisenhower between the Wars*. Westport, CT: Praeger, 2001.

Holland, Norman N. "Spider-Man? Sure! The Neuroscience of Suspending Disbelief." *Interdisciplinary Science Reviews* 33, no. 4 (2008): 312–20.

Horne, Alistair. *The Age of Napoleon*. New York: Random House, 2004.

Hough, John, dir. *Brass Target*. Beverly Hills: Metro-Goldwyn-Mayer Studios, 1978.

Howard, Michael. *Strategic Deception in the Second World War*. New York: W. W. Norton, 1995.

Hymel, Kevin M. "'The Bravest and Best': Patton and the Death of Capt. Richard Jenson in North Africa." *Army History* 91 (Spring 2014): 30–40.

Irzyk, Albin F. *Gasoline to Patton: A Different War*. Oakland, OR: Elderberry Press, 2004.

Johnson, David E. *Fast Tanks and Heavy Bombers: Innovation in the U.S. Army, 1917–1945*. Ithaca, NY: Cornell University Press, 1998.

Jones, Michael. *After Hitler: The Last Ten Days of World War II in Europe*. New York: New American Library, 2015.

Jordan, Jonathan W. *Brothers, Rivals, Victory: Eisenhower, Patton, Bradley, and the Partnership That Drove the Allied Conquest in Europe*. New York: NAL Caliber, 2011.

Junt, Tony. *Postwar: A History of Europe since 1945*. New York: Penguin, 2005.

Kagan, Donald. *The Peace of Nicias and the Sicilian Expedition*. Ithaca, NY: Cornell University Press, 1981.

Keane, Michael. *Patton: Blood, Guts, and Prayer*. Washington, DC: Regnery, 2012.

Kemp, Anthony. *The Unknown Battle: Metz, 1944*. New York: Stein and Day, 1981.

Kershaw, Ian. *The End: The Defiance and Destruction of Hitler's Germany, 1944–1945*. New York: Penguin, 2011.

Kipling, Rudyard. *Kipling: Poems*. Edited by Peter Washington. New York: Alfred A. Knopf, 2007.

Koch, Oscar W., and Robert G. Hayes. *G-2: Intelligence for Patton*. Pittsburgh: Whitmore, 1971.

Komer, Robert W. *Civil Affairs and Military Government in the Mediterranean Theater*. N.p.: Office of the Chief of Military History, 1950.

Letts, Elizabeth. *The Perfect Horse: The Daring U.S. Mission to Rescue the Priceless Stallions Kidnapped by the Nazis*. New York: Ballantine Books, 2016.

Linn, Brian McAllister. *The Echo of Battle: The Army's Way of War*. Cambridge, MA: Harvard University Press, 2007.

Ludewig, Joachim. *Rückzug: The German Retreat from France, 1944*. Lexington: University Press of Kentucky, 2012.

MacDonald, Charles B. *The Battle of the Hürtgen Forest*. Philadelphia: University of Pennsylvania Press, 2003.

Manchester, William. *American Caesar: Douglas MacArthur, 1880–1964*. Boston: Little, Brown, 1978.

Mansoor, Peter R. *The GI Offensive in Europe: The Triumph of American Infantry Divisions, 1941–1945*. Lawrence: University Press of Kansas, 1999.

Matheny, Michael, R. *Carrying the War to the Enemy: American Operational Art to 1945*. Norman: University of Oklahoma Press, 2011.

McManus, John C. *Alamo in the Ardennes: The Untold Story of the American Soldiers Who Made the Defense of Bastogne Possible*. Hoboken, NJ: John Wiley & Sons, 2007.

Mellenthin, F. W. von. *Panzer Battles: A Study of Employment of Armor in the Second World War*. Norman: University of Oklahoma Press, 1954.

Meller, Sidney L. *The Desert Training Center and C-AMA, Study No. 15*. Washington, DC: Historical Section—Army Ground Forces, 1946.

Millett, Allan R., Peter Maslowski, and William B. Feis. *For the Common Defense: A Military History of the United States from 1607 to 2012*. 3rd ed. New York: Free Press, 2012.

Morelock, Jerry D. *Generals of the Bulge: Leadership in the U.S. Army's Greatest Battle*. Mechanicsburg, PA: Stackpole Books, 2015.

Morgenthau, Henry, Jr. *Germany Is Our Problem*. New York: Harper & Brothers, 1945.

Morison, Samuel Eliot. *History of United States Naval Operations in World War II.* Vol. 2, *Operations in North African Waters, October 1942–June 1943.* Boston: Little, Brown, 1947.

———. *History of United States Naval Operations in World War II.* Vol. 9, *Sicily-Salerno-Anzio, January 1943–June 1944.* Boston: Little, Brown, 1954.

Morningstar, James Kelly. *Patton's Way: A Radical Theory of War.* Annapolis, MD: Naval Institute Press, 2017.

Mosby, John S. *The Memoirs of Colonel John S. Mosby.* Boston: Little, Brown, 1917.

Murray, Williamson, and Richard Hart Sinnreich, eds. *The Past as Prologue: The Importance of History to the Military Profession.* Cambridge: Cambridge University Press, 2006.

Muth, Jörg. *Command Culture: Officer Education in the U.S. Army and the German Armed Forces, 1901–1940, and the Consequences for World War II.* Denton: University of North Texas Press, 2011.

Neiberg, Michael. *Potsdam: The End of World War II and the Remaking of Europe.* New York: Basic Books, 2015.

Ninkovich, Frank. *The Wilsonian Century: U.S. Foreign Policy since 1900.* Chicago: University of Chicago Press, 1999.

Nolan, Fredrick. *The Algonquin Project.* New York: William Morrow, 1974.

Nye, Roger H. *The Challenge of Command: Reading for Military Excellence.* New York: Berkley, 1986.

———. *The Patton Mind: The Professional Development of an Extraordinary Leader.* Garden City Park, NY: Avery, 1993.

———. "Whence Patton's Military Genius?" *Parameters* 21 (Winter 1991–92): 60–73.

O'Connell, Robert L. *The Ghosts of Cannae: Hannibal and the Darkest Hour of the Roman Republic.* New York: Random House, 2010.

"Operation 'Eclipse': Appreciation and Outline Plan." Supreme Headquarters Allied Expeditionary Force, November 1944.

O'Reilly, Bill, and Martin Dugard. *Killing Patton: The Strange Death of World War II's Most Audacious General.* New York: Henry Holt, 2014.

Orlando, Robert, dir. *Silence Patton: The First Victim of the Cold War.* Los Angeles: Unified Pictures, 2015.

Pacheco, Ferdie. *Who Killed Patton?* Indianapolis: AuthorHouse, 2004.

Patton, Beatrice Ayer. "A Soldier's Reading." *Armor* 61 (November–December): 10–11.

Patton, Benjamin, and Jennifer Scruby. *Growing Up Patton: Reflections on Heroes, History, and Family Wisdom.* New York: Berkley, 2011.

Patton, George S., Jr. "Cavalry Work of the Punitive Expedition." *Cavalry Journal* 27 (January 1917a): 426–33.

———. "Comments on Cavalry Tanks." *Cavalry Journal* 30, no. 124 (July 1921): 251–52.

———. "The Desert Training Corps." *Cavalry Journal* 51 (September–October 1942): 2–5.

———. *Diary of the Instructor in Swordsmanship*. Fort Riley, KS: Mounted Service School, 1915.

———. "The Effects of Weapons on War." *Cavalry Journal* (November 1930).

———. "The Form and Use of the Saber." *Cavalry Journal* 23 (March 1913): 752–59.

———. "Present Saber: Its Form and Use for Which It Was Designed." *Cavalry Journal* 27 (April 1917): 577–80.

———. "The Probable Characteristics of the Next War and the Organization, Tactics, and Equipment Necessary to Meet Them." Master's thesis, Army War College, 1932.

———. "Report of Operations of the Army Polo Team of 1922." *Cavalry Journal* 32 (April 1923): 230–33.

———. "Success in War." *Cavalry Journal* 40 (January 1931): 26–30.

———. "Tanks in Future Wars." *Infantry Journal* 16 (May 1920): 958–62.

———. *War as I Knew It*. Boston: Houghton Mifflin Harcourt, 1995.

———. "War Department Document No. 463, 'Saber Exercise.'" Washington, DC: Government Printing Office, 1914.

Patton, Robert H. *The Pattons: A Personal History of an American Family*. New York: Crown, 1994.

Paxton, Robert O. *Vichy France: Old Guard and New Order, 1940–1944*. New York: Alfred A. Knopf, 1972.

Pershing, John J. "Punitive Expedition Report." October 10, 1916.

Pogue, Forrest C. *CMH Publication 7-1, United States Army in World War II European Theater of Operations: The Supreme Command*. Washington, DC: Office of the Chief of Military History, 1954.

Porch, Douglas. *The Path to Victory: The Mediterranean Theater in World War II*. New York: Farrar, Straus and Giroux, 2004.

Price, Martin. "I Was Paid to Kill Patton: Exclusive Interview with OSS 'Hitman.'" *Spotlight*, October 22, 1979b.

———. "Who Killed Patton? Super Spy Says He Was Paid $10,000 to Murder World War II Hero." *Spotlight*, October 15, 1979a.

Prioli, Carmine, ed. *Lines of Fire: The Poems of General George S. Patton Jr.* Lewistown, NY: Edwin Mellen Press, 1991.

Rhea, Gordon C. *The Battle of the Wilderness, May 5–6, 1864*. Baton Rouge: Louisiana State University Press, 1994.

Rickard, John Nelson. *Advance and Destroy: Patton as Commander in the Bulge*. Lexington: University Press of Kentucky, 2011.

———. *Patton at Bay: The Lorraine Campaign, September to December, 1944*. Westport, CT: Praeger, 1999.

Riggsby, Andrew. *Caesar in Gaul and Rome: War in Words*. Austin: University of Texas Press, 2006.

Roberts, Andrew. *The Storm of War: A New History of the Second World War*. New York: HarperCollins, 2011.

Robertson, William G. *The Staff Ride*. Washington, DC: US Army Center of Military History, 1987.

Rush, Robert S. *Hell in Hürtgen Forest: The Ordeal and Triumph of an American Infantry Regiment.* Lawrence: University Press of Kansas, 2001.

Ryan, Cornelius. *A Bridge Too Far.* New York: Simon and Schuster, 1974.

Sarantakes, Nicholas Evan. *Making "Patton": A Classic Film's Epic Journey to the Silver Screen.* Lawrence: University Press of Kansas, 2012.

Schaffner, Franklin J., dir. *Patton.* Film. Los Angeles: 20th Century Fox, 1970.

Schultz, Duane. *Patton's Last Gamble: The Disastrous Raid on POW Camp Hammelburg in World War II.* Guilford, CT: Stackpole, 2018.

Semmes, Harry H. *Portrait of Patton.* New York: Appleton-Century-Crofts, 1955.

The Seventh Army in Sicily. After-action report. Staff of the Seventh Army, 1943.

Shamir, Eitan. *Transforming Mission Command: The Pursuit of Mission Command in the U.S., British, and Israeli Armies.* Stanford, CA: Stanford University Press, 2011.

Showalter, Dennis E. *Patton and Rommel: Men of War in the Twentieth Century.* New York: Berkley, 2005.

———. *Railroads and Rifles: Soldiers, Technology, and the Unification of Germany.* Solihull, UK: Helion, 2016.

Sigal, Clancy. "Blood and Guts." *New York Review of Books,* August 20, 1964.

Skates, John Ray. *Invasion of Japan: Alternative to the Bomb.* Columbia: University of South Carolina Press, 1994.

Smith, Jean Edward. *Eisenhower in War and Peace.* New York: Random House, 2012.

Sobel, Brian M. *The Fighting Pattons.* Westport, CT: Praeger, 1997.

Sorley, Lewis. *Thunderbolt: General Creighton Abrams and the Army of His Times.* New York: Simon and Schuster, 1992.

Spires, David N. *Air Power for Patton's Army: The XIX Tactical Air Command in the Second World War.* Washington, DC: Air Force History and Museums Program, 2002.

Staff Group D, Section 4. *CSI Battle Book 4-D: The Battle of Sidi Bou Zid.* Fort Leavenworth, KS: Combat Studies Institute, 1984.

Stein, George S. *The Waffen SS: Hitler's Elite Guard at War, 1939–1945.* Ithaca, NY: Cornell University Press, 1984.

Stowe, Leland. "Old Blood-and-Guts Off the Record." *Esquire,* October 1, 1949.

Sullivan, John J. *Air Support for Patton's Third Army.* Jefferson, NC: McFarland, 2003.

Sumida, Jon Tetsuro. *Decoding Clausewitz: A New Approach to "On War."* Lawrence: University Press of Kansas, 2008.

Taylor, A. J. P. *War by Timetable: How the First World War Began.* London: MacDonald, 1969.

"Theatre General Board, Headquarters Fifteenth US Army Roster of Officers." October 4, 1945.

Toland, John. *The Last 100 Days: The Tumultuous and Controversial Story of the Final Days of the War in Europe.* New York: Modern Library, 2003.

Totten, Ruth Ellen Patton. *The Button Box: A Daughter's Loving Memoir of Mrs. George S. Patton.* Columbia: University of Missouri Press, 2012.

"Training in the Ground Army, 1942–1945, Study No. 11." Army Historical Section, 1948.

Trudeau, Noah Andre. *The Last Citadel: Petersburg, Virginia, June 1864–April 1865*. Rev. ed. El Dorado Hills, CA: Savas Beatie, 2014.

Tucker-Jones, Anthony. *Falaise—the Flawed Victory: The Destruction of Panzergruppe West, August, 1944*. Barnsley, UK: Pen & Sword Military, 2008.

The United States Army in World War II: The War against Germany: Europe and Adjacent Areas. Washington, DC: US Army Center of Military History, 1951.

United States Department of Labor. Bureau of Labor and Statistics inflation calculator. https://www.bls.gov/data/inflation_calculator.htm.

United States Military Academy. *The Howitzer, 1909 Edition*. West Point, NY: Corps of Cadets of the United States Military Academy, 1909.

"United States Military Academy Webpage." n.d. http://www.usma.edu/pv/pointer%20view%20archive/09may21.pdf.

Van Creveld, Martin. *Fighting Power: German and US Army Performance, 1939–1945*. Westport, CT: Greenwood Press, 1982.

Vegetius, Flavius. *On Roman Military Matters: A 5th Century Training Manual in Organization, Weapons and Tactics*. Translated by Lieutenant John Clarke. St. Petersburg, FL: Red and Black, 2013.

Von Hassell, Agostino, and Ed Breslin. *Patton: The Pursuit of Destiny*. Nashville, TN: Thomas Nelson, 2010.

Watts, Barry D. *Clausewitzian Friction and Future War*. Revised Edition. Washington, DC: Institute for National Strategic Studies, National Defense University Press, 2004.

Weigley, Russell. *Eisenhower's Lieutenants: The Campaign of France and Germany, 1944–1945*. Bloomington: Indiana University Press, 1981.

Welsome, Eileen. *The General and the Jaguar: Pershing's Hunt for Pancho Villa, a True Story of Revolution and Revenge*. Lincoln: University of Nebraska Press, 2006.

Wightman, Edith Mary. *Roman Trier and the Treveri*. New York: Praeger, 1971.

Wilcox, Robert K. *Target Patton: The Plot to Assassinate General George S. Patton*. Washington, DC: Regnery, 2008.

Williams, Vernon L. *Lieutenant Patton: George S. Patton, Jr. and the American Army in the Mexican Punitive Expedition, 1915–1916*. Austin, TX: Presidial Press, 1983.

Wilmot, Chester *The Struggle for Europe: An Account of the War in Europe, 1940–45*. New York: HarperCollins, 1952.

Wilson, Harold E., Jr. "A Legend in His Own Mind: The Olympic Experience of General George S. Patton, Jr." *OLYMPIKA: The International Journal of Olympic Studies* 6 (1997): 99–114.

Winters, Harold A., et al. *Battling the Elements: Weather and Terrain in the Conduct of War*. Baltimore: Johns Hopkins University Press, 2001.

Winton, Harold R. *Corps Commanders of the Bulge: Six American Generals and Victory in the Ardennes*. Lawrence: University Press of Kansas, 2007.

Wood, C. E. *Mud: A Military History*. Washington, DC: Potomac Books, 2006.

Wragg, David. *Sink the French: The French Navy after the Fall of France, 1940*. Barnsley, UK: Pen & Sword, 2007.

Yeide, Harry. *Fighting Patton: George S. Patton Jr. through the Eyes of His Enemies*. Minneapolis: Zenith Press, 2011.

Zabecki, David T. *The German 1918 Offensives: A Case Study in the Operational Level of War*. New York: Routledge, 2006.

Ziemke, Earl F. *The U.S. Army Occupation of Germany, 1944–1946*. Washington, DC: US Army Center of Military History, 1975.

Zumbro, Derek S. *Battle for the Ruhr: The German Army's Final Defeat in the West*. Lawrence: University Press of Kansas, 2001.

INDEX

Note: page numbers in italics refer to figures